STL Tutorial and
Reference Guide,
Second Edition

Addison-Wesley Professional Computing Series

Brian W. Kernighan, Consulting Editor

Please see our web site (http://www.awl.com/cseng/series/professionalcomputing) for more information on these titles.

STL Tutorial and Reference Guide, Second Edition

C++ Programming with the Standard Template Library

David R. Musser
Gillmer J. Derge
Atul Saini

ADDISON–WESLEY

Boston • San Francisco • New York • Toronto • Montreal
London • Munich • Paris • Madrid
Capetown • Sydney • Tokyo • Singapore • Mexico City

Many of the designations used by manufacturers and sellers to distinguish their products are claimed as trademarks. Where those designators appear in this book, and Addison-Wesley was aware of the trademark claim, the designations have been printed in initial capital letters or all capital letters.

The authors and publisher have taken care in preparation of this book, but make no expressed or implied warranty of any kind and assume no responsibility for errors or omissions. No liability is assumed for incidental or consequential damages in connection with or arising out of the use of the information or programs contained herein. The publisher offers discounts on this book when ordered in quantity for special sales.

For more information, please contact:

Pearson Education Corporate Sales Division
201 W. 103rd Street
Indianapolis, IN 46290
(800) 428-5331
corpsales@pearsoned.com

Library of Congress Cataloging-in-Publication Data
Musser, David R.
    STL Tutorial and reference guide: C++ programming with the standard template
library / David R. Musser, Gillmer J. Derge, Atul Saini.--2nd ed.
        p.cm. --(Addison-Wesley professional computing series)
    Includes bibiographical references and index.
        ISBN 0-201-37923-6
        1. C++ (Computer program language) 2. Standard template library. I. Derge,
Gillmer J. II. Saini, Atul, 1963- III. Title. IV. Series

QA76.73.C153.M87 2001
005.13'3--dc21   00-068935

ISBN: 0-201-37923-6

Text printed on recycled and acid-free paper.

ISBN 0201379236

2 3 4 5 6 7   MA   04 03 02 01

2nd Printing   September 2001

To Paul, Eric and Martha
　　　　　—David R. Musser

To Mom and Dad
　　　　　—Gillmer J. Derge

For Ayrton Senna (1960–1994)
　　　　　—Atul Saini

Contents

List of Examples

Foreword

When Dave Musser asked me to write an extended foreword to the second edition of this book, I jumped on the opportunity. First, Dave is my closest professional friend; we have been collaborating for over 20 years, and without Dave there would be no STL. So honoring his request is by itself a privilege. It also gives me an opportunity to say a few words about what I had in mind while designing STL.

To use a tool, it is useful to understand not just the instructions for using it but also the principles that guided its designers. The main goal of this foreword is to present you with the principles behind STL. I'll conclude with some musings.

STL was designed with four fundamental ideas in mind:

- Abstractness

- Efficiency

- Von Neumann computational model

- Value semantics

Abstractness. Some of you might have heard that STL is an example of a programming technique called "generic programming." This is so. Some of you might have also heard that generic programming is a style of programming using C++ templates. This is not so. Generic programming has nothing to do with C++ or templates. Generic programming is a discipline that studies systematic organization of abstract software components. Its objective is to develop a taxonomy of algorithms, data structures, memory allocation mechanisms, and other software artifacts in a way that allows the highest level of reuse, modularity, and usability.

To allow the greatest degree of usability, one has to try to analyze all possible extensions. For example, when a famous computer scientist saw my version of Euclid's algorithm for finding the greatest common divisor of two quantities,

```
template <typename T> T gcd(T m, T n) {
  while (n != 0) {
    T t = m % n;
    m = n;
    n = t;
  }
  return m;
}
```

he objected that the algorithm is not correct since it returns -1 when called with 1 and -1 as its arguments, and therefore the common divisor returned is not the greatest. He suggested that I fix the problem by changing the last line to

```
return m < 0 ? -m : m;
```

Unfortunately, if you do this the algorithm will not work for many important extensions: polynomials, Gaussian integers, and so on. It would require the set of elements on which we operate to be totally ordered. The problem disappears if we use a more abstract (and algorithmically more meaningful) definition of greatest common divisor: a divisor that is divisible by any other divisor. That definition allows for nonunique solutions: in the case of integers both 6 and -6 are greatest common divisors of 24 and 30. This actually corresponds to what mathematicians have been doing for the last several hundred years.

The classification of software components should deal only with useful components. It would be ridiculous to introduce a concept of semisequence— a sequence that has multiple beginnings but only one end—since we do not know any data structures that look like that nor any algorithms that could operate on them.

After we organize things systematically, we can ensure the consistency of their interfaces. That is, interfaces to two components should be the same to the same degree that the behavior of the components is the same. That allows us to implement algorithms that work on multiple components—generic algorithms. It also makes it possible to use the library. If a programmer masters STL's `vector`, it is not going to be too hard to learn to use STL's `list` and even easier to learn to use `deque`. It is my belief that the interfaces that allow the greatest possible degree of abstract programming are also the interfaces that are easiest to learn. (This presupposes that a person is learning things from scratch. It is hard to convince a hardened Lisp programmer that comparing with the past-the-end iterator is a better way than testing for `nil`.)

In many respects the ideas of generic programming are very similar to the ideas of abstract algebra. Those of you who took a course dealing with groups, rings, and fields should be able to see where classification of iterators is coming from.[1]

As mathematics organizes theorems around different abstract theories, generic programming organizes algorithms around different abstract concepts. So the task of the library designer is to find all interesting algorithms, find the minimal requirements that allow these algorithms to work, and organize them around these requirements. In general requirements are described through a set of acceptable expressions and their semantics. For example, STL does not state that `++` on an iterator must be defined as a member function of a class. It just states that if `i` is an iterator and if it can be dereferenced, then `++i` is a valid expression.

Efficiency. While mathematics often deals with objects that cannot be constructed at all or could be constructed only if given an arbitrarily long time, computer science makes efficiency an explicit concern. It is not enough to know that an operation can be done. It is important to know that it will be done reasonably fast. To assure that, STL does several things.

First, it makes complexity requirements a part of each interface. When concepts such as iterators are specified, certain complexity requirements are given. A programmer can be certain that doing `++` on an iterator does not depend dramatically on where in the sequence it is. Dereferencing should be equally fast—it is not legal to implement list iterators with a structure

---

[1] In general, I believe that mathematical culture is essential for a good software engineer. Sadly enough, nowadays one goes through college—and through graduate school—without any exposure to real mathematics. I would urge all of you to keep reading mathematics throughout your career. There are some remarkable books out there—I highly recommend the following three books by John Stillwell: *Numbers and Geometry*, *Mathematics and Its History*, and *Elements of Algebra*; after you are done with them, consider *Geometry: Euclid and Beyond* by Robin Hartshorne and *Visual Complex Analysis* by Tristan Needham.

containing the pointer to the list's head and the integer index. (It should be noted that while the operational semantics of the operations can be specified rigorously by specifying the set of valid expressions and their semantics, the complexity is specified informally; a totally new insight is needed to find a way for specifying complexity requirements in a rigorous but practically useful way.)

Second, STL takes great care not to hide any part of a data structure that allows efficient access. Instead of providing get and put methods for operating on a container—the favorite method of textbook writers—the pointer to the value is exposed so that fields could be modified in place. One can write

```
i->second = 5;
```

instead of

```
pair<int, int> tmp = my_vector.get(i);
tmp.second = 5;
my_vector.put(i, tmp);
```

The fact that iterators to elements of a vector do not survive the periodic reallocations is noted, and it is assumed that STL users can learn to deal with it by either preallocating enough storage or storing indices and not iterators.

Great care was taken to see that all the generic algorithms in STL are state of the art and as efficient as hand-coded ones (being quite precise, that they are as efficient as hand-coded ones when a good optimizing compiler—such as Kuck and Associates' C++ compiler—is used).

Von Neumann Computational Model. Although abstract mathematics uses simple numeric facts as its basis of abstraction—one should not forget that mathematics is an experimental science—what should we use as our basis of abstraction to come up with a generic abstract framework? It is my firm belief that the only solid basis is the architectures of real computers. It is important to remember that modern computer architectures are a result of many years of evolution guided by the need to solve more and more diverse problems. Byte-addressable memory and pointers are not the artifacts we inherited from some archaic hardware designs—archaic hardware designs did not have bytes and there were no pointers; one wrote loops with the help of self-modifying code—but the results of architecture catching up with the needs of applications.[2] If we are interested in designing a generic framework for numerical types, it is important to understand the working of built-in numeric types, not just the mathematical theory of integers and real numbers.

The most important new concept in computer science that was not already present in mathematics is the concept of address. Making addresses, not just values, a part of our computational model was the revolutionary step that enabled all the progress from 72 addresses in the Mark I to millions of Internet addresses. In many respects, the most controversial part of STL is the fact that it makes addresses and their conceptual classification the cornerstone of the whole edifice. (This statement might appear strange to a practical programmer, but the academic community has spent decades trying to eliminate addresses altogether in doing what is called "functional programming.") In mathematical terms, the idea underlying STL is that different data structures correspond to different address algebras, different ways of connecting addresses together. A set of operations that move from one address in the data structure to the next corresponds to iterators. A set of operations that add and delete addresses to and from the data structure corresponds to containers.

While the STL classification of iterators (input, output, forward, bidirectional, random access) is sufficient for all the fundamental sequence algorithms, further categories of iterators need to be defined for STL to be properly extended to deal with multidimensional structures. (As a matter of fact, even for many fundamental sequence algorithms, two-dimensional iterators are needed to speed them up in cases of (1) nonuniform accesses as, for example, is the case with deque iterators or cache lines and (2) multiprocessor implementations.)

Value Semantics. STL views containers as a generalization of structures. As the structure owns its components, so does a container own its components. When you copy structures, all their components are copied. When

---

[2] It is very important for a good programmer to understand what really goes under the hood of a high-level programming language. It is important to know at least a couple of different architectures well. Since I recommended a bunch of mathematical books, let me also suggest a couple of computer books: John Hennessy and David Patterson's *Computer Architecture: A Quantitative Approach* is, in my opinion, the most important computer science book; one gets, however, a wonderful additional perspective if it is supplemented with *Computer Architecture: Concepts and Evolution*, by Gerrit Blaauw and Fred Brooks, especially the second part of the book, "The Computer Zoo," which covers some remarkable historical designs.

a structure is destroyed, all its components are destroyed. The same happens with containers. These properties are essential features that allow structures and containers to model the key attribute of real-life things—the relationship between whole and part. Of course, the whole-part relationship is not the only kind of relationship in the real world, and the rest of the relationships need to be modeled with iterators.[3] It is my belief that the confusion between a part and a relation, which is so common in object-oriented languages and libraries, is a major source of conceptual confusion in the modeling of the real world as well as the main reason that they absolutely require garbage collection. STL is not object-oriented—not only in the way it uses global generic algorithms, but more significantly, in the fact that it separates the notions of having an object as a part and pointing to an object. It assumes that

```
T a = b;
```

creates a copy of an object, with all parts being distinct, not just another pointer to the same object. Specifications of those algorithms in STL that use assignment (`sort`, `partition`, `remove`, and so on) require this value semantics. In the STL universe objects never share parts (unless, of course, one object is a part of the other).

In general, STL assumes that for any type on which it operates the semantics of copy constructors, destructors, assignment, and equality and their relations are the same as for built-in types. In addition, STL assumes that for those objects for which operators `<`, `>`, `<=`, and `>=` are defined, their semantics is the same as for built-in types, or, mathematically speaking, they define a total ordering. (One of the gripes I have against C++ is that C++ does not require the semantics of fundamental operations to be consistent with the semantics of built-in types; one can define an operator `=` to do multiplication. Operator overloading is good only if used in a highly disciplined way; otherwise, it can cause great harm.)

Musings. STL was not designed to be a part of the C++ Standard Library. It was designed to be the first library of generic algorithms and data structures. It so happened that C++ was the only language in which I could implement such a library to my personal satisfaction. In the five

---

[3]For example, while my leg is my part, my lawyer is not. If I am destroyed, my leg is destroyed; if I am copied, my leg is copied. My lawyer is another human being, and while my death might affect him in various ways—like a lot of pointers to a dead client, known as dangling pointers—he is not going to be automatically destroyed.

years since STL has been widely available, many people have made claims that they can do STL-like things in their favorite language: Ada-95, ML, Dylan, Eiffel, Java, and so on. Maybe they can. As far as I can see, they have not. I wish they could. I wish someone would construct a language more suitable to generic programming than C++. After all, one gets by in C++ by the skin of one's teeth. Fundamental concepts of STL, things like iterators and containers, are not describable in C++ since STL depends on rigorous sets of requirements that do not have any linguistic representation in C++. (They are, of course, defined in the standard, but they are defined in English.)

The whole point of STL is that it is an extensible framework. While STL is widely used, my hopes for the creation of many libraries of generic components have not been fulfilled. As far as I can determine the reason that such libraries are not created is that there are no financial mechanisms for supporting the work. One cannot make money out of fundamental algorithms. They have to be designed for the entire industry by small teams of component craftsmen. While I have been lucky, on a couple of occasions, to receive funding from large computer companies to do STL work, it cannot be done in a serious way until some reliable way of funding the work is found. It is my hope that the U.S. government or alternatively the EU will fund a small but effective organization dedicated to producing generic software components. And I mean not research but actual production of well-organized, documented, generic, and efficient components. Please write to your elected representatives.

STL presupposes a very different way of teaching computer science. What 99 percent of programmers need to know is not how to build components but how to use them. STL presupposes a different way of running software organizations. People who write their own code, instead of using standard components, should be dealt with like people who propose designing nonstandard, proprietary CPUs. Can we ever move software into the industrial age? I wonder ...

Alexander Stepanov
January 2001

Foreword to the First Edition

What is STL? STL, or the Standard Template Library, is a general-purpose library of generic algorithms and data structures. It makes a programmer more productive in two ways: first, it contains a lot of different components that can be plugged together and used in an application, and more importantly, it provides a framework into which different programming problems can be decomposed.

The framework defined by STL is quite simple: two of its most fundamental dimensions are algorithms and data structures. The reason that data structures and algorithms work together seamlessly is, paradoxically enough, the fact that they do not know anything about each other. Algorithms are written in terms of iterator categories: abstract data-accessing methods. To enable different algorithms to work in terms of these conceptual categories, STL establishes rigid rules that govern the behavior of iterators. For example, if any two iterators are equal then the results of dereferencing them must be equal. It is only because in STL all such rules are stated explicitly that it is possible to write code that knows nothing about a particular implementation of a data structure.

While it is my experience that using STL can dramatically improve programming productivity, such an improvement is possible only if a programmer is fully cognizant of the structure of the library and is familiar with a style of programming that it advocates. How can a programmer learn this style? The only way is to use it and extend it. To do this, however, one needs a place to start. This book is such a place.

The authors bring special qualifications to the writing of this book. Dave Musser has been doing research that led to STL for over fifteen years. Quoting from the original STL manual: "Dave Musser ... contributed to all aspects of the STL work: design of the overall structure, semantic requirements, algorithm design, complexity analysis, and performance measurements." Atul Saini was the first person to recognize the commercial potential of STL and committed his company to selling its production version even before it was accepted by the C++ standards committee.

I hope that this book's publication will help programmers enjoy using STL as much as I do.

Alexander Stepanov
October 1995

Preface

In the five years since the first edition of *STL Tutorial and Reference Guide* appeared, the C++ language standard has been finalized and officially accepted, C++ compiler vendors have made great progress in bringing their compilers into compliance with the standard, and dozens of other books and magazine articles have appeared that describe and explain the standardized language and libraries. Many of these books and articles have highlighted the Standard Template Library (STL) as the most significant addition to the standard. Some hailed it, as we did in this book's first edition, as having the potential to revolutionize the way a large number of people program. The past five years have already seen much of that potential realized, with the first edition of this book playing a key role for tens of thousands of programmers. We wrote in the preface of the first edition that there are five reasons why the STL components could become some of the most widely used software in existence:

- C++ is becoming one of the most widely used programming languages (in large part due to the support it provides for building and using component libraries).

- Since STL has been incorporated into the ANSI/ISO standard for C++ and its libraries, compiler vendors are making it part of their standard distributions.

- All components in STL are generic, meaning that they are adaptable (by language-supported compile-time techniques) to many different uses.

- The generality of STL components has been achieved without sacrificing efficiency.

- The design of STL components as fine-grained, interchangeable building blocks makes them a suitable basis for further development of components for specialized areas such as databases, user interfaces, and so forth.

We have enjoyed seeing these statements borne out by the developments of the past five years.

Changes in the Second Edition

In this new edition we have added substantially more tutorial material including expanded chapters in Part I on function objects and container, iterator, and function adaptors, and two entirely new chapters in Part II containing substantial new examples. We have also gone through all example code and surrounding discussion, including the reference material in Part III, to bring them up to date with the final standard. (Although some ambiguities in the standard have been discovered since it was finalized, we believe that in most cases the remaining uncertainties about the meaning of STL component specifications have no important consequences for the practicing programmer. In the few cases where they might, we point them out.) We also added a new chapter in Part III describing utility components such as the pair and comparison classes, and a new appendix describing the STL-related features of the standard string class.

In this edition we have also adopted the "literate programming" style for presenting example programs and code fragments. For readers unfamiliar with this approach to simultaneous programming and documenting, a brief explanation is given in Chapter 2 and more details are presented in Chapter 12. One benefit of the literate programming approach is that coding details can be presented once and then referred to (by name and page number) many times, so readers do not have to read through the same details repeatedly. Another major benefit is that we have been able check even more thoroughly than before that all code is syntactically and logically correct, since literate programming tools make it easy to extract the code directly from the manuscript and compile and test it. A list of the compilers the code has been compiled and tested with is given in Appendix D.

Some History, from the Preface to the First Edition

Virtually all C++ programmers know that this language was originated by one person, Bjarne Stroustrup, who began thinking of how to extend the C language to support definition of classes and objects as early as 1979. So too, the architecture of STL is largely the creation of one person, Alexander Stepanov.

It is interesting that it was also in 1979, at about the same time as Stroustrup's initial research, that Alex began working out his initial ideas of generic programming and exploring their potential for revolutionizing software development. Although Dave Musser had developed and advocated some aspects of generic programming as early as 1971, it was limited to a rather specialized area of software development (computer algebra). Alex recognized the full potential for generic programming and persuaded his then-colleagues at General Electric Research and Development (including, primarily, Dave Musser and Deepak Kapur) that generic programming should be pursued as a comprehensive basis for software development. But at that time there was no real support in any programming language for generic programming. The first major language to provide such support was Ada, with its generic units feature, and by 1987 Dave and Alex had developed and published an Ada library for list processing that embodied the results of much of their research on generic programming. However, Ada had not achieved much acceptance outside the defense industry, and C++ seemed more likely to become widely used and provide good support for generic programming, even though the language was relatively immature (it did not even have templates, added only later). Another reason for turning to C++, which Alex recognized early on, was that the C/C++ model of computation, which allows very flexible access to storage (via pointers), is crucial to achieving generality without losing efficiency.

Still, much research and experimentation were needed, not just to develop individual components, but more important to develop an overall architecture for a component library based on generic programming. First at AT&T Bell Laboratories and later at Hewlett-Packard Research Labs, Alex experimented with many architectural and algorithm formulations, first in C and later in C++. Dave Musser collaborated in this research, and in 1992 Meng Lee joined Alex's project at HP and became a major contributor.

This work undoubtedly would have continued for some time as just a research project or at best would have resulted in an HP proprietary library, if Andrew Koenig of Bell Labs had not become aware of the work and asked Alex to present the main ideas at a November 1993 meeting of the ANSI/ISO committee for C++ standardization. The committee's response was overwhelmingly favorable and led to a request from Andy for a formal proposal in time for the March 1994 meeting. Despite the tremendous time pressure, Alex and Meng were able to produce a draft proposal that received preliminary approval at that meeting.

The committee had several requests for changes and extensions (some of them major), and a small group of committee members met with Alex and Meng to help work out the details. The requirements for the most significant extension (associative containers) had to be shown to be consistent by fully implementing them, a task Alex delegated to Dave Musser. It would have been quite easy for the whole enterprise to spin out of control at this point, but again Alex and Meng met the challenge and produced a proposal that received final approval at the July 1994 ANSI/ISO committee meeting. (Additional details of this history can be found in an interview Alex gave in the March 1995 issue of *Dr. Dobb's Journal*.)

Spreading the Word

Subsequently, the Stepanov and Lee document [17] was incorporated into the ANSI/ISO C++ draft standard ([1], parts of clauses 17 through 27). It also influenced other parts of the C++ Standard Library, such as the string facilities, and some of the previously adopted standards in those areas were revised accordingly.

In spite of STL's success with the committee, there remained the question of how STL would make its way into actual availability and use. With the STL requirements part of the publicly available draft standard, compiler vendors and independent software library vendors could of course develop their own implementations and market them as separate products or as selling points for their other wares. One of the first edition's authors, Atul Saini, was among the first to recognize the commercial potential and began exploring it as a line of business for his company, Modena Software Incorporated, even before STL had been fully accepted by the committee.

The prospects for early widespread dissemination of STL were considerably improved with Hewlett-Packard's decision to make its implementation freely available on the Internet in August 1994. This implementation, developed by Stepanov, Lee, and Musser during the standardization process, became the basis of all implementations offered by compiler and library vendors today.

Also in 1994, Dave Musser and Atul Saini developed the *STL++ Manual*, the first comprehensive user-level documentation of STL, but they soon recognized that an even more comprehensive treatment of STL was needed, one that would have better and more complete coverage of all aspects of the library. In an attempt to meet this goal, and with much encouragement and assistance from their editor, Mike Hendrickson, they wrote the first edition of this book.

In the second edition, the two original authors are joined by Gillmer J. Derge, President and CEO of the consulting firm Toltec Software Services, Inc. He has been developing applications with C++ for more than a decade, including seven years with General Electric Corporate R&D, where he received a Whitney Award for technical achievement.

Acknowledgments for the First Edition

We gratefully acknowledge the encouragement and assistance of many people. First and foremost, Alex Stepanov and Meng Lee offered continuous encouragement and were always available to help straighten out any misconceptions we had about the design of the library. Invaluable assistance with code development and testing was provided by several Modena staff members, including Atul Gupta, Kolachala Kalyan, and Narasimhan Rampalli. Several reviewers of earlier drafts gave us much valuable feedback and helped us find ways to present the most crucial ideas more clearly. They include Mike Ballantyne, Tom Cargill, Edgar Chrisostomo, Brian Kernighan, Scott Meyers, Larry Podmolik, Kathy Stark, Steve Vinoski, and John Vlissides. Others who also made valuable suggestions include Dan Benanav, Bob Cook, Bob Ingalls, Nathan Schimke, Kedar Tupil, and Rick Wilhelm. Finally, we thank the team at Addison-Wesley for their expert editorial and production assistance: Kim Dawley, Katie Duffy, Rosa Gonzalez, Mike Hendrickson, Simone Payment, Avanda Peters, John Wait, and Pamela Yee.

Acknowledgments for the Second Edition

For assistance with this edition, we wish first of all to thank the reviewers for pointing out errors in the discussion and examples and suggesting many other improvements in the presentation. The extensive comments of Max A. Lebow, Lawrence Rauchwerger, and Jan Christiaan van Winkel were especially helpful. We are greatly indebted to the following people who brought to our attention errors in the first printing: Arthur Ault and Robert Allan Schwartz. We also thank Deborah Lafferty, our editor, and Julie DeBaggis, who served as editor during the early planning of the second edition. Several other members of the production and marketing teams at Addison Wesley helped in many ways, including Jacquelyn Doucette, Chanda Leary-Coutu, Curt Johnson, Jennifer Lawinski, and Marty Rabinowitz.

D.R.M.
Loudonville, NY

G.J.D.
Cohoes, NY

A.S.
Los Gatos, CA

October 2000

Part I

Tutorial Introduction to STL

In Part I, we introduce the key ideas and principles of the Standard Template Library and describe most of its components. In most cases the components are illustrated with small example programs.

CHAPTER 1

Introduction

The Standard Template Library—STL—provides a set of C++ container classes and template algorithms designed to work together to produce a wide range of useful functionality. Though only a small number of container classes are provided, they include the most widely useful containers, such as vectors, lists, sets, and maps. The template algorithm components include a broad range of fundamental algorithms for the most common kinds of data manipulations, such as searching, sorting, and merging.

The critical difference between STL and all other C++ container class libraries is that STL algorithms are *generic*: every algorithm works on a variety of containers, including built-in types, and many work on all containers. In Part I we look at the why and how of generic algorithms and other key concepts that give STL many advantages over other software libraries. One of the most important concepts of STL is the way generic algorithms are defined in terms of *iterators*, which generalize C/C++ pointers, together with the way different kinds of iterators are defined for traversing the different kinds of containers. Besides containers, generic algorithms, and iterators, STL also provides *function objects*, which generalize ordinary C/C++ functions and allow other components to be efficiently adapted to a variety of tasks. The library also includes various other kinds of *adaptors* for changing the interfaces of containers, iterators, or function objects. Storage management in STL is controlled by yet another component type, *allocators*. All these components are discussed in the STL overview in Chapter 2 and in more detail in later chapters of Part I.

Just reading about STL may be interesting, but to become really proficient in using the library, you'll have to get some actual programming experience with it. Our descriptions in Part I include many small examples that show how individual components work, and Part II presents and explains a series of more substantial programs. Though still small, these examples perform some nontrivial and useful tasks, displaying some of the power that a good software library makes available. Part III contains a complete reference guide to the library.

STL is only one part of a larger software library, the C++ Standard Library approved by the ANSI/ISO C++ committee in the International Standard for C++ [5].[1] Nevertheless, STL remains a coherent framework of fine-grained, interchangeable components that deserve treatment separate from the rest of the C++ Standard Library. In this book we attempt to provide a complete and precise *user-level description* of STL. (For a thorough description of one widely used implementation of STL, see [17].)

1.1   Who Should Read This Book

Don't let unfamiliarity with other software libraries stop you from reading this book. Although comparisons with other libraries are made in a few places, the main points should be understandable without that background. All that's assumed is that you have some experience with the major C++ concepts: functions, classes, objects, pointers, templates, and stream input/output. Many books on C++ provide the needed background. Crucial features of templates with which some readers might not be familiar are described in Section 1.3.

1.2   What Generic Programming Is
and Why It's Important

STL is the embodiment of years of research on generic programming. The purpose of this research has been to explore methods of developing and organizing libraries of generic—or reusable—software components. Here the meaning of *reusable* is, roughly, "widely adaptable but still efficient," where the adaptation is done by preprocessor or programming language mechanisms rather than manual text editing. There has been a substantial amount of other work in software reuse (other terms often used in this connection are "software building blocks" or "software ICs"), but two distinguishing char-

---

[1]See the Preface for more information on the background of STL and how it came to be included in the C++ Standard.

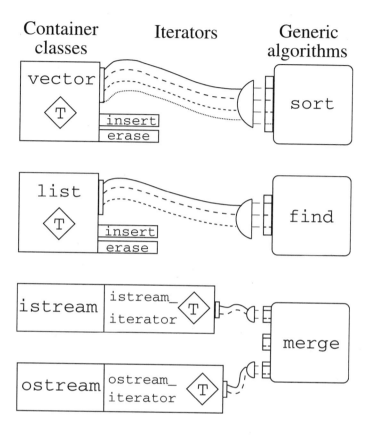

Figure 1.1: Connecting containers and algorithms with iterators

acteristics of the work that led to STL are the high degree of *adaptability* and *efficiency* of the components.

The essential ideas of the generic component construction approach are shown in Figure 1.1 in the depiction of library components and the way they "plug together." On the right are components called *generic algorithms*, for operations such as sequence merging, sorting, and copying. But these algorithms are not self-contained; they are written in terms of *container access operations*, which are assumed to be provided externally. Providing these container access operations is the role of the components called *iterators* (depicted in Figure 1.1 as "ribbon cables"). Each kind of iterator defines container access operations for a particular data representation, such as a linked list representation of sequences or an array representation.

The "sockets" on the left side of the generic algorithm components in

Figure 1.1 are inputs to or outputs from the algorithm. With `merge`, for example, there are two inputs, intended to come from input iterators, such as the `istream_iterator` shown next to the first socket, and one output, intended to go to an output iterator, such as the `ostream_iterator` shown next to the third socket.

For this fine-grained component approach to work well, there must be a certain minimal level of support from the base programming language. Fortunately, C++ provides such support, especially with its template mechanism. Programmers who want to use one of the generic algorithms need only select the algorithm and the container with which it is to be used. The C++ compiler takes care of the final step of plugging together the algorithm, which is expressed as a function template, with the iterators, which are classes that are associated with the container class.

Programmers can write their own iterator class definitions, perhaps in terms of some particular list node structure already in use in existing code. An important point is that it's generally a lot easier to program such an iterator definition than it would be to recode all the generic algorithms to work with that existing data structure.

Not every generic algorithm and iterator pair can be plugged together; you could say that they must be "plug compatible." (The enforcement of this compatibility in C++ is by means of the normal type checking that C++ compilers do when templates are instantiated. Attempts to combine incompatible components result in compile-time errors.) While it would be possible to make all pairs interface together, it is better not to, because some algorithms are efficient only when using a particular data representation. For example, a sort algorithm may be efficient only for a random access data structure like an array, not for a linked list. In such a case the library should provide a separate algorithm that is suitable for use with lists.

The software library designs that have resulted from this generic programming approach are markedly different from other software libraries.

- The precisely organized, interchangeable building blocks that result from this approach permit many more useful combinations than are possible with more traditional component designs.

- The design is also a suitable basis for further development of components for specialized areas such as databases, user interfaces, and so on.

- By employing compile-time mechanisms and paying due regard to algorithm issues, component generality can be achieved without sacrificing efficiency, in sharp contrast to the inefficiencies often introduced by other C++ library structures involving complex inheritance hierarchies and extensive use of virtual functions.

The bottom-line result of these differences is that generic components are far more useful to programmers, and therefore far more likely to be used, in preference to programming every algorithmic or data structure operation from scratch.

These are tall promises, and you may well be skeptical that STL or any library can fully live up to them. As you read on, though, and start putting this remarkable library to use in your own programming, we believe you will agree that STL truly does fulfill the promise of generic programming.

1.3 How C++ Templates Enable Generic Programming

Adaptability of components is essential to generic programming, so now let's look at how C++ templates enable it. There are two kinds of templates in C++: *class templates* and *function templates*.

1.3.1 Class Templates

Class templates have many uses, but the most obvious one is to provide adaptable storage containers. To take a very simple example, suppose we want to create objects that can store two values, an integer and a character. For this purpose we could define

```
class pair_int_char {
 public:
   int first;
   char second;
   pair_int_char(int x, char y) : first(x), second(y) { }
};
```

We could then write, for example,

```
pair_int_char pair1(13, 'a');
cout << pair1.first << endl;
cout << pair1.second << endl;
```

If we also want objects that can store, say, a Boolean value and a double-precision floating-point number, we could define

```
class pair_bool_double {
 public:
   bool first;
   double second;
   pair_bool_double(bool x, double y) : first(x), second(y){}
};
```

and write, for example,

```
pair_bool_double pair2(true, 0.1);
cout << pair2.first << endl;
cout << pair2.second << endl;
```

The same could be repeated for any of the other infinitely many pairs of types, but a class template permits them all to be expressed with a single definition:

```
template <typename T1, typename T2>
class pair {
 public:
   T1 first;
   T2 second;
   pair(T1 x, T2 y) : first(x), second(y) { }
};
```

Here we've written the class definition in terms of two arbitrary type names, T1 and T2, which are *type parameters*. The names are introduced into the definition as type parameters by the clause

```
template <typename T1, typename T2>
```

which means that we can substitute *actual types* for T1 and T2 to obtain a particular *instantiation* of the **pair** class template. For example, writing

```
pair<int, char> pair3(13, 'a');
pair<bool, double> pair4(true, 0.1);
```

declares **pair3** and **pair4** with structure equivalent to **pair1** and **pair2**, respectively. But now we can also use **pair** in countless other ways with other combinations of actual types, such as

```
pair<double, long> pair5(3.1415, 999);
pair<bool, bool> pair6(false, true);
```

Types defined by other classes can be used as the actual types, for instance,

```
    pair<pair_int_char, float> pair7(pair1, 1.23);
```

or, equivalently,

```
    pair<pair<int, char>, float> pair8(pair3, 1.23);
```

As illustrated here, we can use types produced as class template instantiations anywhere ordinary types can be used.

The class template definition of **pair** is a very simple example of a *generic container class* since it is adaptable to many different uses. However, there is usually more to making an ordinary class into a generic one (in the sense of being truly useful in the widest range of applications) than just adding the **template** keyword and type parameter list. Some modifications may be necessary to ensure that the resulting instances are as efficient as ones defined by ordinary means, no matter what actual types are substituted. Even in the case of a class template definition as simple as **pair**, an improvement can be made. In defining the template class, we wrote the constructor declaration a little too simply:

```
    pair(T1 x, T2 y) : first(x), second(y) { }
```

The problem with this is that **x** and **y** are passed *by value*, which means that if they are large objects, an expensive extra copy will be made when the constructor is called. Instead, **x** and **y** should be passed as *constant reference parameters* so that only an address is passed. And this is, in fact, the way **pair** is defined as an STL component:

```
    template <typename T1, typename T2>
    class pair {
     public:
      T1 first;
      T2 second;
      pair() : first(T1()), second(T2()) { }
      pair(const T1& x, const T2& y) : first(x), second(y) { }
    };
```

One other thing added here is the default constructor, **pair()**, which is useful in situations where a default initialization of **pair** objects is needed in another class definition. In any class definition in which no other constructor is defined, the compiler defines the default constructor for us, but in this case we have defined another constructor and the language rules require us to define the default constructor explicitly.

In the case of more complex class definitions, there are usually many other factors involved in making them widely adaptable and efficient. In this book we will not examine in depth the way STL is implemented, but STL's originators gave careful consideration to maintaining efficiency while making components general.

1.3.2 Function Templates

Function templates can be used to define generic algorithms. Consider a function for computing the maximum of two integers:

```
int intmax(int x, int y)
{
  if (x < y)
    return y;
  else
    return x;
}
```

This function can be used only to compute the maximum of two ints, but we can easily generalize it by making it a function template:

```
template <typename T>
T max(T x, T y)
{
  if (x < y)
    return y;
  else
    return x;
}
```

A big difference from class templates is that you do not have to tell the compiler which types you are using; the compiler can infer them from the types of the arguments.

```
int u = 3, v = 4;
double d = 4.7;
cout << max(u, v) << endl;    // type int is inferred
cout << max(d, 9.3) << endl; // type double is inferred
```

The compiler requires that values of the same type be passed for x and y since the same template type parameter, T, is used for both in the declaration. Thus the following is an error:

```
cout << max(u, d) << endl;
```

It also requires a definition of the < operator taking two parameters of type **T**. For example, recalling one of the uses of the **pair** class template definitions given in the previous section

```
pair<double, long> pair5(3.1415, 999);
```

the following will not compile because there is no definition of **operator<** on two **pair<double, long>** objects:

```
return max(pair5, pair5);
```

But it would compile if we first defined some meaning for **operator<** on objects of this type, such as

```
bool operator<(const pair<double, long>& x,
               const pair<double, long>& y)
  // Compare x and y on their first members:
{
  return x.first < y.first;
}
```

The way the compiler can infer types and match up operator or function calls with the proper overloaded definitions makes template functions an extremely useful feature for generic programming. We'll see more evidence of this later, especially in Section 2.2 when we examine how STL generic algorithms are defined by function templates.

Before we leave the **max** example, though, we should note that the definition of this function template can be improved just as we discussed for the constructor in the **pair** class template definition, by using constant reference parameters:

```
template <typename T>
const T& max(const T& x, const T& y) {
  if (x < y)
    return y;
  else
    return x;
}
```

This is essentially the definition used in STL.

1.3.3   Member Function Templates

In class definitions, whether templated or not, member functions may have template parameters (in addition to any template parameters at the class level). This C++ feature is used in the class templates defining STL containers. For example, the STL vector class has an `insert` member function template whose template parameter specifies the type of iterators to be used:

```
template <typename T>
class vector {
  // ...
 public:
  template <typename InputIterator>
  void insert(iterator position,
              InputIterator first, InputIterator last);
  // ...
};
```

Here `iterator` is the vector iterator type defined within the `vector` class and `position` is an iterator pointing somewhere within the vector object on which insert is invoked. The second and third arguments are also iterators but not necessarily vector iterators. As we'll see in Section 6.1, this `insert` member function can be used to insert elements copied from some other container, such as a list, using iterators supplied by the other container. List iterators are quite different from vector iterators. Defining a function such as `insert` as a member function template, with `InputIterator` as a type parameter, makes it much more generic than if its second and third arguments were of a fixed iterator type.

1.3.4   Explicit Specification of Template Arguments

Suppose we would like to define a function for converting a character array to an STL container such as `vector<char>`. We intend the vector to hold the same character sequence as the given character array. One way to code such a function is

```
vector<char> vec(const char s[])
{
  return vector<char>(&s[0], &s[strlen(s)]);
}
```

In the body of this function we use a constructor of the `vector<char>` class which, like the `insert` function discussed in Section 1.3.3, is a member function template:

```
template <typename InputIterator>
vector(InputIterator first, InputIterator last);
```

In the same way we could define a function to convert a character array into an STL `list` container, with

```
list<char> lst(const char s[])
{
  return list<char>(&s[0], &s[strlen(s)]);
}
```

since `list<char>` also has a constructor member function template of the required form:

```
template <typename InputIterator>
list(InputIterator first, InputIterator last);
```

A major goal of generic programming is to write function definitions as generally as possible, so we might check at this point to see if it is possible to write a single generic conversion function that will convert a `string` to any STL container. In fact, that can be done with the following definition,

```
template <typename Container>
Container make(const char s[])
{
  return Container(&s[0], &s[strlen(s)]);
}
```

This will in fact work with all STL containers because all the classes defining them have a constructor member function template like that shown for vector and list. There is a twist here, though, because although this definition is legal, we cannot instantiate `make` in the same simple way as for other function templates. If we write, for example,

```
list<char> L = make("Hello, world!");  // Incorrect
```

we get a compile-time error. The complaint is that the template parameter, `Container`, is used only in the function's return type, not in its parameters. The language rules say that in such a case, the function cannot be used as we have described. Instead we have to say explicitly which instantiation we intend:

```
list<char> L = make< list<char> >("Hello, world!");
```

That is, we append to the function name the type expression we are substituting for the type parameter `Container`, enclosed in `<` and `>`, just as we do when instantiating a class template. This is called *explicit specification of the template argument*.

Thus we can write a conversion from a character array as `vector<char>` as

```
vector<char> V = make< vector<char> >("Hello, world!");
```

and—as we'll see in many example programs we construct to illustrate operations on containers—we can do conversions from character arrays to any other container type using this single generic `make` function.

1.3.5 Default Template Parameters

Another C++ template feature used in container class definitions and a few other places is default template parameters. For example, the actual form of the STL `vector` class template definition is

```
template <typename T, typename Allocator = allocator<T> >
class vector {
  // ...
};
```

The second template parameter, `Allocator`, has a default value, given by `allocator<T>`. All STL container classes use storage management facilities as provided by `Allocator`, and `allocator` is a type (defined by a class) that provides a standard form of these facilities. Since `Allocator` has a default value, we do not have to pass any allocator when we create an instance of `vector`; that is, `vector<int>` is equivalent to `vector<int, allocator<int> >`.

Allocators are discussed again briefly in Section 2.6 and are covered in detail in Chapter 24.

1.3.6 Partial Specialization

Finally, another C++ template feature used in STL definitions is *partial specialization*. This feature can be used to override a generic class or function template with a version that is more specialized (for reasons of efficiency) but still generic (that is, still has one or more template parameters). We defer further discussion and illustration of this feature until Section 6.1.7, which provides a good example in terms of a generic algorithm for swapping two containers.

1.4 The "Code Bloat" Problem with Templates

When different instantiations of class templates or template functions are used in the same program, the compiler in effect creates different versions of the source code and compiles each one into executable code. (Actually, different versions are usually produced not at the source code level but rather at some intermediate level of code representation.) The main benefit is that each copy is specialized for the types used and thus can be just as efficient as if the specialized code had been written directly. But there is also a potentially severe drawback: if many different instances are used, the many copies can make the executable file huge. This "code bloat" problem is exacerbated by the generality of class templates and functions in a library such as STL, since they are intended to have many useful instantiations and since programmers are encouraged to use them as frequently as possible.

Fortunately, there are techniques for avoiding the most severe consequences of the code bloat problem, at some (usually minor) cost in efficiency. We discuss these techniques in Sections 11.3 and 17.2.

1.5 Understanding STL's Performance Guarantees

STL is unusual among software libraries in that performance guarantees are included in the interface requirements of all of its components. Such guarantees are in fact crucial to making wise choices among components, such as choosing whether to use a list, vector, or deque to represent a sequence in a particular application. The component performance characteristics are stated using big-Oh notation.

1.5.1 Big-Oh Notation and Related Definitions

In most cases, talking about the computing time of an algorithm is simplified by classifying all inputs to the algorithm into subsets characterized by some simple parameter(s). For algorithms that work on containers, usually the size N of the container is a convenient choice of parameter. For inputs of size N, we then consider the *maximum time*, $T(N)$, the algorithm takes. $T(N)$ is also called the *worst-case time* for inputs of size N.

To simplify matters further, we focus on how $T(N)$ behaves for large N, and instead of trying to write a precise formula for $T(N)$, we look for a simple function that provides an *upper bound* on the function. For example, we might have

$$T(N) \leq cN$$

for some constant c and all sufficiently large N. We say in this case that "the time grows at worst linearly with the size of the input." The constant c might have to be chosen differently when the algorithm is compiled and run on different machines, so one last simplification that is frequently made is to express such bounds in a way that hides the constant.

This is done using *big-Oh notation*; for example, the foregoing relation is written

$$T(N) = O(N)$$

In general, if there is some function f such that

$$T(N) \leq cf(N)$$

for some constant c and all sufficiently large N, we write

$$T(N) = O(f(N))$$

In this book the five main cases of this notation are as follows.

- $T(N) = O(N)$ This is the case just mentioned. The algorithm is said to have a *linear time bound* or, more simply, to be *linear time* or just *linear*.

- $T(N) = O(N^2)$ The algorithm is said to have a *quadratic time bound* or to be *quadratic time* or just *quadratic*.

- $T(N) = O(\log N)$ The algorithm is said to have a *logarithmic time bound* or to be *logarithmic time* or just *logarithmic*.

- $T(N) = O(N \log N)$ The algorithm is said to have an *$N \log N$ time bound*.

- $T(N) = O(1)$ The algorithm is said to have an *$O(1)$ time bound* or *a constant time bound* or to be *constant time*. Note that in this case the big-Oh notation is shorthand for $T(N) \leq c$ for some constant c and all sufficiently large N.

In each of these cases, it is important to keep in mind that we are characterizing computing times with upper bounds on *worst-case computing times*. This can be misleading if the worst case occurs extremely rarely, as is the case, for example, with the quicksort algorithm for sorting sequences in place. The worst-case time for this algorithm is quadratic, which is much slower than other sorting algorithms such as heapsort or mergesort. Yet for most situations the quicksort algorithm is the best choice, since it is faster on average than the other algorithms. In such cases, the descriptions we give of computing times go beyond the simple big-Oh bounds on worst-case times to discuss the average times. The average time for an algorithm on inputs of size N is usually calculated by assuming that all inputs of size N occur with equal probability. However, other probability distributions might be more appropriate in some situations.

1.5.2   Amortized Time Complexity

In several cases, the most useful characterization of an algorithm's computing time is neither worst-case time nor average time but *amortized time*. This notion is similar to the manufacturing accounting practice of amortization, in which a one-time cost (such as design cost) is divided by the number of units produced and then attributed to each unit. Amortized time can be a useful way to describe the time an operation on some container takes in cases where the time can vary widely as a sequence of the operations is done, but the total time for a sequence of N operations has a better bound than just N times the worst-case time.

For example, the worst-case time for inserting at the end of an STL vector is $O(N)$, where N is the size of the container, because if there is no extra room the insert operation must allocate new storage and move all the existing elements into the new storage. However, whenever a vector of length N needs to be expanded, $2N$ spaces are allocated, so no such reallocation and copying are necessary for the next $N-1$ insertions. Each of these next $N-1$ insertions can be done in constant time for a total of $O(N)$ time for the N insertions, which is $O(1)$ time for the insertion operation when averaged over the N operations. Thus, we say that the amortized time for insertion is constant or that the time is *amortized constant*.[2] In this example, the amortized constant time bound for insertion more accurately reflects the true cost than does the linear time bound for the worst case. In general, the amortized time for an operation is the total time for a sequence of N

---

[2]Actually, implementations might increase the block size to $1.5N$ or by some other factor besides 2, but as long as the increase is by a constant factor greater than 1, rather than by some constant additional amount, a similar argument can be made that the time for an insertion is amortized constant.

operations divided by N. Note that although amortized time is an average, there is no notion of probability involved, as there is with average computing time.

1.5.3 Limitations of Big-Oh Notation

Big-Oh notation has well-known limitations. The time for an $O(N)$ algorithm might grow at a rate slower than linear growth since it is only an upper bound, or it might grow faster than a linear rate for small N, since the bound holds only for large N. Two $O(N)$ algorithms can differ dramatically in their computing times. One could be uniformly 2 or 10 or 100 times faster than the other, but big-Oh notation suppresses all such differences.

With $O(\log N)$ algorithms even small differences in constant factors can make a dramatic difference. For example, if algorithms 1 and 2 are both $O(\log N)$ but algorithm 2 has a c that is twice as large as that of algorithm 1, then the running time for algorithm 2 with a certain N will be the same as when using algorithm 1 with N^2 (since $\log N^2 = 2 \log N$).

As one moves from one compiler or hardware architecture to another, the hidden constants can change, perhaps enough to alter the case for choosing one algorithm over another.

For these and many other reasons, it is advisable to do empirical performance testing of programs under situations that approximate, to the extent possible, the environment and data that are likely to be encountered in production runs.

Chapter 2

Overview of STL Components

STL contains six major kinds of components: *containers*, *generic algorithms*, *iterators*, *function objects*, *adaptors*, and *allocators*. In this chapter we will cover just the highlights of each kind of component, saving the details for later chapters.

2.1 Containers

In STL, containers are objects that store collections of other objects. There are two categories of STL container types: *sequence containers* and *sorted associative containers*.

2.1.1 Sequence Containers

Sequence containers organize a collection of objects, all of the same type T, into a strictly linear arrangement. The STL sequence container types are as follows:

- `vector<T>` Provides random access to a sequence of varying length (*random access* means that the time to reach the ith element of the sequence is constant; that is, the time doesn't depend on i), with amortized constant time insertions and deletions at the end.

- `deque<T>` Also provides random access to a sequence of varying length, with amortized constant time insertions and deletions at both the beginning and the end.

- `list<T>` Provides only linear time access to a sequence of varying length ($O(N)$, where N is the current length), but with constant time insertions and deletions at *any* given position in the sequence.

Before discussing these sequence container types, we note that in many respects an ordinary C++ array type `T a[N]` can be used as a sequence container, because *all STL generic algorithms are designed to work with arrays in the same way they work with other sequence types.* And another important type, the library-provided `string` type (from header `<string>`), represents sequences of characters in a way that fits together well with STL algorithms and conventions. For example, STL provides a generic algorithm called `reverse` that can reverse many kinds of sequences, including `string` objects and arrays. Here is an example of its use on both a `string` and a character array.

Example 2.1: Using the STL generic `reverse` algorithm with a string and an array

`"ex02-01.cpp"` 20 ≡

```
    #include <iostream>
    #include <string>
    #include <cassert>
    #include <algorithm> // For reverse algorithm
    using namespace std;

    int main()
    {
      cout << "Using reverse algorithm with a string" << endl;
      string string1 = "mark twain";
      reverse(string1.begin(), string1.end());
      assert (string1 == "niawt kram");
      cout << " --- Ok." << endl;

      cout << "Using reverse algorithm with an array" << endl;
      char array1[] = "mark twain";
      int N1 = strlen(array1);
      reverse(&array1[0], &array1[N1]);
      assert (string(array1) == "niawt kram");
      cout << " --- Ok." << endl;
      return 0;
    }
```

The arguments to the first call of `reverse`, namely `string1.begin()` and `string1.end()`, are calls to member functions `begin` and `end` defined by the

string class. These member functions return *iterators*, which are pointer-like objects, referring to the beginning and end of **string1**. The **reverse** function reverses the order of the characters in the range specified by these iterators in place (i.e., the result replaces the original contents of **string1**). The **assert** macro call that follows is a simple check that the result in **string1** is indeed the reverse of the original string. (The sidebar "The Assert Macro" contains more discussion of this and other uses of **assert**.)

The Assert Macro.

In Example 2.1, we check the results of calling **reverse** by using the **assert** macro from the **cassert** header (which corresponds to the C header **assert.h**). This macro takes a Boolean-valued expression as its single argument and does nothing if that expression evaluates to true, but it prints an informative message and terminates the program if the expression evaluates to false. In the first use of **assert**, the argument is **string1 == "niawt kram"**, in which the == operator defined on **string** is used to compare two **string** objects character by character. One **string** involved in the comparison is **string1** and the second is the result of a compiler-inserted call of the **string** constructor that takes **"niawt kram"** and constructs a **string** object.

   In the second **assert** call the argument is **string(array1) == "niawt kram"**, in which we use the aforementioned **string** constructor on the character array **array1** so that the **string** == operator is used. Note that if we had written **array1 == "niawt kram"**, the == operator would have had the wrong meaning. (It would check equality of pointers, not the string values to which they point.)

   In many of the example programs in Part I we use the **assert** macro in a similar way to show the results we expect from algorithm or data structure operations.

   In the second call of **reverse** we pass pointers to the beginning and end of the character array **array1**. Note that **&array1[N1]** is actually the address of the location one position past where the last character is stored. The convention with every STL algorithm is that whenever two iterators **first** and **last** are passed to the algorithm, they are expected to define the location at which to start traversing a sequence (**first**) and a location at which to stop traversing (**last**)—without attempting to process the element at which **last** points. This stopping point is thus referred to as a "past-the-end" pointer or iterator. For the **string** class and the STL sequence container classes, the **end** member function is defined to return a past-the-end iterator rather than one that actually points at the last element of the sequence.

Vectors provide all the standard features of arrays but are also expandable and have many other useful features, as will be discussed in Sections 2.1.1 and 6.1. In the case of **reverse**, a **vector** example is the following.

Example 2.2: Using the STL generic **reverse** algorithm with a vector

```
"ex02-02.cpp" 22a ≡
    #include <iostream>
    #include <vector>
    #include <cassert>
    #include <algorithm> // For reverse
    using namespace std;
    ⟨Define make function (builds a container of characters) 22b⟩
    int main()
    {
      cout << "Using reverse algorithm with a vector" << endl;
      vector<char> vector1 = make< vector<char> >("mark twain");
      reverse(vector1.begin(), vector1.end());
      assert (vector1 == make< vector<char> >("niawt kram"));
      cout << " --- Ok." << endl;
      return 0;
    }
```

In writing this example program we include a reference to a "program part" that is separately defined:

```
⟨Define make function (builds a container of characters) 22b⟩ ≡
    template <typename Container>
    Container make(const char s[])
    {
      return Container(&s[0], &s[strlen(s)]);
    }
```
Used in parts 22a, 24, 27, 28, 29, 31, 32, 99, 116, 120, 135, 141, 142, 148, 153, 155, 157, 158, 164, 165, 168, 170, 203.

This is the function template definition we already saw in Section 1.3.3. We use this function template in many of the small example programs throughout Part I of this book to construct containers from strings. See the sidebar

"A Little Literate Programming" for more on how program parts are defined and used in this book.

A Little Literate Programming.

In the definition of the part "Define make function (builds a container of characters)," the small label 22b is the "part number" assigned to it. A part number is the current page number and if more than one is defined on the same page, a letter is appended. The purpose of the part number is to help readers locate the definition of the part when they see references to it on other pages in the book. If you turn to any of the pages listed in the line "Used in parts ..." that follows the part definition, you will see a reference to this part included in the text of an example program or other part definition. This practice is a simple case of D. E. Knuth's "literate programming" style of simultaneous coding and documenting. In Part I of this book our use of this style is limited to the labeling of example programs and definitions and references to only a few parts defining functions or classes, but in Part II we explain literate programming more fully (Chapter 12) and use it extensively in presenting more complex example programs.

In the call of `reverse`, the program uses the `vector` member functions `begin` and `end`, which return the beginning and ending positions of a `vector` object. Again the convention is that the ending position is the first position past the end of the actual contents.

In the assertion we check to see if the vector resulting from the `reverse` call is equal to the `vector` constructed with the call of our generic `make` function,

```
make< vector<char> >("niawt kram");
```

For the comparison of the two vectors, we use the `==` operator, since STL defines this operator as an equality test for vectors. In general, STL defines the `==` operator for all its container classes. (We have previously used the fact that it is defined for objects of the standard `string` class.)

Our `reverse` example can also be written using a `list` instead of a `vector`.

Example 2.3: Demonstrating generic `reverse` algorithm on a list

"ex02-03.cpp" 24 ≡

```
#include <iostream>
#include <cassert>
#include <list>
#include <algorithm>  // For reverse
using namespace std;
⟨Define make function (builds a container of characters) 22b⟩

int main()
{
  cout << "Demonstrating generic reverse algorithm on a list"
      << endl;
  list<char> list1 = make< list<char> >("mark twain");
  reverse(list1.begin(), list1.end());
  assert (list1 == make< list<char> >("niawt kram"));
  cout << " --- Ok." << endl;
  return 0;
}
```

The example could be written equally well using deques. As we'll see, vectors, lists, and deques are not completely interchangeable, but in this case each one works as well as the other. That's because each defines `begin` and `end` member functions with the same abstract meaning, though the implementations are quite different: vectors are represented using arrays; lists are represented using doubly linked nodes; and deques are typically implemented with a two-level array structure. The only difference that might be apparent to the user in the example of using the generic `reverse` function would be in performance. In this simple case there wouldn't be a noticeable difference in performance, but in other cases, using different algorithms and larger sequences, there can be a tremendous performance advantage to using one kind of sequence over another. (But none is a winner in all cases, which is why more than one is provided in the library.)

2.1.2   Sorted Associative Containers

Sorted associative containers provide an ability for fast retrieval of objects from the collection based on keys. The size of the collection can vary at run time. STL has four sorted associative container types:

- `set<Key>` Supports unique keys (contains at most one of each key value) and provides for fast retrieval of the keys themselves.

- `multiset<Key>` Supports duplicate keys (possibly contains multiple copies of the same key value) and provides for fast retrieval of the keys themselves.

- `map<Key, T>` Supports unique keys (of type `Key`) and provides for fast retrieval of another type `T` based on the keys.

- `multimap<Key, T>` Supports duplicate keys (of type `Key`) and provides for fast retrieval of another type `T` based on the keys.

An example of a sorted associative container is `map<string, long>`, which might be used to hold associations between names and telephone numbers, for example, to represent a telephone directory. Given a name, such a map would provide for fast retrieval of a phone number, as in the following example program.

Example 2.4: Demonstrating an STL map

"ex02-04.cpp" 25 ≡

```cpp
#include <iostream>
#include <map>
#include <string>
using namespace std;

int main()
{
  map<string, long> directory;
  directory["Bogart"] = 1234567;
  directory["Bacall"] = 9876543;
  directory["Cagney"] = 3459876;
  // And so on

  // Read some names and look up their numbers:
  string name;
  while (cin >> name)
    if (directory.find(name) != directory.end())
      cout << "The phone number for " << name
           << " is " << directory[name] << "\n";
    else
      cout << "Sorry, no listing for " << name << "\n";
  return 0;
}
```

In this program, we use the C++ Standard Library **string** class from the header file **string**. We declare **directory** as a **map** with **string** as the **Key** type and **long** as the associated type **T**.

We next insert some names and numbers in the directory with array-like assignments such as **directory["Bogart"] = 1234567**. This notation is possible because the **map** type defines **operator[]** analogously to the corresponding operator on arrays. If we know **name** is in the directory, we can retrieve the associated number with **directory[name]**. In this program we first check to see if **name** is a key stored in **directory** using **find**, a member function of the **map** container (and all the sorted associative containers). The **find** function returns an iterator that refers to the entry in the table with **name** as its key if there is such an entry; otherwise it returns an "off-the-end" iterator, which is the same iterator returned by the **end** member function. Thus, by comparing the iterator returned by **find** with that returned by **end**, we are able to determine whether there is an entry in the table with key **name**.

The STL approach to containers differs in a major way from other C++ container class libraries: STL containers do not provide many operations on the data objects they contain. Instead, STL provides *generic algorithms*, the next topic.

2.2   Generic Algorithms

Two of the simplest generic algorithms in STL are **find** and **merge**.

2.2.1   The Generic Find Algorithm

As a simple example of the flexibility of STL algorithms, consider the **find** algorithm, used to search a sequence for a particular value. It's possible to use **find** with any of the STL containers. With arrays, we might write the following program.

Example 2.5: Demonstrating the generic **find** algorithm with an array

```
"ex02-05.cpp" 26 ≡
    #include <iostream>
    #include <cassert>
    #include <algorithm>  // for find
    using namespace std;
```

```
int main()
{
  cout << "Demonstrating generic find algorithm with "
       << "an array." << endl;
  char s[] = "C++ is a better C";
  int len = strlen(s);

  // Search for the first occurrence of the letter e:
  const char* where = find(&s[0], &s[len], 'e');

  assert (*where == 'e' && *(where+1) == 't');
  cout << " --- Ok." << endl;
  return 0;
}
```

This program uses **find** to search the elements in s[0], ..., s[len-1] to see if any is equal to 'e'. If 'e' does occur in the array s, the pointer **where** is assigned the first position where it occurs so that *where == 'e'. In this case it does occur in the array, but if it didn't, then **find** would return &s[len]. This return value is the location one position past the end of the array.

Now, instead of an array, our data might be stored in a **vector**, a type of container that provides fast random access like arrays but also can grow and shrink dynamically. To find an element in a vector, we can use the same **find** algorithm we used for arrays.

Example 2.6: Demonstrating the generic **find** algorithm with a vector

"ex02-06.cpp" 27 ≡

```
#include <iostream>
#include <cassert>
#include <vector>
#include <algorithm>  // For find
using namespace std;
⟨Define make function (builds a container of characters) 22b⟩

int main()
{
  cout << "Demonstrating generic find algorithm with "
       << "a vector." << endl;

  vector<char> vector1 =
    make< vector<char> >("C++ is a better C");
```

```
// Search for the first occurrence of the letter e:
vector<char>::iterator
  where = find(vector1.begin(), vector1.end(), 'e');

assert (*where == 'e' && *(where + 1) == 't');
cout << " --- Ok." << endl;
return 0;
}
```

This time we construct a vector containing the same characters as array s, using a constructor member of class **vector** that initializes the vector using the sequence of values in an array. Instead of **char***, the type of **where** is **vector<char>::iterator**. *Iterators* are pointer-like objects that can be used to traverse a sequence of objects. When a sequence is stored in a **char** array, the iterators *are* C++ pointers (of type **char***), but when a sequence is stored in a container such as **vector**, we obtain an appropriate iterator type from the container class. Each STL container type **C** defines **C::iterator** as an iterator type that can be used with type **C** containers.

In either case, when the **find** algorithm is called as in

```
where = find(first, last, value);
```

it assumes the following:

- Iterator **first** marks the position in a sequence where it should *start* processing.

- Iterator **last** marks the position where it can *stop* processing.

Such starting and ending positions are exactly what the **begin** and **end** member functions of the **vector** class (and all other STL classes that define containers) supply.

If the data elements are in a list, once again we can use the same **find** algorithm.

Example 2.7: Demonstrating the generic **find** algorithm with a list

```
"ex02-07.cpp" 28 ≡
    #include <iostream>
    #include <cassert>
    #include <list>
    #include <algorithm> // for find
```

```
using namespace std;
⟨Define make function (builds a container of characters) 22b⟩

int main()
{
    cout << "Demonstrating generic find algorithm with "
         << "a list." << endl;

    list<char> list1 = make< list<char> >("C++ is a better C");

    // Search for the first occurrence of the letter e:
    list<char>::iterator
        where = find(list1.begin(), list1.end(), 'e');

    list<char>::iterator next = where;
    ++next;
    assert (*where == 'e' && *next == 't');
    cout << " --- Ok." << endl;
    return 0;
}
```

There is one subtle difference between this program and the previous one using a vector because the iterators associated with list containers do not support the operator + used in the expression *(where + 1). The reason is explained in Chapter 4. All STL iterators are required to support ++, however, and that is what we use here to advance another iterator next to the next position past where.

If our data is in a deque, which is a random access container similar to arrays and vectors but allowing even more flexibility in the way it can grow and shrink, we can once again use find.

Example 2.8: Demonstrating the generic find algorithm with a deque

```
"ex02-08.cpp" 29 ≡
    #include <iostream>
    #include <cassert>
    #include <deque>
    #include <algorithm>  // For find
    using namespace std;
    ⟨Define make function (builds a container of characters) 22b⟩

    int main()
    {
```

```
        cout << "Demonstrating generic find algorithm with "
            << "a deque." << endl;
        deque<char> deque1 =
          make< deque<char> >("C++ is a better C");

        // Search for the first occurrence of the letter e:
        deque<char>::iterator
          where = find(deque1.begin(), deque1.end(), 'e');
        assert (*where == 'e' && *(where + 1) == 't');
        cout << " --- Ok." << endl;
        return 0;
    }
```

This program is identical to the vector version except for the substitution of `deque` for `vector` throughout (deque iterators, unlike list iterators, do support the + operator).

In fact, the `find` algorithm can be used to find values in all STL containers. The key point with `find` and all other STL generic algorithms is that since they can be used by many or all containers, individual containers do not have to define as many separate member functions, resulting in reduced code size and simplified container interfaces.

2.2.2 The Generic Merge Algorithm

The flexibility of STL generic algorithms is even greater than the examples involving `find` have indicated. Consider an algorithm such as `merge`, which combines the elements of two sorted sequences into a single sorted sequence. In general, if `merge` is called as

```
        merge(first1, last1, first2, last2, result);
```

it assumes the following:

- `first1` and `last1` are iterators marking the beginning and end of one input sequence whose elements are of some type T.

- `first2` and `last2` are iterators delimiting another input sequence whose elements are also of type T.

- The two input sequences are in ascending order according to the `<` operator for type T.

- `result` marks the beginning of the sequence where the result should be stored.

Under these conditions the result contains all elements of the two input sequences and is also in ascending order. *This interface is flexible enough that the two input sequences and the result sequence can be in different kinds of containers,* as the next example shows.

Example 2.9: Demonstrating the generic `merge` algorithm with an array, a list, and a `deque`

"ex02-09.cpp" 31 ≡

```
#include <iostream>
#include <cassert>
#include <list>
#include <deque>
#include <algorithm>  // For merge
using namespace std;
⟨Define make function (builds a container of characters) 22b⟩

int main()
{
  cout << "Demonstrating generic merge algorithm with "
       << "an array, a list, and a deque." << endl;
  char s[] = "aeiou";
  int len = strlen(s);
  list<char> list1 =
     make< list<char> >("bcdfghjklmnpqrstvwxyz");

  // Initialize deque1 with 26 copies of the letter x:
  deque<char> deque1(26, 'x');

  // Merge array s and list1, putting result in deque1:
  merge(&s[0], &s[len], list1.begin(), list1.end(),
        deque1.begin());
  assert (deque1 ==
          make< deque<char> >("abcdefghijklmnopqrstuvwxyz"));
  cout << " --- Ok." << endl;
  return 0;
}
```

In this program we create a deque to hold the result of merging array `s` and `list1`. Note that the character sequences in both `s` and `list1` are in ascending order, as is the result produced by `merge` in `deque1`.

We can even merge portions of one sequence with portions of another. For example, we can modify the program in Example 2.9 to merge the first five characters of **s** with the first ten characters of **deque1**, putting the result into **list1** (note that we reverse the roles of **list1** and **deque1**).

Example 2.10: Demonstrating generic **merge** algorithm, merging parts of an array and a **deque**, putting the result into a list

```
"ex02-10.cpp" 32 ≡
        #include <iostream>
        #include <string>
        #include <cassert>
        #include <list>
        #include <deque>
        #include <algorithm>   // For merge
        using namespace std;
        ⟨Define make function (builds a container of characters) 22b⟩
        int main()
        {
           cout << "Demonstrating generic merge algorithm,\n"
                << "merging parts of an array and a deque, putting\n"
                << "the result into a list." << endl;
           char s[] = "acegikm";

           deque<char> deque1 =
             make< deque<char> >("bdfhjlnopqrstuvwxyz");

           // Initialize list1 with 26 copies of the letter x:
           list<char> list1(26, 'x');

           // Merge first 5 letters in array s with first 10 in
           // deque1, putting result in list1:
           merge(&s[0], &s[5], deque1.begin(), deque1.begin() + 10,
                   list1.begin());

           assert (list1 ==
                      make< list<char> >("abcdefghijlnopqxxxxxxxxxxx"));
           cout << " --- Ok." << endl;
           return 0;
        }
```

These are simple examples, but they already hint at the immense range of possible uses of such generic algorithms.

2.3 Iterators

Understanding iterators is the key to understanding fully the STL framework and learning how to best make use of the library. STL generic algorithms are written in terms of iterator parameters, and STL containers provide iterators that can be plugged into the algorithms, as we saw in Figure 1.1. Figure 2.1 again depicts this relationship, together with relationships between other major categories of STL components. These very general components are designed to "plug together" in a myriad of different useful ways to produce the kind of larger and more specialized components found in other libraries. The main kind of "wiring" for connecting components together is the category called iterators (drawn as ribbon cables in Figures 2.1 and 2.2, which depicts the hierarchical relationship among different iterator categories). One kind of iterator is an ordinary C++ pointer, but iterators other than pointers may exist. These other kinds of iterators are required, however, to behave like pointers in the sense that one can perform operations like `++` and `*` on them and expect them to behave similarly to pointers: for instance, `++i` advances an iterator `i` to the next location, and `*i` returns the location into which a value can be stored, as in `*i = x`, or its value can be used in an expression, as in `x = *i`.

Consider the STL generic function `accumulate`. When called with iterators `first` and `last` and a value `init`,

```
accumulate(first, last, init);
```

adds up `init` plus the values in positions `first` up to but not including `last` and returns the sum. For example, we could write the following program to compute and print the sum of the values in a vector.

Example 2.11: Demonstrating the generic `accumulate` function

```
"ex02-11.cpp" 33 ≡
    #include <iostream>
    #include <vector>
    #include <cassert>
    #include <numeric>  // for accumulate
    using namespace std;

    int main()
    {
        cout << "Demonstrating the accumulate function." << endl;
```

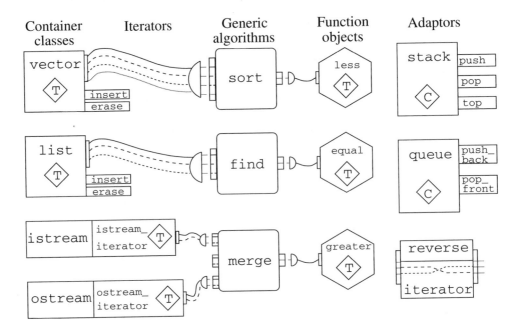

Figure 2.1: Five of the six major categories of STL components (not shown are allocators)

```
int x[5] = {2, 3, 5, 7, 11};
// Initialize vector1 to x[0] through x[4]:
vector<int> vector1(&x[0], &x[5]);

int sum = accumulate(vector1.begin(), vector1.end(), 0);

assert (sum == 28);
cout << " --- Ok." << endl;
return 0;
}
```

This program uses **accumulate** to add up the integers in **vector1**, which is traversed using iterators **vector1.begin()** and **vector1.end()**. We could also use **accumulate** with the array **x** by writing

```
sum = accumulate(&x[0], &x[5], 0);
```

or, say, with a list of **doubles**, as in

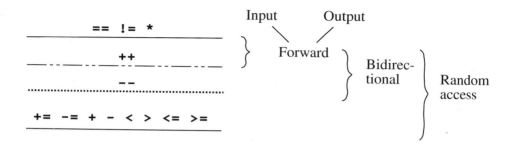

Figure 2.2: Hierarchical relationship among STL iterator categories

```
double y[5] = {2.0, 3.0, 5.0, 7.0, 11.0};
list<double> list1(&y[0], &y[5]);
double sum = accumulate(list1.begin(), list1.end(), 0.0);
```

In each case, the abstract meaning is the same—adding to the initial value the values in the range indicated by the iterators—but the type of iterators and the type of the initial value determine how `accumulate` is adapted to the specific task.

Let's look more closely at the way `accumulate` uses iterators. It can be defined as follows:

```
template <typename InputIterator, typename T>
T accumulate(InputIterator first, InputIterator last, T init)
{
  while (first != last) {
    init = init + *first;
    ++first;
  }
  return init;
}
```

The only operations it performs on iterators are inequality checking with `!=`, dereferencing with `*`, and incrementing with prefix `++`. These operations, together with postfix `++` and equality checking, `==`, are the only operations required by the category of iterators called *input iterators*. One other characteristic of input iterators, from which they get their name, is that the `*` operation is required only to be able to read from positions in a container, not to write into them. With *output iterators*, on the other hand, `*` is required only to be able to write, not to read, and equality and inequality checking are not required.

STL defines three other categories of iterators: *forward iterators, bidirectional iterators,* and *random access iterators.* Except for input and output iterators, the relationship between all these categories is hierarchical, as shown in Figure 2.2. That is, each category adds new requirements to those imposed by the previous category, which means that iterators in a later category are also members of earlier ones. For example, a bidirectional iterator is also a forward iterator, and a random access iterator is also a bidirectional and a forward iterator.

Algorithms, such as `accumulate`, `find`, and `merge`, that are written to work with input iterators are more generic than those that require more powerful iterators, as with `sort`, which requires random access iterators. For example, `sort` cannot be used with STL list containers, because list iterators are only bidirectional and not random access. Instead, STL provides a list member function for sorting that works efficiently with its bidirectional iterators. As we will see in Chapter 4, STL's goal of efficiency motivates placing limitations on the generality of some generic algorithms, and the organization of iterators into categories is the chief means of achieving this goal.

2.4   Function Objects

The `accumulate` function discussed in the previous section is very general in terms of its use of iterators but not as general as it might be in terms of the assumptions it makes about the type of values to which the iterators refer (called the *value type* of the iterators). The `accumulate` definition assumes that there is a + operator defined on the value type by its use of + in the expression

```
init = init + *first;
```

This allows the function to be used with any of the C++ built-in numeric types or with any user-defined type `T` in which such an operator is defined to add up the values in a sequence. But the abstract notion of accumulation applies to more than just addition; one can equally well accumulate a product of a sequence of values, for example. Thus STL provides another, more general, version of `accumulate`:

```
template <typename InputIterator, typename T,
          typename BinaryOperation>
T accumulate(InputIterator first, InputIterator last,
```

```
                    T init, BinaryOperation binary_op)
{
  while (first != last) {
    init = binary_op(init, *first);
    ++first;
  }
  return init;
}
```

Instead of being written in terms of +, this definition introduces another parameter, binary_op, as the binary operation used to combine values.

How can this more general version of accumulate be used to compute a product? If we define a function mult as in the following program, we can use it as the binary_op parameter to accumulate.

Example 2.12: Using the generic accumulate algorithm to compute a product

"ex02-12.cpp" 37 ≡

```cpp
#include <iostream>
#include <vector>
#include <cassert>
#include <numeric>  // For accumulate
using namespace std;

int mult(int x, int y) { return x * y; }

int main()
{
  cout << "Using generic accumulate algorithm to "
       << "compute a product." << endl;

  int x[5] = {2, 3, 5, 7, 11};

  // Initialize vector1 to x[0] through x[4]:
  vector<int> vector1(&x[0], &x[5]);

  int product = accumulate(vector1.begin(), vector1.end(),
                           1, mult);

  assert (product == 2310);
  cout << " --- Ok." << endl;
  return 0;
}
```

(Note that we also changed the initial value from 0 to 1, which is the proper "identity element" for multiplication.) Here we are passing to `accumulate` an ordinary function, `mult`. What is actually passed is the address of the function, which we could have written explicitly as `&mult`. This is only one of the ways C++ supports passing functions to other functions. More generally, one can pass any *function object,* which is any entity that can be applied to zero or more arguments to obtain a value and/or modify the state of the computation. Besides ordinary functions, another kind of function object is *an object of a type defined by a class or struct in which the function call operator is overloaded.* Here's an example of defining and passing such a function object.

Example 2.13: Using the generic `accumulate` algorithm to compute a product, using a function object

```
"ex02-13.cpp" 38 ≡
     #include <iostream>
     #include <vector>
     #include <cassert>
     #include <numeric>  // For accumulate
     using namespace std;

     class multiply {
      public:
        int operator()(int x, int y) const { return x * y; }
     };

     int main()
     {
       cout << "Using generic accumulate algorithm to "
            << "compute a product." << endl;

       int x[5] = {2, 3, 5, 7, 11};

       // Initialize vector1 to x[0] through x[4]:
       vector<int> vector1(&x[0], &x[5]);

       int product = accumulate(vector1.begin(), vector1.end(),
                                1, multiply());

       assert (product == 2310);
       cout << " --- Ok." << endl;
       return 0;
     }
```

By defining the function call operator, `operator()`, in class `multiply`, we define a type of object that can be applied to an argument list, just as a function can. Note that the object passed to `accumulate` is obtained by a call of the default constructor of the class, `multiply()`, which is supplied automatically by the compiler since we didn't explicitly define it in the class definition. Note also that this object has no storage associated with it, just a function definition. (In some cases, though, it is useful to store data in function objects.)

What's the advantage, if any, of using class-defined function objects rather than ordinary functions? We'll answer this question in detail in Chapter 8, but one of the main points is that class-defined function objects can carry with them additional information that an ordinary function cannot, and this information can be used by generic algorithms or containers that need more complex knowledge about a function than `accumulate` does. There are also advantages of efficiency and generality.

Before leaving this topic, we should mention that in Example 2.11 it wasn't really necessary to define class `multiply`, since STL includes such a definition, although in a more general form:

```cpp
template <typename T>
class multiplies : public binary_function<T, T, T> {
public:
  T operator()(const T& x, const T& y) const {
    return x * y;
  }
};
```

This class inherits from another STL component, `binary_function`, whose purpose is to hold extra information about the function, as will be discussed in Chapter 8. Using this definition, the program can be written as follows.

Example 2.14: Using the generic `accumulate` algorithm to compute a product, using `multiplies`

"ex02-14.cpp" 39 ≡

```cpp
#include <iostream>
#include <vector>
#include <cassert>
#include <numeric>  // For accumulate
#include <functional>  // For multiplies
using namespace std;

int main()
```

```
{
    cout << "Using generic accumulate algorithm to "
         << "compute a product." << endl;

    int x[5] = {2, 3, 5, 7, 11};

    // Initialize vector1 to x[0] through x[4]:
    vector<int> vector1(&x[0], &x[5]);

    int product = accumulate(vector1.begin(), vector1.end(),
                             1, multiplies<int>());

    assert (product == 2310);
    cout << " --- Ok." << endl;
    return 0;
}
```

With `multiplies<int>()`, we just call the default constructor of class `multiplies` instantiated with type `int`. A few of the other STL-provided function objects are shown in the fourth column of Figure 2.1.

2.5 Adaptors

A component that modifies the interface of another component is called an *adaptor*. Adaptors are depicted in the last column of Figure 2.1. For example, `reverse_iterator` is a component that adapts an iterator type into a new type of iterator with all the capabilities of the original but with the direction of traversal reversed. This is useful because sometimes the standard traversal order is not what's needed in a particular computation. For example, `find` returns an iterator referring to the first occurrence of a value in a sequence, but we might want the last occurrence instead. We could use `reverse` to reverse the order of the elements in the sequence and then use `find`, but we can do it without disturbing or copying the sequence by using reverse iterators. In Figure 2.1, a reverse iterator component is depicted as having the "wires" for `++` and `--` crossed.

Continuing with `accumulate` as an example, it might not appear too useful to traverse a sequence in reverse order to accumulate its values, since the sum should be the same as with a forward traversal. That's true of a sequence of integers with `+` as the combining function, since on integers `+` obeys the laws $(x + y) + z = x + (y + z)$ (associativity) and $x + y = y + x$ (commutativity), but these properties can fail for floating-point numbers because of round-off and overflow errors (associativity can fail even with ints because of overflow). With floating-point numbers, round-off errors are usually smaller if the numbers are added in order of increasing size; otherwise, values that are very small relative to the running sum may have no effect at all on the sum. Suppose we have a vector of values in descending order and we want to accumulate their sum. To add them in ascending order, we can use accumulate with reverse iterators.

Example 2.15: Demonstrating the generic accumulate algorithm with a reverse iterator

```
"ex02-15.cpp" 41 ≡
    #include <iostream>
    #include <vector>
    #include <cassert>
    #include <numeric>  // For accumulate
    using namespace std;

    int main()
    {
      cout << "Demonstrating generic accumulate algorithm with "
           << "a reverse iterator." << endl;

      float small = (float)1.0/(1 << 26);
      float x[5] = {1.0, 3*small, 2*small, small, small};

      // Initialize vector1 to x[0] through x[4]:
      vector<float> vector1(&x[0], &x[5]);

      cout << "Values to be added: " << endl;

      vector<float>::iterator i;
      cout.precision(10);
      for (i = vector1.begin(); i != vector1.end(); ++i)
        cout << *i << endl;
      cout << endl;

      float sum = accumulate(vector1.begin(), vector1.end(),
                             (float)0.0);

      cout << "Sum accumulated from left = " <<  sum << endl;

      float sum1 = accumulate(vector1.rbegin(), vector1.rend(),
```

```
                              (float)0.0);

    cout << "Sum accumulated from right = "
         << (double)sum1 << endl;
    return 0;
}
```

In computing `sum1`, we use `vector` member functions `rbegin` and `rend` to obtain iterators of type `vector<float>::reverse_iterator`, which, like `vector<float>::iterator`, is defined as part of the `vector` interface. The output of this program will vary depending on the precision used in type `float`, but the value of `small` was chosen to make a difference between `sum` and `sum1` for a precision of about eight decimal places.[1] In this case, the output is as follows.

Output from Example 2.15

```
Demonstrating accumulate function with a reverse iterator.
Values to be added:
1
4.470348358e-08
2.980232239e-08
1.490116119e-08
1.490116119e-08
Sum accumulated from left = 1
Sum accumulated from right = 1.000000119
```

The sum accumulated from the right, using the smaller values first, is the more accurate one.

The type `vector<float>::reverse_iterator` is actually defined using an iterator adaptor. We could have used this adaptor directly in our program by writing

```
reverse_iterator<vector<float>::iterator> start(vector1.end()),
                                  finish(vector1.begin());
float sum1 = accumulate(start, finish, (float)0.0);
```

Here `start` and `finish` are declared as variables of type

```
reverse_iterator<vector<float>::iterator>
```

---

[1]The output shows ten significant digits, but that is an artifact of the output routine.

CHAPTER 3

How STL Differs from Other Libraries

Before going on to the more detailed discussion of STL components in the following chapters, let's briefly examine some of the major differences between STL and other C++ libraries.

First, most C++ libraries have containers that are intrusive in that they require the objects contained to be derived from some common ancestor. STL containers do not assume this kind of inheritance; they can hold anything, including built-in types.

Second, in traditional container class libraries, all algorithms are associated with particular classes and are implemented as member functions. If a list class in such a library has a search algorithm like `find`, it is distinct from the search algorithm of the vector class. This kind of organization has a major problem: each class in the library must contain a huge amount of source code and documentation. With m containers and n operations (like `find`) defined on them, you need to define and document mn operations. Otherwise, the library classes will simply not have many of the operations we may need to perform. In this case, we are forced either to abandon one class for another or to convert back and forth between two data representations to do certain operations. Such conversions not only increase the number of classes we have to understand (and in some cases maintain) but are often the cause of serious run-time performance problems.

The STL approach goes a long way toward solving this problem. Instead of m containers and mn operations to define and document, we have to deal with only m containers and n generic operations. Thus we have a much greater range of flexibility in choosing algorithms and containers than with traditional class libraries, yet the number of interfaces to be understood and the total amount of source code to be maintained in the library remains small.

3.1 Extensibility

No software library does everything, and no one claims that STL is an exception. But in comparison with traditional class libraries, it is relatively easy to extend STL when necessary.

In traditional libraries, where algorithms are associated with particular classes, it may be possible to add an algorithm by deriving a new class from a library class. This approach has some drawbacks:

- It works only if the original designer of the class anticipated such extensions and carefully provided hooks for them (e.g., making some data members protected rather than private or some functions virtual rather than nonvirtual).

- More often than not, one must modify the source code of the classes—assuming the source is even available—possibly introducing subtle bugs or causing other problems in testing, maintenance, and version control.

STL, on the other hand, has an *open and orthogonal structure* that allows programmers to design their own algorithms to work with the library's containers or even their own containers to work with the library's algorithms, without touching (or even reading) the source code.

3.2 Component Interchangeability

How is this openness and orthogonality of STL components achieved? Basically, the solution is one with which we are already familiar in many manufacturing industries: *component interchangeability*, achieved by making the component interfaces as simple and uniform as possible.

We're all familiar with the benefits of interchangeability in tools and parts industries, and many attempts at it have been made even in the software industry. Beginning with some of the current STL's ancestors several years ago, the push toward software component interchangeability has been greater than in any other library design.

We've already seen some aspects of the interchangeability of STL components in the STL `find` and `merge` algorithms (Sections 2.2.1 and 2.2.2). These algorithms work with such a wide variety of containers because their interfaces are designed to access the sequences involved in the computation only in very limited ways, through the pointer-like objects called iterators.

The key point to be made here is that algorithms in STL are not specified directly in terms of the data structures on which they operate. Rather, algorithms and containers in STL are combined as follows:

- For each container, we specify which category of iterators it provides.

- For each algorithm, we state with which category of iterators it works.

By specifying algorithms in terms of iterators rather than in terms of the data structures directly, data structure independence becomes possible. This is what allows the algorithms to be so "generic," allowing each algorithm to operate on a variety of data structures. No other library allows this to the extent STL does.

Furthermore, conventions about how iterators mark the beginning and end of the data are uniformly observed. Consider the `sort` algorithm, which, like `find`, works with the data in a single sequence (it stores the sorted result in the same sequence). Like `find`, `sort` obtains access to the sequence through two iterators, marking the beginning and stopping points:

```
long a[10000];
vector<int> v;
deque<double> d;

// ... Code to insert values in a, v, and d

// Sort all the elements in array a:
sort(&a[0], &a[10000]);

// Sort all the elements in vector v:
sort(v.begin(), v.end());

// Sort all the elements in deque d:
sort(d.begin(), d.end());

// Sort the first 100 elements in deque d:
sort(d.begin(), d.begin() + 100);
```

In short, the algorithms are uniform in the assumptions they make about how to access data, and the way containers provide access to the data is entirely consistent with the algorithms' assumptions.

The iterator concept is explained in much more detail in Chapter 4.

3.3 Algorithm/Container Compatibility

Now we come to one of the most crucial points in understanding STL. *Although some STL algorithms, like* find *and* merge, *are completely generic— that is, they work with any kind of container—it is not possible to plug together every algorithm with every container in the library.*

In theory, all STL algorithm and container components could be made to interface together, but it was deliberately decided not to do so simply because some algorithms would not be efficient when used with some containers.

The sort algorithm is a good example. The algorithm that's used (a variation of quicksort) is efficient only when random access to the data is possible. Random access is provided by arrays, vectors, and deques but not by lists or other STL containers. So it is not possible to say

```
list<int> list1;
// ... Code to insert values in list1

sort(list1.begin(), list1.end());  // incorrect
```

The list class provides a member function sort that sorts lists efficiently. For example, in the foregoing code one can efficiently sort list1 by calling list1.sort().

At this point, you may be beginning to suspect that STL may not be that different from traditional class libraries after all—maybe it has its own proliferation of separate algorithms in different classes. That's not really the case for a couple of reasons. First, many STL algorithms (like find and merge) are completely generic. There are only a few algorithms in STL, like list's sort member function, that are specific to a single container class. Many, like the generic sort, work with several kinds of containers, though not all do.

Second, for the algorithms that work only with certain kinds of containers, it is not difficult to tell with which containers they can be used. We just have to look at how algorithms and containers are combined with each other using iterators, which is the topic of the next chapter.

CHAPTER 4

Iterators

Iterators are pointer-like objects that STL algorithms use to traverse the sequence of objects stored in a container. Iterators are of central importance in the design of STL because of their role as intermediaries between containers and generic algorithms. They enable generic algorithms to be written without concern for how data sequences are stored, and they enable containers to be written without having to code a large number of algorithms on them. However, as discussed in the preceding chapter, for reasons of efficiency it is not possible to have every generic algorithm work with every container. But then how do we know which combinations are possible? For the answer to this question, we have to examine one of the key technical ideas behind STL, the classification of iterators into five categories: *input, output, forward, bidirectional*, and *random access* (recall Figure 2.1). We begin this chapter by defining precisely what these categories are, and then we show how they are used in specifying which algorithms can be used with which containers.

Before we get to the categories, there is another particularly useful concept and notation related to the way STL algorithms use iterators, namely iterator ranges. All STL algorithms gain access to a sequence via iterators, usually through a pair of iterators `first` and `last` that mark the beginning and end of the sequence. To capture concisely the way in which such an iterator pair determines a sequence, the concept of an *iterator range* is used. The range from `first` to `last` consists of the iterators obtained by starting with `first` and applying `operator++` until `last` is reached, but it does not include `last`. This range is written[1]

$$[\texttt{first}, \texttt{last})$$

and is said to be *valid* if and only if `last` is in fact reachable from `first`. All STL algorithms assume that the ranges they work with are valid; the result of application to invalid ranges is undefined.

An important special case, an *empty range*, occurs when `first == last`. An empty range is valid but includes no iterators that refer to valid data.

4.1 Input Iterators

The definitions of STL iterator categories are motivated by considering the needs of certain algorithms. As shown in Chapter 2, the STL generic `find` algorithm can be used to find values in a variety of data structures, including arrays, vectors, and lists. It can even be used to search an input stream with the aid of special iterators called istream iterators, discussed later in this chapter. The `find` algorithm has a simple definition as a template function:

```
template <typename InputIterator, typename T>
InputIterator find(InputIterator first, InputIterator last,
                   const T& value)
{
  while (first != last && *first != value)
    ++first;
  return first;
}
```

Note the expressions in this code in which `InputIterator` objects appear:

- `first != last`

- `++first`

- `*first`

For `find` to work correctly, these expressions should be defined and have the following meanings:

- `first != last` should return true if `first` is not equal to `last`, false otherwise.

---

[1]The notation is based on a similar usage in mathematics of $[a, b)$, where a and b are real numbers, to denote the set of all real numbers x such that $a \leq x < b$. This set is called a half-open interval.

- ++first should increment first and return the incremented value.

- *first should return the value referred to by first.

Furthermore, for find to work efficiently, each of these operations should work in constant time.

These requirements are almost exactly the requirements given in the definition of the *input iterator* category. The main additional requirements are that == also be defined with the meaning of an equality test and that postfix ++ also be defined, with the same meaning as prefix ++ except that it returns the value the iterator had before incrementing (as is the case with built-in pointer types).

These requirements are, of course, met by built-in pointer types. Note, however, that built-in pointer types have many other properties that are not required by the definition of input iterators. In particular, input iterators are not required to support writing into a position with *first = ... A particular input iterator may support this operation, but it's not required. (As we'll see in the next section, output iterators have the opposite requirement; that is, it must be possible to write with operator* but not necessarily to be able to read with it.)

Note that the term input iterator does not refer to a type. Instead, it refers to a family of types, all of which satisfy the basic requirements outlined earlier. To see that several different types satisfy input iterator requirements simultaneously, consider the following example program.

Example 4.1: Demonstrating the generic find algorithm with input iterators associated with arrays, lists, and iostreams

"ex04-01.cpp" 51 ≡

```
#include <iostream>
#include <cassert>
#include <algorithm>
#include <list>
using namespace std;

int main()
{
  // Initialize array a with 10 integers:
  int a[10] = {12, 3, 25, 7, 11, 213, 7, 123, 29, -31};

  // Find the first element equal to 7 in the array:
  int* ptr = find(&a[0], &a[10], 7);
```

```
        assert (*ptr == 7 && *(ptr+1) == 11);

        // Initialize list1 with the same integers as in array a:
        list<int> list1(&a[0], &a[10]);

        // Find the first element equal to 7 in list1:
        list<int>::iterator i = find(list1.begin(),
                                     list1.end(),7);

        assert (*i == 7 && *(++i) == 11);

        cout << "Type some characters, including an 'x' followed\n"
          << "by at least one nonwhite-space character: " << flush;

        istream_iterator<char> in(cin);
        istream_iterator<char> eos;
        find(in, eos, 'x');

        cout << "The first nonwhite-space character following\n"
             << "the first 'x' was '" << *(++in) << "'." << endl;
        return 0;
    }
```

In the first part of this program, we use the **find** algorithm with ordinary pointers, which behave as input iterators for C++ arrays. The second part uses **find** with list iterators, which also satisfy the conditions outlined. Finally, STL provides special input iterators called *istream iterators*, which are used to read values from an input stream. The last part of the program fragment keeps reading the standard **cin** input stream until the character **x** is found or the end of the stream is reached. It then increments the istream iterator to the next nonwhite-space character and outputs that character.

In the cases of array and list iterators, other operations besides input iterator operations are supported, such as storing into positions to which an iterator refers. With istream iterators, however, the only operations supported are those of input iterators. Istream iterators are explained in greater detail in Section 4.8.

4.2 Output Iterators

In the previous section, we saw that input iterator objects can be used to read values from a sequence, but we are not necessarily able to write into it. *Output iterators* have the opposite functionality: they allow us to write values into a sequence, but they do not guarantee that we can read from it. That is, if `first` is an output iterator, we can say `*first = ...`, but it is not guaranteed that we can use `*first` in an expression to obtain the value it refers to. One other difference from the requirements for input iterators is that there is no requirement that `==` or `!=` be defined on output iterators. Output iterators have the same requirements as input iterators for prefix and postfix `++` operations. As with input iterators, the term output iterator does not in itself represent a type. Instead, it can be applied to any type that satisfies these requirements.

For example, consider the STL `copy` algorithm, which copies from one sequence to another:

```
template <typename InputIterator, typename OutputIterator>
OutputIterator copy(InputIterator first, InputIterator last,
                    OutputIterator result)
{
  while (first != last) {
    *result = *first;
    ++first;
    ++result;
  }
  return result;
}
```

Once again, ordinary pointers can be used as output iterators for built-in C++ arrays:

```
int a[100], b[100];
// ... Code to store values in a[0], ..., a[99]

copy(&a[0], &a[100], &b[0]);
```

This copies the values in `a[0]`, ..., `a[99]` into `b[0]`, ..., `b[99]`.

STL provides special output iterators called *ostream iterators*, which are used to write values to an output stream. For example, the following code fragment writes the elements of a list to the `cout` output stream:

```
list<int> list1;
// ... Code to insert values in list1

// Declare an ostream iterator object, out:
ostream_iterator<int> out(cout, "\n");

copy(list1.begin(), list1.end(), out);
```

The arguments to the ostream_iterator constructor are an output stream object and a string to be written between values on the output stream; in this case a newline is used so that each value appears on a separate line. Ostream iterators are explained in greater detail in Section 4.8.

The array pointers used in the first example of copy allow reading from the positions they refer to, but ostream iterators do not, so we could not have used ostream iterators in the first two argument positions of copy.

4.3 Forward Iterators

We have seen that input iterators can be used to read values from a sequence and that output iterators can be used to write to them. A *forward iterator* is one that is both an input iterator and an output iterator, and it thus allows both reading and writing and traversal in one direction. Forward iterators also have a property that input and output iterators are not required to have: it is possible to save a forward iterator and use it to start traversing again from the same position. This property allows forward iterators to be used in multipass algorithms as opposed to single-pass algorithms (like find and merge).

As an example of an algorithm that does both reading from and writing to positions in a sequence, consider the STL replace algorithm, for replacing all occurrences of a value x in a range [first, last) by another value y:

```
template <typename ForwardIterator, typename T>
void replace(ForwardIterator first, ForwardIterator last,
             const T& x, const T& y)
{
  while (first != last) {
    if (*first == x)
      *first = y;
    ++first;
  }
}
```

This algorithm can be used to replace values in a variety of data structures, provided the type used to instantiate ForwardIterator satisfies the requirements of the forward iterator category.

Built-in pointer types, used with arrays, satisfy these requirements:

```
int a[100];
// ... Code to store values in a[0], ..., a[99]

// Replace all values in the array equal to 5 by 6:
replace(&a[0], &a[100], 5, 6);
```

Since the type `deque<T>::iterator` also satisfies all forward iterator requirements, we can also use this algorithm to replace elements in a deque:

```
deque<char> deque1;
// ... Code to insert characters in deque1

// Replace all occurrences of 'e' by 'o' in deque1:
replace(deque1.begin(), deque1.end(), 'e', 'o');
```

4.4 Bidirectional Iterators

In the last section we saw that forward iterators allow us to read values from and write values into a data structure while traversing it in a single direction. A *bidirectional iterator* is similar to a forward iterator, except that it allows traversal in either direction. That is, bidirectional iterators must support all forward iterator operations plus the `--` operation, making it possible to reverse direction in a sequence.

Both prefix and postfix versions of `operator--` are required, where the prefix version decrements the iterator and returns the new value and the postfix version decrements the iterator but returns the old value. Both the prefix and the postfix `operator--` must be constant time operations.

The ability to traverse a data structure in the reverse direction is important because it would not otherwise be possible for certain algorithms to work efficiently. For example, the STL `reverse` algorithm can be used to reverse the order of elements in a sequence, provided that bidirectional iterators are available. For example, built-in pointer types used with arrays satisfy all the requirements of bidirectional iterators, and we can write

```
int a[100];
// ... Code to store values in a[0], ..., a[99]

// Reverse the order of the values in the array:
reverse(&a[0], &a[100]);
```

But STL's `list` containers are also required to provide bidirectional iterators, and we can use them with `reverse`:

```
list<int> list1;
// ... Code to insert values in list1

// Reverse the order of the values in the list:
reverse(list1.begin(), list1.end());
```

As you might expect, the requirement that the `list` class support bidirectional iterators implies that the list representation must be doubly linked. With singly linked lists, it would not be possible to implement `operator--` efficiently (in constant time).

Thus, the requirements for bidirectional iterators allow us to ensure that algorithms such as `reverse`, that need to traverse a sequence in either direction, will operate efficiently.

4.5   Random Access Iterators

In the previous sections, we have seen four different categories of iterators, which allow us to express varying constraints that different algorithms impose on the data structures they work with to operate efficiently. We have seen examples of algorithms that require data structures that can at least be

- read and traversed in one direction (expressed by saying that the algorithm accepts *input* iterators).

- written and traversed in one direction (expressed by saying that the algorithm accepts *output* iterators).

- read and written and traversed in one direction, with the additional ability to save iterators and resume scanning from saved positions (expressed by saying that the algorithm accepts *forward* iterators).

- read and written and traversed in either direction (expressed by saying that the algorithm accepts *bidirectional* iterators).

It turns out that these four different categories of data structures are not enough to account for all algorithms. There are some algorithms that impose even stronger requirements on iterators. To operate efficiently, these algorithms require that any position in a sequence be reachable from any other in constant time.

For example, consider the STL generic `binary_search` algorithm. When called as

```
binary_search(first, last, value)
```

where `first` and `last` delimit a sequence that is sorted into ascending order, the algorithm returns true if there is a position in the sequence where `value` occurs, false otherwise. This is similar to the specification of `find`, but `binary_search` takes advantage of the ordering of the sequence to produce its answer in $O(\log N)$ time rather than $O(N)$, where N is the length of the sequence. It is able to do this by comparing the value in the middle of the sequence with `value` and confining its search to the first half if the middle value is larger than `value` or to the second half if the middle value is smaller. That is, the search space is cut in half with each comparison, so at most $\log_2 N$ comparisons are required. But for the overall computing time to be $O(\log N)$, getting to the middle element must be a constant time operation.

Clearly, lists do not have this property. Given pointers to the beginning and end of a list, the only way to get to the middle element is to traverse elements one by one. This takes time proportional to the length of the list.

On the other hand, vectors and arrays allow constant time access to an arbitrary element in the container. Thus, the `binary_search` algorithm works efficiently for vectors and arrays:

```
vector<int> vector1;
// ... Code to insert values in vector1

// Search vector1 for the value 5; if found,
// return true; otherwise, return false:
bool found = binary_search(vector1.begin(), vector1.end(), 5);
```

From this example, we see the need for yet another iterator category—a random access iterator category.

Random access iterators are required to support all operations supported by bidirectional iterators, plus (where `r` and `s` are a random access iterators and `n` is an integer expression) the following:

- Additions and subtractions of an integer, expressed with `r + n`, `n + r`, and `r - n`

- Access to a location `n` elements away with `r[n]`, which means `*(r + n)`

- Bidirectional "big jumps," expressed with `r += n` and `r -= n`

- Iterator subtraction, expressed as `r - s`, producing an integer value

- Comparisons, expressed as `r < s`, `r > s`, `r <= s`, and `r >= s`, producing `bool` values

STL random access data structures, such as vectors and deques, require their iterators to satisfy these requirements so that any location in the data structure may be reached in constant time.

4.6 The STL Iterator Hierarchy: Combining Algorithms and Containers Efficiently

The key to understanding iterators and their role in STL is understanding why it is useful to classify iterators into the categories input/output, forward, bidirectional, and random access. This classification is an iterator hierarchy:

- Forward iterators are also input and output iterators.

- Bidirectional iterators are also forward iterators and therefore also input and output iterators.

- Random access iterators are also bidirectional iterators and therefore also forward iterators and input and output iterators.

This hierarchy essentially implies the following:

- Algorithms that require only input or output iterators can also be used with forward, bidirectional, or random access iterators.

- Algorithms that require forward iterators can also be used with bidirectional or random access iterators.

- Algorithms that require bidirectional iterators can also be used with random access iterators.

Iterator categories are thus used in the specifications of the containers and algorithms as follows:

- The description of container classes includes the category of the iterator types they provide.

- The description of generic algorithms includes the iterator categories with which they work.

Here are some examples:

- **lists** provide bidirectional iterators, and the **find** algorithm just requires input iterators; hence **find** can be used with **lists**.

- While **lists** provide bidirectional iterators, the **sort** algorithm requires random access iterators. Since bidirectional iterators are not required to have all the properties of random access iterators, **sort** cannot be used with **lists**. Code such as

  ```
  list<int> list1;
  // ... Code to insert values in list1
  sort(list1.begin(), list1.end());
  ```

will not compile.

- A **deque** provides random access iterators, as required by **sort**. This means that **sort** will work with a **deque**; furthermore, the combination will be efficient.

- **Set** iterators are bidirectional, and the **merge** algorithm requires input iterators or greater. Since bidirectional iterators are greater in the iterator hierarchy, we can immediately see that the **merge** algorithm can be applied to **sets**. The combination will be efficient and is allowed.

The iterator hierarchy highlights the fundamental idea behind the design of STL: *STL container and algorithm interfaces are designed to encourage combinations that are efficient and to discourage combinations that are inefficient.* The encouragement comes from efficient combinations compiling without errors. Although some inefficient combinations will also compile, in most cases they cause compilation errors and require more effort because the programmer must write extra code to compensate for missing operations.

Iterator categories and efficiency issues are further discussed in Section 4.11.

4.7   Insert Iterators

An *insert iterator* puts a generic algorithm into "insert mode" rather than its usual "overwrite mode." This means that instead of *i = ... causing the object at position i to be *overwritten*, *i = ... causes an *insertion* into that position, using one of the container's insertion member functions. Insert iterators are especially useful for transferring a data sequence from an input stream or container to another container without having to know in advance the length of the sequence. STL provides three insert iterator types, each parameterized by a `Container` type:

- `back_insert_iterator<Container>`   Uses `Container`'s `push_back` member function.

- `front_insert_iterator<Container>` Uses `Container`'s `push_front` member function.

- `insert_iterator <Container>`   Uses `Container`'s `insert` member function.

Such insertions force the container to expand the space currently allocated for it, unlike assignments, which must have space for their results already available. For example, the following code will fail because there is no space in `vector1` into which `copy`'s assignments can store their results:

```
vector<int> vector1; // vector1 is empty
deque<int> deque1(200, 1); // deque1 holds 200 1's.
copy(deque1.begin(), deque1.end(), vector1.begin());// ERROR
```

During the copying, a run-time error will occur when doing

```
*(vector1.begin()) = *(deque1.begin())
```

But by using an insert iterator as its third argument, we can make `copy` work correctly because `vector1`'s `push_back` function is used, causing storage for `vector1` to be expanded as necessary:

```
copy(deque1.begin(), deque1.end(),
        back_insert_iterator< vector<int> >(vector1));
```

Here `back_insert_iterator< vector<int> >(vector1)` calls a constructor of the class template

```
template <typename Container>
class back_insert_iterator;
```

instantiated with `vector<int>` as the `Container` type. To make it more convenient to use this insert iterator, STL defines a generic function template, `back_inserter`.

```
template <typename Container>
inline
back_insert_iterator<Container>  // This is the return type
back_inserter(Container& x) {
  return back_insert_iterator<Container>(x);
}
```

Thus we can write our call of `copy` more succinctly as

```
copy(deque1.begin(), deque1.end(), back_inserter(vector1));
```

and the compiler automatically instantiates `back_inserter`'s type parameter, `Container`, with `vector<int>`. The `back_inserter` function then plugs that type into `back_insert_iterator<Container>` for us.

`Back_insert_iterator` and therefore `back_inserter` can be used with `vector`, `list`, and `deque` container types, since they all provide a **push_back** member function. This insert iterator takes any container `C1` that has a **push_back** function and produces an iterator type whose * and = operators are defined so that the code

```
*i = x;
```

executes by performing

```
C1.push_back(x);
```

instead. Furthermore, `i` is essentially always pointing at the end of its associated container, and `++i` and `i++` operations do nothing.

Similarly, `front_insert_iterator` and its related `front_inserter` function template cause insertions at the front of a container. They can be used with `list` and `deque` containers, since these containers all provide a **push_front** function:

```
int array1[100];
deque<int> deque1;
// Assign values to array1[0], ..., array1[99]:
copy(&array1[0], &array1[100], front_inserter(deque1));
```

The elements of **array1** will appear at the front of **deque1** (in the reverse of their order in **array1**).

No **push_front** member function is provided by `vector` since it would have to be a linear time operation (just as we'll see with **pop_front** in the discussion of the queue container adaptor in Section 9.2). Thus `front_inserter` cannot be used with a `vector`.

The most general insert iterator is `insert_iterator`, which has a corresponding function template `inserter` and allows insertions at any point in a container's current sequence of elements, as indicated by an iterator argument:

```
copy(&array1[0], &array1[100],
     inserter(deque1, deque1.begin()+1));
```

In this case, the elements of **array1** would be inserted after the first element of **deque1** and would be in the same order as in **array1** (that is, the iterator is incremented with **++** after each insertion so that it moves over the element just inserted).

The **insert_iterator** and **inserter** function use a container's **insert** member function, **insert(iterator, value)**. Since all of STL's container types provide such a function, **inserter** can be applied to any type of container (including sorted associative containers).

Other examples of the use of insert iterators appear in the next section and in Chapters 5 and 12.

4.8   Revisiting Input and Output: Stream Iterators

We now take a slightly more detailed look at the input and output iterator categories. An important reason for including the input and output iterator categories in STL is to allow us to identify algorithms that can be used on iterators associated with I/O streams. Such iterators are provided by STL classes called **istream_iterator** (for input) and **ostream_iterator** (for output). Iterators constructed by **istream_iterator** are input iterators, but they are not output iterators. This means that **istream_iterator** objects can read data only in a single direction, and data cannot be written through an istream iterator object.

The constructor **istream_iterator(istream&)** provided by the type **istream_iterator<T>** produces an input iterator for values of type **T** from a given input stream (such as the standard input stream, **cin**, in the next example).

The constructor **istream_iterator<T>()** produces an input iterator that works as an *end marker* for istream iterators. This is simply a value to which istream iterators become equal when the istream they are scanning reports an end-of-stream condition.

An algorithm such as **merge** can be used with istream iterators because it needs to make only a single pass over the data and only read each data object, not assign to it. For example:

```
vector<int> vector1;
list<int> list1;
// ... Code to insert values in vector1

merge(vector1.begin(), vector1.end(),
      istream_iterator<int>(cin),
      istream_iterator<int>(),
      back_inserter(list1));
```

This merges the integers in `vector1` with those on the standard input stream, `cin`, putting the result in `list1` with the help of an insert iterator constructed with **back_inserter**.

The istream iterators in the preceding example could also be used for the first pair of arguments to `merge`,

```
merge(istream_iterator<int>(cin), istream_iterator<int>(),
      vector1.begin(), vector1.end(), back_inserter(list1));
```

but we could not put an istream iterator in the last argument position, since **merge** needs to be able to assign new values through that iterator, and it is not possible to do so through **istream_iterator** objects.

Iterators constructed by **ostream_iterator** are output iterators, but they are not input iterators. Again, an algorithm such as **merge** can be used with them. This time, though, the iterator must be used as the result parameter of **merge**:

```
vector<int> vector1;
list<int> list1;
// ... Code to insert values in vector1
// ... Code to insert values in list1

merge(vector1.begin(), vector1.end(),
      list1.begin(), list1.end(),
      ostream_iterator<int>(cout, " "));
```

This example merges the integers in `vector1` with those in `list1` and places the result on the standard output stream, `cout`, inserting blanks between the values as they are output (that's what the second argument of the **ostream_iterator** constructor designates).

We cannot use an ostream iterator in any of the first four argument positions of **merge**, because **merge** needs to be able to read from objects obtained by dereferencing those iterators, and the **ostream_iterator** type does not provide such a capability.

4.9   Specification of Iterator Categories Required by STL Algorithms

Let us take a closer look at how we determine from the interface specifications of STL algorithms which iterators can be used with an algorithm. Chapter 22, "Generic Algorithm Reference Guide," gives this interface for `merge`:

```
template <typename InputIterator1,
          typename InputIterator2,
          typename OutputIterator>
OutputIterator merge(InputIterator1 first1,
                     InputIterator1 last1,
                     InputIterator2 first2,
                     InputIterator2 last2,
                     OutputIterator result);
```

The conventions used in Chapter 22 are as follows:

- Template class parameter names that end in `Iterator` or `Iterator`N for some integer N signify that parameters of that type must be iterators.

- The first part of the name is used to describe the category to which the iterator must belong.

This interface description says that `merge` requires its first two parameters to be input iterators of the same type; its third and fourth parameters also must be input iterators of the same type (but a type possibly different from that of the first two parameters); and its last parameter must be an output iterator.

Just from reading this specification, without having to know exactly how `merge` is implemented, we can see that all the ways we've used it in previous examples are legal, including those using `istream_iterator` and `ostream_iterator` objects.

The `find` algorithm has this interface:

```
template <typename InputIterator, typename T>
InputIterator find(InputIterator first,
                   InputIterator last,
                   const T& value);
```

Thus, `find` requires its first two parameters to be input iterators, and it returns an input iterator. This means `find` works with virtually all iterators—input, forward, bidirectional, or random access. Only output iterators are excluded.

The specification of another algorithm, `search`, shows it to be a little more restrictive than `find`. The `search` algorithm looks for a subsequence within another sequence; it generalizes substring matching algorithms like `strstr`:

```
template<typename ForwardIterator1, typename ForwardIterator2>
ForwardIterator1 search(ForwardIterator1 first1,
                        ForwardIterator1 last1,
                        ForwardIterator2 first2,
                        ForwardIterator2 last2);
```

This says that the arguments must be forward iterators, but why must they not be input iterators? The reason is simply that the algorithm `search` is multipass: it saves iterators and uses them to rescan. So it would not work to try to use this algorithm with an `istream_iterator`.

4.10   Designing Generic Algorithms

Once we understand how the interface specification for an algorithm tells us which iterators can be used, we don't really need to know the implementation of the algorithms. But let's reinforce our understanding of iterator categories by looking inside one algorithm and examining some of the design decisions that are dictated by the goal of making it as generic as possible while still retaining its efficiency. Here again is the definition of the STL generic `find` algorithm:

```
template <typename InputIterator, typename T>
InputIterator find(InputIterator first,
                   InputIterator last,
                   const T& value) {
  while (first != last && *first != value)
    ++first;
  return first;
}
```

We see that such an implementation does indeed work with any input iterator:

- It applies only `!=`, `*`, and `++` to its iterator parameters.

- It never tries to assign to objects it obtains using *.

- It is a single-pass algorithm.

This `find` implementation makes the algorithm as generic as possible, but that's not true of other possible implementations. Suppose we make just one tiny change, using < instead of != in the iterator comparison:

```
while (first < last && *first != value)
  ++first;
```

If we call this modified algorithm `find1`, we can see that many uses of `find1` would still work, such as with ordinary arrays, vectors, and deques. But if we try to use it with lists, as in

```
list<int> list1;
// ... Code to insert values in list1

list<int>::iterator where = find1(list1.begin(),list1.end(),7);
```

it will fail because the implementation is trying to compute

```
list1.begin() < list1.end()
```

but no < operator is defined for `list` iterators (because a < operator would be highly inefficient, as we will soon see). The failure shows up as a compile-time error.[2]

Put another way, since the presence of the operator < is guaranteed only by random access iterators, the interface to `find1` would have to be expressed as

```
template <typename RandomAccessIterator, typename T>
RandomAccessIterator find1(RandomAccessIterator first,
                           RandomAccessIterator last,
                           const T& value);
```

One of the key achievements in the design of STL is its demonstration that many algorithms like `find` can be coded with minimal requirements for access to data, thus making them generic. In all cases of implementations like that of `find1`, in which unnecessarily restrictive requirements are placed on their iterators, the implementations have been refined and reduced to ones like that of `find`—those that make the minimal possible assumptions and therefore are of the broadest possible utility.

---

[2]The compiler error message is something similar to "Could not find a match for `list<int>::iterator::operator<(list<int>::iterator)`."

4.11   Why Some Algorithms Require More Powerful Iterators

Some algorithms in the library require more of iterators than the minimal capabilities that input, output, or forward iterators provide. Such algorithms need the iterators supplied to them to be of the bidirectional or random access category; otherwise they simply won't compile. For example, `sort` has the following interface:

```
template <typename RandomAccessIterator>
void sort(RandomAccessIterator first,
          RandomAccessIterator last);
```

meaning that `sort` requires two iterators, both of the random access category. That's just what is supplied when we write

```
vector<int> vector1;
// ... Code to insert values in vector1

sort(vector1.begin(), vector1.end());
```

As with the not-so-generic `find1` implementation, we now see why we run into problems when we try to apply `sort` to a `list`:

```
list<int> list1;
// ... Code to insert values in list1

sort(list1.begin(), list1.end());  // incorrect
```

Since `list1.begin()` and `list1.end()` are only bidirectional iterators, they do not provide all the operations that the implementation of `sort` tries to use, such as `+=`, so this code will not compile.

Why not extend `list` iterators and those for the other container categories to have operators `+=` and `<` and the other operations that random access iterators have? That would seem to simplify the task of writing generic algorithms, since we wouldn't have to worry so much about which operations we could apply to iterators. Again, the answer is efficiency. With `lists`, there's no way to do computations such as `list1.begin() + n` in constant time; we have only the obvious method of stepping through the list nodes one by one, taking time proportional to `n` (that is, linear time) to do it. So even if we programmed that method and called it `+`, we would not have achieved true random access. Algorithms such as `sort` would then run much more slowly than other sorting algorithms that take special advantage of lists (such as the algorithm used by the `list` class `sort` member function).

4.12   Choosing the Right Algorithm

One final point about algorithm/container compatibility: although STL's iterator classification scheme encourages efficient combinations and discourages inefficient ones, it does not completely eliminate combinations that could be inefficient in some cases. That is, it may be possible to apply a generic algorithm to a container, but it is not always wise to do so.

Perhaps the simplest example is once again the `find` algorithm, in combination with random access containers such as arrays, vectors, or deques. As we've seen, `find` just steps through the objects in a sequence one by one, so it is a linear time algorithm (that is, the time taken to `find` a value in a container of size N is proportional to N). If the objects in the sequence are not ordered in any particular way, this kind of search may be the best we can do. However, if we happen to have the objects in a random access container in sorted order, then another STL algorithm, `binary_search`, will do the job far more efficiently (in logarithmic time, that is, proportional to the logarithm of the size of the container).

A slightly more subtle case comes up when we consider the possibility of searching an associative container. Again, the generic `find` algorithm could be used, since associative containers provide a bidirectional iterator type, but STL associative containers are organized internally in such a way that they can be searched in logarithmic time. And they all provide a member function (it's also called `find` and takes one argument, specifying the value for which to search) that does this efficient search. So for a large associative container, it would be inefficient to use the generic `find` on the entire range of positions in the container:

```
set<int> set1;
// ... Code to insert some values in set1

set<int>::iterator where;
where = find(set1.begin(), set1.end(), 7);
```

This works, but it works in linear time. It would be much better to write the following, since it runs in logarithmic time:

```
where = set1.find(7);
```

4.13   Constant Versus Mutable Iterator Types

There is an additional distinction that applies to forward, bidirectional, and random access iterators—they can be *mutable* or *constant* depending on whether the result of `operator*` is a reference or a constant reference.

All STL container types define not only the identifier `iterator` but also `const_iterator`. For example, `vector<T>::iterator` is a mutable random access iterator type, and `vector<T>::const_iterator` is the corresponding constant random access iterator type.

When the result of `operator*` on an iterator `i` is a reference, it is possible to do assignments `*i = ....` Such assignments, however, are impossible with a constant reference (such as in the case when the iterator is actually a constant iterator). The compiler will flag attempts to do such assignments as errors.

Other uses that might result in changing the object to which `*i` refers, such as passing `*i` to a function in place of a nonconstant reference parameter (`T&` but not `const T&`), are also disallowed.

In most cases we can use a container type's `iterator` type when declaring iterator variables:

```
vector<int> vector1;
// ... Code to insert values in vector1

vector<int>::iterator i = vector1.begin(); // OK
```

This is correct because the `begin` member function returns an `iterator` when applied to a mutable container (i.e., a container that is not declared constant). Actually, it would also work to write

```
vector<int>::const_iterator j = vector1.begin(); // OK
```

since a conversion from `iterator` to `const_iterator` is provided.

But if we have a constant container, we have to use constant iterators with it:

```
// initialize vector2 with 100 zeros:
const vector<int> vector2(100, 0);

vector<int>::iterator i = vector2.begin();  // incorrect
```

Instead, the declaration should be

```
vector<int>::const_iterator i = vector2.begin();
```

In this case, using `iterator` is incorrect because the `begin` member function returns a `const_iterator` when applied to a container declared `const`.

No conversion from `const_iterator` to `iterator` is provided, so the attempt to initialize `i` with the `const_iterator` returned by `begin` results in a compilation error message.

We won't often directly declare a container constant, since we usually want to insert elements into or erase elements from the container after it's created. But any time we pass a container to a function through a constant reference parameter, it is as though the container were declared constant:

```
template <typename T>
void print(const vector<T>& v)
{
  for (vector<T>::const_iterator i = v.begin();
       i != v.end(); ++i)
    cout << *i << endl;
}
```

Attempting to use `vector<T>::iterator` in this example would produce a compile-time error message, as would any attempt to use the container's `insert` or `erase` member functions.

If we have a function with an iterator parameter, the parameter should be declared `const_iterator` if possible:

```
template <typename T>
void foo(list<T>::const_iterator i,
         deque<T>& d, deque<T>::iterator j)
{
  if (*i > *j++)
    *j = *i++;
  d.insert(j, *i);
}
```

Here we use `*` only to read the value to which `i` refers, not to assign through it, so declaring `i` to be a `const_iterator` is permissible. It could also be declared `iterator`, but then for the corresponding actual parameter we would be able to use only `iterator` values. On the other hand, `j` must be declared `iterator`, since we assign through it and use it as a parameter to `insert` (either one alone would require an `iterator`).

Note that both `i` and `j` are subjected to incrementing with `++` in this example. The "const" in `const_iterator` doesn't mean that the iterator itself can't be changed; it only inhibits changing the value to which the iterator refers.

4.14 Iterator Categories Provided by STL Containers

Table 4.1 shows the category of each iterator type that the different containers in STL provide. Note that for `sets` and `multisets`, both the `iterator` and `const_iterator` types are constant bidirectional types—in fact, they are the same type. The reason for this is as follows: for sets and multisets, the only allowed method of changing a stored key is to first delete it (using the `erase` member function) and then insert a different key (with the `insert` member function). If the set and multiset iterators were not constant iterators, then it would be possible to modify the keys without going through the `erase` and `insert` member functions, and such changes could violate the property that the elements are in sorted order. The following example illustrates this point:

```
#include <set>

set<int> s;
s.insert(3);
s.insert(5);
s.insert(7);

set<int>::iterator i = s.begin();
*i = 4;  // incorrect
```

This program will not compile since `i` is a constant iterator and elements cannot be modified through constant iterators. Instead, we must write

```
s.erase(i);
s.insert(4);
```

A similar restriction applies with maps and multimaps. A `map<Key, T>` object stores values of type `pair<const Key, T>`. The key part of such a pair cannot be directly modified but it is possible to modify the value of type `T`. The following example illustrates this idea:

```
#include <map>

typedef multimap<int, double> multimap_1;
multimap_1 m;
m.insert(pair<const int, double>(3, 4.1));

multimap_1::iterator i = m.begin();
*i = pair<const int, double>(3, 5.1);  // incorrect
```

Table 4.1: Category of each iterator type the STL containers provide

Container	Iterator	Iterator category
T a[n]	T*	mutable random access
T a[n]	const T*	constant random access
vector<T>	vector<T>::iterator	mutable random access
vector<T>	vector<T>::const_iterator	constant random access
deque<T>	deque<T>::iterator	mutable random access
deque<T>	deque<T>::const_iterator	constant random access
list<T>	list<T>::iterator	mutable bidirectional
list<T>	list<T>::const_iterator	constant bidirectional
set<T>	set<T>::iterator	constant bidirectional
set<T>	set<T>::const_iterator	constant bidirectional
multiset<T>	multiset<T>::iterator	constant bidirectional
multiset<T>	multiset<T>::const_iterator	constant bidirectional
map<Key,T>	map<Key,T>::iterator	mutable bidirectional
map<Key,T>	map<Key,T>::const_iterator	constant bidirectional
multimap<Key,T>	multimap<Key,T>::iterator	mutable bidirectional
multimap<Key,T>	multimap<Key,T>::const_iterator	constant bidirectional

This is an incorrect method of modifying values in maps and multimaps, and it will not compile. A correct method is to erase the value to which i points, then insert the new pair:

```
m.erase(i);
m.insert(pair<const int, double>(3, 5.1));
```

It would also be correct to write

```
i->second = 5.1;
```

since the values associated with keys in a map or multimap can be modified using nonconstant iterators. This method is preferred, since it is more efficient than using erase and insert. It would not be permitted, though, if we had declared i as a multimap_1::const_iterator, since constant iterators do not allow modification of the values to which they refer.

CHAPTER 5

Generic Algorithms

STL provides a rich set of algorithms that operate on data structures defined within the STL framework. As we saw in Section 2.2, STL algorithms are *generic*: each algorithm can operate not just on a single data structure but on a variety of data structures.

STL generic algorithms fall into four broad categories, based loosely on their semantics. *Nonmutating sequence algorithms* operate on containers without, in general, modifying the contents of the container, while *mutating sequence algorithms* typically modify the containers on which they operate. The *sorting-related algorithms* include sorting and merging algorithms, binary searching algorithms, and set operations on sorted sequences. Finally, there is a small collection of *generalized numeric algorithms*.

The previous chapter explained how iterators are used to allow different classes of algorithms to work with a variety of data structures. In this chapter we explore the various categories of algorithms and explain their use through examples. For further details on each algorithm, see Chapter 22, "Generic Algorithm Reference Guide."

5.1   Basic Algorithm Organization in STL

Before taking a detailed look at the four main categories of STL algorithms, we give a brief overview of the different variations a particular algorithm may have. The different variations include in-place and copying versions and versions that take predicate parameters.

5.1.1   In-Place and Copying Versions

For certain STL algorithms, both in-place and copying versions are provided. An *in-place version* of the algorithm places its result into the same container on which it operates.

Example 5.1: Using an in-place generic `sort` algorithm

"ex05-01.cpp" 74 ≡

```
#include <iostream>
#include <algorithm>
#include <cassert>
using namespace std;

int main() {
  cout << "Using an in-place generic sort algorithm." << endl;
  int a[1000];
  int i;
  for (i = 0; i < 1000; ++i)
    a[i] = 1000 - i - 1;

  sort(&a[0], &a[1000]);

  for (i = 0; i < 1000; ++i)
    assert (a[i] == i);
  cout << " --- Ok." << endl;
  return 0;
}
```

This program sorts the array **a** and puts the sorted sequence back into **a**. That is, the array is replaced with a sorted version of itself, since the generic **sort** algorithm is an in-place algorithm.

A *copying version* of an algorithm copies its result to a different container or to a nonoverlapping portion of the same container on which it operates. For example, in the following program, `reverse_copy` leaves the array **a** unchanged and puts a reversed copy of it into the array **b**.

Example 5.2: Using `reverse_copy`, a copying version of the generic **reverse** algorithm

"ex05-02.cpp" 74 ≡

```
#include <iostream>
#include <algorithm>
```

The version of **sort** with two iterator parameters makes comparisons of values in the sequence using the < operator defined on the value type. The version with two iterator parameters and a binary predicate parameter makes comparisons using the binary predicate. The same name, **sort**, is used for both since the two versions are distinguishable by the difference in their parameter lists. In a few cases, though, there would be an ambiguity that could not be resolved, and different names must be used. For example, the predicate version of **find** is called **find_if** so that there is no ambiguity between the two interfaces:

```
template <typename InputIterator, typename T>
InputIterator
find(InputIterator first, InputIterator last,
     const T& value);

template <typename InputIterator, typename Predicate>
InputIterator
find_if(InputIterator first, InputIterator last,
        Predicate pred);
```

In the example programs in this chapter, we give examples of either the predicate or the nonpredicate versions of an algorithm or in a few cases both. A predicate version whose name ends with _if is discussed in the subsection labeled with the base name; for example, **find_if** is discussed in Section 5.2.1.

5.2 Nonmutating Sequence Algorithms

Nonmutating sequence algorithms are those that do not directly modify the containers on which they operate. They include algorithms to search for elements in sequences, to check for equality, and to count sequence elements. The nonmutating sequence algorithms are **find**, **adjacent_find**, **count**, **for_each**, **mismatch**, **equal**, and **search**.

5.2.1 Find

In Section 2.2 we saw several examples of the generic **find** algorithm. Its predicate version, **find_if**, searches a sequence for the first occurrence of an element for which the given predicate is true.

77

Example 5.4: Illustrating the generic `find_if` algorithm

"ex05-04.cpp" 78 ≡
```cpp
#include <iostream>
#include <algorithm>
#include <cassert>
#include <vector>
using namespace std;

// Define a unary predicate object type:
class GreaterThan50 {
 public:
   bool operator()(int x) const { return x > 50; }
};

int main()
{
  cout << "Illustrating the generic find_if algorithm."
       << endl;
  // Create a vector with values 0, 1, 4, 9, 16, ..., 144:
  vector<int> vector1;
  for (int i = 0; i < 13; ++i)
    vector1.push_back(i * i);

  vector<int>::iterator where;
  where = find_if(vector1.begin(), vector1.end(),
                  GreaterThan50());

  assert (*where == 64);
  cout << " --- Ok." << endl;
  return 0;
}
```

In this program we define a unary predicate object type, `GreaterThan50`, and pass an object constructed with its default constructor to `find_if`. (Instead of defining `GreaterThan50` as a new class, we could assemble an equivalent function object type using STL function objects and function adaptors, as discussed in Chapter 8.)

The time complexity of the `find` and `find_if` algorithms is linear.

5.2.2 Adjacent Find

The `adjacent_find` algorithm searches a sequence for adjacent pairs of equal elements. When it finds two adjacent equal elements, it returns an iterator pointing to the first of the pair.

Example 5.5: Illustrating the generic `adjacent_find` algorithm

"ex05-05.cpp" 79 ≡

```cpp
#include <iostream>
#include <string>
#include <algorithm>
#include <cassert>
#include <functional>
#include <deque>
using namespace std;

int main()
{
  cout << "Illustrating the generic adjacent_find algorithm."
       << endl;
  deque<string> player(5);
  deque<string>::iterator i;

  // Initialize the deque:
  player[0] = "Pele";
  player[1] = "Platini";
  player[2] = "Maradona";
  player[3] = "Maradona";
  player[4] = "Rossi";

  // Find the first pair of equal consecutive names:
  i = adjacent_find(player.begin(), player.end());

  assert (*i == "Maradona" && *(i+1) == "Maradona");

  // Find the first name that is lexicographically
  // greater than the following name:
  i = adjacent_find(player.begin(), player.end(),
                    greater<string>());

  assert (*i == "Platini" && *(i+1) == "Maradona");
  cout << " --- Ok." << endl;
  return 0;
}
```

This program first uses the nonpredicate version of `adjacent_find`, which uses `string::operator==` for the comparisons and thus finds the first pair of equal elements. It then conducts another search using the predicate version of `adjacent_find` and the binary predicate `greater<string>()` to do the comparisons. It thus finds the first pair of consecutive strings in the deque such that the first string is lexicographically greater than the second.

The time complexity of the `adjacent_find` algorithm is linear.

5.2.3 Count

`Count` is a nonmutating sequence algorithm that searches a sequence and counts the number of elements equal to a specified value.

Example 5.6: Demonstrating the generic `count` algorithm

`"ex05-06.cpp"` 80 ≡

```
#include <iostream>
#include <cassert>
#include <algorithm>
#include <functional>
using namespace std;

int main()
{
  cout << "Illustrating the generic count algorithm." << endl;
  int a[] = {0, 0, 0, 1, 1, 1, 2, 2, 2};

  // Count the number of values in the array a
  // that are equal to 1:
  int final_count = count(&a[0], &a[9], 1);

  assert (final_count == 3);

  // Determine the number of array elements that are not
  // equal to 1:
  final_count = count_if(&a[0], &a[9],
                         bind2nd(not_equal_to<int>(), 1));

  // There are 6 elements not equal to 1.
  assert (final_count == 6);
  cout << " --- Ok." << endl;
  return 0;
}
```

The first call to `count` determines the number of elements in the array **a** that are equal to 1. The second call is to `count_if`, the unary predicate version of the algorithm, to determine the number of elements in the array that are not equal to 1. The unary predicate is constructed by passing the binary predicate `not_equal_to<int>` to the function adaptor `bind2nd`, along with the argument 1, as follows:

```
bind2nd(not_equal_to<int>(), 1)
```

Both `not_equal_to` and `bind2nd` are defined in the header file `functional`.

Note that by simply changing the arguments to the predicate, we can easily accomplish a completely different task. For example, to find the number of elements in the array greater than 5, we use the predicate

```
bind2nd(greater<int>(), 5)
```

The time complexity of the `count` and `count_if` algorithms is linear.

5.2.4   For Each

The generic `for_each` algorithm applies a function `f` to each element of a sequence.

Example 5.7: Illustrating the generic `for_each` algorithm

```
"ex05-07.cpp" 81 ≡
    #include <iostream>
    #include <cassert>
    #include <algorithm>
    #include <string>
    #include <list>
    #include <iostream>
    using namespace std;

    void print_list(string s)
    {
      cout << s << endl;
    }

    int main()
    {
      cout << "Illustrating the generic for_each algorithm."
           << endl;
      list<string> dlist;
      dlist.insert(dlist.end(), "Clark");
```

```
    dlist.insert(dlist.end(), "Rindt");
    dlist.insert(dlist.end(), "Senna");

    // Print out each list element:
    for_each(dlist.begin(), dlist.end(), print_list);
    return 0;
}
```

Output from Example 5.7

```
Clark
Rindt
Senna
```

In this example we use the `for_each` algorithm to print all elements of a list. The function `print_list` is applied to the result of dereferencing each iterator in the range [`dlist.begin()`, `dlist.end()`).[2] The result of the function applied by `for_each` on the container elements is ignored.

The time complexity of the `for_each` algorithm is linear.

5.2.5 Mismatch and Equal

The `mismatch` and `equal` algorithms are used to compare two ranges. Each accepts three iterator parameters: `first1`, `last1`, and `first2`. The `equal` algorithm returns true if the elements at corresponding positions `first1` + i and `first2` + i are equal for all positions `first1` + i in the range [`first1`, `last1`), false otherwise. The `mismatch` algorithm returns a `pair` of iterators,[3] `first1` + i and `first2` + i, which are the first corresponding positions where unequal elements occur. If there are no unequal elements in corresponding positions, `last1` and `first2` + (`last1` - `first1`) are returned. Thus

```
    equal(first1, last1, first2)
```

is equivalent to

```
    mismatch(first1, last1, first2).first == last1
```

---

[2] The iterator range concept and notation were introduced in the introduction to Chapter 4.

[3] Recall that the class template `pair` was discussed in Section 1.3.1; it has two data members, `first` and `second`, whose types can be different.

Example 5.8: Illustrating the generic `equal` and `mismatch` algorithms

"ex05-08.cpp" 83 ≡

```cpp
#include <iostream>
#include <cassert>
#include <algorithm>
#include <string>
#include <list>
#include <deque>
#include <vector>
using namespace std;

int main()
{
  cout << "Illustrating the generic equal "
       << "and mismatch algorithms." << endl;
  list<string> driver_list;
  vector<string> vec;
  deque<string> deq;

  driver_list.insert(driver_list.end(), "Clark");
  driver_list.insert(driver_list.end(), "Rindt");
  driver_list.insert(driver_list.end(), "Senna");

  vec.insert(vec.end(), "Clark");
  vec.insert(vec.end(), "Rindt");
  vec.insert(vec.end(), "Senna");
  vec.insert(vec.end(), "Berger");

  deq.insert(deq.end(), "Clark");
  deq.insert(deq.end(), "Berger");

  // Show that driver_list and the first 3 elements of
  // vec are equal in all corresponding positions:
  assert (equal(driver_list.begin(), driver_list.end(),
               vec.begin()));

  // Show that deq and the first 2 elements of driver_list
  // are not equal in all corresponding positions:
  assert (!equal(deq.begin(), deq.end(),
               driver_list.begin()));

  // Find the corresponding positions in deq and driver_list
  // at which unequal elements first occur:
```

```
      pair<deque<string>::iterator, list<string>::iterator>
        pair1 = mismatch(deq.begin(), deq.end(),
                         driver_list.begin());

    if (pair1.first != deq.end())
      cout << "First disagreement in deq and driver_list:\n  "
           << *(pair1.first) << " and " << *(pair1.second)
           << endl;
    return 0;
  }
```

Output from Example 5.8

```
    First disagreement in deq and driver_list:
    Berger and Rindt
```

In this example, although the list `driver_list` is not equal to the entire vector `vec`, the first assertion shows that `equal` determines that `driver_list` does agree with the initial three-element range in `vec`. In the second assertion, `equal` returns false since `deq` and `driver_list` disagree in their second positions. Calling `equal` does not yield any information about where the disagreement occurs, but the final part of the program shows how `mismatch` can be called and its return value used to display the elements that disagree.

Note that neither of these algorithms can serve as a complete check for the equality of two containers, since there is no check for the containers having the same size. To check if two containers `c1` and `c2` have equal contents, we can write

```
    c1.size() == c2.size() &&
    equal(c1.begin(), c1.end(), c2.begin())
```

This works even if `c1` and `c2` are of different types, but if they are of the same type, we have to write only

```
    c1 == c2
```

since, as we'll see in Section 6.1.6, the `==` operator is defined on containers of the same type by exactly the preceding expression using `size` and `equal`.

One other point should be noted about the size of the ranges given to `equal` or `mismatch`. The number of dereferenceable positions reachable from `first2` should be at least the size of [`first1, last1`), or else there should be a disagreement between some reachable, dereferenceable position and the corresponding position in [first1, last1). If neither of these conditions holds, the result of equal or mismatch is undefined. For example, it would be incorrect to write the first call to equal in Example 5.8 as

```
equal(vec.begin(), vec.end(), driver_list.begin())
```

since the end of driver_list would be reached without finding a disagreement.[4]

Both algorithms have predicate versions, in which the meaning of equality can be replaced by a binary predicate given as the fourth argument.

The time complexity of both equal and mismatch is linear.

5.2.6   Search

Given two ranges, the generic search algorithm finds the first position in the first range in which the second range occurs as a subsequence. It generalizes string matching functions like the C library function strstr. Its interface is

```
template <typename ForwardIterator1, typename ForwardIterator2>
ForwardIterator1
    search(ForwardIterator1 first1, ForwardIterator1 last1,
           ForwardIterator2 first2, ForwardIterator2 last2);
```

where the two sequences are determined by the ranges [first1, last1) and [first2, last2). If the second range does occur as a subsequence of the first, the beginning position in [first1, last1) of the first occurrence is returned; otherwise, last1 is returned.

Example 5.9: Illustrating the generic search algorithm

```
"ex05-09.cpp" 85 ≡
    #include <iostream>
    #include <cassert>
    #include <algorithm>
    #include <vector>
    #include <deque>
    using namespace std;

    int main()
```

---

[4]The source code for this incorrect variation, Example 5.8a, is available on the Internet (see Appendix D) as the file ex05-08a.cpp.

```
{
    cout << "Illustrating the generic search algorithm." << endl;
    vector<int> vector1(20);
    deque<int>  deque1(5);
    // Initialize vector1 with 0, 1, ..., 19:
    int i;
    for (i = 0; i < 20; ++i)
      vector1[i] = i;

    // Initialize deque1 with 5, 6, 7, 8, 9:
    for (i = 0; i < 5; ++i)
      deque1[i] = i + 5;

    // Search for first occurrence of deque1's contents
    // as a subsequence of the vector contents:
    vector<int>::iterator k =
      search(vector1.begin(), vector1.end(),
             deque1.begin(), deque1.end());

    // Verify that 5, 6, 7, 8, 9 occur in vector1
    //    starting at the position to which k refers:
    for (i = 0; i < 5; ++i)
      assert (*(k + i) == i + 5);
    cout << " --- Ok." << endl;
    return 0;
}
```

The call to the **search** algorithm looks for the first position in the vector where the deque elements (5, 6, 7, 8, 9) are contained as a range. It returns an iterator object of type **vector<int>::iterator**, pointing to the element 5 within the vector.

The algorithm also has a predicate version, taking a binary predicate as a fifth argument and using it as the meaning of equality.

The time complexity of the **search** algorithm is required to be only $O(mn)$ where m is the size of the first range and n is the size of the second range. This requirement can be met by a naive algorithm that starts searching for the second range element by element beginning in the first position of the first range: if all elements of the second range are matched, the search succeeds; otherwise, a new search begins at the second position of the first range, and so on until either a match is found or the end of the first range is reached. In most cases, the time this naive algorithm takes is much better than $O(mn)$, growing only as $O(m + n)$. The $O(m + n)$ growth can actually be guaranteed as the worst case by a more sophisticated algorithm, but when the time complexity requirement for `search` was specified, it was believed that the more sophisticated algorithms available would be slower than the naive algorithm on most inputs. With recent algorithm improvements, however, it is possible to implement `search` with a worst-case bound of $O(m + n)$ and still be faster than the naive algorithm on average [13]. Thus it would be better if in a future revision of the C++ Standard the time bound required for `search` were tightened to $O(m + n)$. (Other cases in which progress in algorithm design has outmoded the C++ Standard's time complexity bounds are discussed in Section 5.4.)

5.3 Mutating Sequence Algorithms

Mutating sequence algorithms are those that modify the contents of the containers on which they operate. For example, the `unique` algorithm eliminates all consecutive duplicate elements from a sequence. Other algorithms in this category copy, fill, generate, partition, shuffle, remove, replace, reverse, swap, or transform elements stored in sequence containers.

5.3.1 Copy and Copy Backward

The generic `copy` and `copy_backward` algorithms are used to copy elements from one range to another. The call

```
copy(first1, last1, first2)
```

copies from [`first1, last1`) to [`first2, last2`) and returns `last2`, where `last2 == first2 + (last1 - first1)`. The algorithm proceeds forward, copying source elements in the order `first1, first1 + 1, ..., last1 - 1`, with the consequence that the destination range can overlap with the source range provided that the source range doesn't contain `first2`. Thus, for example, `copy` can be used to shift a range one position to the left but not to the right. The opposite is true of `copy_backward`:

```
copy_backward(first1, last1, last2)
```

copies from [`first1, last1`) to [`first2, last2`) and returns `first2`, where `first2 == last2 - (last1 - first1)`. It proceeds backward, copying source elements in the order `last1 - 1, last1 - 2, ..., first1`. The copying thus works properly as long as the source range doesn't contain `last2`.

For example, to shift a range to the left by one position, use

```
copy(first1, last1, first1 - 1)
```

which copies `first1` to `first1 - 1`, `first1 + 1` to `first1`, ..., `last1 - 1` to `last1 - 2`, and returns `last1 - 1`. To shift a range to the right by one position, use

```
copy_backward(first1, last1, last1 + 1)
```

which copies `last1 - 1` to `last1`, `last1 - 2` to `last1 - 1`, ..., `first1` to `first1 + 1`, and returns `first1 + 1`.

Example 5.10: Illustrating the generic `copy` and `copy_backward` algorithms

```
"ex05-10.cpp" 88 ≡
      #include <iostream>
      #include <cassert>
      #include <algorithm>
      #include <vector>
      #include <string>
      #include <iostream>
      using namespace std;

      int main()
      {
        cout << "Illustrating the generic copy "
             << "and copy_backward algorithms." << endl;
        string s("abcdefghihklmnopqrstuvwxyz");
        vector<char> vector1(s.begin(), s.end());

        vector<char> vector2(vector1.size());

        // Copy vector1 to vector2:
        copy(vector1.begin(), vector1.end(),
             vector2.begin());

        assert (vector1 == vector2);

        // Shift the contents of vector1 left by 4 positions:
        copy(vector1.begin() + 4, vector1.end(),
             vector1.begin());

        assert (string(vector1.begin(), vector1.end()) ==
```

```
                    string("efghihklmnopqrstuvwxyzwxyz"));

    // Shift it right by 2 positions:
    copy_backward(vector1.begin(), vector1.end() - 2,
                  vector1.end());

    assert (string(vector1.begin(), vector1.end()) ==
            string("efefghihklmnopqrstuvwxyzwx"));
    cout << " --- Ok." << endl;
    return 0;
}
```

The first example of **copy** copies from **vector1** to **vector2**. The second example illustrates copying to an overlapping range, shifting the contents of **vector1** to the left by four positions. Note that, after the shift, the first four characters, **abcd**, have been lost, and the last four characters, **wxyz**, are repeated at the end.

The example of **copy_backward** is a shift by two positions to the right; this shift could not be done with **copy**. In this case, the first two characters, **ef**, of the previous string are now repeated at the beginning, and the last two, **yz**, are lost.

The **copy** and **copy_backward** algorithms have linear time bounds.

5.3.2   Fill

The **fill** and **fill_n** algorithms put copies of a given value in all positions of a range. The call

```
    fill(first, last, value)
```

puts **last - first** copies of **value** in [**first, last**). The call

```
    fill_n(first, n, value)
```

puts **n** copies of **value** in [**first, first + n**).

Example 5.11: Illustrating the generic **fill** and **fill_n** algorithms

"ex05-11.cpp" 89 ≡
```
    #include <iostream>
    #include <cassert>
    #include <algorithm>
    #include <vector>
    #include <string>
```

```
using namespace std;

int main()
{
    cout << "Illustrating the generic fill "
         << "and fill_n algorithms." << endl;
    string s("Hello there");
    vector<char> vector1(s.begin(), s.end());

    // Fill first 5 positions of vector1 with X's:
    fill(vector1.begin(), vector1.begin() + 5, 'X');

    assert (string(vector1.begin(), vector1.end()) ==
            string("XXXXX there"));

    // Fill 3 more positions with Y's:
    fill_n(vector1.begin() + 5, 3, 'Y');

    assert (string(vector1.begin(), vector1.end()) ==
            string("XXXXXYYYere"));
    cout << " --- Ok." << endl;
    return 0;
}
```

The time complexity for the `fill` and `fill_n` algorithms is linear.

5.3.3 Generate

The `generate` algorithm fills a range [`first, last`) with the values returned by `last - first` successive calls to a function `gen` (a third parameter to generate). It is assumed that `gen` takes no arguments.

Example 5.12: Illustrating the generic **generate** algorithm

```
"ex05-12.cpp" 90 ≡
    #include <iostream>
    #include <cassert>
    #include <algorithm>
    #include <vector>
    using namespace std;

    template <typename T>
    class calc_square {
      T i;
```

```
  public:
    calc_square(): i(0) {}
    T operator()() { ++i; return i * i; }
};

int main()
{
    cout << "Illustrating the generic generate algorithm."
         << endl;
    vector<int> vector1(10);

    // Fill vector1 with 1, 4, 9, 16, ..., 100:
    generate(vector1.begin(), vector1.end(), calc_square<int>());

    for (int j = 0; j < 10; ++j)
      assert (vector1[j] == (j+1)*(j+1));
    cout << " --- Ok." << endl;
    return 0;
}
```

The call to **generate** fills the vector **vector1** with the values returned by ten successive calls of the function object **calc_square<int>()**. Note that each of these calls is

```
    calc_square<int>()()
```

since the function called is the one defined as **operator()** in the class **calc_square<int>**. Though the call is the same each time, it returns a different value because the data member **i** is incremented during each call. Function objects used with **generate** are typically defined to change some data member on which the return value depends so that successive calls produce different values.

The time complexity for the **generate** algorithm is linear.

5.3.4 Partition

When given a range [**first, last**) and a unary predicate **pred**, the generic **partition** algorithm rearranges the elements in the range so that all elements that satisfy **pred** are placed before all elements that do not satisfy it. A version of the algorithm called **stable_partition** guarantees that within each group the relative positions of the elements are preserved. Each function returns an iterator marking the end of the first group and the beginning of the second.

Example 5.13: Illustrating the generic `partition` and `stable_partition` algorithms

```
"ex05-13.cpp" 92 ≡
      #include <algorithm>
      #include <vector>
      #include <string>
      #include <iostream>
      using namespace std;

      bool above40(int n) { return (n > 40); }

      int main()
      {
        cout << "Illustrating the generic partition and"
             << " stable_partition algorithms." << endl;
        const int N = 7;
        int array0[N] = {50, 30, 10, 70, 60, 40, 20};
        int array1[N];
        copy(&array0[0], &array0[N], &array1[0]);
        ostream_iterator<int> out(cout, " ");

        cout << "Original sequence:                    ";
        copy(&array1[0], &array1[N], out); cout << endl;

        // Partition array1, putting numbers greater than 40
        // first, followed by those less than or equal to 40:
        int* split = partition(&array1[0], &array1[N], above40);

        cout << "Result of (unstable) partitioning: ";
        copy(&array1[0], split, out); cout << "| ";
        copy(split, &array1[N], out); cout << endl;

        // Restore array1 to array0 contents:
        copy(&array0[0], &array0[N], &array1[0]);

        // Again partition array1, putting numbers greater than 40
        // first, followed by those less than or equal to 40,
        // preserving relative order in each group:
        split = stable_partition(&array1[0], &array1[N], above40);

        cout << "Result of stable partitioning:     ";
        copy(&array1[0], split, out); cout << "| ";
        copy(split, &array1[N], out); cout << endl;
```

```
    return 0;
}
```

Output from Example 5.13

```
Original sequence:                  50 30 10 70 60 40 20
Result of (unstable) partitioning: 50 60 70 | 10 30 40 20
Result of stable partitioning:      50 70 60 | 30 10 40 20
```

In this program the call to `partition` rearranges the values in `array1` into two groups: first, those that are greater than 40, and second, those that are 40 or less. The `partition` algorithm makes no guarantee about the relative order in each group, and indeed we see that in the result 70 and 60 are permuted. The exact order produced by `partition` might vary with different STL implementations. With `stable_partition`, on the other hand, the elements in each group appear in the result in the same order as in the original sequence.

The time complexity is linear for `partition` and `stable_partition`.

5.3.5   Random Shuffle

The generic `random_shuffle` algorithm randomly shuffles the elements in a range [`first`, `last`), using a function that generates pseudo-random numbers. The permutations produced by `random_shuffle` are approximately uniformly distributed; that is, the probability of each of the $N!$ permutations of a range of size N is approximately $1/N!$.

Example 5.14: Illustrating the generic `random_shuffle` algorithm

```
"ex05-14.cpp" 93 ≡
    #include <algorithm>
    #include <vector>
    #include <functional>
    #include <iostream>
    using namespace std;

    int main() {
      cout << "Illustrating the random_shuffle algorithm." << endl;
      const int N = 20;
      vector<int> vector1(N);
      for (int i = 0; i < N; ++i)
        vector1[i] = i;
```

```
for (int j = 0; j < 3; ++j) {
  // Randomly shuffle the integers in vector1:
  random_shuffle(vector1.begin(), vector1.end());

  // Output the contents of vector1:
  copy(vector1.begin(), vector1.end(),
       ostream_iterator<int>(cout, " "));
  cout << endl;
}
return 0;
}
```

Output from Example 5.14

```
6 11 9 2 18 12 17 7 0 15 4 8 10 5 1 19 13 3 14 16
14 19 18 12 0 2 3 5 4 13 15 8 17 11 1 16 9 6 10 7
15 10 5 14 6 11 17 9 13 8 16 4 1 19 7 12 2 18 3 0
```

The order in the output will, of course, vary depending on the details of the particular pseudo-random number generator used.

There is also a **random_shuffle** version that takes a function as a third argument so that one can supply a different generator. The function passed to **random_shuffle** should take an integer argument N and return a pseudo-randomly chosen integer in the interval $[0, N)$.

The time complexity for **random_shuffle** is linear.

5.3.6   Remove

The generic **remove** algorithm removes from a range those elements that are equal to a particular value. It is a stable algorithm—it preserves the relative order of the elements that are not removed from the sequence.

Example 5.15: Illustrating the generic **remove** algorithm

"ex05-15.cpp" 94 ≡

```
#include <iostream>
#include <cassert>
#include <algorithm>
#include <vector>
using namespace std;

int main()
{
```

```
cout << "Illustrating the generic remove algorithm." << endl;
const int  N = 11;
int array1[N] = {1, 2, 0, 3, 4, 0, 5, 6, 7, 0, 8};
vector<int> vector1;
int i;
for (i = 0; i < N; ++i)
  vector1.push_back(array1[i]);

// Remove the zeros from vector1:
vector<int>::iterator new_end;
new_end = remove(vector1.begin(), vector1.end(), 0);

// The size of vector1 remains the same:
assert (vector1.size() == N);

// The nonzero elements are left in
// [vector1.begin(), new_end).  Erase the rest:
vector1.erase(new_end, vector1.end());

// Show that 3 elements were removed and the
// nonzero elements remain, in their original order:
assert (vector1.size() == N - 3);
for (i = 0; i < (int)vector1.size(); ++i)
  assert (vector1[i] == i+1);
cout << " --- Ok." << endl;
return 0;
}
```

It is important to note that **remove** does not alter the size of the container on which it operates. Thus, in the example, **vector1** still has **N** elements after the **remove** call, which has merely copied the elements not equal to the given value into a smaller range and returned the end of the smaller range. The elements between this new end marker and the end of the vector are left in an unspecified order. Using the new end marker and the **erase** member function of the **vector** class, the program then erases the elements from that point to the end of the vector.

There are also copying and predicate versions of **remove**. The time complexity is linear for all versions of the algorithm.

5.3.7 Replace

The generic **replace** algorithm replaces elements in a range that are equal to a particular value with another value.

Example 5.16: Illustrating the generic `replace` algorithm

"ex05-16.cpp" 96 ≡

```
#include <iostream>
#include <cassert>
#include <algorithm>
#include <vector>
#include <string>
using namespace std;

int main()
{
  cout << "Illustrating the generic replace algorithm."
      << endl;
  string s("FERRARI");
  vector<char> vector1(s.begin(), s.end());

  // Replace all occurrences of R by S:
  replace(vector1.begin(), vector1.end(), 'R', 'S');

  assert (string(vector1.begin(), vector1.end()) ==
      string("FESSASI"));
  cout << " --- Ok." << endl;
  return 0;
}
```

In this example, all occurrences of R are replaced with S. All other characters in the sequence remain the same.

There are copying and predicate versions of **replace**. The time complexity is linear for all versions.

5.3.8 Reverse

The generic **reverse** algorithm reverses the order of elements in a range. The iterators specifying the range must be bidirectional. See Examples 2.1, 2.2, and 2.3. The time complexity for the **reverse** algorithm is linear.

5.3.9 Rotate

The generic **rotate** algorithm rotates a range. The call

```
rotate(first, middle, last)
```

rotates the elements in the range [first, last) to the left by middle −
first positions. After the call the elements originally in [middle, last)
appear in [first, first + k), where k = last − middle, and the elements
originally in [first, middle) appear in [first + k, last). The arguments
to rotate must be bidirectional iterators.

Example 5.17: Illustrating the generic rotate algorithm

```
"ex05-17.cpp" 97 ≡
    #include <iostream>
    #include <cassert>
    #include <algorithm>
    #include <vector>
    #include <string>
    using namespace std;

    int main()
    {
      cout << "Illustrating the generic rotate algorithm." << endl;
      string s("Software Engineering ");
      vector<char> vector1(s.begin(), s.end());

      // Rotate the vector so that "Engineering " comes first:
      rotate(vector1.begin(), vector1.begin() + 9,
             vector1.end());

      assert (string(vector1.begin(), vector1.end()) ==
              string("Engineering Software "));
      cout << " --- Ok." << endl;
      return 0;
    }
```

The time complexity for the rotate algorithm is linear.

5.3.10 Swap

The generic swap algorithm exchanges two values.

Example 5.18: Illustrating the generic swap algorithm

```
"ex05-18.cpp" 97 ≡
    #include <iostream>
    #include <cassert>
    #include <algorithm>
```

```
#include <vector>
using namespace std;

int main()
{
    cout << "Illustrating the generic swap algorithm." << endl;
    int high = 250, low = 0;

    swap(high, low);

    assert (high == 0 && low  == 250);
    cout << " --- Ok." << endl;

    vector<int> vector1(100, 1), vector2(200, 2);

    swap(vector1, vector2);

    assert (vector1 == vector<int>(200, 2) &&
            vector2 == vector<int>(100, 1));
    return 0;
}
```

The time complexity for this operation is constant when applied to built-in types and even when applied to a pair of STL containers, as in the second call in the example program. That is, the exchange of the two vectors is not done in terms of vector assignments, which would take $O(N)$ type int assignments, where N is the size of the larger of the two vectors (200 in this case). Instead, as is discussed in Section 6.1.7, `vector` has a `swap` member function that can be called as `vector1.swap(vector2)` and whose time complexity is constant, since it can be done by swapping internal pointers of the `vector` representation. The library arranges that the call `swap(vector1, vector2)` actually calls the `vector swap` member function instead of a more general version that would do the exchange via assignments. See Section 6.1.7 for more explanation of how this is achieved.

5.3.11   Swap Ranges

The generic `swap_ranges` algorithm exchanges two ranges of values, which can be in different containers. The call

```
swap_ranges(first1, last1, first2)
```

exchanges the contents of [`first1`, `last1`) with that of [`first2`, `first2`$+N$), where $N = $ `last1` $-$ `first1`. It is assumed that these ranges do not overlap.

Example 5.19: Illustrating the generic `swap_ranges` algorithm

"ex05-19.cpp" 99 ≡

```
#include <iostream>
#include <cassert>
#include <algorithm>
#include <vector>
#include <string>
using namespace std;
⟨Define make function (builds a container of characters) 22b⟩

int main()
{
  cout << "Illustrating the generic swap_ranges algorithm."
      << endl;
  vector<char> vector1 = make< vector<char> >("HELLO"),
               vector2 = make< vector<char> >("THERE");

  // Save vector1 and vector2 contents, for checking:
  vector<char> temp1 = vector1, temp2 = vector2;

  // Swap the contents of vector1 and vector2:
  swap_ranges(vector1.begin(), vector1.end(),
              vector2.begin());

  assert (vector1 == temp2 && vector2 == temp1);
  cout << " --- Ok." << endl;
  return 0;
}
```

The time complexity is linear for the **swap_ranges** algorithm.

5.3.12   Transform

The generic **transform** algorithm applies a function to each element in a range and stores the values it returns in another range. One version of the algorithm applies a unary function to each element of a range, while another version applies a binary function to corresponding pairs of elements from two ranges. The binary function version of **transform** is illustrated in the following example.

Example 5.20: Illustrating the generic `transform` algorithm

"ex05-20.cpp" 100 ≡

```
#include <algorithm>
#include <iostream>
using namespace std;

int sum(int val1, int val2) { return val2 + val1; }

int main()
{
   cout << "Illustrating the generic transform algorithm."
        << endl;
   int array1[5] = {0, 1, 2, 3, 4};
   int array2[5] = {6, 7, 8, 9, 10};
   ostream_iterator<int> out(cout, " ");

   // Put sums of corresponding array1 and array2 elements
   // into output stream:
   transform(&array1[0], &array1[5], &array2[0], out, sum);

   cout << endl;
   return 0;
}
```

Output from Example 5.20

```
6 8 10 12 14
```

In this program we use `transform` to produce the sums of corresponding pairs of elements from `array1` and `array2`. The resulting sequence of values is placed on the standard output stream using an ostream iterator.

The time complexity for the `transform` algorithm is linear.

5.3.13   Unique

The generic `unique` algorithm eliminates all consecutive duplicate elements from an input sequence. An element is considered to be a consecutive duplicate if it is equal to the element to its immediate left in the sequence, so all but the first element of a group of consecutive elements is removed. As with the `remove` algorithm (see Section 5.3.6), `unique` does not change the size of the container on which it operates; it merely copies the elements that are not consecutive duplicates into a smaller range and returns the end of the smaller range.

Example 5.21: Illustrating the generic unique algorithm

"ex05-21.cpp" 101 ≡

```cpp
#include <iostream>
#include <cassert>
#include <algorithm>
#include <vector>
#include <iostream>
using namespace std;

int main()
{
  cout << "Illustrating the generic unique algorithm." << endl;
  const int N = 11;
  int array1[N] = {1, 2, 0, 3, 3, 0, 7, 7, 7, 0, 8};
  vector<int> vector1;
  for (int i = 0; i < N; ++i)
    vector1.push_back(array1[i]);

  // Eliminate consecutive duplicates from vector1:
  vector<int>::iterator new_end;
  new_end = unique(vector1.begin(), vector1.end());

  // The size of vector1 remains the same;
  assert (vector1.size() == N);

  // The nonconsecutive duplicate elements are left in
  // [vector1.begin(), new_end).  Erase the rest:
  vector1.erase(new_end, vector1.end());

  // Put the resulting vector1 contents on the
  // standard output stream:
  copy(vector1.begin(), vector1.end(),
       ostream_iterator<int>(cout, " "));
  cout << endl;

  return 0;
}
```

Output from Example 5.21

1 2 0 3 0 7 0 8

None of the occurrences of 0 has been eliminated, because they are not consecutive duplicates. If you want to eliminate all duplicates and you do not need to preserve the order of the nonduplicates, first sort the range so that all duplicates occur in consecutive positions and then apply `unique`.

The time complexity is linear for all versions of `unique`.

5.4   Sorting-Related Algorithms

STL includes several algorithms that are in some way related to sorting. There are algorithms for sorting and merging sequences and for searching and performing set-like operations on sorted sequences. In this section we take a look at all these algorithms. Before doing so, we need to understand some of the means by which the generality of these algorithms is achieved.

5.4.1   Comparison Relations

An essential ingredient for these algorithms is comparison of sequence elements. Each algorithm has a version that uses the < operator, and another version takes a comparison object as one of its parameters. In this section, the requirements on comparison objects are also placed on the < operator.

A comparison object should be a binary predicate object, and the binary relation it defines must obey some fundamental laws in order to obtain well-defined results from the sorting-related algorithms.

Let's first consider a set of requirements that is a bit stronger than actually needed. Let R be a binary relation on a set S; then we say that R is a *strict total ordering* on S if R obeys the following two laws:

- (Transitivity) For every x, y, z in S, if xRy and yRz, then xRz.

- (Trichotomy) For every x and y in S, exactly one of the following is true: xRy, yRx, or $x = y$.

Comparison relations that are strict total orderings may be used with the STL sorting-related algorithms. For example, the requirements are satisfied by the comparison relations defined by the C++ built-in < or > operators on built-in numeric types. (But note that <= and >= are not strict total orderings because the trichotomy law fails: two of the three conditions are satisfied instead of exactly one.) When defining a comparison object, it's usually not difficult to obtain a strict total ordering if we merely define it in terms of some previously defined operator whose relation obeys these laws. STL provides two function object types **less** and **greater** (in header **functional**), with template type parameter T, that use the < or > operator for T, respectively. So, for example,

```
sort(vector1.begin(), vector1.end(), less<int>());
```

sorts the **vector<int>** **vector1** and so does

```
sort(vector1.begin(), vector1.end(), greater<int>());
```

As we'll see, with **less<int>()**, the result is put into ascending order, and with **greater<int>()** it is put into descending order. As another example, the C++ Standard **string** class defines **operator<** on strings as alphabetical ordering, which is a total ordering on strings.

```
sort(vector2.begin(), vector2.end(), less<string>());
```

sorts the **vector<string>** **vector2** into ascending order (normal alphabetical order), and

```
sort(vector2.begin(), vector2.end(), greater<string>());
```

sorts it into descending order (reverse alphabetical order).

A strict total ordering completely defines the order in which elements can appear in a sequence (hence the name "total"), but sometimes we do not care about the order of some elements. For example, if we have

```
struct Person {
  string last_name;
  string first_name;
};
```

we might need to sort only according to last names, not caring about the order in which two people with the same last name but different first names appear. This can be done by defining

```
class LastNameLess {
public:
  bool operator()(const Person& p, const Person& q) const
  {
    return p.last_name < q.last_name;
  }
};
```

and sorting, say, a `deque<Person> deque1` with

```
sort(deque1.begin(), deque1.end(), LastNameLess());
```

The fact that this works does not follow from the previous discussion, since the relation R defined by `LastNameLess()` is not a strict total ordering. It fails to impose any order on some pairs of persons (those with the same last name). That is, for some distinct persons p and q, both pRq and qRp are false. Effectively, it is treating such persons as equivalent, though they are not identical. The need for this kind of sorting operation is common enough that the STL sorting-related algorithms have all been designed to work with a relation weaker than a strict total ordering.

The actual requirements are for what is called a strict weak ordering ([18], p. 33) where "weak" refers to the fact that the requirements are not strong enough to determine the order of all elements. Any two elements whose relative order is not determined are considered equivalent. The precise way in which strict weak ordering is defined is given in Section 22.26. The ordering defined by `LastNameLess()` is a strict weak ordering, as is, for example, any ordering of multimember structs in which one field is compared using a strict total ordering and the other fields are ignored. Another common and useful example is case-insensitive comparison of strings (when strings that differ in case are considered equivalent).

As already noted, comparison objects defined in terms of operators like the built-in `<=` or `>=` operators do not satisfy the requirements of a strict total ordering. Neither do they satisfy the strict weak ordering requirements, and thus they cannot be used with the STL sorting-related algorithms. In fact, if you attempt to do so, say with

```
sort(first, last, less_equal<int>());  // incorrect
```

the computation may even fail to terminate.

Another important point is that the sorting-related algorithms make no use of operator `==`. In describing the results these algorithms produce, we nonetheless often talk about "equivalence" between elements, but here the meaning of equivalence is independent of the meaning of the `==` operator. Instead, if `comp` is the comparison operator, we mean the equivalence defined by

Equiv(x, y) if and only if both comp(x, y) and comp(y, x) are false.

An example is the way we describe the stability property of a sorting algorithm. Usually, a sorting algorithm is said to be *stable* if it preserves the relative order of equal elements. We extend this definition to mean preserving the order of elements that are equivalent as just defined.

5.4.2 Nondecreasing (Ascending) Order Versus Nonincreasing (Descending) Order

The STL sorting and merging algorithms put their results into *nondecreasing order* according to the given comparison relation R. This means that for every iterator i referring to a sequence element, x, and every nonnegative integer N such that i + N refers to a sequence element, y, yRx is false.

Suppose that we need the opposite order—*nonincreasing order*—according to R. For this we need R's *converse relation*. In general, if R is a binary relation on S, its converse is the relation C on S defined by "xCy if and only if yRx." Thus the converse relation of the < operator for built-in types is the same relation as that computed by the > operator. For a user-defined type, if < is defined, then an STL template function definition (in header utility) ensures that > is defined as the converse relation of <:

```
template <typename T>
inline bool operator>(const T& x, const T& y) {
  return y < x;
}
```

(There are similar definitions of <= and >= in terms of <, so one needs to define only <. As already noted, these relations cannot be used with the STL sorting-related algorithms, but they may be useful for other purposes.)

The STL predicate object **greater<T>()** encapsulates the > operator for type T in a function object that can be passed to a sorting algorithm. Thus, for example, we can sort a range [first, last) of integers into nonincreasing order with

```
sort(first, last, greater<int>());
```

Suppose that instead of < we are using a comparison object comp as the less-than relation on some user-defined type U. That is, assume that we have defined

```
class comp {
 public:
  bool operator()(const U& x, const U& y) const
  { // ...
  }
};
```

Then we can code its converse relation explicitly by defining

```
class comp_converse {
 public:
   bool operator()(const U& x, const U& y) const
   {
     return comp()(y, x);
   }
};
```

and we can sort into nonincreasing order with

```
sort(first, last, comp_converse());
```

We sometimes use the terms *ascending* as a synonym for nondecreasing and *descending* for nonincreasing.

5.4.3   Sort, Stable Sort, and Partial Sort

STL provides three generic sorting algorithms, `sort`, `partial_sort`, and `stable_sort`. Each sorts a random access sequence and each places its result into the same container on which it operates. `Partial_sort` requires only a constant amount of extra storage, `sort` a logarithmic amount. Thus both are essentially in-place algorithms, while `stable_sort` can use a linear amount of extra storage. All three are illustrated later in Example 5.22.

These sorting algorithms differ in their computing times and stability. The `sort` function is required to sort a sequence of length N using $O(N \log N)$ comparisons on the average, but it is allowed to take $O(N^2)$ time in the worst case. For *guaranteed* $O(N \log N)$ behavior, one can use a special case of `partial_sort`. Neither algorithm is required to be stable; that is, the relative position of equivalent elements is not necessarily maintained. If stability is required, `stable_sort` will do the job and it has an $O(N \log N)$ time bound unless storage is tight, in which case it can take a bit longer (we'll get to this in a moment).

Readers familiar with sorting algorithms can probably guess from these descriptions that `sort` is intended to be implemented with some version of quicksort, `partial_sort` with some version of heapsort, and `stable_sort` with some version of mergesort. For simple cases of sorting, such as sorting vectors of integers or floating-point numbers, quicksort typically runs two or three times faster than heapsort, but it can blow up to quadratic time, taking many times longer than heapsort on certain kinds of sequences. The specification of `sort` was thus written so that it can be implemented with quicksort, and programmers would thus have this usually fast algorithm available. The standard thus stipulates only $O(N \log N)$ average time for `sort`, then appends the caveat "If the worst-case behavior is important `stable_sort` or `partial_sort` should be used."

This advice may leave programmers somewhat uneasy about choosing between these sorting algorithms, but in a future revision of the standard it will be possible to avoid the dilemma entirely. One of us (Dave Musser) has developed a new sorting algorithm, *introsort* [12], which is just as fast as quicksort on most sequences while meeting an $O(N \log N)$ worst-case bound. Introsort achieves this goal by starting with and normally continuing quicksort's usual partitioning strategy, but it changes strategy if the going gets rough (namely, if it encounters too many "bad partitions," the well-known source of quicksort's quadratic time blow-up). In that case it switches to heapsort. Since the bad partitioning cases are rare, introsort almost always behaves like a straight quicksort algorithm, except that it is much better behaved in a few cases. Thus the `sort` algorithm time bound could now best be expressed as an $O(N \log N)$ worst-case bound, since library implementors can meet it with introsort without giving up the typical speed advantage of quicksort. In fact, several STL implementations currently do or soon will implement `sort` with introsort.

The worst-case time bound for `stable_sort` is $O(N(\log N)^2)$ time. This bound can be satisfied with an algorithm based on the principle of merge sorting with the addition of another significant technique, *adaptation to memory constraints*. If memory for at least $N/2$ elements is available, the time bound is $O(N \log N)$. In some cases, `stable_sort` can be faster even than `sort`. As its name suggests, it also has the advantage of being stable; that is, the relative position of equivalent elements is maintained. This property is often important when the elements have several fields on which they are being sorted, for example, a last name field and a city field. If sorted by city first and then by last name with a stable algorithm, each set of records with the same last name will still be in order according to the city fields. As already noted, neither `sort` nor `partial_sort` has this stability property. An example of the results of a stable versus nonstable sort is given in Example 5.22.

Sometimes we need only partial sorting; for example, we might want to know only the top 100 scores among 20,000 test grades. Calling the `partial_sort` algorithm as

```
partial_sort(first, middle, last)
```

puts into [`first`, `middle`) the $k =$ `middle` $-$ `first` smallest elements of the entire range [`first`, `last`) without actually sorting the entire range. The elements in [`middle`, `last`) are left in an undetermined order. Thus if the test scores are in `vector<float> scores`,

```
partial_sort(scores.begin(), scores.begin() + 100,
             scores.end(), greater<float>())
```

causes the range [`scores.begin()`, `scores.begin() + 100`) to contain the 100 largest scores in descending order.

The computing time for `partial_sort` is $O(N \log k)$, where $N =$ `last` $-$ `first` and $k =$ `middle` $-$ `first`.

It follows from this specification that

```
partial_sort(first, last, last)
```

sorts the entire range [`first`, `last`). This special case is the normal heapsort algorithm, with $O(N \log N)$ computing time.

The following program illustrates all three of these algorithms, applying them to a vector of integers and using a comparison object, `comp_last()`, that compares two integers based on the size of their last base-10 digits. Thus, for example, `comp_last()(13, 6)` is true since 3 < 6, but both `comp_last()(13, 3)` and `comp_last()(3, 13)` are false, so 3 and 13 are considered equivalent. Using `sort`, 3 and 13 may not be left in the same relative order in which they occurred in the sequence before sorting (in fact, we see from the output in this case that they are not), but `stable_sort` leaves these and other groups of equivalent elements in their original relative order.

Example 5.22: Illustrating the generic algorithms `sort`, `stable_sort`, and `partial_sort`

"ex05-22.cpp" 108 $\equiv$
```
#include <vector>
#include <algorithm>
#include <iostream>
using namespace std;

class comp_last {
 public:
  bool operator()(int x, int y) const
    // Compare x and y based on their last base-10 digits:
  {
```

```
      return x % 10 < y % 10;
    }
};

int main()
{
  cout << "Illustrating the generic sort, stable_sort,"
       << " and partial_sort algorithms." << endl;
  const int N = 20;

  vector<int> vector0;
  for (int i = 0; i < N; ++i)
   vector0.push_back(i);

  vector<int> vector1 = vector0;

  ostream_iterator<int> out(cout, " ");

  cout << "Before sorting:\n";
  copy(vector1.begin(), vector1.end(), out);
  cout << endl;

  sort(vector1.begin(), vector1.end(), comp_last());

  cout << "After sorting by last digits with sort:\n";
  copy(vector1.begin(), vector1.end(), out);
  cout << endl << endl;

  vector1 = vector0;
  cout << "Before sorting:\n";
  copy(vector1.begin(), vector1.end(), out);
  cout << endl;

  stable_sort(vector1.begin(), vector1.end(), comp_last());

  cout << "After sorting by last digits with stable_sort:\n";
  copy(vector1.begin(), vector1.end(), out);
  cout << endl << endl;

  vector1 = vector0;
  reverse(vector1.begin(), vector1.end());
  cout << "Before sorting:\n";
  copy(vector1.begin(), vector1.end(), out);
  cout << endl << endl;
```

```
        partial_sort(vector1.begin(), vector1.begin() + 5,
                     vector1.end(), comp_last());

        cout << "After sorting with partial_sort to get\n"
             << "5 values with smallest last digits:\n";
        copy(vector1.begin(), vector1.end(), out);
        cout << endl << endl;
        return 0;
}
```

Output from Example 5.22

```
    Before sorting:
    0 1 2 3 4 5 6 7 8 9 10 11 12 13 14 15 16 17 18 19

    After sorting by last digits with sort:
    10 0 11 1 12 2 13 3 4 14 5 15 6 16 7 17 8 18 9 19

    Before sorting:
    0 1 2 3 4 5 6 7 8 9 10 11 12 13 14 15 16 17 18 19

    After sorting by last digits with stable_sort:
    0 10 1 11 2 12 3 13 4 14 5 15 6 16 7 17 8 18 9 19

    Before sorting:
    19 18 17 16 15 14 13 12 11 10 9 8 7 6 5 4 3 2 1 0

    After sorting with partial_sort to get
    5 values with smallest last digits:
    10 0 11 1 12 19 18 17 16 15 9 8 7 6 5 4 14 13 3 2
```

5.4.4   Nth Element

The generic `nth_element` algorithm places in the Nth position of a sequence an element that could be in that position if the sequence were sorted. The algorithm also partitions the sequence in such a way that all elements to the left of the Nth element are less than or equivalent to those to its right.

Example 5.23: Illustrating the generic `nth_element` algorithm

"ex05-23.cpp" 110 ≡

```
    #include <iostream>
```

```
#include <cassert>
#include <algorithm>
#include <vector>
using namespace std;

int main()
{
  cout << "Illustrating the generic nth_element algorithm."
       << endl;
  vector<int> v(7);

  v[0] = 25; v[1] = 7; v[2] = 9;
  v[3] = 2; v[4] = 0; v[5] = 5; v[6] = 21;

  const int N = 4;

  // Use nth_element to place the Nth smallest
  // element in v in the Nth position, v.begin() + N:

  nth_element(v.begin(), v.begin() + N, v.end());

  // Check that the element at v.begin() + N, v[N], is
  // greater than or equal to each of the preceding elements:
  int i;
  for (i = 0; i < N; ++i)
    assert (v[N] >= v[i]);

  // Check that v[N] is less than or equal to each
  // of the following elements:
  for (i = N + 1; i < 7; ++i)
    assert (v[N] <= v[i]);
  cout << " --- Ok." << endl;
  return 0;
}
```

In this example, the call to **nth_element** places in position **v.begin()** + N the element that would appear there if the vector were completely sorted. This element, **v[N]**, is the Nth smallest element if elements are counted starting with 0, or the (N + 1)st smallest if they are counted starting with 1. That the element in **V[N]** is the Nth smallest element is verified by the assertions, which also show that the elements have been partitioned so that **v[0]**, ..., **v[N]** are all less than or equal to **v[N + 1]**, ..., **v[6]**.

The average computing time for **nth_element** is linear, but the worst-case time is allowed to be quadratic. The worst case can, however, be kept to linear without slowing down the average case by implementing `nth_element` with the introselect algorithm described in [12]. *Introselect*, like introsort, switches to another algorithm if many bad partitions are occurring, in this case an algorithm with a linear worst-case bound. Given the existence of introselect, the worst-case time bound for `nth_element` should be tightened to linear in a future revision of the C++ Standard.

5.4.5 Binary Search, Lower Bound, Upper Bound, and Equal Range

The generic binary search algorithms use a traditional binary search to find an element in a sorted sequence. Given a sorted range [`first, last`) and an element `x`, the generic `binary_search` algorithm returns true if it finds an element equivalent to `x` in the range, false otherwise. With the same inputs the `lower_bound` and `upper_bound` algorithms return an iterator `i` referring to the first or last position, respectively, into which the value can be inserted while still maintaining the sorted ordering. (Note that this specification determines a position in the range regardless of whether or not the there is already an element equivalent to `x` in the range.) The `equal_range` algorithm returns the pair of iterators that would be computed by `lower_bound` and `upper_bound`.

For random access containers, the `binary_search` function makes at most $\log N + 2$ comparisons, `lower_bound` and `upper_bound` make at most $\log N + 1$ comparisons, and `equal_range` makes at most $2\log N + 1$ comparisons. Note that random access containers can also be searched with the generic `find` algorithm, described in Section 2.2. The `find` algorithm takes linear time to determine whether an element is present in a sequence, regardless of whether the sequence is sorted. The advantage of using `find` over the binary search algorithms is that `find` can be used on nonsorted sequences. Also, since `find` requires only input iterators, it can be used to search for elements in data structures such as input streams, singly and doubly linked lists, and so forth, on which the binary search algorithms cannot operate in logarithmic time.

It must be noted that although the binary search algorithms achieve their maximum efficiency (logarithmic time) only for sorted random access sequences, the algorithms are written to work for nonrandom access containers, such as lists, as well. For all nonrandom access data structures, the time the binary search algorithms take is linear, but the number of comparisons is only logarithmic. In cases in which comparisons are expensive, it could be better, by some constant factor, to use one of the binary search algorithms rather than `find`.

All the binary search algorithms are illustrated in the following example.

Example 5.24: Illustrating the generic binary search algorithms

"ex05-24.cpp" 113 ≡

```
#include <iostream>
#include <cassert>
#include <algorithm>
#include <vector>
using namespace std;

int main()
{
  cout << "Illustrating the generic binary search algorithms."
       << endl;
  vector<int> v(5);
  bool found;

  // Initialize:
  int i;
  for (i = 0; i < 5; ++i) v[i] = i;

  // Search for each of the integers 0, 1, 2, 3, 4:
  for (i = 0; i < 5; ++i) {
    found = binary_search(v.begin(), v.end(), i);
    assert (found == true);
  }

  // Try searching for a value that's not present:
  found = binary_search (v.begin(), v.end(), 9);
  assert (found == false);

  v[1] = 7; v[2] = 7; v[3] = 7; v[4] = 8;

  // Vector v now contains 0 7 7 7 8

  // Apply upper_bound, lower_bound and equal_range on v:

  vector<int>::iterator k;
  k = lower_bound(v.begin(), v.end(), 7);
  assert (k == v.begin() + 1 && *k == 7);
```

```
        k = upper_bound(v.begin(), v.end(), 7);
        assert (k == v.end() - 1 && *k == 8);

        pair<vector<int>::iterator, vector<int>::iterator> pi =
            equal_range(v.begin(), v.end(), 7);

        assert (pi.first == v.begin() + 1);
        assert (pi.second == v.end() - 1);
        cout << " --- Ok." << endl;
        return 0;
    }
```

5.4.6 Merge

The generic `merge` algorithm merges two sorted ranges and places the result in a range that does not overlap either of the two input ranges. The `inplace_merge` algorithm merges two consecutive sorted ranges and replaces both ranges with the resulting merged sequence.

For the `merge` algorithm the time complexity is linear. The time complexity for `inplace_merge` depends on the amount of additional memory available. If no additional memory is available, the algorithm can take $O(N \log N)$ time; otherwise, it takes linear time.

Example 5.25: Illustrating the generic `merge` algorithms

"ex05-25.cpp" 114 ≡

```
    #include <iostream>
    #include <cassert>
    #include <algorithm>
    #include <vector>
    using namespace std;

    int main()
    {
      cout << "Illustrating the generic merge algorithms." << endl;
      // Initialize vector of integers:
      vector<int> vector1(5);
      vector<int> vector2(5);
      vector<int> vector3(10);

      int i;
      for (i = 0; i < 5; ++i)
        vector1[i] = 2 * i;
```

```
      for (i = 0; i < 5; ++i)
        vector2[i] = 1 + 2 * i;

      // Merge contents of vector1 and vector2,
      // putting result in vector3:
      merge(vector1.begin(), vector1.end(),
            vector2.begin(), vector2.end(),
            vector3.begin());

      for (i = 0; i < 10; ++i)
        assert (vector3[i] == i);

      for (i = 0; i < 5; ++i)
        vector3[i] = vector1[i];
      for (i = 0; i < 5; ++i)
        vector3[i + 5] = vector2[i];

      // Merge the two sorted halves of vector3
      // in place to obtain a sorted vector3:
      inplace_merge(vector3.begin(), vector3.begin() + 5,
                    vector3.end());

      for (i = 0; i < 10; ++i)
        assert (vector3[i] == i);
      cout << " --- Ok." << endl;
      return 0;
    }
```

5.4.7   Set Operations on Sorted Structures

STL provides five algorithms that perform set-like operations on sorted sequences: includes, set_union, set_intersection, set_difference, and set_symmetric_difference.

The includes algorithm checks whether the elements of one range, [first1, last1) are contained in another, [first2, last2), and returns a Boolean value accordingly.

Given two ranges, [first1, last1) and [first2, last2), representing sets, the set_union algorithm generates the union of the two sets into the range [result, last) and returns last, the past-the-end location of the resulting sequence.

The generic set_difference algorithm creates a set of elements that are in the first range but not in the second; the set_intersection algorithm creates a set from elements that are common to both input sequences; and set_symmetric_difference creates a set of elements that are in one but not in both of the input sequences. Like set_union, all these functions place the resulting sequence into the range [result, last) and return last, the past-the-end location of the resulting sequence.

For all the set operations, the time complexity is linear. Each algorithm performs at most $2(N1 + N2) - 1$ comparisons, where $N1 = \texttt{last1} - \texttt{first1}$ and $N2 = \texttt{last2} - \texttt{first2}$.

Example 5.26: Illustrating the generic set operations

"ex05-26.cpp" 116 ≡

```
#include <iostream>
#include <cassert>
#include <algorithm>
#include <vector>
using namespace std;
⟨Define make function (builds a container of characters) 22b⟩

int main()
{
  cout << "Illustrating the generic set operations." << endl;
  bool result;

  vector<char> vector1 = make< vector<char> >("abcde"),
               vector2 = make< vector<char> >("aeiou");

  // Illustrate includes:
  result = includes(vector1.begin(), vector1.end(),
                    vector2.begin(), vector2.end());
  assert (result == false);

  result = includes(vector1.begin(), vector1.end(),
                    vector2.begin(), vector2.begin() + 2);
  // 'a' and 'e' are contained in vector1
  assert (result == true);

  // Illustrate set_union:
  vector<char> setUnion;
  set_union(vector1.begin(), vector1.end(),
            vector2.begin(), vector2.end(),
            back_inserter(setUnion));
```

```
    assert (setUnion == make< vector<char> >("abcdeiou"));

    // Illustrate set_intersection:
    vector<char> setIntersection;
    set_intersection(vector1.begin(), vector1.end(),
            vector2.begin(), vector2.end(),
            back_inserter(setIntersection));

    assert (setIntersection == make< vector<char> >("ae"));

    // Illustrate set_symmetric_difference:
    vector<char> setDifference;

    set_symmetric_difference(vector1.begin(),
            vector1.end(),
            vector2.begin(), vector2.end(),
            back_inserter(setDifference));

    assert (setDifference == make< vector<char> >("bcdiou"));
    cout << " --- Ok." << endl;
    return 0;
}
```

5.4.8 Heap Operations

A *heap* represents a particular organization of a random access data structure. Given a range [first, last), we say that the range represents a heap if two key properties are satisfied:

- The value pointed to by first is the largest value in the range.

- The value pointed to by first may be removed by a pop operation or a new element added by a push operation in logarithmic time. Both the pop and push operations return valid heaps.

STL provides four algorithms to create and manipulate heaps: make_heap, pop_heap, push_heap, and sort_heap.

The push_heap algorithm assumes that [first, last - 1) contains a valid heap and rearranges [first, last) into a heap (thus pushing the value at last - 1 into the heap). The pop_heap algorithm assumes that [first, last) is a valid heap, swaps the value at first with the value at last - 1, and transforms the range [first, last - 1) into a heap. The time complexity for `push_heap` and `pop_heap` is $O(\log N)$, where N is the size of the range $[\texttt{first}, \texttt{last})$.

The `make_heap` algorithm constructs a heap in the range $[\texttt{first}, \texttt{last})$ using elements in $[\texttt{first}, \texttt{last})$, and `sort_heap` sorts the elements that are stored in the heap. The time complexity for `make_heap` is linear, requiring at most $3N$ comparisons, while the `sort_heap` algorithm requires $O(N \log N)$ time with a maximum of $N \log N$ comparisons. All these algorithms are illustrated in the next example.

Example 5.27: Illustrating the generic heap operations

"ex05-27.cpp" 118 ≡

```cpp
#include <iostream>
#include <cassert>
#include <algorithm>
#include <vector>
using namespace std;

int main()
{
  cout << "Illustrating the generic heap operations." << endl;
  // Initialize a vector of integers:
  vector<int> vector1(5);
  int i;
  for (i = 0; i < 5; ++i)
    vector1[i] = i;

  random_shuffle(vector1.begin(), vector1.end());

  // Sort vector1 using push_heap and pop_heap:
  for (i = 2; i < 5; ++i)
    push_heap(vector1.begin(), vector1.begin() + i);

  for (i = 5; i >= 2; --i)
    pop_heap(vector1.begin(), vector1.begin() + i);

  // Verify that the array is sorted:
  for (i = 0; i < 5; ++i)
    assert (vector1[i] == i);

  // Shuffle the elements again:
  random_shuffle(vector1.begin(), vector1.end());
```

```
    // Sort vector1 using make_heap and sort_heap:
    make_heap(vector1.begin(), vector1.end());
    sort_heap(vector1.begin(), vector1.end());

    // Verify that the array is sorted:
    for (i = 0; i < 5; ++i)
        assert (vector1[i] == i);
    cout << " --- Ok." << endl;
    return 0;
}
```

Sorting with **push_heap** and **pop_heap** is done as follows. The element **v[0]** is assumed to be a valid heap; **push_heap** is then called four times to arrange the vector elements into a heap. Once the heap has been thus created, **pop_heap** is called four times. On each call, **pop_heap** takes the first heap element (which is known to be the largest element in the sequence) and places it at the end of the sequence. After all calls to **pop_heap** are complete, the sequence is sorted.

5.4.9   Minimum and Maximum

The generic **min** and **max** algorithms are passed two elements and they return the one that is smaller or larger, respectively. The **min_element** and **max_element** algorithms return an iterator pointing to a minimum or maximum, respectively, of the elements in an input sequence, as illustrated in the following example.

Example 5.28: Illustrating the generic **min_element** and **max_element** algorithms

"ex05-28.cpp" 119 ≡

```
    #include <iostream>
    #include <cassert>
    #include <algorithm>
    #include <vector>
    using namespace std;

    int main()
    {
      cout << "Illustrating the generic min_element and"
           << " max_element algorithms." << endl;
      // Initialize a vector of integers:
      vector<int> vector1(5);
```

```
    for(int i = 0; i < 5; ++i)
      vector1[i] = i;
    random_shuffle(vector1.begin(), vector1.end());

    // Find the maximum element in vector1:
    vector<int>::iterator k =
      max_element(vector1.begin(), vector1.end());
    assert (*k == 4);

    // Find the minimum element in vector1:
    k = min_element(vector1.begin(), vector1.end());
    assert (*k == 0);
    cout << " --- Ok." << endl;
    return 0;
  }
```

5.4.10 Lexicographical Comparison

The generic `lexicographical_compare` algorithm compares two input sequences as follows. Corresponding pairs of elements, `e1` and `e2` (from sequences 1 and 2), are compared. If `e1 < e2`, then the algorithm returns true immediately; if `e2 < e1`, the algorithm returns false immediately. Otherwise, comparison proceeds to the next pair of elements. If the first sequence is exhausted but the second is not, then the algorithm returns true; otherwise it returns false. The `<` operator must be defined on the sequence elements as a strict weak ordering (or one can pass to `lexicographical_compare` a comparison object that defines a strict weak ordering). If `<` or the comparison object defines a strict total ordering, the ordering determined by `lexicographical_compare` is also a strict total ordering; otherwise, it is a strict weak ordering.

Example 5.29: Illustrating the generic `lexicographical_compare` algorithm

"ex05-29.cpp" 120 ≡

```
    #include <iostream>
    #include <cassert>
    #include <algorithm>
    #include <vector>
    using namespace std;
    ⟨Define make function (builds a container of characters) 22b⟩

    int main()
```

```
    {
      cout << "Illustrating the generic"
           << " lexicographical_compare algorithm." << endl;

      vector<char> vector1 = make< vector<char> >("helio");
      vector<char> vector2 = make< vector<char> >("hello");

      // Show that vector1 is lexicographically
      // less than vector2:
      bool result = lexicographical_compare(vector1.begin(),
           vector1.end(), vector2.begin(), vector2.end());

      assert (result == true);
      cout << " --- Ok." << endl;
      return 0;
    }
```

5.4.11   Permutation Generators

STL provides two permutation generation algorithms: `next_permutation` changes a sequence into the next permutation in lexicographical order, while `prev_permutation` changes a sequence into the previous permutation in lexicographical order. The input sequence must support bidirectional iterators. Because of their definition in terms of lexicographical ordering, < must be defined on the sequence elements as a strict weak ordering (alternatively, one can pass to these algorithms a comparison object that defines a strict weak ordering). The algorithms are illustrated in the following example.

Example 5.30: Illustrating the generic permutation algorithms

```
"ex05-30.cpp" 121 ≡
    #include <iostream>
    #include <cassert>
    #include <algorithm>
    #include <vector>
    using namespace std;

    int main()
    {
      cout << "Illustrating the generic permutation algorithms."
           << endl;
      // Initialize a vector of integers:
      vector<int> vector1(3);
```

```
    for (int i = 0; i < 3; ++i) vector1[i] = i;

    // In lexicographical order the permutations of 0 1 2 are
    // 0 1 2, 0 2 1, 1 0 2, 1 2 0, 2 0 1, 2 1 0.
    // Show that from 0 1 2 next_permutation produces 0 2 1:
    next_permutation(vector1.begin(), vector1.end());
    assert (vector1[0] == 0);
    assert (vector1[1] == 2);
    assert (vector1[2] == 1);

    // Show that from 0 2 1 prev_permutation() produces 0 1 2:
    prev_permutation(vector1.begin(), vector1.end());
    assert (vector1[0] == 0);
    assert (vector1[1] == 1);
    assert (vector1[2] == 2);
    cout << " --- Ok." << endl;
    return 0;
}
```

5.5 Generalized Numeric Algorithms

STL has four generalized numeric algorithms: `accumulate`, `partial_sum`, `adjacent_difference`, and `inner_product`. In this section, we take a look at examples of each of these algorithms.

5.5.1 Accumulate

The generic `accumulate` function adds the values in a given range.

Example 5.31: Illustrating the generic `accumulate` algorithm

```
"ex05-31.cpp" 122 ≡
    #include <iostream>
    #include <cassert>
    #include <algorithm>
    #include <functional>
    #include <numeric>
    using namespace std;

    int main()
    {
      cout << "Illustrating the generic accumulate algorithm."
           << endl;
```

```
    int x[20];

    for (int i = 0; i < 20; ++i)
      x[i] = i;

    // Show that 5 + 0 + 1 + 2 + ... + 19 == 195:
    int result = accumulate(&x[0], &x[20], 5);
    assert (result == 195);

    // Show that 10 * 1 * 2 * 3 * 4 == 240:
    result = accumulate(&x[1], &x[5], 10, multiplies<int>());
    assert (result == 240);
    cout << " --- Ok." << endl;
    return 0;
}
```

In the second call of **accumulate** we use multiplication in place of addition, and we accumulate the values in **x[1]** through **x[4]**. Other illustrations of **accumulate** are given in Examples 2.12, 2.13, and 2.14.

5.5.2 Partial Sum

Given a sequence $x_0, x_1, \ldots, x_{n-1}$, the generic **partial_sum** algorithm computes the sequence of sums $x_0, x_0 + x_1, x_0 + x_1 + x_2, \ldots, x_0 + x_1 + \ldots + x_{n-1}$. The algorithm can store these partial sums either in place of the original sequence or in another range.

Example 5.32: Illustrating the generic **partial_sum** algorithm

```
"ex05-32.cpp" 123 ≡
    #include <algorithm>
    #include <numeric>
    #include <iostream>
    using namespace std;

    int main()
    {
      cout << "Illustrating the generic partial_sum algorithm."
           << endl;
      const int N = 20;
      int x1[N], x2[N];
      int i;
      for (i = 0; i < N; ++i)
        x1[i] = i;
```

```
      // Compute the partial sums of 0, 1, 2, 3, ..., N - 1,
      // putting the result in x2:
      partial_sum(&x1[0], &x1[N], &x2[0]);

      for (i = 0; i < N; ++i)
        cout << x2[i] << " ";
      cout << endl;
      return 0;
    }
```

Output from Example 5.32

```
0 1 3 6 10 15 21 28 36 45 55 66 78 91 105 120 136 153 171 190
```

5.5.3 Adjacent Difference

Given a sequence $x_0, x_1, \ldots, x_{n-1}$, the generic `adjacent_difference` algorithm calculates the difference between adjacent pairs of values in a sequence and places the result, $x_1 - x_0, x_2 - x_1, \ldots, x_{n-1} - x_{n-2}$, into the same or another sequence.

Example 5.33: Illustrating the generic `adjacent_difference` algorithm

```
"ex05-33.cpp" 124 ≡
    #include <iostream>
    #include <cassert>
    #include <algorithm>
    #include <numeric>
    using namespace std;

    int main()
    {
      cout << "Illustrating the generic "
           << "adjacent_difference algorithm." << endl;
      const int N = 20;
      int x1[N], x2[N];
      int i;
      for (i = 0; i < N; ++i)
        x1[i] = i;

      // Compute the partial sums of 0, 1, 2, 3, ..., N - 1,
      // putting the result in x2:
```

```
partial_sum(&x1[0], &x1[N], &x2[0]);

// Compute the adjacent differences of elements in x2,
// placing the result back in x2:
adjacent_difference(&x2[0], &x2[N], &x2[0]);

// The result is the original 0, 1, 2, 3, ..., N - 1:
for (i = 0; i < N; ++i)
    assert (x2[i] == i);
cout << " --- Ok." << endl;
return 0;
}
```

This program first calls `partial_sum` on a sequence 0, 1, ..., N - 1. When `adjacent_difference` is applied to the resulting sequence of partial sums (see the Output from Example 5.32), the original sequence is reproduced.

5.5.4 Inner Product

The generic `inner_product` algorithm computes the inner product of two input sequences. The following program first computes the inner product of 1, 2, 3, 4, 5, and 2, 3, 4, 5, 6 using its normal definition in terms of + and *, obtaining

$$1 * 2 + 2 * 3 + 3 * 4 + 4 * 5 + 5 * 6 == 70$$

The algorithm uses the two operators involved in this calculation, + and *, by default, but other operators can be used instead by passing function objects to `inner_product`. The program illustrates this fact in a second call of `inner_product` that reverses the roles of + and * to compute

$$(1 + 2) * (2 + 3) * (3 + 4) * (4 + 5) * (5 + 6) == 10395$$

Example 5.34: Illustrating the generic `inner_product` algorithm

"ex05-34.cpp" 125 ≡
```
#include <algorithm>
#include <iostream>
#include <functional>
#include <numeric>
using namespace std;
```

```
int main()
{
  cout << "Illustrating the generic inner_product algorithm."
       << endl;
  const int N = 5;
  int x1[N], x2[N];
  for (int i = 0; i < N; ++i) {
    x1[i] = i + 1;
    x2[i] = i + 2;
  }

  // Compute inner product of 1, 2, ..., N and 2, 3, ..., N+1:
  int result = inner_product(&x1[0], &x1[N], &x2[0], 0);

  cout << "Inner product as normally defined: "
       << result << endl;

  // Again compute "inner product," with roles of + and *
  // reversed:
  result = inner_product(&x1[0], &x1[N], &x2[0], 1,
                         multiplies<int>(), plus<int>());

  cout << "Inner product with roles of + and * reversed: "
       << result << endl;
  return 0;
}
```

Output from Example 5.34

```
Inner product as normally defined: 70
Inner product with roles of + and * reversed: 10395
```

The fourth argument to **inner_product** is the value for initializing the sum of products. Normally this initial value is the identity element for the first of the two operators involved. Thus we use 0 for this initial value when we compute the sum of products, but we use 1 when we compute the product of sums.

CHAPTER 6

Sequence Containers

In this chapter and the next we take a comprehensive tour of STL containers, describing and illustrating most of their features. More important, we consider criteria for choosing one kind of container in preference to others.

All of STL's container classes are examples of one of the most important concepts in software, *data abstraction* or *abstract data types*. An abstract data type provides a set of objects and a set of operations on those objects, both of which have a publicly defined abstract meaning that is separate from the way the objects are represented and the operations are implemented. By keeping their representation and implementation private (a goal supported by the C++ class feature), abstract data types prevent programmers from writing code that depends on particular internal details, which in turn means greater flexibility in modifying and maintaining the software over its lifetime.

Many software libraries embody the data abstraction concept, but the design of STL's container classes takes an important further step by employing an even higher-level concept, that of a *family of abstractions* that share a core of specifications. STL provides two families of abstractions, *sequence containers* and *sorted associative containers*. The sequence containers are `vector`, `deque`, and `list`, and the sorted associative containers are `set`, `multiset`, `map`, and `multimap`. In terms of functions provided, different members of a family may differ "at the margins"; for example, deques and lists provide a function called `push_front`, but vectors do not. But with the sequence abstraction family, the fundamental differences are in terms of performance, which is what dictates decisions to include or omit certain operations—the reason `push_front` is not included in vectors is that it would have to take linear time, whereas in deques and lists it can be implemented as a constant time operation.

None of the three members of the sequence abstraction family dominates the others in terms of performance of all operations (if one did, there would be little reason to provide all three). When we learn about the differences between vectors, deques, and lists, one of our most important goals should be to understand when one is likely to be superior to the others. That is, when programming some application that involves building and using sequences, we need to think about what mix of operations needs to be done on the sequences and choose the sequence representation accordingly. Of course, in our initial thinking about a problem, we may have only a vague idea of the operation mix, and we may want to start programming experimentally before we know the answer. One of the advantages of the STL library is that it not only provides different representations of sequences, it also provides them with almost the same interfaces—the family of abstractions idea. This allows switching between different representations to experiment with which one gives the best overall performance, with only a few changes in the program. Where there are differences between two interfaces, it's because they're designed that way purposely to make you think about which is the best representation to use.

The `set`, `multiset`, `map`, and `multimap` members of the sorted associative abstraction family have some real differences in the meanings of their operations, rather than differing mainly in terms of performance the way the sequence abstractions do. Between `set` and `multiset`, the main difference is in the meaning of `insert`. Insertion into a set has no effect if the value being inserted is already present, but with a multiset duplicates are stored. The same distinction exists between `map` and `multimap`, and these two containers share a substantial difference from `set` and `multiset` in that they associate values of another type with keys; with `set` and `multiset` just the keys themselves are stored. The performance requirements on all these sorted associative containers are essentially the same, requiring logarithmic time bounds on insertion, deletion, and search operations.[1]

STL also provides several containers that are more restrictive in the access they provide—stacks, queues, and priority queues. However, these are provided by means of container adaptors and are described in Chapter 9.

---

[1] The sorted associative containers described here are those that were accepted as part of the ANSI/ISO C++ Standard Library. Another closely related abstraction family is *hashed associative containers*, which trade some of the functionality of sorted associative containers for improvements in performance. The requirements for these containers permit hash table representations that have *constant average time* performance for storage and retrieval operations. Hashed associative containers are available as extensions to the Standard Library in some C++ implementations, as described in Appendix D.

In describing the sequence containers, we describe vectors in fullest detail and then discuss deques and lists mainly in terms of how they differ from vectors. More self-contained descriptions of all container classes can be found in Chapter 21, "Container Reference Guide."

6.1 Vectors

Vectors are sequence containers that provide fast random access to sequences of varying length in addition to fast insertions and deletions at the end. They are the sequence container of choice when the fastest possible random access is needed, and few if any insertions or deletions are required at any point other than the end. If insertions and deletions must also be done at the beginning of a sequence, they take linear time when using a vector. If many such operations are required, a better choice is a deque, which provides constant time insertions and deletions at both ends, together with random access. (The trade-off is that the constant bound for accessing elements is somewhat larger with a deque than with a vector.) Finally, if insertions and deletions must be done at interior positions, it may be better to use a list than a vector or deque. (With lists one gives up random access, but many kinds of computations can get by with stepping through a container sequentially, which lists support well.)

6.1.1 Types

The template parameters of each of the sequences classes are given by

```
template <typename T, typename Allocator = allocator<T> >
```

The first parameter is the type of data to be stored, and the second is the type of storage allocator to be used, which defaults to a standard allocator.

Each STL container class defines and makes public several types:

- **value_type** Type of elements the container stores (T).

- **pointer** Type of pointers to elements of the container (usually T*, but more generally it is determined by the allocator type).

- **reference** Type of locations of elements of the container (usually T&, but more generally it is determined by the allocator type).

- **iterator** Iterator type referring to values of type **reference**; for vectors this type is of the random access category.

- `difference_type`   Signed integral type that can represent the difference between two iterators.

- `size_type`   Unsigned integral type that can represent any nonnegative value of difference type.

- `reverse_iterator`   Iterator type whose values are of type `reference` and which defines incrementing and decrementing opposite to their normal `iterator` definitions; for vectors this type is of the random access category.

The pointer, reference, and iterator types have corresponding constant pointer, constant reference and constant iterator types, `const_pointer`, `const_reference`, and `const_iterator`. Finally, there is also a constant reverse iterator type, `const_reverse_iterator`.

With vectors the iterator types are all random access types, the most powerful category. This means that all STL generic algorithms can be used with vectors. Consequently, the only operations that the vector class needs to define as member functions are those for constructing vectors, inserting and deleting vector elements, and accessing basic information such as the iterators marking the vector's beginning and end.

6.1.2   Constructing Sequences

Vectors have several kinds of constructors. The default constructor, as used in expressions like `vector<T>()` or in declarations like

```
vector<T> vector1;
```

produces a sequence that is initially empty. An expression `vector<T>(n, value)` or a declaration

```
vector<T> vector1(n, value);
```

produces a sequence initialized with N = n copies of `value`, which must be of type `T` or convertible to type `T`. The second parameter of this constructor is actually a default parameter, with `T()` as the default; that is, `vector<T>(n)` or

```
vector<T> vector1(n);
```

produces a sequence initialized with N = n copies of the result of calling the default constructor of type T.[2]

Constructing an empty sequence with the default constructor takes constant time, and constructing a sequence with N elements takes time proportional to N.

Before looking at two other ways of constructing vectors, let's see some simple examples of the three ways considered so far. The following program illustrates the first two ways; it also makes use of both a member function `size`, which returns the number of elements in a vector, and the ability to use array-like notation for accessing the ith element of a vector.

Example 6.1: Demonstrating the simplest STL vector constructors

"ex06-01.cpp" 131 $\equiv$

```cpp
#include <iostream>
#include <cassert>
#include <vector>
using namespace std;

int main()
{
  cout << "Demonstrating simplest vector constructors"
       << endl;
  vector<char> vector1, vector2(3, 'x');
  assert (vector1.size() == 0);
  assert (vector2.size() == 3);
  assert (vector2[0] == 'x' && vector2[1] == 'x' &&
          vector2[2] == 'x');
  assert (vector2 == vector<char>(3, 'x') &&
          vector2 != vector<char>(4, 'x'));
  cout << " --- Ok." << endl;
  return 0;
}
```

Here's an example of constructing a vector of elements of a user-defined type, including a case of defaulting the initial value by passing only one argument to the constructor. We first define the type U with a data member `id` that holds an identification number for a U object.

---

[2]This works even if T is a built-in type such as `int`, since `int()` and other such expressions are required to be defined (as 0 converted to type T, by default initialization). If T is defined by a class, the class must have a default constructor.

⟨Define type U 132a⟩ ≡

```
    class U {
    public:
      unsigned long id;
      U() : id(0) { }
      U(unsigned long x) : id(x) { }
    };
```

Used in parts 132, 139.

We define the == and != operators on U to compare the identities of objects.

⟨Define == and != on type U 132b⟩ ≡

```
    bool operator==(const U& x, const U& y)
    {
      return x.id == y.id;
    }

    bool operator!=(const U& x, const U& y)
    {
      return x.id != y.id;
    }
```

Used in parts 132, 133.

Example 6.2: Demonstrating STL vector constructors with a user-defined type

"ex06-02.cpp" 132 ≡

```
    #include <iostream>
    #include <cassert>
    #include <vector>
    using namespace std;
    ⟨Define type U 132a⟩
    ⟨Define == and != on type U 132b⟩

    int main()
    {
      cout << "Demonstrating STL vector constructors with "
           << "a user-defined type." << endl;
      vector<U> vector1, vector2(3);
      assert (vector1.size() == 0);
      assert (vector2.size() == 3);
      assert (vector2[0] == U() && vector2[1] == U() &&
```

```
        vector2[2] == U());
   assert (vector2 == vector<U>(3, U()));
   return 0;
}
```

When creating N copies of the initial value, the vector constructor calls the copy constructor of the element type. To demonstrate that this is the case, let's define the copy constructor for type U to keep track of which "generation" a copy is (an originally constructed value is generation 0, a copy of it is generation 1, a copy of a copy of it is generation 2, and so on.). We also keep track in a static variable of the total number of times U's copy constructor has been called.

Example 6.3: Demonstrating STL vector constructors with a user-defined type and showing copying explicitly

"ex06-03.cpp" 133 ≡

```
#include <iostream>
#include <cassert>
#include <vector>
using namespace std;

class U {
public:
  unsigned long id;
  unsigned long generation;
  static unsigned long total_copies;
  U() : id(0), generation(0) { }
  U(unsigned long n) : id(n), generation(0) { }
  U(const U& z) : id(z.id), generation(z.generation + 1) {
    ++total_copies;
  }
};

⟨Define == and != on type U 132b⟩

unsigned long U::total_copies = 0;

int main()
{
  cout << "Demonstrating STL vector constructors with "
       << "a user-defined type and showing copying "
       << "explicitly" << endl;
  vector<U> vector1, vector2(3);
```

```
    assert (vector1.size() == 0);
    assert (vector2.size() == 3);

    assert (vector2[0] == U() && vector2[1] == U() &&
            vector2[2] == U());

    for (int i = 0; i != 3; ++i)
      cout << "vector2[" << i << "].generation: "
            << vector2[i].generation << endl;

    cout << "Total copies: " << U::total_copies << endl;
    return 0;
}
```

Output from Example 6.3

```
Demonstrating STL vector constructors with a user-defined type
and showing copying explicitly.
vector2[0].generation: 1
vector2[1].generation: 1
vector2[2].generation: 1
Total Copies: 3
```

This program's output shows that each U value stored in the vector is a generation 1 copy, and U's copy constructor was called once for each of the three values stored.

Of course, the vector class itself provides a copy constructor for copying another vector. The following program shows uses of the copy constructor along with uses of another constructor for copying any range of values from another vector.

Example 6.4: Demonstrating STL vector copying constructors

"ex06-04.cpp" 134 ≡

```
    #include <iostream>
    #include <cassert>
    #include <vector>
    using namespace std;

    int main()
    {
        cout << "Demonstrating STL vector copying constructors"
```

```
            << endl;
    char name[] = "George Foreman";
    vector<char> George(name, name + 6);

    vector<char> anotherGeorge(George.begin(), George.end());
    assert (anotherGeorge == George);

    vector<char> son1(George); // Uses copy constructor
    assert (son1 == anotherGeorge);

    vector<char> son2 = George; // Also uses copy constructor
    assert (son2 == anotherGeorge);
    return 0;
}
```

The constructor for copying a range of values via iterators is more general than this example illustrates; as mentioned in Section 1.3.3, it can be used with iterators for other containers to copy, for example, a range of values from a list, deque, or string:

```
list<char> list1;
// ... code to insert characters in list1;
vector<char> vector1(list1.begin(), list1.end());
```

The vector constructor member that permits this code is a template member function with the following interface:

```
template <typename InputIterator>
vector(InputIterator first, InputIterator last);
```

6.1.3 Insertion

The most useful vector member function for inserting elements is **push_back**, which inserts a single element at the end of the sequence. This function has been used several times in earlier chapters. The following program contains yet another use, along with a use of the more general **insert** member function.

Example 6.5: Demonstrating STL vector **push_back** and **insert** functions

"ex06-05.cpp" 135 ≡
```
#include <iostream>
#include <cassert>
#include <vector>
```

```
#include <string>
#include <algorithm>  // for reverse
using namespace std;
⟨Define make function (builds a container of characters) 22b⟩

int main()
{
  vector<char> vector1 =
                   make< vector<char> >("Bjarne Stroustrup"),
             vector2;
  vector<char>::iterator i;

  cout << "Demonstrating vector push_back function" << endl;
  for (i = vector1.begin(); i != vector1.end(); ++i)
    vector2.push_back(*i);
  assert (vector1 == vector2);

  vector1 = make< vector<char> >("Bjarne Stroustrup");
  vector2 = make< vector<char> >("");

  cout << "Demonstrating vector insertion at beginning"
       << endl;
  for (i = vector1.begin(); i != vector1.end(); ++i)
    vector2.insert(vector2.begin(), *i);
  assert (vector2 ==
          make< vector<char> >("purtsuortS enrajB"));

  // Show that vector2 is the reverse of vector1, by using
  // the generic reverse function to reverse vector1:
  reverse(vector1.begin(), vector1.end());
  assert (vector2 == vector1);
  cout << " --- Ok." << endl;
  return 0;
}
```

In the first part of this program we use **push_back** to build a vector by inserting characters one by one at its end. The second part reinitializes and inserts the same characters one by one at the beginning of **vector2**, which makes **vector2** hold the reverse of the original string. We can see that from the assertion

```
assert (vector2 == make< vector<char> >("purtsuortS enrajB"));
```

but we also show it in another way by using the generic **reverse** function to reverse the original string and then asserting equality between the result and `vector2`.

Inserting elements into a vector at positions other than the end works in a small example like this, but it should be avoided when working with large vectors since it requires linear time (because every element at or past the insertion point has to be moved over to make room for the new element). If your application requires such insertions, a deque or a list probably should be used instead.

By the way, `vector1.push_back(x)` is functionally equivalent to the expression `vector1.insert(vector1.end(), x)`; the performance might be slightly different, but both take constant time (amortized).

Vectors also provide `insert` member functions for inserting n = N copies of an element or a range of elements from another sequence:

```
vector1.insert(position, n, x);
```

This call to `insert` is functionally equivalent to a loop:

```
for (p = position, k = 0; k < n; ++k)
    p = vector1.insert(p, x) + 1;
```

but is much faster if `position` is not at the end. (If there are M elements at or past `position`, then in the loop version each of the N `insert` calls causes these M elements to be moved, requiring a total of NM moves. The `insert` member function with parameter N is allowed to take only $O(N + M)$ time, but it can do so by moving the M elements only once, making space for the N new elements, for a total of $N + M$ element moves. If, say, $M = N = 1,000$, there are only 2,000 moves rather than 1 million.)

There is also a vector member function for inserting a range of elements from another sequence: if `first` and `last` are iterators of some type `iterator_type` and they define a range, then

```
vector1.insert(position, first, last)
```

is functionally equivalent to

```
for (p = position, i = first; i != last; ++i)
    p = vector1.insert(p, *i) + 1;
```

but is much faster if `position` is not at the end—provided `iterator_type` is of the forward, bidirectional, or random access category. With iterators of these categories, it is possible to compute the distance from `first` to

last and reserve that much space for the new elements, but otherwise—with istream iterators, for example—the insertions have to be done one by one, as in the loop.

This insert member function is actually a member function template:

```
template <typename InputIterator>
void insert(iterator position, InputIterator first,
            InputIterator last);
```

Using **insert** can cause reallocation; that is, the vector elements may be stored in a different area after the insertion. The reason is that the elements are stored in a block of contiguous storage. If there is no room left in the current block for the new element, then a larger block is requested from the storage allocator, all of the old elements and the new element are copied to the new block, and the old block is deallocated. The new block size is twice the old size, which means that for a vector holding N elements, reallocation will not be required again until N more elements are inserted. Thus, although reallocation can make the insertions that cause it expensive, they are infrequent enough that the amortized cost of insertion is constant.[3]

You can exercise some control over when reallocation occurs by using the **capacity** and **reserve** member functions. The **capacity** member function returns the size of the currently allocated block (the number of elements it can hold). The call

```
vector1.reserve(n);
```

ensures that **vector1.capacity()** after the call is at least N = **n**; it causes reallocation if (and only if) the current capacity is less than N. In any case, it does not change the current size of the vector (the number of elements actually stored).

If you know in advance that you are about to insert N elements (with **push_back** or one of the forms of **insert**), you can speed up your program by doing the **reserve** call beforehand, rather than letting repeated reallocations occur. It is guaranteed that no reallocations take place during the insertions that happen after **reserve** until the time the vector's size reaches N.

---

[3]If the vector is empty, then a block of some implementation-defined size is allocated. As mentioned in Section 1.5.2, some other expansion factor besides 2 might be used in some implementations, but any constant factor greater than 1 would yield amortized constant time for insertion.

Example 6.6: Demonstrating STL vector `capacity` and `reserve` functions

"ex06-06.cpp" 139 ≡

```cpp
#include <iostream>
#include <cassert>
#include <vector>
using namespace std;
⟨Define type U 132a⟩

int main()
{
  cout << "Demonstrating STL vector capacity and reserve "
          "functions." << endl;

  int N = 10000; // size of vectors

  vector<U> vector1, vector2;

  cout << "Doing " << N << " insertions in vector1,\n"
       << "with no advance reservation.\n";
  int k;
  for (k = 0; k != N; ++k) {
    vector<U>::size_type cap = vector1.capacity();
    vector1.push_back(U(k));
    if (vector1.capacity() != cap)
      cout << "k: " << k << ", new capacity: "
           << vector1.capacity() << endl;
  }

  vector2.reserve(N);
  cout << "\nNow doing the same thing with vector2,\n"
       << "after starting with reserve(" << N << ").\n";
  for (k = 0; k != N; ++k) {
    vector<U>::size_type cap = vector2.capacity();
    vector2.push_back(U(k));
    if (vector2.capacity() != cap)
      cout << "k: " << k << ", new capacity: "
           << vector2.capacity() << "\n";
  }
  return 0;
}
```

Output from Example 6.6

```
Demonstrating STL vector capacity and reserve functions.
Doing 10000 insertions in vector1,
with no advance reservation.
k: 0, new capacity: 1024
k: 1024, new capacity: 2048
k: 2048, new capacity: 4096
k: 4096, new capacity: 8192
k: 8192, new capacity: 16384

Now doing the same thing with vector2,
after starting with reserve(10000).
```

In the loop inserting into **vector1**, the points at which reallocations occur might differ with different implementations of STL. There is no output from the loop inserting into **vector2**, since calling **reserve** prevents reallocations from occurring.

Besides efficiency, there is another reason you may want to use **reserve**. *Reallocation invalidates all iterators and references to positions in the vector*, since the elements may be moved to a different storage area. If no reallocation occurs, though, it is guaranteed that insertions at the end of a vector do not invalidate any iterators or references. And those in the middle invalidate just those iterators and references to or after the insertion point. If there is some section of your program in which you need to maintain several iterators to different parts of a vector while doing insertions, you should use **reserve** with a sufficiently large size in order to avoid reallocations while that section is executing.

6.1.4   Erasure (Deletion)

Just as **push_back** is the most useful vector insertion member function, the most useful member function for erasure is **pop_back**, which removes one element from the end of a sequence in constant time. These two functions together, along with another member function, **back**, allow a vector to be used as a stack—data can be stored and retrieved in a last-in, first-out order. (A true stack data abstraction is much more restricted than a vector, as access is limited to the last element. STL provides the more restricted notion via a container adaptor, as described in Chapter 9.)

Example 6.7: Demonstrating STL vector `back` and `pop_back` operations

`"ex06-07.cpp"` 141 ≡
```
    #include <iostream>
    #include <vector>
    #include <string>
    using namespace std;
    ⟨Define make function (builds a container of characters) 22b⟩

    int main()
    {
      cout << "Demonstrating STL vector back "
           << "and pop_back operations." << endl;
      vector<char> vector1 = make< vector<char> >("abcdefghij");

      cout << "Popping characters off the back produces: ";

      while (vector1.size() > 0) {
        cout << vector1.back();
        vector1.pop_back();
      }
      cout << endl;
      return 0;
    }
```

Output from Example 6.7

```
    Demonstrating STL vector back and pop_back operations.
    Popping characters off the back produces: jihgfedcba
```

This program repeatedly retrieves the last element, prints it, and erases it until the vector becomes empty.

As with insertion, vectors do provide a more general ability to erase an element at any position. For example, we could replace the while loop in the previous program by one that retrieves, prints, and erases the first element rather than the last:[4]

```
    while (vector1.size() > 0) {
      cout << vector1.front();
      vector1.erase(vector1.begin());
    }
```

[4]The source code for this variation, Example 6.7a, is available on the Internet (see Appendix D) as the file `ex06-07a.cpp`.

Note that to erase the first element we use **erase**, as there is no **pop_front** member function corresponding to **pop_back** for vectors. The reason for excluding **pop_front** from vectors (this function is provided for deques and lists) is to discourage using a vector in this way, since erasure at the beginning of a vector is inefficient. With a deque or a list, erasure at the beginning takes only constant time, but with a vector it can be accomplished only by moving all the elements that are past the erasure point over by one to fill the gap, and that takes linear time. That means, for example, that the loop shown would take quadratic time.

Nevertheless, general erasure capability is provided for vectors for situations in which a vector is overall a better choice than a deque or a list but an occasional erasure is needed at positions other than the end. The following program shows various uses of the vector **erase** member function, including one in which the version

```
iterator erase(iterator first, iterator last);
```

is used. This function erases all elements from the range of positions [**first**, **last**) (the element at **last**, if any, is not erased) and returns **last**.

Example 6.8: Demonstrating the STL vector **erase** function

```
"ex06-08.cpp" 142 ≡
    #include <iostream>
    #include <cassert>
    #include <vector>
    #include <string>
    #include <algorithm>  // for find
    using namespace std;
    ⟨Define make function (builds a container of characters) 22b⟩

    int main()
    {
      cout << "Demonstrating STL vector erase function." << endl;

      vector<char> vector1 = make< vector<char> >("remembering");
      vector<char>::iterator j;

      j = find(vector1.begin(), vector1.end(), 'm');

      // j now points to the first 'm':
      assert (*j == 'm' && *(j+1) == 'e');
```

```
        vector1.erase(j--);
        assert (vector1 == make< vector<char> >("reembering"));

        // j now points to the first 'e':
        assert (*j == 'e' && *(j+1) == 'e');

        vector1.erase(j--);
        assert (vector1 == make< vector<char> >("rembering"));
        assert (*j == 'r');

        // Erase first 3 characters:
        vector1.erase(j, j + 3);
        assert (vector1 == make< vector<char> >("bering"));

        vector1.erase(vector1.begin() + 1);
        assert (vector1 == make< vector<char> >("bring"));
        cout << " --- Ok." << endl;
        return 0;
    }
```

This program illustrates a rather subtle point about the interaction between **erase** and iterators. The erase function *invalidates all iterators to all positions past the point of erasure*, but it leaves valid those referring to preceding positions or to the erased position. That's why the line

```
        vector1.erase(j--);
```

works correctly, but the similar code

```
        vector1.erase(j++);
```

doesn't work, because j would be invalid after the erasure.

All STL containers have **insert** and **erase** member functions, but the way they interact with iterators varies considerably. We revisit this issue when we consider other containers in later sections.

The **erase** member for erasing a range (which is used in the next-to-last step of the preceding program) is more efficient than erasing elements one by one. The time it takes is $O(p)$, where p is the number of elements past the erased elements, whereas the time for erasing them one by one would be $O(ep)$, where e is the number of erased elements.

6.1.5 Accessors

Container accessors are member functions that return information about a container without changing it. We've already seen most of the vector accessors in earlier discussions and examples. Here is the complete list.

- `iterator begin()` Returns an iterator referring to the beginning of the vector.

- `iterator end()` Returns an iterator referring to the end of the vector.

- `iterator rbegin()` Returns a reverse iterator referring to the beginning of the vector for reverse order traversal.

- `iterator rend()` Returns a reverse iterator referring to the end of the vector for reverse order traversal.

- `size_type size() const` Returns the number of elements in the vector.

- `size_type max_size() const` Returns the maximum number of elements that could be stored in the vector.

- `size_type capacity() const` Returns the number of elements that can be stored in the vector without reallocation.

- `bool empty() const` Returns true if the vector contains no elements, false otherwise.

- `reference front()` Returns a reference to the element at the beginning of the vector.

- `reference back()` Returns a reference to the element at the end of the vector.

- `reference operator[](size_type n)` Returns a reference to the element n elements from the beginning of the vector.

- `reference at(size_type n)` Returns a reference to the element n elements from the beginning of the vector, if n is in range; otherwise, an exception is raised.

The member functions in this list that return iterators also have versions that return constant iterators when applied to constant vectors; so do reverse iterator and reference-returning member functions:

- `const_iterator begin() const` Returns a constant iterator referring to the beginning of a constant vector.

- `const_iterator end() const` Returns a constant iterator referring to the end of a constant vector.

- `const_iterator rbegin() const` Returns a constant reverse iterator referring to the beginning of a constant vector for reverse order traversal.

- `const_iterator rend() const` Returns a constant reverse iterator referring to the end of a constant vector for reverse order traversal.

- `const_reference front() const` Returns a constant reference to the element at the beginning of a constant vector.

- `const_reference operator[](size_type n) const` Returns a constant reference to the element n elements from the beginning of a constant vector.

- `const_reference at(size_type n) const` Returns a reference to the element n elements from the beginning of the vector, if n is in range; otherwise, an `out_of_range` exception is raised.

All these accessors take constant time.

6.1.6 Equality and Less-Than Relations

We've already seen numerous examples of vector equality in assertions in our example programs. STL employs a general definition of container equality, one that allows equality comparison between any two containers of the same type (not just vectors):

- The sequences they contain must be of the same size.

- Elements in corresponding positions must be equal, as determined by the `==` operator of the element type.

In fact, the official definition of container equality is expressed in terms of the `size` member function and the generic `equal` algorithm: for any two containers `a` and `b` of the same type, `a == b` is defined by

```
a.size() == b.size() && equal(a.begin(), a.end(), b.begin())
```

The number of `==` operations applied to pairs of elements is no more than `a.size()`.

Similarly, a general definition of `<` is used: for any two containers `a` and `b` of the same type, if `T` is the type of elements they contain and there is a `<` on `T` that defines a strict weak ordering relation (see Section 5.4), then `a < b` is defined by

```
lexicographical_compare(a.begin(), a.end(),
                        b.begin(), b.end())
```

This program uses the generic `lexicographical_compare` function on the sequences in `a` and `b`. The number of `<` operations applied to pairs of elements is at most $2\min(\texttt{a.size()},\texttt{b.size()})$.

Both the equality and less-than definitions apply not only to sequence containers but also to associative containers, since associative containers include a notion of containing a sequence.

Other ordering relations (`>`, `<=`, `>=`) are defined in terms of `<`, so the definition given suffices to determine them all.

6.1.7   Assignment

The assignment operator `=` is defined for all STL containers. Immediately after an assignment `x = y`, it is always the case that `x == y`. The computing time is $O(N)$, where $N = \max(\texttt{x.size()}, \texttt{y.size()})$.

For sequence containers there is also an `assign` template member function for assigning from an iterator range:

```
template <typename InputIterator>
void assign(InputIterator first, InputIterator last);
```

It is functionally equivalent to

```
erase(begin(), end());
insert(begin(), first, last);
```

Finally, there is a `swap` member function such that the expression `vector1.swap(vector2)` exchanges the values of `vector1` and `vector2`. It is required to operate in constant time, which can be achieved by swapping internal pointers of the vector representation. The library also arranges that a call of the generic `swap` algorithm on vectors, `swap(vector1, vector2)`, is actually performed using the `vector swap` member function, so it takes place in constant time rather than being linear in the size of the vectors. To see how this works, first consider how the generic `swap` algorithm can be implemented in the usual way with three assignments:

```
template <typename T>
void swap(T& x, T& y)
{
  T temp = x;
  x = y;
  y = temp;
}
```

If instantiated with `vector<int>` as type `T`, this function would perform three vector assignments. But the library also defines[5]

```
template <typename U>
void swap(vector<U>& x, vector<U>& y)
{
  x.swap(y);
}
```

This definition is an example of yet another template feature that C++ supports, called *partial specialization*. The definition specializes the original `swap` function template to the case that `T` is `vector<U>` where `U` is itself a type parameter. The result is thus still templated, which is the reason it is called a partial specialization as opposed to an ordinary specialization of the original function template (which would fully instantiate `T` and leave nothing left to instantiate). When a partial specialization of a function template exists and matches the types of actual parameters in a call, the language rules require using the most specialized version that matches. This is why the call `swap(vector1, vector2)` actually results in the `vector1.swap(vector)` being executed, rather than three vector assignments.

In fact, all the STL container types have `swap` member functions, and the library defines corresponding partial specializations of the generic `swap` algorithm, so `swap` is a constant time operation in every case.

---

[5]In the definition actually used the `vector` arguments also have an allocator template argument, which we omit here for simplicity.

6.2 Deques

Deques have few differences from vectors in terms of functionality. The main difference is in performance: insertion and erasure at the beginning of a deque are much faster than with a vector, taking only constant time rather than linear time, while other operations are the same as or slower by a constant factor than the corresponding vector operations. Like vectors, deques provide random access iterators, and thus all STL generic algorithms can be applied to them. They are therefore the sequence abstraction of choice when enough insertions and deletions are required at both ends of sequences to offset a slowdown in other operations, in comparison with vectors. Although deques also support insertions and deletions in the middle, these operations take linear time. If many such operations are required, the list abstraction may be a better choice.

The deque class interface is so similar to the vector class interface that many programs that use vectors could be converted to using deques instead with only a few syntactic changes, mainly in declarations and other uses of constructors. Certainly all the example programs demonstrating vectors in the preceding section fit this description. Here is one example: we edit the program in Example 6.5 and simply replace all occurrences of **vector** with **deque**. The result compiles and executes properly; no other changes are necessary. In the following version we have also made a change in the section

```
cout << "Demonstrating deque insertion at beginning"
    << endl;
for (i = deque1.begin(); i != deque1.end(); ++i)
  deque2.insert(deque2.begin(), *i);
```

to use the **push_front** member function that deque provides but vector does not:

```
cout << "Demonstrating deque push_front function" << endl;
for (i = deque1.begin(); i != deque1.end(); ++i)
  deque2.push_front(*i);
```

Here is the result.

Example 6.9: Demonstrating STL deque **push_back** and **push_front** functions

`"ex06-09.cpp"` 148 ≡
```
#include <iostream>
#include <cassert>
```

```
#include <string>
#include <deque>
#include <algorithm> // for reverse
using namespace std;
⟨Define make function (builds a container of characters) 22b⟩

int main()
{
  deque<char> deque1 =
              make< deque<char> >("Bjarne Stroustrup"),
        deque2;
  deque<char>::iterator i;

  cout << "Demonstrating deque push_back function" << endl;
  for (i = deque1.begin(); i != deque1.end(); ++i)
    deque2.push_back(*i);
  assert (deque1 == deque2);

  deque1 = make< deque<char> >("Bjarne Stroustrup");
  deque2 = make< deque<char> >("");

  cout << "Demonstrating deque push_front function" << endl;
  for (i = deque1.begin(); i != deque1.end(); ++i)
    deque2.push_front(*i);
  assert (deque2 == make< deque<char> >("purtsuortS enrajB"));

  // Show that deque2 is the reverse of deque1 by using
  // STL generic reverse function to reverse deque1:
  reverse(deque1.begin(), deque1.end());
  assert (deque2 == deque1);
  cout << " --- Ok." << endl;
  return 0;
}
```

Note that the generic **reverse** algorithm works with deque iterators just as it does with vector iterators.

The only essential change required to convert programs using vectors into programs using deques, other than using **deque** instead of **vector** in declarations and constructors, is removing any uses of the vector **capacity** and **reserve** member functions. The deque class does not provide these members, because they are not needed for improving performance as they are for vectors. We must be careful here, though, to examine the way **reserve** is being used. If the only purpose is to improve performance by avoiding repeated reallocations, it will not affect the correctness of the original uses of

149

vectors or the corresponding uses of deques to just drop the **reserve** statements. On the other hand, if the purpose is to avoid reallocations in order to preserve the validity of iterators, then a careful examination of the ways in which iterators are used is necessary, since deque insertions and erasures are not guaranteed to preserve the validity of iterators in the (limited) way that vector insertions and erasures are. This point is discussed in more detail in the sections on insertion (Section 6.2.3) and erasure (Section 6.2.4).

An implementation approach that meets all the deque requirements is to use a two-level storage structure consisting of blocks of fixed size and a directory containing the block addresses. The directory block is initialized so that its active entries occupy the middle and expand toward the directory boundaries. When inserting at the beginning of the deque, if there is no room in the first block, a new block is allocated and a pointer to it added to the directory in the position before the current first directory entry. Inserting at the end is handled symmetrically. It is only when a directory boundary is hit that reallocation must occur, and then only the directory block is reallocated, not the data-containing blocks. Reallocation is thus infrequent and inexpensive in comparison with vector reallocation. Nevertheless, when it does occur, it can invalidate all iterators and references into the deque,[6] so we must be careful not to write code that depends on iterators or references remaining valid while insertions are occurring.

6.2.1 Types

The deque class has the same template parameters, T and Allocator, as the vector class, and it provides definitions of the same types: value_type, iterator, reverse_iterator, pointer, reference, difference_type, size_type, const_iterator, const_reverse_iterator, const_pointer, and const_reference. These types have the same abstract meaning as in the vector class, although the implementation can be quite different. Like vector iterators, deque iterators are of the random access category.

6.2.2 Constructors

The deque class provides exactly the same variety of constructors as the vector class.

---

[6]In this two-level implementation no references are invalidated when reallocation occurs, but they would be if deques were implemented as a single block of memory with the data in the middle and the ability to grow in either direction.

6.2.3 Insertion

Deques provide the same variety of `insert` member functions as vectors, and they add a `push_front` function for inserting at the beginning of a deque, as shown in Example 6.9. As we already noted, however, there is no `reserve` member function. The differences between deques and vectors are in performance and in instances when iterators and references may be invalidated by insertions.

Inserting at either the beginning or the end of a deque is a constant time operation. Inserting in the interior of a deque takes time proportional to the distance from the insertion point to the closest end. Thus, for example,

```
deque1.insert(deque1.begin() + 5, x)
```

would be a constant time operation, whereas the corresponding operation on a vector would take linear time.

As with vectors, insertion may cause reallocation of the storage associated with a deque. See the discussion at the end of the introduction to Section 6.2 of the implications for validity of iterators. Insertions in the interior invalidate all iterators and references, regardless of whether reallocation occurs. This situation is different from the situation with vectors, where insertions that don't cause reallocation leave iterators and references before the insertion point valid.

6.2.4 Erasure (Deletion)

Again, deques have the same variety of `erase` member functions as vectors, plus there is a `pop_front` function for erasing from the beginning of a deque. The same remarks about insertion performance and effect on validity of iterators and references apply to erasures also.

6.2.5 Accessors

The deque class provides all the same container accessors as the vector class except `capacity`—namely `begin`, `end`, `rbegin`, `rend`, `size`, `max_size`, `empty`, `operator[]`, `at`, `front`, and `back`. As with vectors, these are all constant time operations. The `capacity` member is omitted because it is not needed.

6.2.6   Equality and Less-Than Relations

The definitions of equality and ordering relations given in Section 6.1.6 are for all STL containers and thus apply to deques.

6.2.7   Assignment

The definitions of =, `assign`, and `swap` member functions discussed in Section 6.1.7 have corresponding definitions and computing times for deques.

6.3   Lists

We've seen that the vector and deque sequence abstractions are almost identical in terms of functionality; their only essential difference is in performance of insertions at the beginning of a sequence. The `list` sequence abstraction, by contrast, does have some real differences from vectors or deques in terms of member functions provided. The reason is that lists give up random access iterators in order to allow constant time insertions and deletions; without random access, some key generic algorithms, such as those for sorting, cannot be used. Hence, these operations are provided instead as member functions of the list class.

Also provided as member functions are some operations such as reversing a sequence, which can be done using the generic `reverse` algorithm and the bidirectional iterators that the list class provides, but which can be done somewhat more efficiently with special algorithms that take advantage of the linked structures used to represent lists.

Insertion and deletion member functions are provided with essentially the same interface as in vectors and deques, but with major differences in performance. Insertions and deletions at any position in a list are constant time operations, not just at one or both ends. The linked representation of lists also permits some additional operations, called *splicing*, for transferring elements from one sequence to another in constant time, and these are also provided as member functions.

Another major difference from vectors and deques is that list insertions never invalidate any iterators, and deletions invalidate only iterators that refer to the element deleted.

Lists are certainly the sequence abstraction of choice when many insertions and/or deletions are required in interior positions and there is little need to jump around from one position to another some distance away. Such linked structures have also been frequently used in favor of arrays simply for their ability to grow dynamically, but vectors and deques also have this property and probably should be used instead if that is the sole reason for using linked structures.

Let's begin our tour of the list class by taking the same example program we considered when discussing the differences between vectors and deques (Examples 6.5 and 6.9).

Example 6.10: Demonstrating STL list `push_back` and `push_front` functions

```
"ex06-10.cpp" 153 ≡
    #include <iostream>
    #include <cassert>
    #include <list>
    #include <string>
    #include <algorithm>  // for reverse
    using namespace std;
    ⟨Define make function (builds a container of characters) 22b⟩

    int main()
    {
      list<char> list1 = make< list<char> >("Bjarne Stroustrup"),
                 list2;
      list<char>::iterator i;

      cout << "Demonstrating list push_back function" << endl;
      for (i = list1.begin(); i != list1.end(); ++i)
        list2.push_back(*i);
      assert (list1 == list2);

      list1 = make< list<char> >("Bjarne Stroustrup");
      list2 = make< list<char> >("");

      cout << "Demonstrating list push_front function" << endl;
      for (i = list1.begin(); i != list1.end(); ++i)
        list2.push_front(*i);
      assert (list2 == make< list<char> >("purtsuortS enrajB"));

      // Show that list2 is the reverse of list1, by using
      // STL generic reverse function to reverse list1:
      reverse(list1.begin(), list1.end());
      assert (list2 == list1);
```

```
      cout << " --- Ok." << endl;
      return 0;
}
```

This program was obtained from the deque version simply by substituting `list` for every `deque` and `lst` for every `deq`. Note that the generic `reverse` algorithm is still applicable, since the bidirectional iterators it requires are exactly what lists supply. It does the sequence reversal by moving sequence elements from one position to another with assignments, but it may be better for some kinds of data to accomplish the reversal by relinking the list structure instead. When the data are characters, as they are here, the assignments are inexpensive, but relinking would be more efficient for large data elements. The relinking algorithm is provided as a list member function, and the generic `reverse` algorithm call could be replaced by

```
      list1.reverse();
```

In other cases, such changes from using generic algorithms to list member functions may be required rather than optional. We'll see examples as we go through the member functions provided.

6.3.1   Types

The list class has the same template parameters, `T` and `Allocator`, as the vector and deque classes, and it defines the same types: `value_type`, `iterator`, `reverse_iterator`, `pointer`, `reference`, `difference_type`, `size_type`, `const_iterator`, `const_reverse_iterator`, `const_pointer`, and `const_reference`. The list iterator types are bidirectional rather than random access, which means that some generic algorithms, such as those for sorting, cannot be applied to lists.

6.3.2   Constructors

The list class provides exactly the same variety of constructors as the vector and deque classes.

6.3.3   Insertion

The `insert` member functions the list class provides have the same functionality as those the vector and deque provide, but they always take only constant time per element inserted. There is also a significant difference in their abstract meaning: they never invalidate any iterators or references. There is no **reserve** member function, as it is unnecessary with lists. The **splice** member functions (Section 6.3.5) also perform insertion-like operations.

6.3.4 Erasure (Deletion)

The list class provides the same **erase** member functions as the vector and deque classes. With lists they always take only constant time per element erased, and the only iterators and references invalidated are those to the erased elements.

Here is an example similar to one we considered for vectors (Example 6.8).

Example 6.11: Demonstrating STL list **erase** function

```
"ex06-11.cpp" 155 ≡
    #include <iostream>
    #include <cassert>
    #include <list>
    #include <string>
    #include <algorithm>  // for find
    using namespace std;
    ⟨Define make function (builds a container of characters) 22b⟩

    int main()
    {
      cout << "Demonstrating STL list erase function." << endl;
      list<char> list1 = make< list<char> >("remembering");
      list<char>::iterator j;

      j = find(list1.begin(), list1.end(), 'i');

      list1.erase(j++);
      assert (list1 == make< list<char> >("rememberng"));

      // j now points to the 'n':
      list1.erase(j++);
      assert (list1 == make< list<char> >("rememberg"));

      // j now points to the 'g':
      list1.erase(j++);
      assert (list1 == make< list<char> >("remember"));
```

```
        list1.erase(list1.begin());
        assert (list1 == make< list<char> >("emember"));

        list1.erase(list1.begin());
        assert (list1 == make< list<char> >("member"));
        cout << " --- Ok." << endl;
        return 0;
    }
```

In the calls

```
        list1.erase(j++);
```

we are doing something that neither vectors nor deques support, because they would invalidate iterators to the position after the one erased. With lists the iterator returned by j++, which is the iterator j held before it was incremented, is invalidated but the incremented value is not, and we can continue computing with it in subsequent statements (in the vector version we used j-- and carried out a somewhat different computation). Note that the following code

```
        list1.erase(j); j++;
```

which might seem equivalent, is incorrect because the **erase** call invalidates j before we have a chance to increment it.

The **splice** member functions described next also perform erasure-like operations.

6.3.5 Splicing

One of the big performance advantages of linked structures over storing data in contiguous positions is that sequences can be rearranged by relinking, which takes only constant time regardless of the number of elements involved. The list class provides for this kind of rearrangement with these **splice** member functions (Example 6.12):

- list1.splice(i1, list2), where i1 is a valid iterator for list1, inserts the contents of list2 before i1, and leaves list2 empty. list1 and list2 must not be the same list.

- list1.splice(i1, list2, i2), where i1 is a valid iterator for list1 and i2 is a valid dereferenceable iterator for list2, removes the element to which i2 refers and inserts it before i1 in list1. list1 and list2 may be the same list.

- `list1.splice(i1, list2, i2, j2)`, where `i1` is a valid iterator for `list1` and $[i2, j2)$ is a valid range in `list2`, removes the elements of the range and inserts them before `i1` in `list1`. `list1` and `list2` may be the same list.

The first two variants always take constant time. The third does if `list1` and `list2` are the same list; otherwise, it takes linear time.

Example 6.12: Demonstrating STL list `splice` functions[7]

`"ex06-12.cpp"` 157 ≡

```
#include <iostream>
#include <cassert>
#include <list>
#include <string>
#include <algorithm> // for find
using namespace std;
⟨Define make function (builds a container of characters) 22b⟩

int main()
{
  cout << "Demonstrating STL splice functions." << endl;
  list<char> list1, list2, list3;
  list<char>::iterator i, j, k;

  // Example of splice(iterator, list<char>&):
  list1 = make< list<char> >("There is something "
                             "about science.");
  list2 = make< list<char> >("fascinating ");
  i = find(list1.begin(), list1.end(), 'a');
  list1.splice(i, list2);
  assert (list1 ==
      make< list<char> >("There is something fascinating "
                         "about science."));
  assert (list2 == make< list<char> >(""));

  // Example of splice(iterator, list<char>&, iterator):
  list1 =
        make< list<char> >("One gets such wholesale return "
                           "of conjecture");
```

---

[7]In several places in this example (and later in other examples) we break string literals into pieces to make the code fit properly on the printed page. The compiler will concatenate adjacent string literals. For example, `"a"` `"b"` is equivalent to `"ab"`.

```
list2 =
    make< list<char> >("out of ssuch a trifling "
                       "investment of fact.");
list3 = make< list<char> >(" of");
i = search(list1.begin(), list1.end(), list3.begin(),
           list3.end());
// i points to the blank before "of";
j = find(list2.begin(), list2.end(), 's');
list1.splice(i, list2, j);
assert (list1 ==
    make< list<char> >("One gets such wholesale returns "
                       "of conjecture"));
assert (list2 ==
    make< list<char> >("out of such a trifling investment "
                       "of fact."));

// Example of splice(iterator, list<char>&, iterator,
//                   iterator):
list1 = make< list<char> >("Mark Twain");
list2 = make< list<char> >(" --- ");
j = find(list2.begin(), list2.end(), ' ');
k = find(++j, list2.end(), ' ');   // Find second blank.
list1.splice(list1.begin(), list2, j, k);// Move the ---.
assert (list1 == make< list<char> >("---Mark Twain"));
assert (list2 == make< list<char> >("  "));
return 0;
}
```

6.3.6   Sorting-Related Member Functions

As we've already noted, the generic **sort** algorithm requires random access iterators and thus cannot be used with lists, which supply only bidirectional iterators. Instead, to sort a list one can use its **sort** member function. The following example shows a simple use of **sort** along with another member function, **unique**, which removes consecutive duplicate elements.

Example 6.13: Demonstrating STL list **sort** and **unique** functions

"ex06-13.cpp" 158 ≡

```
#include <iostream>
#include <cassert>
#include <string>
#include <list>
using namespace std;
```

⟨Define make function (builds a container of characters) 22b⟩

```
int main()
{
  cout << "Demonstrating STL list sort and unique "
       << "functions." << endl;
  list<char> list1 = make< list<char> >("Stroustrup");

  list1.sort();
  assert (list1 == make< list<char> >("Soprrsttuu"));

  list1.unique();
  assert (list1 == make< list<char> >("Soprstu"));
  cout << " --- Ok." << endl;
  return 0;
}
```

The **sort** member function has another version for sorting with a given comparison function:

```
template <typename Compare>
void sort(Compare comp);
```

Similarly, **unique** has a version with a template parameter to allow the comparison between consecutive elements to be done with a given binary predicate. These member functions differ from the generic **unique** function in that they work by relinking rather than by assignment.

```
template <typename BinaryPredicate>
void unique(BinaryPredicate comp);
```

Another sorting-related operation that is supplied as a list member function is **merge**, which merges the current list with another list, where both lists are assumed to be sorted. Again, it has a template version:

```
void merge(const list<T>& otherList);
template <typename Compare>
void merge(const list<T>& otherList, Compare comp);
```

As in the case of **reverse**, the generic **merge** algorithm can be used with lists (it requires only input iterators), but the merge operation is also supplied as a member function to provide an algorithm based on relinking rather than moving elements by assignment.

159

6.3.7   Removal

One other operation supplied as a member function, for the same reason as `reverse` and `merge`, is `remove`, which erases all elements in the list equal to some given value or for which some given predicate holds:

```
void remove(const T& value);
template <typename Predicate>
void remove_if(Predicate pred);
```

Unlike the application of the generic `remove` algorithm to other kinds of sequences, these `remove` member functions do reduce the size of the list by the number of elements removed.

6.3.8   Accessors

The list class provides all the same container accessors as the vector class—except `capacity`, `operator[]`, and `at`—namely `begin`, `end`, `rbegin`, `rend`, `size`, `max_size`, `empty`, `front`, and `back`. As with vectors, these are all constant time operations. The `capacity` member is omitted because it is not needed, and `at` and `operator[]` are omitted because they would have to take linear time.

6.3.9   Equality and Less-Than Relations

The definitions of equality and ordering relations given in Section 6.1.6 are for all STL containers and thus apply to lists.

6.3.10   Assignment

The definitions of `=`, `assign`, and `swap` member functions discussed in Section 6.1.7 have corresponding definitions and computing times for lists.

CHAPTER 7

Sorted Associative Containers

We now come to sorted associative containers, which are a different family of abstractions from the sequence family we considered in Chapter 6. Whereas sequence containers store data items in a linear arrangement that preserves the relative positions into which the items are inserted, sorted associative containers dispense with this order and instead concentrate on being able to retrieve items as quickly as possible based on *keys* that are stored in the item (or in some cases are the items themselves).

One general approach to associative retrieval is to keep keys sorted according to some total order, such as numeric order if the items are numbers or lexicographical order if the keys are strings, and use a binary search algorithm. Another approach is hashing: dividing the key space into some number of subsets, inserting each key into its designated subset, and correspondingly confining each search to just one subset, with the association of a key to a subset being done by a "hash" function (so-called because it appears to be somewhat arbitrary or random in its assignments). The former approach—called *sorted associative containers*—can be implemented with balanced binary search trees, among other data structures, and the latter—called *hashed associative containers*—can be implemented in any of a variety of hash table representations.

The main advantage of the hashed approach is constant average time for storage and retrieval, while that of the sorted approach is reliable performance. (Worst-case performance of hash table operations can be very bad—linear in the size, N, of the table—under some circumstances, but that of balanced binary trees is always $O(\log N)$.)

Ideally, both sorted and hashed associative containers should be in the C++ Standard Library, but only sorted associative containers are included (unofficial STL-based hash table specifications and implementations are available; see footnote 1 in Chapter 6 and Appendix D).

The STL sorted associative container classes are `set`, `multiset`, `map` and `multimap`. With sets and multisets, the data items are just the keys themselves, and multisets allow duplicate keys while sets do not. With maps and multimaps, the data items are pairs of keys and data of some other type, and multimaps allow duplicate keys while maps do not. We consider sets and multisets together in Section 7.1 and maps and multimaps together in Section 7.2.

Though their fundamental nature is different, sorted associative containers share many features with sequence containers because they support traversal of the data items as a linear sequence using the same container accessors as defined for sequence containers. Bidirectional iterators are provided, and traversals using them produce the items in sorted order. Indeed, in some cases (for example, if the data items are large structures) sorting a sequence of items may be accomplished more efficiently by inserting them in a multiset and traversing the multiset than by using the generic sort algorithm or list sort member function.

7.1 Sets and Multisets

7.1.1 Types

The template parameters of both the `set` and the `multiset` classes are given by

```
template <typename Key, typename Compare = less<Key>,
          class Allocator = allocator<Key> >
```

The first parameter is the type of keys to be stored, the second is the type of comparison function to be used in determining order, and the third is the type of storage allocator to be used.

Both classes provide definitions of the same types as the sequence containers: `value_type` (defined as type Key), `size_type`, `difference_type`, `reference`, `pointer`, `iterator`, `reverse_iterator`, `const_reference`, `const_pointer`, `const_iterator`, and `const_reverse_iterator`, plus the following:

- `key_type` Defined as type Key.

- `key_compare` Defined as type Compare.

- `value_compare`   Defined as type `Compare`.

These classes define both `key_compare` and `value_compare` for compatibility with `map` and `multimap`, where they are distinct types.

The comparison function must define an ordering relation on keys, which is used to determine their order in the linear traversals the container's iterator types support. The requirements on this relation are the same as those already discussed in Section 5.4 for relations used with STL's sorting-related algorithms. The ordering relation is also used to determine when two keys are considered equivalent. That is, two keys `k1` and `k2` are considered equivalent if

```
key_compare(k1, k2) == false && key_compare(k2, k1) == false
```

In most simple cases, this definition of equivalence coincides with that of the `==` operator. For example, if the keys are any built-in numeric type and `key_compare(k1, k2) == (k1 < k2)`, the definition of key equivalence amounts to

```
!(k1 < k2) && !(k2 < k1)
```

which is the same relation as that computed by `k1 == k2`. Certainly, though, it's possible for the two definitions to disagree. As a trivial example, suppose that the keys are `vector<int>` containers and we define `key_compare` to compare just their first elements. Then any two vectors that have the same first element will be considered equal by `key_compare` but not by the `==` operator for vectors if they disagree in any other position.

It's important to keep this (potential) distinction in mind because, as we'll see, the notion of key equivalence comes into play in a variety of ways with all the sorted associative containers. These ways include determining whether to insert an element based on whether its key duplicates (is equivalent to) one already present or the results of searching a multiset for all keys equivalent to a given key. In every case, when we talk about key equivalence, we mean the definition given here, not `==`.

The set and multiset iterator types are bidirectional rather than random access, which means that some generic algorithms, such as those for sorting, cannot be applied to sets or multisets. But there's no need to apply a sorting algorithm anyway, since these containers maintain sorted order at all times.

7.1.2 Constructors

The set constructors are

```
set(const Compare& comp = Compare());
template <typename InputIterator>
set(InputIterator first, InputIterator last,
    const Compare& comp = Compare());
set(const set<Key, Compare, Allocator>& otherSet);
```

The first produces an empty set, the second a set with copies of elements from the range [first, last) (with duplicates eliminated), and the third (the copy constructor) a set with the same elements as otherSet. The first and second constructors take an optional argument of type Compare, which defaults to Compare(). The multiset constructors have the same form and meaning, except that they retain duplicate elements.

7.1.3 Insertion

The simplest insert member function for set and multiset takes a single argument of type value_type, which is type Key, and inserts a copy of the argument.

Example 7.1: Demonstrating set construction and insertion

"ex07-01.cpp" 164 ≡
```
    #include <iostream>
    #include <cassert>
    #include <list>
    #include <string>
    #include <set>
    using namespace std;
    ⟨Define make function (builds a container of characters) 22b⟩

    int main()
    {
      cout << "Demonstrating set construction and insertion."
           << endl;
      list<char> list1 =
          make< list<char> >("There is no distinctly native "
                             "American criminal class");

      // Put the characters in list1 into set1:
      set<char> set1;
```

```
      list<char>::iterator i;
      for (i = list1.begin(); i != list1.end(); ++i)
        set1.insert(*i);

  // Put the characters in set1 into list2:
    list<char> list2;
    set<char>::iterator k;
    for (k = set1.begin(); k != set1.end(); ++k)
      list2.push_back(*k);

    assert (list2 == make< list<char> >(" ATacdehilmnorstvy"));
    return 0;
  }
```

After inserting the characters in `list1` into `set1`, we examine the contents of this set by copying its contents back into `list2` using a loop variable of the iterator type `set<char>::iterator` and the `begin` and `end` member functions, which are provided for associative containers just as they are for sequence containers. The assertion shows that the sequence of characters in `list2` and thus also in `set1` is in sorted order, and there are no duplicates.

Here is a program that does the same thing using a multiset instead of a set.

Example 7.2: Demonstrating `multiset` construction and insertion

```
"ex07-02.cpp" 165 ≡
    #include <iostream>
    #include <cassert>
    #include <list>
    #include <string>
    #include <set>
    using namespace std;
    ⟨Define make function (builds a container of characters) 22b⟩

    int main()
    {
      cout << "Demonstrating multiset construction "
          << "and insertion." << endl;
      list<char> list1 =
          make< list<char> >("There is no distinctly native "
                              "American criminal class");

      // Put the characters in list1 into multiset1:
      multiset<char> multiset1;
```

165

```
list<char>::iterator i;
for (i = list1.begin(); i != list1.end(); ++i)
  multiset1.insert(*i);

// Put the characters in multiset1 into list2:
list<char> list2;
multiset<char>::iterator k;
for (k = multiset1.begin(); k != multiset1.end(); ++k)
  list2.push_back(*k);

assert (list2 ==
        make< list<char> >("       ATaaaacccccdeeeehiiiiiii"
                                  "lllmmnnnnnorrrsssssttttvy"));
cout << " --- Ok." << endl;
return 0;
}
```

In this case, the assertion shows that duplicates are retained.

The `insert` member function used in these examples has different return types in the `set` and `multiset` classes. In class `set`, its interface is

```
pair<iterator, bool> insert(const value_type& x);
```

while in class `multiset` it is

```
iterator insert(const value_type& x);
```

In the `set` version, the iterator returned refers to the position of `x` in the set, whether or not it was already there, and the `bool` value is `true` if the element was inserted, `false` if it was already there. In the `multiset` version, the element is always inserted, and so the `bool` value is unnecessary.

The time required by `insert` is $O(\log N)$, where N is the number of elements stored in the set or multiset.

The `insert` member above differs from any of the sequence `insert` members in that no iterator must be passed to it to tell where the newly inserted element goes. Instead, the new element's position is whatever the comparison function requires to maintain sorted order. There is, however, another set and multiset `insert` member that does take an iterator argument, giving it the same interface as in the sequence containers.

```
iterator insert(iterator position, const value_type& x);
```

This function still puts **x** in the position required to maintain sorted order, treating **position** only as a "hint" as to where to begin searching. It takes only amortized constant time rather than $O(\log N)$ time if **x** is inserted or is already present at **position**. A simple case in which this performance property is useful is copying some already sorted container into a set or multiset, for example, with

```
vector<int>::iterator i;
for (i = vector1.begin(); i != vector1.end(); ++i)
  set1.insert(set1.end(), *i);
```

This code works whether or not **vector1**'s elements are in sorted order, taking $O(N \log N)$ time (where N is **vector1.size()**) if they are not sorted, but only $O(N)$ time if they are.

Since the insert iterator produced by **inserter** is expressed in terms of the **insert** function, the preceding code could also be written as

```
copy(vector1.begin(), vector1.end(),
     inserter(set1, set1.end()));
```

More generally, the "hint" version of set and multiset **insert** is useful in conjunction with the generic algorithms for set operations on sorted structures (**includes**, **set_union**, **set_intersection**, **set_difference**, and **set_symmetric_difference**). For example,

```
set_union(set1.begin(), set1.end(),
          set2.begin(), set2.end(),
          inserter(set3, set3.end()));
```

puts the union of **set1** and **set2** into **set3** in time $O(N1 + N2)$, where $N1$ and $N2$ are the sizes of **set1** and **set2**.

There is one other **insert** member function for sets and multisets for inserting elements from a range:

```
template <typename InputIterator>
void insert(InputIterator first, InputIterator last);
```

It takes time $O(M \log(N + M))$, where M is the size of the range and N is the size of the set or multiset.

7.1.4 Erasure (Deletion)

Elements can be erased from a set or multiset either by key or by position: to erase all elements with key **k** from a set or multiset **set1**, use

```
set1.erase(k);
```

If **set1** is a set, there can be at most one element with key **k**; if there is none, this function call does nothing. If **i** is a valid dereferenceable iterator for **set1**, use

```
set1.erase(i);
```

to erase the element to which **i** refers. In case **set1** is a multiset and there are other copies of ***i** in **set1**, only the copy to which **i** refers is erased. To illustrate this in the following program, we define a new function **make_string** for converting from any STL container of characters to string.

⟨Define make_string function (builds a string from a container) 168⟩ ≡
```
#include <functional>
template <typename Container>
string make_string(const Container& c)
{
  string s;
  copy(c.begin(), c.end(), inserter(s, s.end()));
  return s;
}
```
Used in parts 168, 170.

This example also uses one of the multiset accessor member functions, **find**, for finding an element by key.

Example 7.3: Demonstrating multiset **erase** functions

"ex07-03.cpp" 168 ≡
```
#include <iostream>
#include <cassert>
#include <list>
#include <string>
#include <set>
using namespace std;
```
⟨Define make function (builds a container of characters) 22b⟩
⟨Define make_string function (builds a string from a container) 168⟩

```
int main()
{
  cout << "Demonstrating multiset erase functions" << endl;
  list<char> list1 =
      make< list<char> >("There is no distinctly native "
                         "American criminal class");

  // Put the characters in list1 into multiset1:
  multiset<char> multiset1;
  copy(list1.begin(), list1.end(),
       inserter(multiset1, multiset1.end()));
  assert (make_string(multiset1) ==
      "          ATaaaaccccdeeeehiiiiiiiilllmmnnnnnorrrssssstttvy");
  multiset1.erase('a');
  assert (make_string(multiset1) ==
             "          ATccccdeeeehiiiiiiiilllmmnnnnnorrrssssstttvy");

  multiset<char>::iterator i = multiset1.find('e');

  multiset1.erase(i);
  assert (make_string(multiset1) ==
             "          ATccccdeeehiiiiiiiilllmmnnnnnorrrssssstttvy");
  cout << " --- Ok." << endl;
  return 0;
}
```

The first **erase** call passes a key **a**, and all elements in **multiset1** with that key are erased. The second **erase** call passes an iterator **i** returned by the **find** call, referring to the element containing one of the **e**'s, causing just that element to be erased. By the way, we could have written the **find** call and **erase** call together in one line:

```
multiset1.erase(multiset1.find('e'));
```

This would avoid having to declare an iterator variable.

The **set** and **multiset** classes provide one other **erase** member function, for erasing all elements in a range. For example, we might add the following lines to the end of the program:[1]

---

[1] The source code for this variation, Example 7.3a, is available on the Internet (see Appendix D) as the file ex07-03a.cpp.

```
    i = multiset1.find('T');
    multiset<char>::iterator j = multiset1.find('v');

    multiset1.erase(i, j);
    assert (make_string(multiset1) == "      Avy");
```

All **erase** member functions take $O(\log N + E)$ time, where N is the size of the set or multiset and E is the number of elements erased.

7.1.5 Accessors

Sets and multisets have most of the accessors that are common to the sequence containers for accessing information about the elements as a linear, sorted sequence: **begin**, **end**, **rbegin**, **rend**, **empty**, **size**, and **max_size**. As usual, the iterator-returning accessors also have a version that returns a constant iterator when applied to a constant set or multiset. But these containers also have several member functions for accessing information by key: **find**, **lower_bound**, **upper_bound**, **equal_range**, and **count**.

Examples of **find** given in Section 7.1.4. It's important to understand the differences between this member function and the generic **find** algorithm. As we pointed out in Section 4.12, the major difference is in efficiency: the set or multiset **find** member function takes only $O(\log N)$ time, where N is the size of the container, while the generic **find** algorithm takes $O(N)$ time. The **find** member is more efficient because it can take advantage of the keys' sorted order to do a binary search, while the generic **find** does a linear search.

Another difference between the **find** member and the generic **find**, in the case of multisets, is in the element to which the returned iterator refers. The generic **find** returns the position of the first member with the given key, but it is unspecified which position the **find** member returns, among those containing the given key. If it is important to get the first position, that is what the **lower_bound** member returns, and **upper_bound** returns the past-the-end iterator of the range of positions containing the given key.

Example 7.4: Demonstrating multiset search member functions

"ex07-04.cpp" 170 ≡
```
    #include <iostream>
    #include <cassert>
    #include <list>
    #include <string>
    #include <set>
```

```
using namespace std;
⟨Define make function (builds a container of characters) 22b⟩
⟨Define make_string function (builds a string from a container) 168⟩

int main()
{
  cout << "Demonstrating multiset search member functions."
       << endl;
  list<char> list1 =
      make< list<char> >("There is no distinctly native "
                         "American criminal class"),
             list2 =
      make< list<char> >("except Congress. - Mark Twain");

  // Put the characters in list1 into multiset1:
  multiset<char> multiset1;
  copy(list1.begin(), list1.end(),
       inserter(multiset1, multiset1.end()));

  assert (make_string(multiset1) ==
      "        ATaaaaccccdeeeehiiiiiiiilllmmnnnnnorrrsssstttvy");

  multiset<char>::iterator i = multiset1.lower_bound('c'),
                           j = multiset1.upper_bound('r');

  multiset1.erase(i, j);

  assert (make_string(multiset1) == "        ATaaaasssstttvy");

  list<char> found, not_found;
  list<char>::iterator k;
  for (k = list2.begin(); k != list2.end(); ++k)
    if (multiset1.find(*k) != multiset1.end())
      found.push_back(*k);
    else
      not_found.push_back(*k);

  assert (found == make< list<char> >("t ss  a Ta"));
  assert (not_found ==
          make< list<char> >("excepCongre.-Mrkwin"));
  cout << "  --- Ok." << endl;
  return 0;
}
```

We can think of **lower_bound** as returning the first position where the key could be inserted while still maintaining sorted order and `upper_bound` as returning the last such position. These statements are true regardless of whether the key is already present. (This is the same meaning that the generic `lower_bound` and `upper_bound` algorithms have on sorted sequences.)

The last part of the program searches `multiset1` for each of the characters in `list2` and puts those it finds in `found` and the others in `not_found`.

If we need the results of `lower_bound` and `upper_bound` for the same key, we can get them both in one call with `equal_range`, which returns a pair of iterators. This function gets its name from the fact that the iterators it returns determine the range of elements equivalent to the given key. This range is empty (the iterators are equal) if there are no such elements in the container.

Finally, `count` returns the distance from the `lower_bound` position to the `upper_bound` position, which is the number of elements equivalent to the given key. For examples of both `equal_range` and `count`, we could add the following to the end of the previous program:[2]

```
assert (make_string(multiset1) == "        ATaaaassssttttvy");

i = multiset1.lower_bound('s');
j = multiset1.upper_bound('s');

pair<multiset<char>::iterator,
    multiset<char>::iterator>
    p = multiset1.equal_range('s');

assert (p.first == i && p.second == j);
assert (multiset1.count('s') == 4);

multiset1.erase(p.first, p.second);

assert (multiset1.count('s') == 0);
assert (make_string(multiset1) == "        ATaaaattttvy");
```

Each search function (except `count`) has a version that returns a constant iterator (or, in the case of `equal_range`, a pair of constant iterators) when applied to a constant container. Note that although we've illustrated them only for multisets, each is defined for sets as well. On sets, `count` always returns either 0 or 1.

---

[2]The source code for this variation, Example 7.4a, is available on the Internet (see Appendix D) as the file `ex07-04a.cpp`.

With all search functions, one should keep in mind that their meaning depends on the meaning of equivalence as defined in terms of the `key_compare` function, not as defined by the `==` operator.

All search member functions take $O(\log N)$ time, where N is the size of the set or multiset, except `count`, which takes $O(\log N + E)$ time, where E is the number of elements with the given key.

7.1.6 Equality and Less-Than Relations

Let's recall the definition of container equality that's used with all STL containers (from Section 6.1.6):

- The sequences they contain must be of the same length.

- Elements in corresponding positions must be equal, as determined by the `==` operator of the element type.

When applied to STL set and multiset containers, with their property of maintaining their elements in sorted order, this definition amounts to just what we expect from the names "set" and "multiset" as used in mathematics. That is, two sets are equal if they contain the same elements— order is ignored. Two multisets are equal if they contain the same number of occurrences of each element, again regardless of order. Taken together with the STL generic algorithms for set operations on sorted structures (`includes`, `set_union`, `set_intersection`, `set_difference`, and `set_symmetric_difference`), these properties enable all the most basic and useful computations with sets and multisets.

Actually, though, things are not quite that simple, because the notion of "sameness" here is the key equivalence relation as determined by the `key_compare` function: two keys `k1` and `k2` are considered equivalent if

```
key_compare(k1, k2) == false && key_compare(k2, k1) == false
```

As noted in Section 7.1.1, this is not always identical to the relation computed by the `==` operator on the elements. If the two relations don't agree, we may get some unexpected results from set and multiset equality.

A similar situation exists with `operator<` on sets and multisets, since the general definition of this operator on all containers uses the generic `lexicographical_compare` algorithm, which uses the `<` operator of the element type. If `key_compare` does not compare keys the same way the element type `<` operator does, comparisons of sets and multisets might not give the results you expect.

7.1.7 Assignment

As already noted in Section 6.1.7, `operator=` is defined for all STL containers, such that `x = y` makes it true that `x == y`. This is a linear time operation. There is no `assign` member function for sorted associative containers, but there is a `swap` member function in each case such that `x.swap(y)` exchanges the values of `x` and `y` in constant time. There is likewise a partial specialization of the generic `swap` algorithm to use the corresponding `swap` member function.

7.2 Maps and Multimaps

Map containers can be viewed as arrays that are indexed by keys of some arbitrary type `Key` rather than by integers $0, 1, 2, \ldots$. They are sorted associative containers that provide for fast retrieval of information of some type `T` based on keys of a separate type `Key`, with the keys being stored uniquely. Multimaps do the same but allow duplicate keys. Their relationship to maps is the same as that of multisets to sets.

Maps and multimaps can be understood as sets and multisets in which there is additional information of type `T` along with each key. This additional data does not affect the way the containers are searched or traversed and only comes into play in a few additional operations that are provided specifically for storing or retrieving it. Our discussion in this section will be based on this insight and will therefore be brief.

Alternatively, we could have started with a full treatment of maps and multimaps and then said that sets and multisets could be understood simply as maps and multimaps in which the associated data was not used. This might have been a more natural order of presentation, since maps and multimaps have a wider range of applications than sets and multisets, but we choose to discuss sets and multisets first because they are a little simpler and are easier to illustrate in small example programs. We present only a few examples of maps and multimaps in this chapter, but you'll find them used in a more significant way in Chapters 14, 15, 18, and 19.

Turning around the analogy with which we began, arrays (and vectors and deques) provide a map-like capability in which the keys are integers in some range $0, 1, 2, \ldots, N - 1$ for some nonnegative integer N. While they handle such associations very efficiently, they are severely limited compared to the map container, first by allowing only integers as keys and second by requiring storage proportional to N even if only a small percentage of the integers in the range $0, 1, 2, \ldots, N-1$ have useful data associated with them. Maps and multimaps break away from both these restrictions, allowing keys of almost any type and using storage only in proportion to the number of keys actually stored.

Even with integer keys, the "sparse representation" that maps and multimaps permit can enable huge savings in storage and computing time, as we'll show in Section 7.2.3 in an example of computing the inner product of two sparse vectors (where by vector we mean an N-tuple of numbers; it will be represented as a `map`, not a `vector`). We'll come to examples of maps and multimaps with noninteger keys in Chapters 14 and 15.

7.2.1 Types

The template parameters of both the `map` and the `multimap` classes are given by

```
template <typename Key, typename T,
          typename Compare = less<Key>,
          class Allocator = allocator<pair<const Key, T> > >
```

The first parameter is the type of keys to be stored, the second is the type of objects to be associated with the keys, the third is the comparison function to be used in determining order, and the fourth is the storage allocator to be used. These are the same parameters as for sets and multisets except for the addition of `T`.

Both classes provide definitions of the same types as the sequence containers: `value_type` (which is defined as type `pair<const Key, T>`), `pointer`, `reference`, `iterator`, `reverse_iterator`, `difference_type`, `size_type`, `const_iterator`, `const_reverse_iterator`, `const_pointer`, and `const_reference`, plus the following:

- `key_type` Defined as type `Key`.

- `key_compare` Defined as type `Compare`.

- `value_compare` Function type defined to compare two `value_type` objects based just on their keys:

```
class value_compare
  : public binary_function<value_type, value_type, bool> {
 protected:
  Compare comp;
  value_compare(Compare c) : comp(c) { }
 public:
  bool operator()(const value_type& x,
                  const value_type& y) const {
    return comp(x.first, y.first);
  }
};
```

As with sets and multisets, the map and multimap iterator types are bidirectional rather than random access.

7.2.2 Constructors

The map and multimap constructors have the same form as those for sets and multisets and have the same distinction in their meanings, that constructing a map from a range eliminates copies with duplicate keys but a multimap retains them. Time bounds are the same as for sets and multisets.

7.2.3 Insertion

Insertion into maps and multimaps can be accomplished with `insert` member functions, which have the same interfaces as for sets and multisets. Note, however, that here `value_type` is not just Key but `pair<const Key, T>`; that is, the single `value_type` argument passed to `insert` contains both a Key and a T value. We are allowed to change already inserted pairs by assignment but only in their T members; the `const` in front of Key prevents changing a key. This restriction is crucial to the integrity of the internal map representation.

Another way to insert into a map is with `operator[]`:

```
map1[k] = t;
```

If there is no pair already in **map1** with key k, then the pair (k, t) is inserted. If there is already a pair (k, t0) for some t0, then t0 is replaced by t. Another way to accomplish this replacement (departing for the moment from the subject of insertion) is

```
i->second = t;
```

where i is a map<Key, T>::iterator such that i->first == k. (But we could not write i->first = k1, since i->first is a constant member of value_type.)

Returning to operator[], it is *not* defined for multimaps. This may seem surprising, but if it were defined, there might be bigger surprises in some cases. The associated value would have to redefined for all (key, value) pairs with keys equivalent to the given one to guarantee that the assignment multimap1[k] = v results in the equality multimap1[k] == v afterward. Such an extensive effect might be unwanted in some cases.

Even with maps, there is one perhaps surprising behavior of operator[]: it can cause an insertion into a map even when it just appears in an expression and not only when it appears on the left-hand side of an assignment. That is, an occurrence of

    map1[k]

in any expression returns the T value associated with key k if there is one— but if there isn't, it inserts a pair (k, T()) and returns T(). See also footnote 2 in Chapter 6 regarding the meaning of T() when T is a built-in type like int.

Let's look at some examples of insertion using operator[]. In the process we will note similarities and differences between the map container and the array, vector, and deque containers. Consider the problem of computing the inner product of two vectors of real numbers. Here we are using the word vector in one of its traditional senses, meaning tuples of real numbers, not STL vectors. In the following we use the word tuple for this meaning to avoid confusion. If $x = (x_0, x_1, \ldots, x_{n-1})$ and $y = (y_0, y_1, \ldots, y_{n-1})$, then the inner product of x and y is defined as

$$x \circ y = \sum_{i=0}^{n-1} x_i \cdot y_i$$

If x and y are stored in arrays, vectors, or deques, this is of course easily computed with

```
double sum = 0;
for (int i = 0; i < n; ++i)
  sum += x[i] * y[i];
```

There's also an STL generic inner_product algorithm that could be used (see Section 5.5.4). But suppose we want to deal with sparse tuples, that is, those in which most elements are 0. For example, suppose N is 1 million but there are only a few thousand nonzero elements in either x or y. Neither the preceding `for` loop nor the STL generic `inner_product` algorithm takes advantage of sparseness; both would blindly compute each of the million products and sum them.

By storing x and y in maps rather than vectors and storing only the nonzero elements, first we can cut the storage requirements dramatically. Second, we can make the same kind of reduction in the time for computing the inner product by traversing the nonzero elements in one of the tuples.

Before looking at the version with maps, let's do it with vectors.

Example 7.5: Computing an inner product of tuples represented as vectors

"ex07-05.cpp" 178 $\equiv$

```cpp
#include <vector>
#include <iostream>
using namespace std;

int main()
{
  cout << "Computing an inner product of tuples "
      << "represented as vectors." << endl;

  const long N = 600000; // Length of tuples x and y
  const long S = 10; // Sparseness factor

  cout << "\nInitializing..." << flush;
  vector<double> x(N), y(N);
  long k;
  for (k = 0; 3 * k * S < N; ++k)
    x[3 * k * S] = 1.0;
  for (k = 0; 5 * k * S < N; ++k)
    y[5 * k * S] = 1.0;

  cout << "\n\nComputing inner product by brute force: "
      << flush;
  double sum = 0.0;
  for (k = 0; k < N; ++k)
    sum += x[k] * y[k];

  cout << sum << endl;
  return 0;
}
```

Output from Example 7.5

```
Computing an inner product of tuples represented as vectors.
Initializing...
Computing inner product by brute force: 4000
```

In this program we use the vector constructor that takes two arguments to initialize x and y to have N elements, all equal to 0.0. This is essential since the vector `operator[]` does not grow the vector if the index is larger than the current size. Maps do not require this initialization since there is no bound on the size of indices (keys) other than that imposed by the key type itself. We can simply start off with x and y as empty maps:

```
map<long, double> x, y;
```

The inner product calculation can now be written as

```
map<long, double>::iterator ix, iy;

for (sum = 0.0, ix = x.begin(); ix != x.end(); ++ix) {
  long k = ix->first;
  if (y.find(k) != y.end())
    sum += x[k] * y[k];
}
```

where we use the map **find** member function, which has the same meaning as with sets and multisets: it searches for a given key and returns an iterator referring to the entry with that key if it finds one or to the end position if it doesn't find the given key.

The computation of y[k] involves essentially the same search, but we can avoid repeating it by saving the iterator returned by y.find(k) and dereferencing it to help get the value of y[k]. We can likewise avoid the search implicit in x[k] by dereferencing ix.

Example 7.6: Computing an inner product of tuples represented as maps

```
"ex07-06.cpp" 179 ≡
    #include <map>
    #include <iostream>
    using namespace std;

    int main()
    {
      cout << "Computing an inner product of tuples "
```

```
          << "represented as maps." << endl;

    const long N = 600000; // Length of tuples x and y
    const long S = 10; // Sparseness factor

    cout << "\nInitializing..." << flush;
    map<long, double> x, y;
    long k;
    for (k = 0; 3 * k * S < N; ++k)
      x[3 * k * S] = 1.0;
    for (k = 0; 5 * k * S < N; ++k)
      y[5 * k * S] = 1.0;

    cout << "\n\nComputing inner product taking advantage "
         << "of sparseness: " << flush;

    double sum;
    map<long, double>::iterator ix, iy;
    for (sum = 0.0, ix = x.begin(); ix != x.end(); ++ix) {
      long i = ix->first;
      iy = y.find(i);
      if (iy != y.end())
        sum += ix->second * iy->second;
    }
    cout << sum << endl;
    return 0;
}
```

Output from Example 7.6

```
Computing an inner product of tuples represented as maps.
Initializing...
Computing inner product taking advantage of sparseness: 4000
```

This program performs only 4,000 additions and 4,000 multiplications versus 600,000 of each in the original program. The following table also shows the operation counts for the indexing and iterator operations and the search steps involved in the find operations. The calculations are based on the fact that $600,000/30 = 20,000$ entries are stored in x and $600,000/50 = 12,000$ in y, and the assumption that on average each of the 20,000 find operations performed on y takes $\log_2 12,000 \approx 13.5$ search steps.

Operations	Using vectors	Using maps
Additions	600,000	4,000
Multiplications	600,000	4,000
Incrementing: `++k`	600,000	
Iterating: `++ix`		20,000
Dereferencing: `x[k]`	600,000	
Dereferencing: `*ix`		20,000
Dereferencing: `y[k]`	600,000	
Search steps in `y.find(i)`		270,000
Dereferencing: `*iy`		12,000

7.2.4 Erasure (Deletion)

As with sets and multisets, elements can be erased from a map or multimap either by key or by position. The type **T** data plays no role in erasure operations, and the operations behave exactly as they do for sets and multisets and have the same computing time bound ($O(\log N + E)$ time, where N is the size of the map or multimap and E is the number of elements erased).

7.2.5 Accessors

Again, the story here is very similar to that of sets and multisets. Maps and multimaps have the same accessors as sets and multisets for accessing information about the elements as a linear, sorted sequence: `begin`, `end`, `rbegin`, `rend`, `empty`, `size`, and `max_size`. They also have the same member functions for accessing information by key: `find`, `lower_bound`, `upper_bound`, and `equal_range`, and `count`. Maps have the new accessor `operator[]`. This accessor does not apply to multimaps since there may be more than one element associated with a particular key value. The time bounds for all search operations, including `operator[]`, are all $O(\log N)$, where N is the size of the map or multimap. The single exception is `count`, which takes $O(\log N + E)$ time, where E is the number of elements with the given key.

7.2.6 Equality and Less-Than Relations

Basically, equality and less-than relations on maps and multimaps have all the same properties as sets and multisets do. The only distinction is that the presence of the extra type **T** information means that the key equivalence agrees less often with the meaning of `value_type::operator==`, since the latter (usually) takes the `T` member into account, while `key_compare` cannot. A similar remark applies to the distinction between `key_compare` and `value_type::operator<`.

7.2.7 Assignment

Again, the definitions of = and the `swap` member functions discussed in Section 6.1.7 have corresponding definitions and computing times for maps and multimaps.

CHAPTER 8

Function Objects

We now come to the fourth major kind of components STL provides, function objects. Most STL generic algorithms (and some container classes) accept a function object as a parameter to make it possible to vary their computations in other ways besides those controlled by iterators. A *function object* is any entity that can be applied to zero or more arguments to obtain a value and/or modify the state of the computation. In C++ programming, any ordinary function satisfies this definition, but so does an object of any class (or struct) that overloads the function call operator, `operator()`. As we saw in Section 2.4, either an ordinary function such as

⟨Define multfun 183a⟩ ≡
```
    int multfun(int x, int y) { return x * y; }
```
Used in part 184.

or an object `multfunobj` of the type `multiply` defined by

⟨Define multiply and multfunobj 183b⟩ ≡
```
    class multiply {
     public:
       int operator()(int x, int y) const { return x * y; }
    };

    multiply multfunobj;
```
Used in part 186.

can be applied to a pair of integer arguments as in
```
    int product1 = multfun(3, 7);
    int product2 = multfunobj(3, 7);
```

In the case of the object of type `multiply`, the function applied is the function defined within the class by overloading `operator()` for pairs of `int` arguments. There are several reasons for defining a function object in this way rather than as a simpler and more familiar-looking function definition. Since these reasons all revolve around the idea of having functions that have other functions as parameters to modify their behavior, let's first look at different ways that are available for defining such function parameters.

8.1 Passing Functions via Function Pointers

Consider again the STL generic function `accumulate`, which, when called with iterators `first` and `last` and a value `init`, adds up `init` plus the values in positions `first` up to but not including `last` and returns the sum. It can be programmed as follows:

```
template <typename InputIterator, typename T>
T accumulate(InputIterator first, InputIterator last, T init)
{
  while (first != last) {
    init = init + *first;
    ++first;
  }
  return init;
}
```

But instead of addition, we want to allow any two-argument function to be used by passing the desired function as another argument in a call of `accumulate`. The traditional method of accomplishing this goal in C and C++ programming is to declare the extra parameter to be of a function pointer type; in a call, we would then pass as the actual argument the address of a function, such as `&mult`, as shown in the following example program.[1]

Example 8.1: First extended `accumulate` definition and call

"ex08-01.cpp" 184 ≡
```
#include <iostream>
#include <cassert>
```

---

[1] Readers not already familiar with function pointer passing do not necessarily need to try to decipher the cryptic syntax of the new formal parameter. Even in the cases that will be discussed later where it is desirable to use function pointer passing with STL components, a simpler syntax is enabled by a "pointer-to-function adaptor," as discussed in Section 11.3.

```
#include <vector>
using namespace std;

template <typename InputIterator, typename T>
T accumulate1(InputIterator first, InputIterator last, T init,
              T (*binary_function)(T x, T y)) // New parameter
{
  while (first != last) {
    init = (*binary_function)(init, *first);
    ++first;
  }
  return init;
}
```

⟨Define multfun 183a⟩

```
int main()
{
  cout << "Demonstrating function pointer passing." << endl;
  int x[5] = {2, 3, 5, 7, 11};
  // Initialize vector1 to x[0] through x[4]:
  vector<int> vector1(&x[0], &x[5]);

  int product = accumulate1(vector1.begin(), vector1.end(),
                            1, &multfun);
  assert (product == 2310);
  cout << " --- Ok." << endl;
  return 0;
}
```

One basic problem with this traditional approach is that it is not as general as we might like. For example, the prototype of the function pointer is written

```
    T (*binary_function)(T x, T y)
```

and is matched by `int multfun(int, int)`, but if we had written

```
    T (*binary_function)(const T& x, const T& y)
```

so that we would have more efficient parameter passing if type `T` objects are large, our `multfun` would not match it, and we would have to rewrite it with prototype `int multfun(const int&, const int&)`. Another problem is efficiency: in `accumulate1` we have to dereference a pointer to get to the function that was passed, and then we have to call that function out of line (passing its parameters to it, transferring control to it, and copying its return value back to the calling scope and transferring control back to the call site). In a case like `multfun`, these steps may be much more costly than the computation internal to the function, which requires only one or two machine instructions.

8.2   Advantages of Specifying Function Objects with Template Parameters

Fortunately both the generality problem and the efficiency problem with function pointers are alleviated by another method of declaring a function object parameter: declare it to be a type that is itself a template parameter, as shown in the next example.

Example 8.2: First extended `accumulate` definition and call

```
"ex08-02.cpp" 186 ≡
    #include <iostream>
    #include <cassert>
    #include <vector>
    using namespace std;

    template <typename InputIterator, typename T,
              typename BinaryFunction>
    T accumulate(InputIterator first, InputIterator last, T init,
                 BinaryFunction binary_function)
    {
      while (first != last) {
        init = binary_function(init, *first);
        ++first;
      }
      return init;
    }

    ⟨Define multiply and multfunobj 183b⟩

    int main()
    {
      cout << "Demonstrating function pointer passing." << endl;
      int x[5] = {2, 3, 5, 7, 11};
      // Initialize vector1 to x[0] through x[4]:
      vector<int> vector1(&x[0], &x[5]);
```

```
      int product = accumulate(vector1.begin(), vector1.end(),
                               1, multfunobj);
      assert (product == 2310);
      cout << " --- Ok." << endl;
      return 0;
}
```

With this definition of **accumulate** (which is an acceptable implementation of the STL generic algorithm of that name), the type requirements placed on any actual parameter passed as the last argument are only those imposed by the way it is used within the body of **accumulate**: it must be applicable to two arguments of types T1 and T2, where T is convertible to T1 and the value type of **InputIterator** is convertible to T2, and its return type must be convertible to T. Thus many function prototype variations are acceptable, in contrast to the overly strict type requirements of function pointer passing. Furthermore, function objects defined as objects of a class that overloads the function call operator, like **multfunobj**, are now acceptable but cannot be used with **accumulate1**.

As for efficiency, with function object passing defined using a template parameter and overloading of **operator()** it is possible for the compiler to inline the call of **binary_function** within the body of **accumulate**, completely eliminating the extra steps involved in pointer dereferencing and out of line calling.

In addition to generality and efficiency, there is still another advantage of allowing class objects to be used as function objects. Class objects can carry with them additional information such as type definitions that make it easier for function adaptors to produce variations on the function beyond its basic definition in the **operator()** overloading, as we discuss in Chapter 11. And since class objects can have data members, functions that maintain state between calls can easily be defined. In the following two examples we use this capability to define a comparison function object that not only compares two values but also increments a counter. When used in a call of a sorting algorithm, for example, it records the number of comparisons performed during a sort. In the first version, the counter is maintained as a static data member, **long counter**, of the class that defines the comparison counting function objects.

⟨Define less_with_count class with static member 187⟩ ≡
```
    template <typename T>
    class less_with_count : public binary_function<T, T, bool> {
```

```
public:
  less_with_count() { }
  bool operator()(const T& x, const T& y) {
      ++counter;
      return x < y;
  }
  long report() const {return counter;}
  static long counter;
};


template <typename T>
long less_with_count<T>::counter = 0;
```

Used in part 188.

For static members, there is only one storage location for all of the objects of the class; thus, no matter how many objects are created during a call of the sorting algorithm, they all increment the same counter, and the result left in it at the end is the total number of comparisons done.

Example 8.3: Using a function object for operation counting, first version

"ex08-03.cpp" 188 ≡

```
#include <iostream>
#include <iomanip>
#include <cassert>
#include <vector>
#include <algorithm>
#include <functional>
using namespace std;
⟨Define less_with_count class with static member 187⟩

int main()
{
  cout << "Using a function object for operation counting, "
      << "first version." << endl;
  const long N1 = 1000, N2 = 128000;
  for (long N = N1; N <= N2; N *= 2) {
    vector<int> vector1;
    for (int k = 0; k < N; ++k)
      vector1.push_back(k);
    random_shuffle(vector1.begin(), vector1.end());
    less_with_count<int> comp_counter;
    less_with_count<int>::counter = 0;
```

```
        sort(vector1.begin(), vector1.end(), comp_counter);
        cout << "Problem size " << setw(9) << N
             << ",  comparisons performed: "
             << setw(9) << comp_counter.report() << endl;
    }
    return 0;
}
```

The output might look as follows (although the exact counts will differ with different STL implementations).

Output from Example 8.3

```
Using a function object for operation counting, first version.
Problem size      1000,  comparisons performed:       11833
Problem size      2000,  comparisons performed:       25198
Problem size      4000,  comparisons performed:       58801
Problem size      8000,  comparisons performed:      122815
Problem size     16000,  comparisons performed:      264323
Problem size     32000,  comparisons performed:      583628
Problem size     64000,  comparisons performed:     1204460
Problem size    128000,  comparisons performed:     2709767
```

A well-known problem with static variables is that they are difficult to use properly in multithreaded computations. We therefore next show a different way of keeping track of the comparison count using per-object data members instead of a static data member. This is not as straightforward as it might seem, because the original function object we create in our main program to pass to **sort** might be copied, for example, if it is passed by value to other internal functions in the body of **sort**. In fact, several "generations" of copies might be made. Then each copy has its own **counter** data member, and we must somehow add up all their values to get the total number of comparisons. The solution proposed here is to record in each copy of the function object the address of its *progenitor*, the object from which all the copies descended.

⟨Define less_with_count class with no static member 189⟩ ≡

```
    template <typename T>
    class less_with_count : public binary_function<T, T, bool> {
    public:
      less_with_count() : counter(0), progenitor(0) { }
      // Copy constructor:
      less_with_count(less_with_count<T>& x) : counter(0),
```

```
        progenitor(x.progenitor ? x.progenitor : &x) { }
    bool operator()(const T& x, const T& y) {
      ++counter;
      return x < y;
    }
    long report() const { return counter; }
    ~less_with_count() {  // Destructor
      if (progenitor) {
        progenitor->counter += counter;
      }
    }
  }
private:
  long counter;
  less_with_count<T>* progenitor;
};
```

Used in part 190.

An object created by the default constructor has a null pointer in its progenitor member. The copy constructor copies the progenitor member unless it is null, in which case it records as its progenitor the address of the object being copied. Then, when an object is being destroyed, its last act is to add its own counter to that of its progenitor.[2]

Example 8.4: Using a function object for operation counting, second version

```
"ex08-04.cpp" 190 ≡
    #include <iostream>
    #include <iomanip>
    #include <cassert>
    #include <vector>
    #include <algorithm>
    #include <functional>
    using namespace std;
    ⟨Define less_with_count class with no static member 189⟩
    int main()
    {
      cout << "Using a function object for operation counting, "
           << "second version." << endl;
```

---

[2]This is not a completely general solution, since an object's progenitor might be destroyed before the object itself is. In the way STL sorting algorithms pass around copies of function objects, however, this never happens—the original function object always outlives its descendants.

```
const long N1 = 1000, N2 = 128000;
for (long N = N1; N <= N2; N *= 2) {
  vector<int> vector1;
  for (int k = 0; k < N; ++k)
    vector1.push_back(k);
  random_shuffle(vector1.begin(), vector1.end());
  less_with_count<int> comp_counter;
  sort(vector1.begin(), vector1.end(), comp_counter);
  cout << "Problem size " << setw(9) << N
       << ", comparisons performed: "
       << setw(9) << comp_counter.report() << endl;
}
return 0;
}
```

The output of this program is exactly the same as it was for the previous example (assuming that both programs are compiled with the same library.)

8.3   STL-Provided Function Objects

STL provides a dozen or so function object types for the most common cases. Chapter 23, "Function Object and Function Adaptor Reference Guide," details the function objects STL provides.

CHAPTER 9

Container Adaptors

Adaptors are STL components that can be used to change the interface of another component. They are defined as template classes that take a component type as a parameter. STL provides *container adaptors*, *iterator adaptors*, and *function adaptors*. We'll look at these in turn in this and the next two chapters.

To see the advantages of a mechanism for adapting interfaces, let's first look at the problem of providing basic data structures like stacks and queues.

A *stack* is a simpler kind of container than vector, list, or deque; any one of these containers could be used as a stack, in the sense that each supports the operations one does on a stack:

- Insertion at one end (push, with push_back)

- Deletion from the same end (pop, with pop_back)

- Retrieving the value at that end (top, with back)

- Testing for the stack being empty (with empty or size)

Another important property of the stack type is the fact that it presents only a very limited interface. No other operations besides the basic stack operators are provided.

This is an important point to note because although we might choose to use a list, say, as the current implementation of a stack, we may want the ability to switch, at some later time, to a different implementation of stack operations. So unless we restrict the interface, it is difficult to ensure that we don't inadvertently start using the current implementation in nonstack-like ways.

The usual solution adopted in C++ container class libraries is to define a stack type as a class, **StackAsList**, with a private member holding a list object, and to define public functions **push**, **pop**, **top**, and **empty** in terms of list operations. Then none of the other list operations is available on stack objects, which is just what we want.

However, since in some situations it's better to use a vector instead of a list to represent a stack, such libraries may also provide a **StackAsVector** class. The same approach is used with other containers, resulting in a variety of classes such as **QueueAsVector**, **QueueAsList**, **QueueAsDoubleList**, **PriorityQueueAsVector**, **PriorityQueueAsList**, and so on.

In STL this kind of proliferation is completely avoided by the use of *container adaptors*. STL provides container adaptors to produce **stack**, **queue**, and **priority_queue** containers out of its other sequence containers.

9.1   Stack Container Adaptor

The **stack** container adaptor can be applied to a **vector**, **list**, or **deque**:

- **stack<T>** is a stack of T with a default implementation using a **deque**.

- **stack<T, vector<T> >** is a stack of T with a **vector** implementation.

- **stack<T, list<T> >** is a stack of T with a **list** implementation.

- **stack<T, deque<T> >** is a stack of T with a **deque** implementation (identical to **stack<T>**).

The operations **stack** provides are called **empty**, **size**, **top**, **push**, and **pop**. The pop function's return type is **void**, because it would need to return the popped value by value. Returning a reference would create a dangling pointer to a value that has already been removed from the **stack**. But return by value would require a constructor call, which would often be inefficient if the popped value is not needed. Thus, if the value is required, it should be obtained by using the **top** function prior to calling **pop**.

The stack adaptor can be applied to any container that supports the **empty**, **size**, **push_back**, **pop_back**, and **back** operations. Each of the containers **vector<T>**, **list<T>**, and **deque<T>** does provide these operations, so each can be made into a stack. In fact, if we define some new container class **C<T>** that supports these operations, we can also adapt it to serve as a stack with **stack<T, C<T> >**.

Here is a simple example illustrating how a stack can be created and manipulated with the stack adaptor.

Example 9.1: Illustrating the `stack` adaptor

"ex09-01.cpp" 195 ≡
```cpp
#include <iostream>
#include <stack>
using namespace std;

int main()
{
  cout << "Illustrating the stack adaptor." << endl;
  int thedata[] = {45, 34, 56, 27, 71, 50, 62};
  stack<int> s;
  cout << "The stack size is now " << s.size() << endl;
  int i;
  cout << "Pushing 4 elements " << endl;
  for (i = 0; i < 4; ++i)
    s.push(thedata[i]);
  cout << "The stack size is now " << s.size() << endl;
  cout << "Popping 3 elements " << endl;
  for (i = 0; i < 3; ++i) {
    cout << s.top() << endl;
    s.pop();
  }
  cout << "The stack size is now " << s.size() << endl;
  cout << "Pushing 3 elements " << endl;
  for(i = 4; i < 7; ++i)
    s.push(thedata[i]);
  cout << "The stack size is now " << s.size() << endl;
  cout << "Popping all elements" << endl;
  while (!s.empty()) {
    cout << s.top() << endl;
    s.pop();
  }
  cout << "The stack size is now " << s.size() << endl;
  return 0;
}
```

Output from Example 9.1

```
Illustrating the stack adaptor.
The stack size is now 0
```

```
Pushing 4 elements
The stack size is now 4
Popping 3 elements
27
56
34
The stack size is now 1
Pushing 3 elements
The stack size is now 4
Popping all elements
62
50
71
45
The stack size is now 0
```

9.2   Queue Container Adaptor

A *queue* differs from a stack in that elements are inserted on one end but removed from the opposite end. This is often called first-in, first-out (FIFO) service, in contrast to the last-in, first-out (LIFO) service a stack provides.

STL provides a `queue` container adaptor that can be applied to any container that supports the `empty`, `size`, `front`, `back`, `push_back`, and `pop_front` operations. These operations are supported by `list` and `deque`, implying that we can construct queues out of these containers:

- `queue<T>` is a queue of T with a default implementation using a `deque`.

- `queue<T, list<T> >` is a queue of T with a `list` implementation.

- `queue<T, deque<T> >` is a queue of T with a `deque` implementation (identical to `queue<T>`).

The operations `queue` provides are called `empty`, `size`, `front`, `back`, `push`, and `pop`. The `pop` function, like that of the `stack` adapter, has no return value. To obtain that value, use the `front` member.

Note that the `queue` adaptor cannot be applied to `vector`, because `vector` does not support `pop_front`. Why was `pop_front` omitted from the interface of `vector`? Pop_front could easily be programmed on vectors as `v.erase(v.begin())`, but that kind of operation on vectors should be avoided because it's very inefficient for long vectors—since all of the elements after the first position must be shifted over to fill the hole, it is a linear time operation.

By providing `pop_front` in list and `deque`, where it can be done in constant time, and omitting it from `vector`, where it would require linear time, STL makes it easy to get efficient implementations of queues and difficult to get an inefficient one.

In the following example we (arbitrarily) use `list` as the underlying representation instead of the default, `deque`. We push onto the queue the same data values we used on the stack in the previous example, but the values we get as we pop them off are different because they come from the front, the other end from where we pushed them.

Example 9.2: Illustrating the `queue` adaptor

"ex09-02.cpp" 197 ≡

```
#include <iostream>
#include <queue>
#include <list>
using namespace std;

int main()
{
  cout << "Illustrating the queue adaptor." << endl;
  int thedata[] = {45, 34, 56, 27, 71, 50, 62};
  queue<int, list<int> > q;
  cout << "The queue size is now " << q.size() << endl;
  int i;
  cout << "Pushing 4 elements " << endl;
  for (i = 0; i < 4; ++i)
    q.push(thedata[i]);
  cout << "The queue size is now " << q.size() << endl;
  cout << "Popping 3 elements " << endl;
  for (i = 0; i < 3; ++i) {
    cout << q.front() << endl;
    q.pop();
  }
  cout << "The queue size is now " << q.size() << endl;
  cout << "Pushing 3 elements " << endl;
  for(i = 4; i < 7; ++i)
    q.push(thedata[i]);
  cout << "The queue size is now " << q.size() << endl;
  cout << "Popping all elements" << endl;
  while (!q.empty()) {
    cout << q.front() << endl;
    q.pop();
```

```
  }
  cout << "The queue size is now " << q.size() << endl;
  return 0;
}
```

Output from Example 9.2

```
Illustrating the queue adaptor.
The queue size is now 0
Pushing 4 elements
The queue size is now 4
Popping 3 elements
45
34
56
The queue size is now 1
Pushing 3 elements
The queue size is now 4
Popping all elements
27
71
50
62
The queue size is now 0
```

9.3   Priority Queue Container Adaptor

A *priority queue* is a type of sequence in which the element immediately available for retrieval is the largest of those in the sequence, for some particular way of ordering the elements. The STL `priority_queue` adaptor converts any container that provides random access iterators and `empty`, `size`, `push_back`, `pop_back`, and `front` operations, along with a comparison function object, `comp`, into a priority queue that uses `comp` for comparisons when making the largest element available for retrieval.

Both `vector<T>` and `deque<T>` provide random access iterators and the necessary operations:

- `priority_queue<int>` stores `int`s in a default container implementation (`vector`) and a default comparison object (`less<int>`).

- `priority_queue<int, vector<int>, greater<int> >` stores `int`s in a `vector` and using the built-in `>` operation defined for `int`s.

- `priority_queue<float, deque<float>, greater<float> >` stores `floats` in a `deque` and using the > operation on `floats`.

Since > is used instead of < in the second and third examples, the element available for retrieval in those cases is actually the smallest element rather than the largest.

The operations `priority_queue` provides are called `empty`, `size`, `top`, `push`, and `pop`. The `pop` function, like that of the `stack` and `queue` adapters, has no return value. To retrieve the available value, use the `top` member before using `pop`.

In the following example we push onto the priority queue the same data values we used on the stack and the queue in the previous two examples, but the values we get as we pop them off are different because each one is the largest element currently in the priority queue.

Example 9.3: Illustrating the `priority_queue` adaptor

"ex09-03.cpp" 199 ≡

```cpp
#include <iostream>
#include <queue> // Defines both queue and priority_queue
using namespace std;

int main()
{
  cout << "Illustrating the priority_queue adaptor." << endl;
  int thedata[] = {45, 34, 56, 27, 71, 50, 62};
  priority_queue<int> pq;
  cout << "The priority_queue size is now " << pq.size()
       << endl;
  int i;
  cout << "Pushing 4 elements " << endl;
  for (i = 0; i < 4; ++i)
    pq.push(thedata[i]);
  cout << "The priority_queue size is now " << pq.size()
       << endl;
  cout << "Popping 3 elements " << endl;
  for (i = 0; i < 3; ++i) {
    cout << pq.top() << endl;
    pq.pop();
  }
  cout << "The priority_queue size is now " << pq.size()
       << endl;
  cout << "Pushing 3 elements " << endl;
```

```
        for(i = 4; i < 7; ++i)
          pq.push(thedata[i]);
        cout << "The priority_queue size is now " << pq.size()
             << endl;
        cout << "Popping all elements" << endl;
        while (!pq.empty()) {
          cout << pq.top() << endl;
          pq.pop();
        }
        cout << "The priority_queue size is now " << pq.size()
             << endl;
        return 0;
      }
```

Output from Example 9.3

```
      Illustrating the priority_queue adaptor.
      The priority_queue size is now 0
      Pushing 4 elements
      The priority_queue size is now 4
      Popping 3 elements
      56
      45
      34
      The priority_queue size is now 1
      Pushing 3 elements
      The priority_queue size is now 4
      Popping all elements
      71
      62
      50
      27
      The priority_queue size is now 0
```

CHAPTER 10

Iterator Adaptors

Iterator adaptors are STL components that can be used to change the interface of an iterator component. Only one kind of iterator adaptor is predefined in STL: the *reverse iterator adaptor*, which transforms a given bidirectional or random access iterator into one in which the traversal direction is reversed. The transformed iterator has the same interface as the original. This adaptor is defined by a template class that takes an iterator type as a parameter. An example of direct use of the reverse iterator adaptor is given in Section 2.5. In most cases, though, it is not necessary to use this adaptor directly, since each of the STL container types provides two reverse iterator types (which are predefined with the aid of the adaptor), `reverse_iterator`, a mutable iterator type, and `const_reverse_iterator`, a constant iterator type. Each container also provides member functions called `rbegin` and `rend` that can be used in loops or passed to algorithms to define the beginning and end of a sequence in reverse of the normal order, as shown in the following example.

Example 10.1: Illustrating normal and reverse iteration

```
"ex10-01.cpp" 201 ≡
    #include <iostream>
    #include <vector>
    #include <list>
    using namespace std;

    template <typename Container>
    void display(const Container& c)
    {
```

```
        cout << "Elements in normal (forward) order:   ";
        typename Container::const_iterator i;
        for (i = c.begin(); i != c.end(); ++i)
            cout << *i << "  ";
        cout << endl;

        cout << "Elements in reverse order:              ";
        typename Container::const_reverse_iterator r;
        for (r = c.rbegin(); r != c.rend(); ++r)
            cout << *r << "  ";
        cout << endl;
    }

    int main()
    {
        cout << "Normal and reverse iteration through a vector:\n";
        vector<int> vector1;
        vector1.push_back(2);
        vector1.push_back(3);
        vector1.push_back(5);
        vector1.push_back(7);
        vector1.push_back(11);

        display(vector1);

        cout << "Normal and reverse iteration through a list:\n";
        list<int> list1(vector1.begin(), vector1.end());

        display(list1);
        return 0;
    }
```

Output from Example 10.1

```
    Normal and reverse iteration through a vector:
    Elements in normal (forward) order:  2  3  5  7  11
    Elements in reverse order:              11  7  5  3  2
    Normal and reverse iteration through a list:
    Elements in normal (forward) order:  2  3  5  7  11
    Elements in reverse order:              11  7  5  3  2
```

When reverse iterators are passed to a generic algorithm, they make the algorithm "see in reverse" the container's sequence of elements. Otherwise, all computations proceed as with normal iterators. For example, the find generic algorithm normally returns an iterator to the first location that contains a given value. If we want the last location we can obtain it by calling `find` with reverse iterators.

Example 10.2: Using `find` with normal and reverse iteration

"ex10-02.cpp" 203 ≡

```
#include <iostream>
#include <vector>
#include <algorithm> // for find
using namespace std;
⟨Define make function (builds a container of characters) 22b⟩

int main()
{
  cout << "Using find with normal and reverse iteration:\n";
  vector<char> vector1 =
      make< vector<char> >("now is the time");
  ostream_iterator<char> out(cout, " ");

  vector<char>::iterator i =
    find(vector1.begin(), vector1.end(), 't');
  cout << "chars from the first t to the end: ";
  copy(i, vector1.end(), out); cout << endl;

  cout << "chars from the last t to the beginning: ";
  vector<char>::reverse_iterator r =
    find(vector1.rbegin(), vector1.rend(), 't');
  copy(r, vector1.rend(), out); cout << endl;

  cout << "chars from the last t to the end: ";
  copy(r.base() - 1, vector1.end(), out); cout << endl;
  return 0;
}
```

The last step in this program uses a member function `base` defined by the `reverse_iterator` class, which returns the underlying iterator that the reverse iterator is adapted from. A fundamental relation between the reverse iterator `r` and this underlying iterator `r.base()` is `&*r == &*(r.base() - 1)`. That is, if `r` is a reverse iterator that we logically consider to be pointing at some position `p`, `r` internally holds an iterator `i` that actually points to position p+1.[1] Thus, to include the value to which r points in the last output line, we use r.base() - 1 as the first normal iterator pass to copy along with vector1.end().

Output from Example 10.2

```
Using find with normal and reverse iteration:
chars from the first t to the end: t h e   t i m e
chars from the last t to the beginning: t   e h t   s i   w o n
chars from the last t to the end: t i m e
```

Notice that the characters from the last 't' to the beginning are listed in reverse order, since we printed them with reverse iterators. If we wanted to print them in forward order, we could use the same technique of subtracting 1 from a reverse iterator's underlying iterator. If we print those characters with

```
copy(vector1.begin(), r.base() - 1, out);
```

our output would show

```
chars from the beginning to the last t: n o w   i s   t h e   t
```

Although reverse iterators are the only iterator adaptors predefined in STL, the concept of an iterator adaptor has many other applications. A simple example of a user-defined iterator adaptor is discussed in Chapter 16.

---

[1]This offset by 1 is required by the fact that we need to be able to use an iterator to the first position of a sequence as the internal value of the past-the-end iterator when traversing in reverse: with arrays, in particular, there is no guarantee of any storage location being available that actually precedes the first position in the array, as there is with the last position.

CHAPTER 11

Function Adaptors

We've seen how many generic STL algorithms can take a function object as an argument and perform differently depending on the argument. Both function objects and iterators can be viewed as algorithm adaptors.

Just as iterator adaptors help us construct a wider variety of iterators to use with generic algorithms, *function adaptors* help us construct a wider variety of function objects. Using function adaptors is often easier than directly constructing a new function object type with a struct or class definition. STL provides three categories of function adaptors: *binders, negators,* and *adaptors for pointers to functions.* These adaptors are defined by class templates, but they are also accompanied by function templates that make it more convenient to use the classes. It is also convenient in describing the adaptors to concentrate on the accompanying functions and speak of them as function adaptors also.

11.1 Binders

A *binder* is a kind of function adaptor used to convert binary function objects into unary function objects by binding an argument to some particular value. For example,

```
int* where = find_if(&array1[0], &array1[1000],
                     bind2nd(greater<int>(), 200));
```

finds the first integer in `array1` that is greater than 200. The `find_if` algorithm is similar to `find`, but instead of a value to search for it takes a unary predicate function object p (that is, a function object that encapsulates a one-argument function that returns a `bool` value):

```
where = find_if(first, last, p);
```

assigns to **where** an iterator pointing to the first position in the range from **first** to **last** for which **p** returns true or **last** if no such position exists. In the example, we construct the predicate for our search by starting with **greater<int>()**, a function object that defines a binary function

```
bool operator()(int x, int y) const { return x > y; }
```

By applying **bind2nd** to this function object and 200, we produce a function object that defines a unary function

```
bool operator()(int x) const { return x > 200; }
```

just as if we had programmed another function object type

```
struct Greater200 : unary_function<int, bool> {
    bool operator()(int x) const { return x > 200; }
};
```

directly. Function adaptor **bind1st** can be used in a similar way to bind the first argument of a binary function object. More examples of the use of both binders and negators appear in the next section and in Part II.

11.2   Negators

A *negator* is a kind of function adaptor used to reverse the sense of predicate function objects. There are two negator adaptors, **not1** and **not2**. For example,

```
where = find_if(&array1[0], &array1[1000],
                not1(bind2nd(greater<int>(), 200)));
```

searches for the first integer in **array1** that is not greater than 200 (**<=** 200). In general, given a unary predicate object **p**, **not1** returns a unary predicate object defining a function

```
bool operator()(const T& x) const { return !(p(x)); }
```

where **T** is the type of **p**'s argument. In this case we could have obtained the same function object a bit more easily using another STL-provided function object, **less_equal<T>()**:

```
where = find_if(&array1[0],&array1[1000],
                bind2nd(less_equal<int>(),200));
```

The other negator similarly negates a binary predicate. As an example of the use of **not2**, suppose we have a type U of objects with a binary predicate member function that compares objects based on **id** members (identification numbers).

```
class U : public binary_function<U, U, bool> {
public:
  int id;
  bool operator()(const U& x, const U& y) const {
    return x.id >= y.id;
  }
  friend ostream& operator<<(ostream& o, const U& x) {
    o << x.id;
    return o;
  }
};
```

Note that since the class overloads the function call operator and we have derived the class from **public binary_function<U, U, bool>**, objects of type U can be used as function objects, in fact as binary predicate objects.

Now suppose we also have **vector1** defined as follows:

```
vector<U> vector1(1000);
for (int i = 0; i != 1000; ++i)
  vector1[i].id = 1000 - i - 1;
```

If we want to sort **vector1** into ascending order of **id** members, we can't use the default ordering, because that would require operator < to be defined on type U objects. We also can't use the overloaded operator defined in the type, because it uses >= to compare **id** members, not <. But we can do the job easily with the aid of **not2**:

```
sort(vector1.begin(), vector1.end(), not2(U()));
```

Following is the the complete example.

Example 11.1: Sort a vector into ascending order of `id` members

"ex11-01.cpp" 208 ≡

```cpp
#include <iostream>
#include <cassert>
#include <vector>
#include <algorithm>
#include <functional>
using namespace std;

class U : public binary_function<U, U, bool> {
public:
  int id;
  bool operator()(const U& x, const U& y) const {
    return x.id >= y.id;
  }
  friend ostream& operator<<(ostream& o, const U& x) {
    o << x.id;
    return o;
  }
};

int main()
{
  vector<U> vector1(1000);
  for (int i = 0; i != 1000; ++i)
    vector1[i].id = 1000 - i - 1;
  sort(vector1.begin(), vector1.end(), not2(U()));
  for (int k = 0; k != 1000; ++k)
    assert (vector1[k].id == k);
  cout << " --- Ok." << endl;
  return 0;
}
```

11.3   Adaptors for Pointers to Functions

Adaptors for pointers to functions are provided to allow pointers to unary and binary functions to work with the other function adaptors provided in the library. These adaptors may also be useful by themselves in avoiding one form of "code bloat" (see Section 1.4) as we show by example in this section.

Although function objects can always be used in place of the older, less efficient technique of passing a pointer to a function, there are times when pointers to functions still should be used. Suppose, for example, that within the same program we need to use two different sets that differ only in the comparison functions passed to them:

```
set<string, less<string> > set1;
set<string, greater<string> > set2;
```

The problem with this is that the compiler is likely to duplicate most or all of the code that implements sets, even though most of it is identical in the two instances.

To avoid duplication, we can instead work with a single instance of **set** by using an adaptor for pointers to functions as the type of comparison function to be used in maintaining sorted order in the set:

```
set<string,
    pointer_to_binary_function<const string&,
                               const string&, bool> >
```

When constructing sets of this type, we supply an instance of this adaptor type created from a particular pointer to a binary function using **ptr_fun**, as in the following program.

Example 11.2: Illustrating the use of an adaptor for pointers to functions

```
"ex11-02.cpp" 209 ≡
    #include <iostream>
    #include <string>
    #include <set>
    using namespace std;

    bool less1(const string& x, const string& y)
    {
      return x < y;
    }

    bool greater1(const string& x, const string& y)
    {
      return x > y;
    }

    int main()
    {
      cout << "Illustrating the use of an adaptor"
           << " for pointers to functions." << endl;
```

```
typedef
  set<string,
      pointer_to_binary_function<const string&,
                                 const string&, bool> >
    set_type1;

set_type1 set1(ptr_fun(less1));

set1.insert("the");
set1.insert("quick");
set1.insert("brown");
set1.insert("fox");

set_type1::iterator i;
for (i = set1.begin(); i != set1.end(); ++i)
  cout << *i << " ";
cout << endl;

set_type1 set2(ptr_fun(greater1));

set2.insert("the");
set2.insert("quick");
set2.insert("brown");
set2.insert("fox");

for (i = set2.begin(); i != set2.end(); ++i)
  cout << *i << " ";
cout << endl;
return 0;
}
```

Output from Example 11.2

```
Illustrating the use of an adaptor for pointers to functions.
brown fox quick the
the quick fox brown
```

In this example there is only one instance of the **set** type, **set_type1**. Two **set_type1** objects are constructed: **set1**, which uses **ptr_fun(less1)** for its comparison object, and **set2**, which uses **ptr_fun(greater1)**. Because of the extra level of indirection involved with pointers to functions, programs such as this will run slightly slower than the corresponding programs with separate instances of `set` but with a considerable savings in executable file size.

Additional examples of the use of function adaptors appear in Chapters 13 and 15.

Part II

Putting It Together: Example Programs

In this part, we solve some simple but nontrivial programming problems using STL components. In Chapters 12 through 15 we explore variations on the theme of searching a dictionary for anagrams (words that can be formed by transposing the letters of a given word). In these chapters we repeatedly tackle the same or similar problems using different approaches, including (in Chapter 13) combining STL components with user-defined types. Chapter 16 gives a small example of defining a new iterator type and using it with existing STL components. The example program in Chapter 17 illustrates issues of combining STL with object-oriented programming. Chapter 18 uses STL to implement more complex data structures than are found in the previous examples. Finally, in Chapter 19 we discuss an approach to timing algorithms, giving insight into some of the performance-related design decisions involved in using STL.

CHAPTER 12

Program for Searching a Dictionary

In Part I the examples were small ones designed to illustrate individual STL components. Now, in Part II, we look at some slightly larger examples, ones that simultaneously demonstrate several STL components.

12.1 Finding Anagrams of a Given Word

Let's start with the problem of finding, in a given dictionary, all the anagrams of a given word. We'll develop a program that reads a dictionary from a file, then repeatedly accepts a word (or arbitrary string of letters) from the standard input stream, looks up all permutations of its letters in the dictionary, and outputs the words it finds. Following is an example of how we might interact with the program (all user input is underlined).

Output from Example 12.1

```
Anagram finding program:
finds all words in a dictionary that can
be formed with the letters of a given word.

First, enter the name of the file containing
the dictionary: diction

Reading the dictionary ...
The dictionary contains 20159 words.

Now type a word (or any string of letters),
```

and I'll see if it has any anagrams: <u>rseuce</u>
  cereus
  recuse
  rescue
  secure

Type another word (or the end-of-file char to stop): <u>nadeirga</u>
  drainage
  gardenia

Type another word (or the end-of-file char to stop): <u>grinch</u>
  Sorry, none found.

Type another word (or the end-of-file char to stop): <u>gonar</u>
  argon
  groan
  organ

Type another word (or the end-of-file char to stop):

The exact results will, of course, depend on the dictionary. The 20,159-word dictionary used in this example is available with the source code for all examples in this book, as described in Appendix D.

Here is an overview of the program, which we expand and explain in detail in the rest of the chapter.

Example 12.1: Program to find all anagrams of a given word, using a dictionary read from a file

"ex12-01.cpp" 216 ≡

```
#include <iostream>
#include <fstream>
#include <string>
#include <vector>
#include <algorithm>
#include <iterator>
using namespace std;

int main()
{
  cout << "Anagram finding program:\n"
    << "finds all words in a dictionary that can\n"
    << "be formed with the letters of a given word.\n" << endl;
  ⟨Get the dictionary name, and prepare to read it in 218⟩
```

⟨Copy words from dictionary file to a vector for random access 219⟩
⟨Repeatedly ask the user for a word and check it for anagrams 219a⟩
```
    return 0;
}
```

Literate Programming.

In presenting the example programs in Part II we use the "literate programming" style [10], in which code and its documentation are interspersed. In this style, no separate version of the code is maintained; instead, a computer program is used to extract from a single source file the file(s) needed for preparing the printed document (in this case, the LaTeX files from which this book is printed) and the file(s) containing the code to be compiled (in this case, C++ source files). The main idea behind literate programming is that many programs are more often read by humans than executed, so it's vitally important to make them readable and to ensure that documentation remains consistent with the code. When presenting a program in the literate programming style, we break it into small parts, define and describe the role of each part, and assemble the parts to make up the whole program. Another key idea is that the parts can be arranged in any order, including top-down or bottom-up development or some mixture (rather than the order required by the programming language rules).

With the literate programming support tool we use, Briggs's Nuweb [3], the program parts are named by phrases and are also automatically numbered (by Nuweb) according to the page number on which they appear, with parts on the same page distinguished by an appended letter. Parts are referred to in other code by their name and number.

For Example 12.1, we proceed top down, first presenting the overall program structure with several references to parts that are defined afterward. For example, part

⟨Copy words from dictionary file to a vector for random access 219⟩

is defined on page 219. In Chapter 14, on the other hand, we mostly define the parts first and then assemble them into the whole program at the end.

A few other points about literate programming are discussed in other sidebars in this chapter.

12.2 Interacting with the Standard String and I/O Streams Classes

We read the name of the file as a string, using the standard **string** class, then prepare to read the dictionary from the specified file using an **ifstream**.

⟨Get the dictionary name, and prepare to read it in 218⟩ ≡

```
cout << "First, enter the name of the file containing\n"
    << "the dictionary: " << flush;
string dictionary_name;
cin >> dictionary_name;
ifstream ifs(dictionary_name.c_str());
if (!ifs.is_open()) {
  cout << "Eh? Could not open file named "
      << dictionary_name << endl;
  exit(1);
}
```

Used in parts 216, 228, 238, 245.

In creating the input file stream **ifs** we are using the **string** class member function **c_str** to get the C-style character array that the **ifstream** constructor expects.

Literate Program Parts Can Often Be Used in Several Related Programs.

One of the advantages of the literate programming style is that a program part can be defined once and used in constructing different programs that are variations on a theme. The preceding part is used not only in the current program but also in three others in later chapters, on the pages noted in the "Used in ..." list just below the part definition.

For use here and later in the program, we define the type **string_input** as an istream iterator type. We then copy the dictionary file into a **vector** container using the generic **copy** algorithm and the **back_inserter** insert iterator to insert the words of the dictionary one by one at the end of the vector. Values are read from the dictionary stream until the **stream_input** iterator equals **string_input()**, the end-of-stream value.

⟨Copy words from dictionary file to a vector for random access 219⟩ ≡

```
cout << "\nReading the dictionary ..." << flush;
typedef istream_iterator<string> string_input;
vector<string> dictionary;
copy(string_input(ifs), string_input(),
    back_inserter(dictionary));
cout << "\nThe dictionary contains "
  << dictionary.size() << " words.\n\n";
```

Used in part 216.

After the dictionary has been read in, we report its size. The program is now ready to accept letter strings from the user and look them up. The look-ups are conducted using the generic **binary_search** algorithm, which requires the dictionary to be in alphabetical order. It's assumed here that the dictionary file was already in alphabetical order. (If not, the **sort** algorithm could be used to sort it by inserting the line

```
sort(dictionary.begin(), dictionary.end());
```

just after the dictionary is read.)

Input of the candidate words (or arbitrary letter strings) is controlled by an istream iterator j, set up for traversing the standard **cin** input stream until an end-of-stream indicator is hit:

⟨Repeatedly ask the user for a word and check it for anagrams 219a⟩ ≡

```
cout << "Now type a word (or any string of letters),\n"
  << "and I'll see if it has any anagrams: " << flush;
for (string_input j(cin); j != string_input(); ++j) {
  string word = *j;
  ⟨Search the dictionary for anagrams of word 219b⟩
  cout << "\nType another word "
      << "(or the end-of-file char to stop): " << flush;
}
```

Used in part 216.

In the body of the preceding loop, we generate all permutations of the letters of the given word and search the dictionary for each one.

⟨Search the dictionary for anagrams of word 219b⟩ ≡
    ⟨Start with letters of word in alphabetical order 220a⟩
    ⟨Repeatedly generate the next permutation and search for it 220b⟩

Used in part 219a.

A Literate Programming Part Can Refer to Other Parts.

As demonstrated in the preceding parts, a program part can contain references to other parts to any depth, but cycles in the part reference chain are not allowed. (The Nuweb processor issues a warning if it detects a cycle.)

We use repeated calls of the generic **next_permutation** algorithm to generate the permutations. The initial letter string given to **next_permutation** should be the one in which the letters appear in alphabetical order, so we use the generic **sort** algorithm to sort the characters. As Appendix B explains, the **string** class provides a random access iterator type and **begin** and **end** members. (A **string** is quite similar to a **vector<char>**).

⟨Start with letters of word in alphabetical order 220a⟩ ≡
```
    sort(word.begin(), word.end());
```

Used in part 219b.

The sorted word is the first permutation of the letters that the program will look for in the dictionary. So, for example, if the letters in **word** are **gonar**, then after sorting **word** will contain **agnor**.

12.3 Generating Permutations and Searching the Dictionary

The inner loop tests each permutation for membership in the dictionary:

⟨Repeatedly generate the next permutation and search for it 220b⟩ ≡
```
    bool found_one = false;
    do {
      if (binary_search(dictionary.begin(),
                        dictionary.end(),
                        word)) {
        cout << "  " << word << endl;
        found_one = true;
      }
    } while (next_permutation(word.begin(), word.end()));
    if (!found_one)
      cout << "  Sorry, none found.\n";
```

Used in part 219b.

The generic `binary_search` algorithm returns `true` if it finds the current candidate word in the dictionary, `false` otherwise.[1] The time for this search is proportional to the logarithm of the size of the dictionary.

If `word` is found in the dictionary, we send this permutation of the original letter sequence to the standard output stream.

The generic `next_permutation` algorithm is then used to change `word` into the next permutation of its characters, the permutation that follows in the lexicographical ordering of all permutations. (We sorted `word` initially, to start with the first permutation in this ordering.)

For example, with the letters `agnor`, the permutations in lexicographical order are `agnor`, `agnro`, `agonr`, `agorn`, `angor`, `angro`, ..., `argon`, ..., `groan`, ..., `organ`, ..., `ronga`. (The total number is $5! = 120$.)

If the last permutation in lexicographical order hasn't been reached, `next_permutation` puts the next permutation into `word` and returns `true`; otherwise it reverts `word` back to the first permutation in lexicographical order—the sorted one, that is—and returns `false`, terminating the inner loop.

12.4 Complete Program

The complete program file assembled from all the program parts looks like this:

```
#include <iostream>
#include <fstream>
#include <string>
#include <vector>
#include <algorithm>
#include <iterator>
using namespace std;

int main()
{
  cout << "Anagram finding program:\n"
    << "finds all words in a dictionary that can\n"
    << "be formed with the letters of a given word.\n" << endl;
  cout << "First, enter the name of the file containing\n"
```

---

[1] As noted in Chapter 5, STL provides three other generic algorithms based on binary searching: `lower_bound`, `upper_bound`, and `equal_range`. These algorithms return iterators that pinpoint the position or range of positions that contain values equal to the given value. They all run in logarithmic time.

```
          << "the dictionary: " << flush;
    string dictionary_name;
    cin >> dictionary_name;
    ifstream ifs(dictionary_name.c_str());
    if (!ifs.is_open()) {
      cout << "Eh? Could not open file named "
           << dictionary_name << endl;
      exit(1);
    }
    cout << "\nReading the dictionary ..." << flush;
    typedef istream_iterator<string> string_input;
    vector<string> dictionary;
    copy(string_input(ifs), string_input(),
         back_inserter(dictionary));
    cout << "\nThe dictionary contains "
      << dictionary.size() << " words.\n\n";
    cout << "Now type a word (or any string of letters),\n"
      << "and I'll see if it has any anagrams: " << flush;
    for (string_input j(cin); j != string_input(); ++j) {
      string word = *j;
      sort(word.begin(), word.end());
      bool found_one = false;
      do {
        if (binary_search(dictionary.begin(),
                          dictionary.end(),
                          word)) {
          cout << "  " << word << endl;
          found_one = true;
        }
      } while (next_permutation(word.begin(), word.end()));
      if (!found_one)
        cout << "  Sorry, none found.\n";
      cout << "\nType another word "
           << "(or the end-of-file char to stop): " << flush;
    }
    return 0;
}
```

In subsequent chapters we won't show the complete code assembled by Nuweb from the parts, since with a little practice one can read and understand programs more easily from their literate programming style development by parts. In any case, though, the program files are available on the Internet as discussed in Appendix D.

12.5   How Fast Is It?

This program is reasonably fast for short strings, but note that the number of permutations of a string of length N is $N!$, so it takes quite a while when N is greater than 8 or so. Although we don't revisit this look-up program per se in the following chapters, it could be reprogrammed for much faster operation using the approach taken in those chapters. (Exercise for the reader!)

Origins of Literate Programming.

Both the concept of literate programming and the first tools supporting it were introduced by D. E. Knuth, who invented the approach while constructing and documenting source code of his TeX documentation processing system (on top of which LaTeX was later developed by L. Lamport as a preprocessor). Knuth's original literate programming system, Web, has separate tools for extracting the code and the documentation, called `tangle` and `weave`, respectively. The programming language supported by Web is Pascal. Later S. Levy developed CWeb, supporting C programming initially and eventually C++ also. Nuweb is language independent, since, unlike Web or CWeb, it doesn't highlight keywords or use other special formatting conventions in typsetting the program code. This makes it somewhat simpler to use than CWeb.

CHAPTER 13

Program for Finding All Anagram Groups

The program developed in this chapter, like the program of Chapter 12, uses a dictionary, but the operations on the dictionary are more elaborate. The program searches the dictionary for all anagram groups, that is, groups of words that are permutations of each other, like `caret`, `carte`, `cater`, `crate` and `trace`.

In most of our previous examples, all the types were either built-in C++ types or types provided by the STL library. In the present example, we use library components with a type we define.

13.1   Finding Anagram Groups

The main idea of the program is to create an internal dictionary vector containing pairs of strings (see Sections 1.3.1 and 25.3 for discussion of the `pair` template class). These pairs of strings are set up as follows:

- The second member of a pair holds a word `w` from the dictionary file.

- The first member holds the string that results from sorting the letters of `w` into alphabetical order.

When these pairs are sorted using their first members as keys, all the words that are anagrams come together in consecutive positions of the vector. (Actually, the pairs containing those words come together.) For example, if the dictionary file contains the words

```
argon cater cereus groan maker organ
secure trace
```

then the vector of pairs will initially contain the words shown in the following table:

first	second
agnor	argon
acert	cater
ceersu	cereus
agnor	groan
aekmr	maker
agnor	organ
ceersu	secure
acert	trace

After sorting on the first members of these pairs it will contain these words:

first	second
acert	cater
acert	trace
aekmr	maker
agnor	argon
agnor	groan
agnor	organ
ceersu	cereus
ceersu	secure

Thus, anagram groups like **argon**, **groan**, and **organ** come together. The program can then make a single pass through the dictionary to find groups of pairs that agree in their first member and output the list of their second members as an anagram group. Singletons like

first	second
aekmr	maker

are ignored.

13.2 Defining a Data Structure to Work with STL

To implement this approach, we first define the following data structure:

⟨Define a structure, PS, for holding pairs of strings 227a⟩ ≡

```
struct PS : pair<string, string> {
  PS() : pair<string, string>(string(), string()) { }
  PS(const string& s) : pair<string, string>(s, s) {
    sort(first.begin(), first.end());
  }
  operator string() const { return second; }
};
```

Used in part 228.

This structure defines type **PS** as a struct derived from **pair<string, string>** using the STL **pair** template class (described in Sections 1.3.1 and 25.3). In general, if **p** is a **pair<T1, T2>** object, **p.first** refers to one member of the pair, of type **T1**, and **p.second** refers to the other, of type **T2**. The second constructor takes a string argument, stores copies of it in the **first** and **second** members of the pair, then sorts the characters of the **first** member. This constructor serves as a type conversion from **string** to **PS**, and **operator string()** provides a type conversion from **PS** back to **string**. The presence of these type conversions allows us to use the generic **copy** algorithm to copy strings from an input string into a vector of **PS** objects and from the vector to an output stream.

We could use type **pair<string, string>** itself instead of defining the **PS** structure. But then we would not be able to define the type conversions needed to use **copy**, and we would have to code the I/O with explicit loops.

13.3   Creating Function Objects for Comparisons

To use STL components to do operations like sorting and searching **PS** objects, we need to create two function objects—**firstLess** and **firstEqual**—to communicate to the components how we want to compare two **PS** objects.

⟨Define a function object for less-than comparisons of PS objects 227b⟩ ≡

```
struct FirstLess : binary_function<PS, PS, bool> {
  bool operator()(const PS& p, const PS& q) const
  {
    return p.first < q.first;
  }
} firstLess;
```

Used in part 228.

Thus, when **firstLess** is passed to algorithms such as **binary_search** or **sort**, it makes them base comparisons of **PS** objects on comparisons of their **first** members. Since the type of the **first** members of **PS** objects is **string**, the algorithms use the < operator defined on string objects. This is lexicographical ordering, precisely the normal alphabetical ordering we want.

In the same way, we define a function object **firstEqual** to handle equality of **PS** objects.

⟨Define a function object for equality comparisons of PS objects 228⟩ ≡

```
struct FirstEqual : binary_function<PS, PS, bool> {
  bool operator()(const PS& p, const PS& q) const
  {
    return p.first == q.first;
  }
} firstEqual;
```

Used in part 228.

We gather these definitions together in a small header file (which will also be used in Chapter 14).

"ps.h" 228 ≡

```
#include <functional>
using namespace std;
```
⟨Define a structure, PS, for holding pairs of strings 227a⟩
⟨Define a function object for less-than comparisons of PS objects 227b⟩
⟨Define a function object for equality comparisons of PS objects 228⟩

13.4   Complete Anagram Group Finding Program

We present the program in overview here and then explain the remaining details of its operation in the remainder of this chapter.

Example 13.1: Find all anagram groups in a dictionary, and print them to standard output stream

"ex13-01.cpp" 228 ≡

```
#include <algorithm>
#include <iostream>
#include <fstream>
#include <string>
#include <vector>
```

```
#include <iterator>
using namespace std;
#include "ps.h" // Definitions of PS, firstLess, firstEqual

int main() {
  cout << "Anagram group finding program:\n"
       << "finds all anagram groups in a dictionary.\n\n"
       << flush;

  ⟨Get the dictionary name, and prepare to read it in 218⟩
  ⟨Copy words from dictionary file to a vector of PS objects 229⟩
  ⟨Bring all anagram groups together 230a⟩
  ⟨Prepare to output the anagram groups 230b⟩
  ⟨Output all of the anagram groups 230c⟩
  return 0;
}
```

13.5   Reading the Dictionary into a Vector of PS Objects

The first part of the program is very similar to that of the program in Chapter 12: we read in the dictionary from a file and store it into a vector. However, instead of just storing each string read in, we store a **PS** object constructed from the string. The conversion from **string** to **PS** happens implicitly during the **copy** operation:

⟨Copy words from dictionary file to a vector of PS objects 229⟩ ≡

```
      cout << "\nReading the dictionary ..." << flush;
      typedef istream_iterator<string> string_input;

      vector<PS> word_pairs;
      copy(string_input(ifs), string_input(),
           back_inserter(word_pairs));
      cout << "\nSearching " << word_pairs.size()
        << " words for anagram groups..." << flush;
```

Used in parts 228, 238.

As part of the definition of the **PS(const string&)** constructor, the first member of the object is sorted, putting the letters in the string in alphabetical order. Thus, the **word_pairs** vector starts out with the structure shown in the first table in Section 13.1.

13.6   Using a Comparison Object to Sort Word Pairs

The next step of the algorithm is to use the function object `firstLess` to tell the generic `sort` algorithm how to order the PS objects based on the first member of every pair:

⟨Bring all anagram groups together 230a⟩ ≡
```
        sort(word_pairs.begin(), word_pairs.end(), firstLess);
```
Used in parts 228, 238.

This sort operation rearranges the vector element pairs so that all the pairs containing words that are anagrams come together in consecutive positions of the vector. At this point, the `word_pairs` vector has the structure shown in the second table in Section 13.1.

13.7   Using an Equality Predicate Object to Search for Adjacent Equal Elements

Finally, we prepare to output the anagram groups by setting up constant iterators pointing to the beginning and end of the vector:

⟨Prepare to output the anagram groups 230b⟩ ≡
```
        vector<PS>::const_iterator j = word_pairs.begin(),
                              finis = word_pairs.end(), k;
```
Used in part 228.

In the output loop that follows, we use iterator j to scan the vector, looking for the beginning of an anagram group.

⟨Output all of the anagram groups 230c⟩ ≡
```
        cout << "\n\nThe anagram groups are:" << endl;
        while (true) {
            ⟨Advance j to the start of the next anagram group (if any) 231a⟩
            ⟨Test for completion 231b⟩
            ⟨Find the end position, k, of the anagram group that begins at j 232a⟩
            ⟨Output the anagram group in positions j to k 232b⟩
            j = k;
        }
```
Used in part 228.

We first use `adjacent_find`, a generic search algorithm. Although j is a `vector<PS>::const_iterator`, recall that this means that the value j points to is constant, not that j itself is constant. Therefore it is perfectly reasonable to assign a new value to j:

⟨Advance j to the start of the next anagram group (if any) 231a⟩ ≡
```
    j = adjacent_find(j, finis, firstEqual);
```
Used in parts 230c, 239.

This advances j to the first position in **word_pairs** where `firstEqual(*j, *(j+1))` is **true**; if no such adjacent values are in the range, then `finis` is returned.

If the end of the dictionary has been reached, the loop and the program both terminate:

⟨Test for completion 231b⟩ ≡
```
    if (j == finis) break;
```
Used in parts 230c, 239, 245.

Otherwise, we need to search from the position j+1 onward for the pair whose first element is not equal to the first element of the pair pointed to by j. The details of how this is done are presented in the next section.

13.8 Using a Function Adaptor to Obtain a Predicate Object

We could conduct the necessary search with the generic `find` algorithm, except that we want to consider the search successful when we find a value not equal to a given value rather than equal to it. So we use `find_if`, the version of `find` that takes a predicate object. Since we don't already have a suitable predicate object available to pass to `find_if`, we use a couple of function adaptors to manufacture one out of `firstEqual`.

We first apply `bind1st` to `firstEqual` and the value *j to produce a function object that takes a single argument x and returns true if *j == x, false otherwise.

The resulting predicate function object is the opposite of the sense needed, so we apply to it another function adaptor, `not1`. The result is a predicate function object that returns **true** if *j != x and **false** otherwise, which is precisely what we need:

⟨Find the end position, k, of the anagram group that begins at j 232a⟩ ≡

```
    k = find_if(j + 1, finis, not1(bind1st(firstEqual, *j)));
```

Used in parts 230c, 239.

13.9 Copying the Anagram Group to the Output Stream

Thus the iterator j returned by `adjacent_find` and the iterator k returned by `find_if` delimit the range of word pairs containing words that are anagrams in their second components, and we next

⟨Output the anagram group in positions j to k 232b⟩ ≡

```
    cout << "  ";
    copy(j, k, ostream_iterator<string>(cout, " "));
    cout << endl;
```

Used in part 230c.

to put the words on the standard output stream. Note that during the `copy` operation there is an implicit conversion of a `PS` word pair to a `string`: when a `PS` object is converted to a `string`, its second element is returned.

Finally, we advance j to k to continue looking for the next anagram group.

13.10 Output of the Anagram Program

Here is the output of this program (user input is underlined) when given the dictionary in the `diction` file available with the source code (see Appendix D).

Output from Example 13.1

```
    Anagram group finding program:
    finds all anagram groups in a dictionary.

    First, enter the name of the file containing
    the dictionary: diction

    Reading the dictionary ...
    Searching 20159 words for anagram groups...

    The anagram groups are:
```

232

```
hasn't shan't
drawback backward
bacterial calibrate
cabaret abreact
bandpass passband
abroad aboard
banal nabla
balsa basal
saccade cascade
coagulate catalogue
ascertain sectarian
activate cavitate
vacuolate autoclave
caveat vacate
charisma archaism
maniac caiman
caviar variac
scalar lascar rascal sacral
causal casual
drainage gardenia
emanate manatee
```

and so on. The program finds a total of 865 anagram groups in this 20,159-word dictionary.

CHAPTER 14

Better Anagram Program: Using the List and Map Containers

One problem we might have with the anagram finder we developed in Chapter 13 is that the output is a bit unorganized; we might like to see the anagram groups in order of maximum size first. In this chapter we extend the program so that it organizes its output in this way, and in the process we illustrate the use of both another of the sequence containers, `list`, and one of the sorted associative containers, `map`.

14.1 Data Structure Holding Iterator Pairs

In this program we create another data structure using the template class `pair`. This pair is called PPS, and its objects hold pairs of iterators that point into a vector of PS structures (which we developed in the last chapter).

⟨Define a data structure for holding iterator pairs 235⟩ ≡

```
typedef vector<PS>::const_iterator PSi;
typedef pair<PSi, PSi> PPS;
```

Used in part 238.

A PPS iterator pair will be used to delimit a range of dictionary entries whose second members are the words of an anagram group. This is shown in Figure 14.1. Note that the diagram shows the second iterator in a PPS pair pointing to the position past the end of the positions with equal words, in keeping with the standard convention for STL iterator ranges.

235

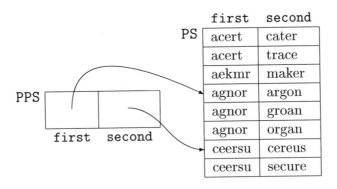

Figure 14.1: PPS indicating an anagram group

14.2 Storing Information in a Map of Lists

Now, after sorting the dictionary vector to get the anagram groups together, we scan it as before, but instead of outputting each anagram group as we find it, we save its range in a PPS pair. To make it easy to output the groups according to their size, we save all the ranges of a given size s in a list of PPS pairs, and we store the list as the value associated with s in a map:

⟨Set up the map from group sizes to lists of groups of that size 236⟩ ≡
```
    typedef map<int, list<PPS>, greater<int> > map_1;
    map_1 groups;
```
Used in part 238.

That is, for a given integer group size s, groups[s] will hold a list of PPS objects, and the map is organized so that iterating through it from groups.begin() to groups.end() produces the entries in order from largest to smallest. (To get smallest-to-largest order we would have used the default less<int> as the function type passed to map.)

Figure 14.2 illustrates this data structure. Recall that each PPS pair indicates an anagram group in the vector of PS entries, as shown in Figure 14.1.

So when we generate a PPS(j, k) object, we just have to insert it into the list groups[k-j], since k-j is the size of the range (and therefore of the anagram group):

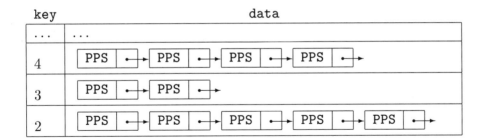

Figure 14.2: **groups** map, associating integers with lists of PPS

⟨Store the pair j, k in the groups map 237a⟩ ≡
```
if (k-j > 1)
    // Save the positions j and k delimiting the anagram
    // group in the list of groups of size k-j:
    groups[k-j].push_back(PPS(j,k));
```

Used in part 239.

14.3 Outputting the Anagram Groups in Order of Size

Once the whole vector of pairs has been scanned, we iterate through the groups map as follows:

⟨Output the anagram groups in descending order of size 237b⟩ ≡
```
map_1::const_iterator m;
for (m = groups.begin(); m != groups.end(); ++m) {
    cout << "\nAnagram groups of size " << m->first << ":\n";
    list<PPS>::const_iterator l;
    for (l = m->second.begin(); l != m->second.end(); ++l) {
        cout << "    ";
        j = l->first;  // beginning of the anagram group
        k = l->second; // end of the anagram group
        copy(j, k, ostream_iterator<string>(cout, " "));
        cout << endl;
    }
}
```

Used in part 238.

The size of group **m** is given by **m->first**, and **m->second** is the corresponding entry, a **list<PPS>** object. With the inner for loop, we iterate over the

237

elements of the list. Each list entry *l is a pair whose first and second members are **vector<PS>** iterators giving a range in the **word_pairs** vector of entries that represents an anagram group, so we just have to copy those entries to the output stream. Again, during the copy there is an implicit conversion of pairs to strings.

14.4   Better Anagram Program

Putting all this together, we have the following example program.

Example 14.1: Finding all anagram groups in order of decreasing size

"ex14-01.cpp" 238 ≡

```
#include <algorithm>
#include <iostream>
#include <fstream>
#include <string>
#include <vector>
#include <list>
#include <map>
#include <iterator>
using namespace std;
#include "ps.h" // Definitions of PS, firstLess, firstEqual

⟨Define a data structure for holding iterator pairs 235⟩

int main() {
  cout << "Anagram group finding program:\n"
       << "finds all anagram groups in a dictionary.\n\n"
       << flush;

  ⟨Get the dictionary name, and prepare to read it in 218⟩
  ⟨Copy words from dictionary file to a vector of PS objects 229⟩
  ⟨Bring all anagram groups together 230a⟩

  ⟨Set up the map from group sizes to lists of groups of that size 236⟩
  ⟨Find all of the groups and save their positions in the groups map 239⟩
  ⟨Output the anagram groups in descending order of size 237b⟩
  return 0;
}
```

Recall that the header file **ps.h** was defined in Chapter 13. The only part remaining to be defined is the following, expressed mainly in terms of constituent parts presented earlier in this or the previous chapter.

⟨Find all of the groups and save their positions in the groups map 239⟩ ≡

```
cout << "\n\nThe anagram groups are" << endl;
PSi j = word_pairs.begin(), finis = word_pairs.end(), k;
while (true) {
    ⟨Advance j to the start of the next anagram group (if any) 231a⟩
    ⟨Test for completion 231b⟩
    ⟨Find the end position, k, of the anagram group that begins at j 232a⟩
    ⟨Store the pair j, k in the groups map 237a⟩
    j = k;
}
```

Used in part 238.

14.5   Output of the Program

When this program is applied to the 20,159-word dictionary available with
the source code (see Appendix D), the first part of the output is as follows
(user input is underlined).

Output from Example 14.1

```
Anagram group finding program:
finds all anagram groups in a dictionary.

First, enter the name of the file containing
the dictionary: diction

Reading the dictionary ...
Searching 20159 words for anagram groups...

The anagram groups are

Anagram groups of size 5:
   crate carte cater caret trace

Anagram groups of size 4:
   scalar lascar rascal sacral
   bate beat beta abet
   glare lager large regal
   mantle mantel mental lament
   peal pale leap plea
   leapt plate pleat petal
   slate steal stale least
   mane name mean amen
   mate team tame meat
```

```
        pare pear reap rape
        tea ate eat eta
        cereus recuse rescue secure
        edit tide tied diet
        vile live evil veil
        item mite emit time
        rinse siren resin risen
        stripe sprite esprit priest

Anagram groups of size 3:
        abed bead bade
        bread debar beard
        brad bard drab
        brae bare bear
        garb grab brag
        tuba tabu abut
        came mace acme
        cavern carven craven
        secant stance ascent
        avocet octave vocate
        care acre race
        infarct frantic infract
        gander danger garden
```

and so on. In this dictionary the program finds a total of 79 anagram groups of size 3 and 768 of size 2.

14.6   Why Use a Map Container?

Looking back over this example, what were the advantages of using a **map** to associate lists of word groups with integer sizes? It would appear that we could have just used a small array or vector, since we aren't likely to have very large groups of anagrams, even with a large dictionary (the maximum size is 5 with the **diction** file). The key advantages of maps are as follows:

- *No size dependence.* With an array, we would have to worry about how big it should be (is 20 big enough?), and no matter how big we made it, someone might come along with an anomalous dictionary with larger groups of anagrams (for example, one in which a word is simply repeated many times).

- *Automatic expansion.* Using a **vector**, with its expansion capability, would help to avoid the problem with arrays but not entirely automatically. Whenever we found a group larger than the current vector size, we would have to expand the vector to that size and initialize the new entries to empty lists.

By using a **map**, we avoid these problems completely.

CHAPTER 15

Faster Anagram Program: Using Multimaps

Often when we first start thinking about implementing an application, we are not sure which of several possible approaches would be the most efficient. As we pointed out in Chapter 6, one of the great advantages of building implementations with STL is that it is possible to try different data structures and algorithms in the implementations without making drastic changes to the code. In this chapter we will illustrate this point by modifying the anagram group finding program once more. Our goal this time is not to enhance the output, as it was in Chapter 14, but to see if a different way of storing the dictionary makes the program any faster (it turns out that it does).

15.1 Finding Anagram Groups, Version 3

The pair-of-strings data structure PS used in the anagram programs of the preceding two chapters provides a way to associate a string s with another string that results from sorting the letters of s. Let's now look at another way to make such associations using a multimap, one of the STL sorted associative containers. Since these containers are designed for efficient handling of the associations, it seems worth exploring whether using one in the anagram finding application might be more efficient than storing the PS objects in a vector.

A multimap allows us to store multiple keys of a given type Key and to efficiently retrieve values of another type T based on the stored Key. In the program developed in this chapter, both Key and T are the string type. We make an entry into the multimap for each word in the dictionary using

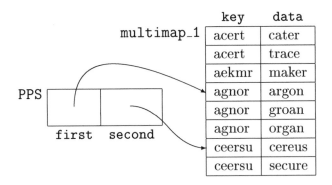

Figure 15.1: PPS indicating an anagram group

the letter-sorted version of the word as the key and the original word as the associated value.

This is essentially the same approach as with the vector of PS objects used in Chapters 13 and 14. Indeed, as shown in Figure 15.1, the data structure is virtually identical to the one in the previous chapter, but with a multimap the entries are automatically kept in sorted order, so *there is no need to explicitly sort them* as we did with the vector. The iterator type provided by a multimap takes us through the entries according to their sorted order, so carrying out the search for anagram groups is very similar to the way we did it in the previous chapters using a vector.

Sorting the dictionary according to the first members of the PS objects is the main part of the computation that might be made faster. Why do we suspect that it might be faster to use a multimap than a vector? Putting objects into a vector and sorting the vector can be one of the most efficient sorting methods, but only if the objects are small enough to be easily moved around in the vector. With large objects, it is more efficient to work with pointers, which are smaller than the objects. Although the PS objects are not particularly large, they could be large enough that sorting methods based on pointer manipulations would be faster than methods based on moving the objects. Since multimaps (and the other STL sorted associative containers) achieve sorted order using pointer manipulations, it is worth exploring whether they can speed up the sorting required in the anagram program.

We now present the program, followed by details about key points in the implementation.

Example 15.1: Finding all anagram groups in a given dictionary of words

"ex15-01.cpp" 245 ≡

```
#include <algorithm>
#include <iostream>
#include <fstream>
#include <string>
#include <list>
#include <map>
#include <iterator>
using namespace std;

typedef multimap<string, string> multimap_1;
⟨Define PS as multimap_1::value_type 247a⟩
typedef multimap_1::const_iterator PSi;

typedef pair<PSi, PSi> PPS;

int main() {
  cout << "Anagram group finding program:\n"
    << "finds all anagram groups in a dictionary.\n\n";

  ⟨Get the dictionary name, and prepare to read it in 218⟩

  cout << "\nReading the dictionary ..." << flush;

  // Copy words from dictionary file to
  // a multimap:
  typedef istream_iterator<string> string_input;
  multimap_1 word_pairs;
  ⟨Copy the dictionary to the multimap 247b⟩

  cout << "\nSearching " << word_pairs.size()
    << " words for anagram groups..." << flush;

  // Set up the map from anagram group sizes to lists of
  // groups of that size:
  typedef map<int, list<PPS>, greater<int> > map_1;
  map_1 groups;

  // Find all the anagram groups and save their
  // positions in the groups map:
  cout << "\n\nThe anagram groups are: " << endl;
  ⟨Prepare to iterate through the multimap entries 247c⟩
```

```
while (true) {
  // Make j point to the next anagram
  // group, or to the end of the multimap:
  ⟨Find adjacent map entries that are equal 248a⟩
  ⟨Test for completion 231b⟩

  ⟨Find the end of a series of equal map entries 248b⟩
  ⟨Get the size of the range of equal items and store the range 249a⟩

  // Prepare to continue search at position k:
  j = k;
}

// Iterate through the groups map to output the anagram
// groups in order of decreasing size:
map_1::const_iterator m;
for (m = groups.begin(); m != groups.end(); ++m) {

  cout << "\nAnagram groups of size "
    << m->first << ":\n";

  list<PPS>::const_iterator l;
  for (l = m->second.begin();
       l != m->second.end(); ++l) {
    cout << "    ";
    ⟨Print the anagram groups 249b⟩
    cout << endl;
  }
}
return 0;
}
```

15.2 Declaration of the Multimap

In the declaration

```
typedef multimap<string, string> multimap_1;
```

we define `multimap_1` as a type abbreviation for a type of multimap whose types `Key` and `T` are both strings and whose entries are ordered according to the usual less-than ordering of the keys. The type of the entries in a `multimap_1` container is

```
pair<const string, string>
```

and this type is given by `multimap_1::value_type`. In the next declaration we use this type to define another type abbreviation, PS, to be used later in the program:

⟨Define PS as `multimap_1::value_type` 247a⟩ ≡
```
    typedef multimap_1::value_type PS;
```

Used in part 245.

This PS type is similar to the PS type defined in the previous chapter, but this time we do not have to define any conversions between PS objects and `strings` or any function objects for comparing PS objects. Instead, we can use facilities that are provided automatically by the `multimap` type.

15.3   Reading the Dictionary into the Multimap

In the first phase of the program, after creating an empty multimap called `word_pairs`, we read each string from the input stream and create a sorted version of it in another `string word`. We then insert an entry in multimap `word_pairs` with `word` as the key and the original string as the associated value. The code that carries out the reading, sorting, and inserting is

⟨Copy the dictionary to the multimap 247b⟩ ≡
```
    for (string_input in(ifs); in != string_input(); ++in) {
      string word = *in;
      sort(word.begin(), word.end());
      word_pairs.insert(PS(word, *in));
    }
```
Used in part 245.

15.4   Finding the Anagram Groups in the Multimap

Next we set up the `groups` map as in the previous version and prepare to iterate through the `word_pairs` multimap to find all the groups of adjacent entries with equal keys.

⟨Prepare to iterate through the multimap entries 247c⟩ ≡
```
    PSi j = word_pairs.begin(), finis = word_pairs.end(), k;
```
Used in part 245.

This declaration sets up iteration through the multimap entries in the order corresponding to the comparison function supplied in the definition of multimap_1, which in this case defaults to less<string>.

In the while loop that follows the initialization, the basic strategy used is the same as that in previous versions of the anagram program; in fact, we could have programmed the loop almost identically if we had defined a function object similar to firstEqual for comparing PS objects.

With multimaps, however, we can take advantage of the value_comp member function, which provides a function object for comparing entries based on comparison of their keys using the given key comparison object, which for multimap_1 is the default comparison less<string>. This function is used in constructing the predicate, which, when passed to the STL adjacent_find function, allows us to determine the next anagram group.

The goal is to determine a predicate that allows us to find the next multimap entry that is greater than the previous entry. This is done by taking advantage of the following fact: in the multimap, for any two adjacent entries u and v, either u is less than v or u is equal to v. Hence, by searching for adjacent entries u and v such that u is not less than v, we can find the first ones that are equal.

Since the word_pairs.value_comp() predicate object returns true for operands u and v such that u is less than v, all we need to do is negate it using the binary function adaptor not2 to obtain the predicate object we need to pass to adjacent_find:

⟨Find adjacent map entries that are equal 248a⟩ ≡
```
    j = adjacent_find(j, finis,
                      not2(word_pairs.value_comp()));
```
Used in part 245.

This call to adjacent_find locates the beginning of a run of entries that are equal in their keys. As in the previous versions, find_if can be used to locate the end of the run, this time constructing the predicate object using word_pairs.value_comp() and bind1st:

⟨Find the end of a series of equal map entries 248b⟩ ≡
```
    k = find_if(j, finis,
                bind1st(word_pairs.value_comp(), *j));
```
Used in part 245.

As in the version in Chapter 14, we then compute the distance from the beginning position j and the ending position k and save this pair of iterators for later output. In Chapter 14 we could compute this distance as k - j, but that was possible only because j and k were random access iterators, for which the - operator is provided. Here j and k are bidirectional iterators, and thus the - operator is not available. Instead, we call the generic distance function:

⟨Get the size of the range of equal items and store the range 249a⟩ ≡
```
multimap_1::size_type n = distance(j, k);
if (n > 1)
    // Save the positions j and k delimiting the anagram
    // group in the list of groups of size n:
    groups[n].push_back(PPS(j, k));
```
Used in part 245.

The distance function takes linear time and is generally to be avoided, but it is available for special cases such as this, in which we expect the searches to be short. Section 20.7 discusses the distance function.

15.5 Outputting the Anagram Groups in Order of Size

This phase of the program is quite similar to the one in Chapter 14. The only difference is that now we cannot use copy to place the PS objects on the output stream, since we don't have a type conversion from our current PS objects to strings. Instead we use a for loop:

⟨Print the anagram groups 249b⟩ ≡
```
j = l->first;  // Beginning of the anagram group
k = l->second; // End of the anagram group
for (; j != k; ++j)
    cout << j->second << " ";
```
Used in part 245.

15.6 Output of the Program

The output of this version of the anagram group finding program is the same as that from the version given in Chapter 14.

15.7   How Fast Is It?

Timings of this version of the program show it to be about 30% faster than the version of Chapter 14. The second and third phases of the program may be slightly slower in the new version (because iteration with multimap iterators is slower than with vector iterators), so the speed gain comes in the first phase where the internal dictionary is stored in a multimap, with sorting occurring implicitly rather than in a vector, which has to be sorted explicitly.

Chapter 16

Defining an Iterator Class

As we hope the examples of the preceding chapters have shown, one of the most attractive features of STL is the way its component interfaces are designed, allowing algorithms and data structures to be fitted together in a myriad of different ways.

This structure not only provides a huge amount of functionality relative to the size of the library source code, it is also the reason that STL is better suited than other software libraries to be the basis for developing more extensive and more specialized libraries. Of course, most STL users will probably not become developers of major new extensions, but many will at some point have occasion to develop simple new components. In this chapter we go through a small exercise of developing such a component, an iterator adaptor that is useful for debugging or optimizing programs that use iterators.

16.1 New Kind of Iterator: Counting Iterator

We define a new kind of iterator called a *counting iterator*, which does just what a normal iterator does plus keeping track of how many operations, such as ++ operations, are done on the iterator. Upon request, this counting iterator can print out the count(s) it has accumulated, thereby providing usage statistics. Consider the following code.

Example 16.1: Demonstrating a counting iterator class

"ex16-01.cpp" 251 ≡
```
    #include <iostream>
    #include <algorithm>
```

```
#include <string>
using namespace std;

⟨Define counting iterator class 253a⟩

int main()
{
    cout << "Demonstrating a counting iterator class." << endl;
    int x[] = {12, 4, 3, 7, 17, 9, 11, 6};
    counting_iterator<int*> i(&x[0], "Curly"),
                            j(&x[0], "Moe"),
                            end(&x[8], "Larry");
    cout << "Traversing array x\n"
         << "  from i (Curly) to end (Larry)\n";
    while (i != end) {
       cout << *i << endl;
       ++i;
    }
    cout << "After the traversal:\n";
    i.report(cout);
    end.report(cout);
    cout << "Assigning j (Moe) to i (Curly)."
         << endl;
    i = j;
    cout << "Searching the array\n"
         << "  from i (Moe) to end (Larry)\n"
         << "  using find\n";
    counting_iterator<int*> k = find(i, end, 9);
    cout << "After the find:\n";
    k.report(cout);
    i.report(cout);
    end.report(cout);
    return 0;
}
```

In this program the calls of the **report** member function are supposed
to print the identity of the iterator in terms of the name given to it in the
constructor call, the version number (initially 1 and incremented each time
a copy is made of the iterator), and the number of **++** operations that have
been done on the iterator. For example, the first call, `i.report(cout)`,
should print

```
Iterator Curly, version 1, reporting 8 ++ operations
```

because in the while loop `++i` is executed eight times. To make this work, we must define `counting_iterator` as a class whose objects behave as iterators but also keep track of how many times `++` has been performed on them.

For the sake of brevity, we restrict our attention to the forward iterator category. That is, we provide an iterator adaptor that converts any forward iterator (an iterator that provides at least the operations of a forward iterator and could provide more) into a forward iterator that traverses a sequence in the same way as the original iterator does while also keeping track of how many times `++` operations are applied to it. This new iterator also has a `report` member function capable of displaying its accumulated statistics.

16.2 Counting Iterator Class

Here is the form of the class definition:

⟨Define counting iterator class 253a⟩ ≡
```
    template <typename ForwardIterator>
    class counting_iterator {
    private:
      ⟨Define private data members 253b⟩
    public:
      typedef counting_iterator<ForwardIterator> self;
      ⟨Define types required for adaptation by other iterator adaptors 254⟩
      ⟨Define default constructor 255c⟩
      ⟨Define main constructor 255a⟩
      ⟨Define copy constructor 255b⟩
      ⟨Define *, ==, !=, and prefix and postfix ++ 255d⟩
      ⟨Define statistics reporting member function 256⟩
    };
```
Used in part 251.

This class definition begins with the declaration of the private data members needed to keep track of the state of the iterator (`current`), the number of times `++` has been applied to it (`plus_count`), and the name and version number used to identify the iterator in the copy constructor and report function.

⟨Define private data members 253b⟩ ≡
```
    ForwardIterator current;
    int plus_count;
    string name;
    int version;
```
Used in part 253a.

To properly define some members of `counting_iterator`, we need to know some of the types associated with the `ForwardIterator` template parameter, such as its `value_type` and `reference` type. We can extract this information using the `iterator_traits` class. In turn, we can define these types and other useful types for `counting_iterators`, thus providing this type information for later use by adaptors that might be applied to this kind of iterator. (In general, providing these typedefs in an STL component is part of what's required to make the component "adaptable.")

⟨Define types required for adaptation by other iterator adaptors 254⟩ ≡
```
    typedef typename iterator_traits<ForwardIterator>::value_type
            value_type;
    typedef typename iterator_traits<ForwardIterator>::reference
            reference;
    typedef typename iterator_traits<ForwardIterator>::pointer
            pointer;
    typedef typename
            iterator_traits<ForwardIterator>::difference_type
            difference_type;
    typedef forward_iterator_tag iterator_category;
```
Used in part 253a.

For any iterator type, including pointers, `iterator_traits<Iterator>` defines various nested types that indicate the properties of the iterator. See Chapter 20 for a more detailed discussion of `iterator_traits`.

Notice that since we are restricting our implementation to the forward iterator operations, we explicitly use `forward_iterator_tag` for the iterator category. Even if the original iterator type is a random access iterator, the counting iterator will merely be a forward iteratory. If we were creating a more general iterator adaptor, we might want our new iterator to be in the same category as the original adapted iterator. In this case, we would say

```
    typedef typename iterator_traits<Iterator>::iterator_category
            iterator_category;
```

We would, of course, also need to implement all the random access iterator operations.

The primary constructor takes an iterator that will be adapted and a name for the counting iterator. The count is initialized to 0, and the version number is set to 1.

⟨Define main constructor 255a⟩ ≡
```
    counting_iterator(ForwardIterator first, const string& n)
      : current(first), plus_count(0), name(n), version(1) {}
```
Used in part 253a.

The copy constructor copies these data members, except that **version** is incremented, and reports the name and new version number on the standard output stream.

⟨Define copy constructor 255b⟩ ≡
```
    counting_iterator(const self& other) : current(other.current),
      plus_count(other.plus_count), name(other.name),
      version(other.version + 1)
    {
       cout << "copying " << name
            << ", new version is "
            << version << endl;
    }
```
Used in part 253a.

Having a "talking copy constructor" like this can aid greatly in understanding where and how many times iterator objects are being copied.

Although it's not needed for the program in this chapter, we define a default constructor in order to meet the requirements for forward iterators.

⟨Define default constructor 255c⟩ ≡
```
    counting_iterator()
      : current(0), plus_count(0), name("null"), version(1) {}
```
Used in part 253a.

Operators ==, !=, and both prefix and postfix versions of ++ are provided, according to the STL requirements on forward iterators (see Section 20.3). We simply apply the same operation to the underlying iterator, **current**. In the function for **operator++**, however, we also increment the operation count, **plus_count**.

⟨Define *, ==, !=, and prefix and postfix ++ 255d⟩ ≡
```
    reference operator*()
      // dereference
    {
       return *current;
```

```
        }

        bool operator==(const self& other) const
          // test for equality
        {
          return current == other.current;
        }

        bool operator!=(const self& other) const
          // test for inequality
        {
          return current != other.current;
        }

        self& operator++()
         // prefix ++
        {
          ++current;
          ++plus_count;
          return *this;
        }

        self operator++(int)
          // postfix ++
        {
          self tmp = *this;
          ++(*this);
          return tmp;
        }
```

Used in part 253a.

Note that the postfix ++ is defined simply in terms of the prefix version.

The reporting function takes an **ostream** argument and writes its statistics to that output stream.

⟨Define statistics reporting member function 256⟩ ≡

```
        void report(ostream& o) const
          // Display statistics on stream o
        {
          o << "Iterator " << name << ", version " << version
            << ", reporting  " << plus_count
            << "  ++ operations " << endl;
        }
```

Used in part 253a.

With this definition of `counting_iterator`, here is the complete output of the sample program given at the beginning of the chapter.

Output from Example 16.1

```
Demonstrating a counting iterator class.
Traversing array x
  from i (Curly) to end (Larry)
12
4
3
7
17
9
11
6
After the traversal:
Iterator Curly, version 1, reporting  8  ++ operations
Iterator Larry, version 1, reporting  0  ++ operations
Assigning j (Moe) to i (Curly).
Searching the array
  from i (Moe) to end (Larry)
  using find
Copying Moe, new version is 2
Copying Larry, new version is 2
Copying Moe, new version is 3
After the find:
Iterator Moe, version 3, reporting  5  ++ operations
Iterator Moe, version 1, reporting  0  ++ operations
Iterator Larry, version 1, reporting  0  ++ operations
```

Note that calling the `find` function causes `i` and `end` to be copied (because the iterator parameters to `find` are value parameters), and the final value of the copy of `i` (Moe, version 2) is copied when returning the result in `k` (Moe, version 3).

Since we defined `counting_iterator` as an iterator adaptor (it has an iterator class as a template parameter), we can use it to convert the iterator type associated with any of the STL container classes into a counting iterator. For example, to declare a counting iterator `i` usable with `list<char>`, we can say,

```
list<char> l;
counting_iterator<list<char>::iterator> i(l.begin(), "Shemp");
```

As we have defined it, `counting_iterator` produces iterators of the forward category (it would more properly be called `forward_counting_iterator`). Thus the iterators it produces cannot be used with STL algorithms that require bidirectional or random access iterators, but defining counting iterator adaptors for these categories is a straightforward exercise (if you are interested in trying this exercise, see Sections 20.4 and 20.5 for discussion of the requirements on iterators of these categories).

In summary, an iterator adaptor such as `counting_iterator` can confirm or reveal a great deal of information about the way an STL generic algorithm or user code uses iterators, and such information can be very useful in debugging or optimizing programs. We hope this example also illustrates some of the main issues in defining other kinds of iterator adaptors or other new software components that are compatible with STL.

CHAPTER 17

Combining STL with Object-Oriented Programming

Many people's initial reaction to STL is "But it's not object-oriented!" It's true that STL makes little use of class inheritance and none at all of virtual functions, two of the hallmarks of C++ object-oriented programming.[1] But STL gives up little in omitting use of these language features. Through its innovative use of templates and framework of fine-grained, interchangeable components, STL achieves most of the flexibility that one ordinarily finds in programs that make heavy use of inheritance and virtual functions while gaining a great deal in terms of efficiency.

Nevertheless, there remain valid reasons for using derived classes and virtual functions in some settings, and it is quite possible to combine these techniques with STL to good advantage. Two reasons to do so are as follows:

- *Having containers that hold objects of different types.* We may need to store objects of different types in a single container; this is known as *heterogeneous storage*, versus the *homogeneous storage* directly provided by STL's template container classes.

- *Avoiding "code bloat."* Even if we need only homogeneous storage in any one container, we may need many different instances of the same container type, leading to the problem of "code bloat." For example, having `list<int>`, `list<string>`, `list<vector<int> >`, and so on,

---

[1]The other two language features that are usually included among those considered essential for full-blown object-oriented programming are data abstraction (encapsulation) and polymorphism, both of which are heavily ingrained in STL.

in the same program results in several slightly different copies of the `list` class code present in our executable file.[2]

In this chapter we show in a simple example how STL components and generic programming techniques can be combined with class inheritance and virtual functions to achieve one or both of these goals at some cost in efficiency and compile-time checking.

17.1   Using Inheritance and Virtual Functions

The example is based on the "shapes" example in Section 6.4 of *The C++ Programming Language* by Bjarne Stroustrup [20]. This is a simple program for drawing geometric shapes on a screen, used to illustrate object-oriented programming techniques. It consists of the following:

- *Screen manager:* low-level routines and data structures defining the screen. It knows about points and straight lines only.

- *Shape library:* set of definitions of general shapes, such as rectangles and circles, and standard routines for manipulating them.

- *Application program:* set of application-specific definitions and code that uses them.

The shape library organizes the different shapes it supports into a simple class hierarchy consisting of a **shape** base class and derived **line** and **rectangle** classes. Operations for drawing and moving shapes are defined as virtual functions in class **shape** and are given specific meanings for each derived shape in their respective derived classes. This organization allows all shapes to be drawn or moved via the interface provided by class **shape**. It also happens to allow objects of different types (**rectangles** and **lines**) to be stored in the same container, since they can be stored using **shape*** pointers.

The details of the screen manager and shapes library can be found in *The C++ Programming Language*. The header files **screen.h** and **shape.h** and corresponding implementation files **screen.cpp** and **shape.cpp** are replicated in Appendix C. The exact details are not particularly important for

---

[2]In theory, compilers could do "code sharing" in many cases. For example, if `sizeof(T1) == sizeof(T2)`, then most of the code for `list<T1>` and `list<T2>` could be shared, since most of it is independent of the type of elements stored. But current production C++ compilers seem to make little or no use of code sharing.

this discussion, but the key point is that **draw** and **move** are defined as virtual functions in **shape**, so application-level functions (such as stacking one shape over another) written in terms of **draw** and **move** will work for all shapes. For example, since **draw** is a virtual function, when we apply it to a **shape** object that is a rectangle, the function that is used is the **draw** defined within the derived **rectangle** class and similarly for **line** or other derived classes that might be added.

The application program in *The C++ Programming Language* is an extremely simple one that merely draws a stylized "face" and moves it around. In our adaptation of the example, we define an STL **vector<shape*>** and show how to manipulate specific shapes in a vector of this type with a combination of (nonvirtual) STL vector member function calls, STL generic algorithm calls, and **shape** virtual function calls.

Example 17.1: Combining STL components with inheritance and virtual functions

```
"ex17-01.cpp" 261 ≡
     #include "shape.h"
     #include <vector>
     #include <algorithm>
     #include <iostream>
     #include <functional>
     using namespace std;

     class myshape : public rectangle {
      /* Define a new shape, a simple "face," derived from
         rectangle.
       */
       line* l_eye;
       line* r_eye;
       line* mouth;
      public:
       myshape(point, point);
       void draw();
       void move(int, int);
     };

     myshape::myshape(point a, point b) : rectangle(a,b)
     {
       int ll = neast().x - swest().x+1;
       int hh = neast().y - swest().y+1;
       l_eye =
```

```
     new line(point(swest().x+2,swest().y+hh*3/4),2);
  r_eye =
     new line(point(swest().x+ll-4,swest().y+hh*3/4),2);
  mouth =
     new line(point(swest().x+2,swest().y+hh/4),ll-4);
}

void myshape::draw()
  // Draw it by drawing the rectangle and a point for the
  // "nose"; the eye and mouth objects are refreshed
  // separately by the shape_refresh function.
{
  rectangle::draw();
  int a = (swest().x + neast().x)/2;
  int b = (swest().y + neast().y)/2;
  put_point(point(a,b));
}

void myshape::move(int a, int b)
  // Move it by moving the base rectangle and secondary
  // objects.
{
  rectangle::move(a,b);
  l_eye->move(a,b);
  r_eye->move(a,b);
  mouth->move(a,b);
}

// Beginning of definitions added in order to use STL
// with shape classes.

struct CompWestX : binary_function<shape*, shape*, bool> {

  bool operator()(shape* p, shape* q) const
    // Compare shapes based on the x-coordinate of
    // west point. The west function is virtual in the
    // shape class, so the comparison is made based on
    // how it is defined for a more specific shape.
  {
    return p->west().x < q->west().x;
  }
} compWestX;

void outputWestX (const vector<shape*>& vs)
```

```
    // Output the x-coordinate of the west point of each
    // shape in vs.
{
  vector<shape*>::const_iterator i;
  for (i = vs.begin(); i != vs.end(); ++i)
    cout << "The x-coordinate of the west point of shape "
         << i - vs.begin() << " is " << (*i)->west().x
         << endl;
}

// End of definitions added in order to use STL.

int main()
{
// First part is same as in Stroustrup's book:
  screen_init();
  shape* p1 = new rectangle(point(0,0),point(10,10));
  shape* p2 = new line(point(0,15),17);
  shape* p3 = new myshape(point(15,10),point(27,18));
  shape_refresh();
  p3->move(-10,-10);
  stack(p2,p3);
  stack(p1,p2);
  shape_refresh();

// This part is added as a tiny example of use of STL
// along with code that uses a class hierarchy and
// virtual functions. First put points into an STL vector:
  vector<shape*> vs;
  vs.push_back(p1);
  vs.push_back(p2);
  vs.push_back(p3);

// Use STL-provided iterator to move all points
// horizontally 20 units:
  vector<shape*>::iterator i;
  for (i = vs.begin(); i != vs.end(); ++i)
    (*i)->move(20, 0);
  shape_refresh();

// Demonstrate use of STL generic sorting algorithm with
// objects in a class hierarchy:
  outputWestX(vs);
  cout << "Sorting the shapes according to the "
```

```
         << "x-coordinate of their west points." << endl;
      sort(vs.begin(), vs.end(), compWestX);
      cout << "After sorting:" << endl;
      outputWestX(vs);
      screen_destroy();
      return 0;
    }
```

First, the different shapes are output in their original positions:

Output from Example 17.1

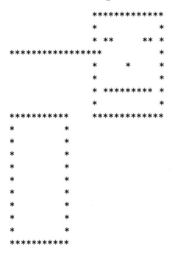

Then these shapes are moved around to form

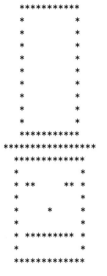

These shapes are all moved over 20 spaces by putting them in a vector and traversing the vector, moving each shape it contains.

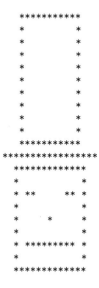

The last part shows the west point x-coordinates of each shape in the vector before and after sorting with STL's generic `sort` algorithm:

```
The x-coordinate of the west point of shape 0 is 26
The x-coordinate of the west point of shape 1 is 23
The x-coordinate of the west point of shape 2 is 25
Sorting the shapes according to the x-coordinate of their west
points.
After sorting:
The x-coordinate of the west point of shape 0 is 23
The x-coordinate of the west point of shape 1 is 25
The x-coordinate of the west point of shape 2 is 26
```

17.2 Avoiding "Code Bloat" from Container Instances

The `vector<shape*>` type introduced in Example 17.1 allows different shapes (rectangles, lines, and so on) to be stored in the same container. In some cases we might not have any need for this kind of heterogeneous storage, but we might need several different vector instances, each holding some specific shape, such as

```
vector<rectangle> vr;
vector<line> v1, v12;
vector<circle> vc;
vector<myshape> ms1, ms2, ms3;
// and so on
```

The problem this introduces is that the compiler may insert a separate copy of the vector class code for each instance of **vector**, resulting in an unacceptably large executable file. One way to avoid this "code bloat" is to use **vector<shape*>** as the type of all shape vectors we declare:

```
vector<shape*> vr;
vector<shape*> v1, v12;
vector<shape*> vc;
vector<shape*> ms1, ms2, ms3;
// and so on
```

Then only one copy of the **vector** code will be included in the executable file. What we give up is some of the type checking that the compiler was able to do using the first set of declarations and some run-time speed (due to the extra level of indirection involved in calling virtual functions).

Of course this technique only works if the types of objects we want to store in containers are all derived from the same base class. If not, we would have to try to reorganize them into such an arrangement.

As a final note, these techniques can be applied to help avoid code bloat that arises from instances of *any* template class, not just STL container classes. The amount of reduction in executable file size will depend on how much of the class implementation is independent of the exact type of its template parameters. With container-defining template classes there is typically more independence than with other kinds of template classes. See also Section 11.3 for other techniques of avoiding code bloat that arises from template classes or functions.

CHAPTER 18

Program for Displaying Theoretical Computer Science Genealogy

The SIGACT Theoretical Computer Science Genealogy page[1] lists information on earned doctoral degrees (advisor, university, and year) of theoretical computer scientists worldwide. The Web site provides a convenient means of looking up individuals a few at a time. To get the "big picture," though, it's useful to display the entire forest of academic ancestor trees represented in the TCS Genealogy data base.

The program presented in this chapter does so, working from an ASCII file version (76k) of the data[2] and producing a listing (102K) that displays the tree structure using indentation. The students of each Ph.D. advisor are listed in order of date of the students' Ph.D.'s (oldest first).

The output contains many fascinating details, but it is also instructive to examine the program to see how it combines several components of STL (vectors, maps, multisets, the generic `find` algorithm, and library and user-defined function objects) to do the job efficiently and succinctly.

18.1 Sorting Students by Date

Since we want the output to list the students in the order of their graduation, we need to define a function that can compare two students based on the

---

[1] *http://sigact.acm.org/genealogy*
[2] Obtained from *http://sigact.acm.org/genealogy/textfile.html* and slightly updated.

date their degrees were awarded. For the sake of this example, we assume that all the years contain four digits (allowing years between 1000 and 9999, which should be sufficient). This simplifying assumption permits us to treat the dates as strings, avoiding conversion to an integer and also allowing us to use the same data structure to store both the place and date of the degree.

Since the function needs to access the dates, we store the dates and places as part of the comparison class. We define a type called `data_map` which is simply a map associating two strings. We use this with students' names as the keys and the dates and places as the associated values.

⟨Define a type of map from strings to strings 268a⟩ ≡

```
typedef map<string, string> data_map;
```

Used in part 277.

Now we can define the comparison relation using the `data_map` type to store the dates and places.

⟨Define a function object to compare persons based on date of Ph.D. 268b⟩ ≡

```
struct earlier: binary_function<string, string, bool> {
  bool operator()(const string& name1,
                  const string& name2) const {
    return dates[name1] < dates[name2];
  }
  static data_map dates;
      // dates[name] holds year in which Ph.D. degree was
      // granted to name
  static data_map places;
      // places[name] holds institution that granted Ph.D.
};

data_map earlier::dates;
data_map earlier::places;
```

Used in part 277.

As an example, Brian Kernighan graduated from Princeton in 1969: `dates["Brian Kernighan"] = "1969"` and `places["Brian Kernighan"] = "Princeton"`.

18.2   Associating Students with Advisors

The output that we eventually want is a tree whose roots are any students whose advisor is unknown. For each person, we will print the name, university, and year, followed by an indented listing of any students he may have had. An excerpt from the output is shown below.

Output from Example 18.1

```
Displaying the SIGACT Theoretical Computer Science Genealogy
Peter Weiner ( )
       Brian Kernighan (Princeton 1969)
D.H. Younger ( )
       C L. Lucchesi (Waterloo 1976)
Dean Arden ( )
       C.L. Liu (MIT 1962)
              Andy Yao (Harvard 1972)
                     Scot Drysdale (Stanford 1979)
                            David Levine (Dartmouth 1986)
                            Barry Schaudt (Dartmouth 1991)
                     Ken Clarkson (Stanford 1984)
                     Joan Feigenbaum (Stanford 1986)
                     Weizhen Mao (Princeton 1990)
              Don Friesen (UIUC 1978)
                     Mike Langston (Texas A&M 1981)
              Shmuel Zaks (UIUC 1979)
              Hon Wai Leong (UIUC 1986)
              Pravin Vaidya (UIUC 1986)
              Ran Libeskind-Hadas (UIUC 1993)
```

This shows, for example, that Brian Kernighan graduated from Princeton in 1969, and his advisor was Peter Weiner (the database does not say where or when he graduated, so the parentheses after his name are empty).

To accomplish this output, we use a map that associates the name of an advisor with the set of his students. We order the set by the date of the degree using the **earlier** relation defined previously. We use a **multiset** since more than one student of an advisor could graduate in the same year. Those students, even with different names, would compare equally in terms of the **earlier** relation.

⟨Define a multiset containing **strings** ordered by dates 269a⟩ ≡
```
        typedef multiset<string, earlier> date_ordered_mset;
```

Used in part 277.

⟨Define a map from **strings** to date_ordered_msets 269b⟩ ≡
```
        typedef map<string, date_ordered_mset> relation_map;
```

Used in part 277.

key	data
Andy Yao	Scot Drysdale, Ken Clarkson, Joan Feigenbaum, Weizhen Mao
C.L. Liu	Andy Yao, Don Friesen, Shmuel Zaks, Hon Wai Leong, Pravin Vaidya Ran Libeskind-Hadas
D.H. Younger	C L. Lucchesi
Dean Arden	C.L. Liu
Don Friesen	Mike Langston
Peter Weiner	Brian Kernighan
Scot Drysdale	David Levine, Barry Schaudt

Figure 18.1: Sample `relation_map` showing the names in the output from Example 18.1, associating advisors with their students

The key in the map is the advisor's name, and the set will contain his students. As an example, the table in Figure 18.1 shows the map entries for the advisors shown in the sample output. Note that the keys are sorted alphabetically by first name. The sets of students are sorted by date via the `earlier` relation. Of course, the actual map contains many additional entries.

18.3   Finding the Roots of the Tree

The roots of the tree are the students whose advisor is not known. Many of those students are entered in the database as having the advisor --- (or ?, which we convert to --- when we read the file). Thus, we can look up the students of --- to find the tree roots.

However, not all of the roots will be in that set. When nothing is known about a student's Ph.D.—not even the university or year—the student is omitted from the database completely. For example, Brian Kernighan's advisor was Peter Weiner. There is no entry in the genealogy database stating explicitly that Peter Weiner's advisor was ---. Therefore, to find all of the tree roots, we need to look for people listed as advisors but who do not have a database record of their own.

To do so, we maintain another `relation_map` that is the converse of the one we discussed previously. In this map, the keys are the names of students, and the associated data is a set containing that student's advisor(s). Normally there will be only one element in the set, since most students have

key	data
Joan Feigenbaum	Andy Yao
Ken Clarkson	Andy Yao
Scot Drysdale	Andy Yao
Weizhen Mao	Andy Yao

Figure 18.2: Sample `relation_map` associating students with their advisors

just one Ph.D. advisor, but in some cases there may be multiple advisors for one student.

In Section 18.2, we had a map entry listing the students of Andy Yao as Scot Drysdale, Ken Clarkson, Joan Feigenbaum, and Weizhen Mao. In the new map, this entry corresponds to four entries, one for each student as shown in Figure 18.2. Again, the map entries are sorted alphabetically by first name, and it should be understood that many additional entries are not shown.

Given these two `relation_maps`, which we will refer to as `students` (Figure 18.1) and `advisors` (Figure 18.2), we can now proceed to find the remaining roots of the tree. After initializing the set of tree roots, we iterate over the list of students, determining for each student whether he or she can be reached from one of the roots we have already determined. If not, we add the student's first advisor to the set of tree roots.

⟨Find persons with unknown advisor and add a root entry for each 271a⟩ ≡
```
        ⟨Initialize the set of tree roots to the students of --- 271b⟩
        relation_map::iterator i;
        date_ordered_mset::iterator j;
        bool any_advisor;
        for (i = advisors.begin(); i != advisors.end(); ++i) {
          ⟨Check if this person has an advisor in the database 272⟩
          ⟨If not, add an entry to the set of roots 273a⟩
        }
```
Used in part 277.

We initialize the set of roots to the students whose advisor is listed in the database as ---.

⟨Initialize the set of tree roots to the students of --- 271b⟩ ≡
```
        date_ordered_mset& roots = students["---"];
```
Used in part 271a.

key	data
Brian Kernighan	Peter Weiner

Figure 18.3: Brian Kernighan's entry in the `advisors` map

The goal is to ensure that all the students in the database will be printed by traversing the hierarchy of students from the tree roots. If a student is reachable from an existing, known root advisor, then we do nothing. Otherwise, we need to add one of the student's advisors as a root.

There are two ways in which a student can be reached from an existing root. First, if the student's advisor is --- (unknown), then the student will already be in the list of roots, due to our initialization. Second, if any of the student's advisors is in the database, then this student can be reached via that path. Therefore, we iterate through the list of advisors checking first for equality to --- and second whether the name appears in the list of students (the keys of the advisors map).

⟨Check if this person has an advisor in the database 272⟩ ≡
```
    any_advisor = false;
    for (j = i->second.begin(); j != i->second.end(); ++j) {
      if (*j == string("---") ||
          advisors.find(*j) != advisors.end())
        any_advisor = true;
    }
```
Used in part 271a.

This is better explained by an example. As we mentioned earlier, Brian Kernighan's advisor, Peter Weiner, is not in the database. Therefore, at some point during the iteration through the `advisors` map, i points to the pair shown in Figure 18.3. In the second loop, we iterate through the set of Brian Kernighan's advisors (in this case it is a set containing only one element). The first time through the loop, j points to `"Peter Weiner"`. Since he is not in the database, his advisor is not ---, meaning that he is not already in the list of tree roots. Furthermore, `advisors.find("Peter Weiner")` will not succeed, so `any_advisor` remains `false`.

At this point, we have determined that none of the current student's advisors is in the database, so we need to add a new entry to the set of tree roots. By adding only the first advisor, we avoid duplicating portions of the tree in our output. If we added all the advisors, then this student (and all

his students and their students and so on) would be listed separately under
each advisor.

⟨If not, add an entry to the set of roots 273a⟩ ≡

```
    if (!any_advisor) {
      string first_advisor = *(i->second.begin());
      // Check if it is already there:
      //    must do linear search with generic find, since multiset
      //    is ordered based on dates rather than names (but the
      //    multiset size is not big enough for this to be a
      //    problem).
      if (find(roots.begin(), roots.end(), first_advisor)
          == roots.end())
        roots.insert(first_advisor);
    }
```

Used in part 271a.

18.4   Reading the File

The data is stored in an ASCII text file with one line per student. A line that
begins with a **#** character is treated as a comment and ignored. All other
lines contain four tab-separated fields: the student's name, the advisor's
name, the name of the university, and the year the degree was conferred. In
some cases, when the information is incomplete, one or more of the fields
(but not the student's name) may be **?** or **---**.

We write a utility function that reads the next field of data from the file
by reading until the next tab character or the end of the file.[3] We first erase
any previous contents of the **string** result variable (this makes it easier to
use the function in a loop, where the same variable will be used repeatedly).
Then we reserve some space to avoid frequent reallocations. Finally, we read
the characters in a loop.

⟨Function to get a string of all the characters up to next terminator 273b⟩ ≡

```
    void get_chunk(istream& in, string& s, char terminator = '\t')
    {
      s.erase(s.begin(), s.end());
      s.reserve(20);
      string::value_type ch;
```

---

[3]This function is essentially equivalent to the standard **getline** function, which is not
discussed in this book. That function, however, requires templated streams that are not
yet supported by many compilers.

```
  while (in.get(ch) && ch != terminator)
    s.insert(s.end(), ch);
}
```
Used in part 277.

Now we can construct the loop for reading the data. We define variables to store the two **relation_maps** we discussed earlier: one, **students**, associating advisors with their students and another, **advisors**, for the converse relation, associating students with their advisors.

We define variables to store each of the four fields when a line is read. The loop first checks whether the next line is a comment, ignoring those lines. If the line is not a comment, the values are read and stored into the data structures. We break out of the loop when the end of the file is reached.

⟨Scan the theory database file and build the maps 274a⟩ ≡
  ⟨Get the genealogy file name, and prepare to read it in 274b⟩

```
    relation_map advisors, students;
    string name, advisor, place, date;
    while (true) {
      // ignore comments
      if (ifs.peek() == '#') {
        get_chunk(ifs, name, '\n');
        continue;
      }
      ⟨Read a line of data, terminate on end of file 275a⟩
    }
```
Used in part 277.

Opening the file is straightforward and is nearly identical to the code used for opening the dictionary file in Chapters 12 through 15.

⟨Get the genealogy file name, and prepare to read it in 274b⟩ ≡
```
    cout << "First, enter the name of the file containing\n"
        << "the genealogy data: " << flush;
    string file_name;
    cin >> file_name;
    ifstream ifs(file_name.c_str());
    if (!ifs.is_open()) {
      cout << "Eh?  Could not open file named " << file_name
          << endl;
      exit(1);
    }
```
Used in part 274a.

To process a single line of the input file, we read the four fields, making sure that we don't reach the end of the file while trying to read the name. Then we insert the date and place into the **data_maps** in the **earlier** class and add the advisor/student relationship to the **relation_maps**. Additionally, we change any occurrences of ? for the advisor to ---, so that there is only one map key indicating an unknown advisor.

⟨Read a line of data, terminate on end of file 275a⟩ ≡

```
get_chunk(ifs, name);
if (!ifs) break;
get_chunk(ifs, advisor);
get_chunk(ifs, place);
get_chunk(ifs, date, '\n');

earlier::places[name] = place;
earlier::dates[name] = date;
if (advisor == "?")
  advisor = "---";
students[advisor].insert(name);
advisors[name].insert(advisor);
```

Used in part 274a.

18.5 Printing the Results

The last piece we need is a function to print the results. We do this recursively with a function that prints the information for a single student. After indenting the line properly, we print the name, place, and date of the degree. Finally, we invoke the function recursively to print any students the person might have.

⟨Function to output a single branch of the tree, rooted at **name** 275b⟩ ≡

```
void output_tree(const string& name, relation_map& students,
                 data_map& places, data_map& dates,
                 int indentation_level = 0)
{
  ⟨Indent the line according to the indentation_level 276a⟩
  ⟨Print the student's Ph.D. degree information 276b⟩
  ⟨Print this person's students, indented one additional level 276c⟩
}
```

Used in part 277.

Each of the remaining parts is relatively straightforward. We indent simply by repeatedly printing a series of spaces (we used four).

⟨Indent the line according to the indentation_level 276a⟩ ≡
```
    for (int k = 0; k != indentation_level; ++k)
        cout << "    ";
```
Used in part 275b.

The degree information is printed with the university and date in parentheses, such as **Brian Kernighan (Princeton 1969)**.

⟨Print the student's Ph.D. degree information 276b⟩ ≡
```
    cout << name << " (" << places[name] << " " << dates[name]
         << ")" << endl;
```
Used in part 275b.

And to print the students, we iterate over the set, ordered by date, increasing the indentation level by one.

⟨Print this person's students, indented one additional level 276c⟩ ≡
```
    date_ordered_mset& L = students[name];
    date_ordered_mset::const_iterator j;
    for (j = L.begin(); j != L.end(); ++j)
      output_tree(*j, students, places, dates,
                  indentation_level + 1);
```
Used in part 275b.

To print the entire result set, we want to print all the trees that were found earlier when we searched for students without an advisor. Thus, we iterate over the **roots** set, printing each of those trees, using the default argument for the indentation level.

⟨Output all the trees rooted at --- 276d⟩ ≡
```
    for (j = roots.begin(); j != roots.end(); ++j)
        output_tree(*j, students, earlier::places, earlier::dates);
```
Used in part 277.

18.6   Complete "Genealogy" Program

Finally, we can assemble all the pieces into a complete program. See Appendix D for information on obtaining the source code on the Internet.

Example 18.1: Displaying the SIGACT Theoretical Computer Science Genealogy

"ex18-01.cpp" 277 ≡

```
#include <algorithm>
#include <iostream>
#include <fstream>
#include <string>
#include <vector>
#include <iomanip>
#include <map>
#include <set>
using namespace std;
```

⟨Define a type of map from strings to strings 268a⟩
⟨Define a function object to compare persons based on date of Ph.D. 268b⟩
⟨Define a multiset containing **strings** ordered by dates 269a⟩
⟨Define a map from **strings** to **date_ordered_msets** 269b⟩

⟨Function to output a single branch of the tree, rooted at **name** 275b⟩
⟨Function to get a string of all the characters up to next terminator 273b⟩

```
int main()
{
  cout << "Displaying the SIGACT "
       << "Theoretical Computer Science Genealogy" << endl;
```
⟨Scan the theory database file and build the maps 274a⟩
⟨Find persons with unknown advisor and add a root entry for each 271a⟩
⟨Output all the trees rooted at --- 276d⟩
```
  return 0;
}
```

CHAPTER 19

Class for Timing Generic Algorithms

It is useful to measure the execution time computer algorithms take, either to compare two or more algorithms for the same task, or to understand how the time for a single algorithm grows as a function of its input parameters. For example, how does the time for a given sorting algorithm grow with the length N of the input sequence: as $O(N)$ (linearly), $O(N^2)$ (quadratically), or $O(N \log N)$? Beyond the big-Oh formulas (which might already be known analytically anyway), how do two algorithms that both take, say, $O(N \log N)$ time compare in terms of actual times? In this chapter we present a class that can be used to automate much of the work of running timing experiments. We then use this class to demonstrate some interesting performance properties of the various STL sorting algorithms.

19.1   Obstacles to Accurate Timing of Algorithms

While it would seem straightforward to write programs to time algorithms, simple programs to set up timing experiments often do not give very accurate or repeatable results. For example, the C/C++ Standard Library provides a function called `clock` (in the header file `ctime`) that can sometimes be used in a simple way to time computations:

```
clock_t start, finish;
start = clock();
sort(x.begin(), x.end());  // Call the generic sort algorithm
finish = clock();
cout << "Time for sort (seconds): "
    << ((double)(finish - start))/CLOCKS_PER_SEC << endl;
```

The type `clock_t` and the constant `CLOCKS_PER_SEC` are defined in `ctime`. On a typical Unix system `CLOCKS_PER_SEC` is 1 million, which might lead one to believe that the clock ticks every microsecond. Usually the clock granularity is much larger, however, such as every 1/100 of a second. (But the number reported by `clock` is 10,000 larger than on the previous tick, making it appear that microseconds are being measured.) Although 1/100 of a second may sound fairly accurate for timing normal human activities, in terms of computation it is grossly long. Modern processors can execute millions of instructions between ticks. In the example, if the algorithm is any good, the sequence being sorted may have to be 10,000 or more elements long before a nonzero time is measured. If the time is to be measured for shorter sequences, the algorithm call will have to be put in a loop to build up the accumulated time to a measurable value, which is then divided by the number of loop iterations.

Even if the input sequence is large enough (or the repetitions high enough) for the algorithm to take a measurable time, the times reported may not be very accurate. For example, one might see a time reported for sorting a 20,000-element sequence greater than the time reported for a 30,000-element sequence. There are two main reasons for such inaccuracy.

First, although the `clock` function is supposed to report only time used by the user's process, not system time, there is inevitably some fluctuation in times reported when the processor has to attend to a lot of other activity. And even on a single-user workstation or PC, modern operating systems are often running a score or more different processes to handle network activity and other, often invisible actions. Second, the `clock` function is often poorly implemented, with the result that it "misses ticks" and can accumulate enough error over several seconds to make the times measured inaccurate, perhaps by as much as 50%.

19.2   Overcoming the Obstacles

Timing fluctuations severely limit the usefulness of algorithm timing experiments unless care is taken to reduce their effect. Fortunately, there is a way of overcoming the main problems. Although it is a bit more complicated than the simple timing code shown, it can be packaged in a class definition so that it is simple to use.

The key idea is to put the algorithm in a loop and count the number of iterations between ticks. This is then repeated for, say, ten times, so that even if some of the durations between ticks vary, we can pick out one that is likely to be accurate. Let's look at an example. We set up a timing experiment in which we investigate the generic **sort** algorithm. We repeat the algorithm execution r times on a randomly generated array of size N, where N and r are taken from user input. Note that to ensure that each iteration is identical, we copy the original array before sorting it. This way, iterations after the first one are operating from the same starting point rather than with a presorted array.

Example 19.1: First attempt at timing the **sort** algorithm

```
"ex19-01.cpp" 281 ≡
    #include <cmath>
    #include <cstdlib>
    #include <ctime>
    #include <iostream>
    #include <vector>
    #include <algorithm>
    using namespace std;

    int main()
    {
      cout << "First attempt at timing the sort algorithm."
          << endl;
      double* A, *B;
      unsigned long N;
      unsigned int reps;
      cout << "Input array size and repetitions: ";
      cin >> N >> reps;

      A = new double[N];
      B = new double[N];

      srand(time(0));

      for (unsigned int i = 0; i < N; ++i)
        A[i] = (double)rand();

      vector<long> iterations;
      iterations.reserve(reps);

      time_t start, finish;

      start = time(0);
      while (iterations.size() < reps) {
```

```
          int count = 0;
          do {
            ++count;
            copy(A, A + N, B);
            sort(B, B + N);
            finish = time(0);
          }
          // Continue as long as clock hasn't ticked:
          while (finish == start);
          // Record the number of iterations:
          iterations.push_back(count);
          start = finish;
        }
      cout << "Iteration counts: " << endl;
      unsigned int k;
      for (k = 0; k < iterations.size(); ++k)
        cout << iterations[k] << " ";
      cout << endl;
      cout << "Sorted iteration counts: " << endl;
      sort(iterations.begin(), iterations.end());
      for (k = 0; k < iterations.size(); ++k)
        cout << iterations[k] << " ";
      cout << endl;
      cout << "Selected value: " << iterations[reps/2] << endl;
      cout << "Time: " << 1000.0/iterations[reps/2]
            << " ms " << endl;
      return 0;
    }
```

Here is a sample run of this program (user input is underlined).

Output from Example 19.1

```
    First attempt at timing the sort algorithm.
    Input array size and repetitions: 10000 10
    Iteration counts:
    53 103 128 134 127 126 126 128 135 128
    Sorted iteration counts:
    53 103 126 126 127 128 128 128 134 135
    Selected value: 128
    Time: 7.8125 ms
```

In this program, instead of the standard clock function we use the standard time function, which ticks once every second. The program records the iteration counts in an STL vector. Note the wide variations in the number of iterations, evidence of the inaccuracies we have been discussing. However, if we sort these values, we notice that the middle values are closely grouped. The values at the end of the sorted range may vary widely, but we can completely ignore them by simply choosing the central value of the sorted values, 128, which is the median of the original sequence, as a good representative of the middle group. The time per loop iteration is then reported as

$$1/128 = .0078125 \text{ seconds} = 7.8125 \text{ milliseconds.}$$

Of course, the actual time depends on the platform the program is compiled and run on. The result shown was obtained on laptop with a 400 Mhz Pentium processor and 128 megabytes of memory running Windows 98, with the program compiled by **g++** with optimization turned on. If we run the same test several times on the same platform, we get results that differ only by a few percent. In general, this timing method produces much more repeatable results than simple timing runs or even taking the median or average of the results of several timing runs.

19.3   Refining the Approach

An additional adjustment needs to be made in this basic strategy. The time per loop iteration is not really the time for the algorithm call, since it includes the overhead of the timing loop itself—the time for calling the **time** function, the normal loop overhead (incrementing and testing the loop index variable, and so on), and most important, copying the array once per iteration. Thus, we must measure this baseline time by separately running the loop without the algorithm call. If we comment out the algorithm call in the above program[1]

```
//      sort(B, B + N);
```

and recompile and rerun it, we might get the following output.

Output from Example 19.1a

```
Baseline for timing the sort algorithm.
Input array size and repetitions: 10000 10
Iteration counts:
128 656 1036 1048 1044 1050 1102 1045 1045 1033
```

---

[1]The source code for this variation, Example 19.1a, is available on the Internet (see Appendix D) as the file ex19-01a.cpp.

```
Sorted iteration counts:
128 656 1033 1036 1044 1045 1045 1048 1050 1102
Selected value: 1045
Time: 0.956938 ms
```

Thus the baseline time is 0.956938 ms and the time for the algorithm call is actually

$$7.8125 \text{ ms} - 0.956938 \text{ ms} = 6.855562 \text{ ms}$$

We don't need to report these times to this many decimal places because probably only a couple are significant.

19.4   Automated Analysis with a Timer Class

We now present the class `timer`, which automates most of the work involved in this type of analysis. Since we are running each experiment in the amount of time it takes for one clock tick (1 second), this approach is most accurate for computations that take up to about 100 milliseconds. The basic usage of our class follows.

```
timer tim;              // Declare a timer, tim
// ...

// Start baseline timing, with 10 trials
tim.start_baseline(10);
do {
  // Set-up computation (leave blank if no set up is required):
} while (tim.check());
// Baseline time is recorded and reported on cout;
// replace false by true for more output:
tim.report(false);

tim.start(10, 1000); // Start the actual timing, 10 trials,
                     // problem size 1000
do {
  // Set-up computation (leave blank if no set up is required):
  // algorithm call:
} while (tim.check());
// Algorithm time is recorded and reported on cout;
// replace false by true for more output:
tim.report(false);
```

This usage corresponds to the following interface. We have also provided a method, `results`, for accessing the timing results directly. They are represented as a `map` of times (in milliseconds) indexed by problem size.

⟨Interface of the timer class 285⟩ ≡

```
#include <iostream>
#include <iomanip>
#include <vector>
#include <map>
#include <algorithm>
using namespace std;

class timer {
public:
  timer();  // Default constructor
  // Start a series of r trials for problem size N:
  void start(unsigned int r, unsigned long N);
  // Start a series of r trials to determine baseline time:
  void start_baseline(unsigned int r);
  // Returns true if the trials have been completed, else false
  bool check();
  // Report the results of the trials on cout
  // with additional output if verbose is true:
  void report(bool verbose);
  // Returns the results for external use
  const map<unsigned int, double>& results() const;

private:
  unsigned int reps;  // Number of trials
  // For storing loop iterations of a trial
  vector<long> iterations;
  // For saving initial and final times of a trial
  time_t initial, final;
  // For counting loop iterations of a trial
  unsigned long count;
  // For saving the problem size (N) for current trials
  unsigned int problem_size;
  // For storing (problem size, time) pairs
  map<unsigned int, double> result_map;
  // true if this is a baseline computation, false otherwise
  bool baseline;
  // For recording the baseline time
  double baseline_time;
};
```

Used in part 289.

The constructor is quite trivial and simply sets the `baseline` variable to `false` until the `start_baseline` method is called.

⟨timer default constructor implementation 286a⟩ ≡

```
      timer::timer() { baseline = false; }
```

Used in part 289.

The **start** method sets the number of repetitions and the problem size. It also initializes the iterations vector, the count, and the start time. This method should be invoked to begin a timing trial.

⟨timer **start** method implementation 286b⟩ ≡

```
      void timer::start(unsigned int r, unsigned long N)
      {
        reps = r;
        problem_size = N;
        count = 0;
        iterations.clear();
        iterations.reserve(reps);
        initial = time(0);
      }
```

Used in part 289.

The **start_baseline** method simply sets the **baseline** variable to **true** and invokes **start** to initialize the other class members. This method should be invoked to begin calculating the baseline time taken by the loop overhead operations.

⟨timer **start_baseline** method implementation 286c⟩ ≡

```
      void timer::start_baseline(unsigned int r)
      {
        baseline = true;
        start(r, 0);
      }
```

Used in part 289.

The **check** is used to determine whether a trial has completed. It will return **true** as long as the trial continues. When the trial completes (when the clock ticks), the number of iterations is stored, and the timer state is reset for the next trial.

⟨timer **check** method implementation 286d⟩ ≡

```
      bool timer::check()
      {
```

```
    ++count;
    final = time(0);
    if (initial < final) {
      iterations.push_back(count);
      initial = final;
      count = 0;
    }
    return (iterations.size() < reps);
  }
```
Used in part 289.

The **results** method simply returns a map containing the timing results. This can be useful for printing more elaborate reports than those generated by **report**.

⟨timer **results** method implementation 287a⟩ ≡
```
    const map<unsigned int, double>& timer::results() const
    {
      return result_map;
    }
```
Used in part 289.

19.4.1   Reporting the Results

Most of the work of the **timer** class is done by the **report** method. This is where the times are calculated and printed for each problem size. Furthermore, we've added a feature that wasn't present in the earlier examples. Although any sequence of problem sizes can be used, if we double the problem size at each step, the **report** function shows the growth ratio of the time for problem size N to the time for problem size $N/2$. This growth ratio is one way of looking at algorithm performance that is, like big-Oh notation, independent of the platform on which the algorithm is run. We look at this further in the next section.

The **report** function sorts the iteration counts, choosing the median value for computing the time. In verbose mode, the counts are printed both before and after sorting. If the trial was a baseline trial, the time is saved for later use. Otherwise the time is added to the result map and printed.

⟨timer **report** method implementation 287b⟩ ≡
```
    void timer::report(bool verbose)
    {
      if (verbose) {
```

⟨Print the iteration counts, breaking lines every 10 numbers 289b⟩
```
}
sort(iterations.begin(), iterations.end());
if (verbose) {
   cout << "Sorted counts:" << endl;
```
⟨Print the iteration counts, breaking lines every 10 numbers 289b⟩
```
}
```

⟨Choose the median of the counts as the most accurate 288⟩

```
if (baseline) {
   baseline_time = 1000.0/selected_count;
   cout << "Baseline time: " << baseline_time << endl;
   baseline = false;
} else {
   double calculated_time, growth_factor;
   result_map[problem_size] = calculated_time =
      1000.0/selected_count - baseline_time;
   cout << setiosflags(ios::fixed) << setprecision(4)
        << setw(35) << problem_size << setw(12)
        << calculated_time << " ms ";
```
⟨Compute the growth factor, if possible 289a⟩
```
   cout << endl;
   }
}
```

Used in part 289.

We find the median value of the iterations by taking the middle value after sorting. In verbose mode, this number is reported.

⟨Choose the median of the counts as the most accurate 288⟩ ≡
```
      int selected_count = iterations[reps/2];
      if (verbose)
         cout << "Selected count: " << selected_count << endl;
```
Used in part 287b.

Again, the growth factor is based on a comparison of the results for problem size N to those for problem size $N/2$. Therefore the first step to computing the growth factor is to determine whether results are available for that problem size. If so, the growth factor is the ratio of the computing times.

⟨Compute the growth factor, if possible 289a⟩ ≡

```
    if (result_map.find(problem_size/2) != result_map.end()) {
      growth_factor = calculated_time / result_map[problem_size/2];
      cout << setiosflags(ios::fixed) << setprecision(4)
           << setw(8) << growth_factor;
    }
```

Used in part 287b.

We print the iteration counts with a simple loop. We could use the STL
`copy` algorithm with an `ostream_iterator`, but writing our own loop allows
us to break the lines every ten values, which makes for better formatting.
This code is used for printing both the original, unsorted values and for the
values after they are sorted.

⟨Print the iteration counts, breaking lines every 10 numbers 289b⟩ ≡

```
    for (unsigned int k = 0; k < iterations.size(); ++k) {
      cout << iterations[k] << " ";
      if ((k+1) % 10 == 0)
        cout << endl;
    }
    cout << endl;
```

Used in part 287b.

We place this class in a file called `timer.h` which will be used in the remainder of the chapter to analyze the STL sorting algorithms.

```
"timer.h" 289 ≡
    ⟨Interface of the timer class 285⟩

    ⟨timer default constructor implementation 286a⟩
    ⟨timer start method implementation 286b⟩
    ⟨timer start_baseline method implementation 286c⟩
    ⟨timer check method implementation 286d⟩
    ⟨timer report method implementation 287b⟩
    ⟨timer results method implementation 287a⟩
```

19.5 Timing the STL Sort Algorithms

We can now use our `timer` class to compare different STL sorting algorithms.
The program that follows times the `sort` algorithm with random vectors in
sizes that increase by a factor of 2 in each iteration. Thus, the growth factor
for `sort` will be computed.

Example 19.2: Timing **sort** on random vectors

"ex19-02.cpp" 290 ≡

```cpp
#include <cmath>
#include <cstdlib>
#include <ctime>
#include <iostream>
#include <vector>
#include <algorithm>
#include "timer.h"
using namespace std;

int main()
{
  cout << "Timing sort on random vectors." << endl;
  srand(time(0));
  vector<double> v, v0;
  unsigned long N, N1, N2;
  unsigned int reps;
  cout << "Repetitions, initial size, and final size: ";
  cin >> reps >> N1 >> N2;

  timer tim;

  for (N = N1; N <= N2; N *= 2) {
    v.clear();
    v.reserve(N);
    for (unsigned int i = 0; i < N; ++i)
      v.push_back((double)rand());

    v0 = v;    // save the input vector in v0

    // Compute the baseline time for N
    tim.start_baseline(reps);
    do {
      // Include the vector assignment in baseline time
      v = v0;
    } while (tim.check());
    tim.report(false);

    tim.start(reps, N);
    do {
      v = v0;    // Restore the saved vector v0 into v
      sort(v.begin(), v.end());
```

```
      }
      while (tim.check());
      tim.report(false);
   }
   return 0;
}
```

Sample output follows.

Output from Example 19.2

```
Timing sort on random vectors.
Repetitions, initial size, and final size: 11 1000 64000
Baseline time: 0.148522
                              1000        0.5115 ms
Baseline time: 0.2119
                              2000        1.0885 ms     2.1279
Baseline time: 0.3472
                              4000        2.3337 ms     2.1439
Baseline time: 0.6498
                              8000        5.1642 ms     2.2128
Baseline time: 1.7953
                             16000       11.0252 ms     2.1349
Baseline time: 4.1667
                             32000       27.0833 ms     2.4565
Baseline time: 8.3333
                             64000       58.3333 ms     2.1538
```

As expected, since **sort** is $O(N \log N)$ the growth rate is slightly larger than 2. If we modify the algorithm to use **stable_sort**[2] we get the following results. Recall that **stable_sort** is also $O(N \log N)$, and as we see, the growth rates are similar; however, the actual times are roughly 1.5 times longer for **stable_sort**.

Output from Example 19.2a

```
Timing stable_sort on random vectors.
Repetitions, initial size, and final size: 11 1000 64000
Baseline time: 0.148017
                              1000        0.7901 ms
Baseline time: 0.2418
                              2000        1.5034 ms     1.9028
```

---

[2]The source code for this variation, Example 19.2a, is available on the Internet (see Appendix D) as the file **ex19-02a.cpp**.

Baseline time: 0.3427

4000	3.6734 ms	2.4434

Baseline time: 0.6618

| 8000 | 7.2747 ms | 1.9804 |

Baseline time: 1.7606

| 16000 | 17.4702 ms | 2.4015 |

Baseline time: 4.1494

| 32000 | 41.3052 ms | 2.3643 |

Baseline time: 8.4034

| 64000 | 134.4538 ms | 3.2551 |

Similarly, if we apply the timing algorithm to `partial_sort` (sorting the entire vector using `partial_sort(v.begin(), v.end(), v.end())`)[3] we get the following results. Like `sort` and `stable_sort`, `partial_sort` is $O(N \log N)$, and the growth rates more or less mirror those of `sort`. But the times are again roughly 1.5 times longer.

Output from Example 19.2b

```
Timing partial_sort on random vectors.
Repetitions, initial size, and final size: 11 1000 64000
```
Baseline time: 0.152416

1000	0.8251 ms	

Baseline time: 0.2437

| 2000 | 1.7444 ms | 2.1142 |

Baseline time: 0.3525

| 4000 | 3.7459 ms | 2.1474 |

Baseline time: 0.6423

| 8000 | 8.2073 ms | 2.1910 |

Baseline time: 1.8519

| 16000 | 17.3789 ms | 2.1175 |

Baseline time: 4.2194

| 32000 | 41.2351 ms | 2.3727 |

Baseline time: 8.3333

| 64000 | 116.6667 ms | 2.8293 |

This exercise demonstrates the value of understanding the true performance of an algorithm, based on actual time results. Big-Oh notation is a useful measure of an algorithm's efficiency, but the implied constant factor can often hide important performance trade-offs between algorithms.

---

[3]The source code for this variation, Example 19.2b, is available on the Internet (see Appendix D) as the file `ex19-02b.cpp`.

Part III

STL Reference Guide

Part III is a complete description of all STL components, including some details not mentioned in Parts I or II. This guide does not contain examples, but examples and tutorial descriptions of almost all components can be located in Parts I and II by consulting the entry for the component in the index at the back of the book.

CHAPTER 20

Iterator Reference Guide

This chapter is a reference guide to STL iterator components:

- The requirements that must be satisfied by a class or a built-in type to be used as an iterator of a particular iterator category (input iterators, output iterators, forward iterators, bidirectional iterators, or random access iterators)

- Stream iterator classes for using generic algorithms with input streams or output streams

- Iterator adaptors (reverse iterators and insert iterators)

The following terminology is used in the statement of iterator requirements.

- *Value type*   Type (either a class or a built-in type) of the value returned when `operator*` is applied to an iterator.

- *Difference type*   Signed integral type representing the distance between two iterators for which equality is defined.

- *Past-the-end values*   Iterator value that points past the last element of a corresponding container. Just as a regular pointer to an array guarantees that there is a valid pointer value pointing past the last element of the array, STL iterators guarantee that there is a past-the-end value.

- *Dereferenceable values*   Values of the iterator for which `operator*` is defined. STL components never assume that past-the-end values are dereferenceable.

- *Singular values* Values that are not associated with any container. For example, after the declaration of an uninitialized pointer x (as with int* x), x should always be assumed to have a singular value of a pointer. Results of most expressions are undefined for singular values. The only exception is an assignment of a nonsingular value to an iterator that holds a singular value. In this case the singular value is overwritten the same way as any other value. Dereferenceable and past-the-end values are always nonsingular.

- *Reachability* An iterator j is called reachable from an iterator i if and only if there is a finite sequence of applications of operator++ to i that makes i == j. If an iterator j is reachable from another iterator i, the iterators refer to the same container.

- *Ranges* Pair of iterators that serve as beginning and end markers for a computation. A range [i, i) is an empty range; in general, a range [i, j) consists of the iterators obtained by starting with i and applying operator++ until j is reached, but does not include j. Range [i, j) is *valid* if and only if j is reachable from i. All of the library's algorithmic templates that operate on containers have interfaces that use ranges. The result of the application of the algorithms in the library to invalid ranges is undefined.

- *Mutable* versus *constant* Depends on whether the result of operator* behaves as a reference (mutable) or as a reference to a constant (constant). Constant iterators do not satisfy the requirements for output iterators.

For all iterator operations that are required in each category, the computing time requirement is *constant time* (amortized). For this reason, we will not mention computing times separately in any of the following sections on requirements.

20.1 Input Iterator Requirements

As Stepanov and Lee [19] stress, it is important to state the requirements on the components as generally as possible. For example, instead of saying "class X must define a member function operator++()," we say "for any object x of type X, ++x is defined." (We leave open the possibility that X is a built-in type and that the operator is globally defined rather than a class member function.)

In this and the following four requirements sections in this chapter, for each iterator type X we will assume the following:

- a and b denote values of type X.

- n denotes a value of the difference type for X.

- r and s denote a value of X&.

- t denotes a value of type T, the iterator's value_type.

- u, tmp, and m denote identifiers.

A class or a built-in type X satisfies the requirements of an input iterator for the value type T if and only if the following expressions are defined and meet the requirements specified for them:

X(a)	Copy constructor, which makes X(a) == a. A destructor is assumed.
X u(a);	Results in u == a.
X u = a;	Same as X u(a).
u = a;	Results in u == a.
a == b	Return type must be convertible to bool, and == must be an equivalence relation.
a != b	Return type must be convertible to bool, and the result must be the same as !(a == b).
*a	Return type is T. It is assumed that a is dereferenceable. If a == b, then it must be the case that *a == *b.
a->m	Equivalent to (*a).m, assuming that the latter expression is well defined.
++r	Return type is X&. It is assumed that r is dereferenceable. The result is that r is dereferenceable or r is the past-the-end value of the container, and &r == &++r.
(void)r++	Equivalent to (void)++r.
*r++	Result must be the same as that of {T tmp = *r; ++r; return tmp;}.

For input iterators, a == b does not imply ++a == ++b. The main consequence is that algorithms on input iterators should be *single-pass* algorithms; that is, they should never attempt to copy the value of an iterator and use it to pass through the same position twice. Furthermore, value type T is not required to be a reference type, so algorithms on input iterators should not attempt to assign through them. (Forward iterators remove these restrictions.)

20.2   Output Iterator Requirements

A class or a built-in type X satisfies the requirements of an output iterator for the value type T if and only if the following expressions are defined and meet the requirements specified for them:

X(a)   *a = t is equivalent to *X(a) = t. Further, a destructor is assumed in this case.

X u(a);   Result is that u is a copy of a. Note, however, that equality and inequality are not necessarily defined, and algorithms should not attempt to use output iterators to pass through a position twice (they should be single-pass).

X u = a;   Same as X u(a).

*a = t   t is assigned through the iterator to the position to which a refers. The return value of this operation is not used.

++r   Return type is X&. It is assumed that r is dereferenceable on the left-hand side of an assignment. The result is that either r is dereferenceable on the left-hand side of an assignment or r is the past-the-end value of the container, and &r == &++r.

r++   Return type must be convertible to const X&. The result must be the same as that of {X tmp = r; ++r; return tmp;}.

*r++ = t   Result must be the same as that of {*r = t; ++r;}. The return value of this operation is not used.

The only valid use of **operator*** on output iterators is on the left-hand side of an assignment statement. As with input iterators, algorithms that use output iterators should be single-pass. Equality and inequality operators might not be defined. Algorithms that use output iterators can be used with ostreams as the destination for placing data via the **ostream_iterator** class as well as with insert iterators and insert pointers.

298

20.3 Forward Iterator Requirements

A class or a built-in type X satisfies the requirements of a forward iterator for the value type T if and only if the following expressions are defined and meet the requirements specified for them:

X u;   Resulting value of u might be singular. A destructor is assumed.

X()   X() might be a singular value.

X(a)   Result must satisfy a == X(a).

X u(a);   Result must satisfy u == a.

X u = a;   Same as X u(a).

a == b   Return type must be convertible to bool, and == must be an equivalence relation.

a != b   Return type must be convertible to bool, and the result must be the same as !(a == b).

r = a   Return type is X&, and the result must satisfy r == a.

*a   Return type is T&. It is assumed that a is dereferenceable. If a == b, then it must be that *a == *b. If X is mutable, *a = t is valid.

a->m   Equivalent to (*a).m, assuming that the latter expression is well defined.

++r   Return type is X&. It is assumed that r is dereferenceable, and the result is that r either is dereferenceable or is the past-the-end value, and &r == &++r. Moreover, r == s and r is dereferenceable imply that ++r == ++s.

r++   Return type must be convertible to const X&. The result must be the same as that of {X tmp = r; ++r; return tmp;}.

*r++   Return type is T&.

Two properties of forward iterators contribute to allowing the use of multipass, one-directional algorithms: first, the condition that a == b implies ++a == ++b (which is not true for input or output iterators), and second, the removal of the restrictions on the number of the assignments through the iterator (which applies to output iterators).

20.4 Bidirectional Iterator Requirements

A class or a built-in type X satisfies the requirements of a bidirectional iterator for the value type T if and only if the following expressions are defined and meet the requirements specified for them, in addition to the requirements that are described in the previous section for forward iterators:

`--r`	Return type is `X&`. It is assumed that there exists `s` such that `r == ++s`; then `--r` refers to the same position as `s`. Also `--r` is dereferenceable and `&r == &--r`. Both of the following properties must hold: `--(++r) == r`, and if `--r == --s`, then `r == s`.
`r--`	Return type must be convertible to `const X&`. The result must be the same as that of `{X tmp = r; --r; return tmp;}`.
`*r--`	Return type must be convertible to `T`.

20.5 Random Access Iterator Requirements

A class or a built-in type `X` satisfies the requirements of a random access iterator for the value type `T` if and only if the following expressions are defined and meet the requirements specified for them, in addition to the requirements of a bidirectional iterator type:

`r += n`	Return type must be `X&`. The result must be the same as would be computed by

```
{
    Distance m = n;
    if (m >= 0)
        while (m--) ++r;
    else
        while (m++) --r;
    return r;
}
```

	but is computed in constant time.
`a + n`	Return type must be `X`. The result must be the same as would be computed by `{X tmp = a; return tmp += n;}`.
`n + a`	Same as `a + n`.
`r -= n`	Return type must be `X&`. The result must be the same as would be computed by `r += -n`.
`a - n`	Return type must be `X`. The result must be the same as would be computed by `{X tmp = a; return tmp -= n;}`.

b - a   Return type must be the iterator's difference type. It is assumed that there exists a value n of the difference type such that a + n == b; the result returned is n.

a[n]   Return type must be convertible to T. The result is *(a + n).

a < b   Return type must be convertible to bool, and < must be a total ordering relation (see Section 5.4 for a discussion or ordering relations).

a > b   Return type must be convertible to bool, and > must be a total ordering relation opposite to <.

a >= b   Return type is convertible to bool, and the result must be the same as !(a < b).

a <= b   Return type is convertible to bool, and the result must be the same as !(b < a).

20.6 Iterator Traits

Within an algorithm defined in terms of an iterator, it is often necessary to determine properties of the iterator: its value type, its difference type, its category, and so forth. As a result for a type Iterator, five types must be defined:

- iterator_traits<Iterator>::difference_type   Type that can be used to represent the distance between two iterators.

- iterator_traits<Iterator>::value_type   Type resulting from dereferencing the iterator.

- iterator_traits<Iterator>::pointer   Pointer to value_type.

- iterator_traits<Iterator>::reference Reference to value_type.

- iterator_traits<Iterator>::iterator_category Defines the category (input, output, forward, etc.) of the iterator. See Section 20.6.2 for details on the possible definitions for iterator_category.

The template class iterator_traits is defined as follows.

```
template <typename Iterator> struct iterator_traits {
  typedef typename Iterator::difference_type difference_type;
  typedef typename Iterator::value_type value_type;
  typedef typename Iterator::pointer pointer;
  typedef typename Iterator::reference reference;
  typedef typename Iterator::iterator_category
                   iterator_category;
};
```

Thus, an iterator class must define the types `difference_type`, `value_type`, `reference`, `pointer`, and `iterator_category`. The base class `iterator` (see Section 20.6.1 for details) can be used to define these types.

For this mechanism to work properly for pointer types (which are random access iterators), two specializations are defined for `iterator_traits`.

```
template <typename T> struct iterator_traits<T*> {
  typedef ptrdiff_t difference_type;
  typedef T value_type;
  typedef T* pointer;
  typedef T& reference;
  typedef random_access_iterator_tag iterator_category;
};

template <typename T> struct iterator_traits<const T*> {
  typedef ptrdiff_t difference_type;
  typedef T value_type;
  typedef const T* pointer;
  typedef const T& reference;
  typedef random_access_iterator_tag iterator_category;
};
```

See Example 16.1 for a use of `iterator_traits`.

20.6.1   Iterator Base Class

To simplify the definition of the types required for iterator types by `iterator_traits`, a template class is provided that makes the required definitions. An iterator class may use `iterator` as a base class to automatically generate the necessary definitions.

```
template <typename Category, typename T,
        typename Difference = ptrdiff_t,
        typename Pointer = T*, typename Reference = T&>
struct iterator {
  typedef T           value_type;
```

```
    typedef Difference  difference_type;
    typedef Pointer     pointer;
    typedef Reference   reference;
    typedef Category    iterator_category;
};
```

20.6.2   Standard Iterator Tags

The `iterator_category` defined by `iterator_traits` can be used to select a different algorithm based on the type of iterator provided as a function argument. Five types are provided to be used as iterator categories. An iterator should use the most specific tag as its iterator category.

```
struct input_iterator_tag {};
struct output_iterator_tag {};
struct forward_iterator_tag: public input_iterator_tag {};
struct bidirectional_iterator_tag :
  public forward_iterator_tag {};
struct random_access_iterator_tag :
  public bidirectional_iterator_tag {};
```

An example of using the iterator category to select from alternative implementations follows.

```
template <typename InputIterator>
void my_algorithm(InputIterator start, InputIterator finish) {
  typedef iterator_traits<InputIterator> traits;
  my_algorithm_impl(start, finish,
                    typename traits::iterator_category());
}


template <typename RandomAccessIterator>
void my_algorithm_impl(RandomAccessIterator start,
                       RandomAccessIterator finish,
                       random_access_iterator_tag) {
  // Specialized implementation for random access iterators
}


template <typename InputIterator>
void my_algorithm_impl(InputIterator start,
                       InputIterator finish,
                       input_iterator_tag) {
  // Default implementation for any input iterator
}
```

The `my_algorithm` function is defined for input iterators, but we have a specialized implementation for random access iterators that is more efficient. When `my_algorithm` is called on a range, it invokes `my_algorithm_impl` passing an instance of the iterators' category as an additional argument. If the iterators are random access, the first version of `my_algorithm_impl` is used. For any other category of iterators, the second version is used.

20.7   Iterator Operations

Since only random access iterators provide + and – operations, the library provides template functions that perform the same computations for input, forward, and bidirectional iterators (and also for random access iterators). When applied to a random access iterator, the functions use the existing + and – operations to perform the computation, and therefore they take constant time. For other iterator categories, they complete in linear time using the ++ operation.

```
template <typename InputIterator, typename Difference>
void advance(InputIterator& i, Difference n);
```

> Increments (or decrements if `n < 0`) `i` by `n`. `n` may be negative only for random access and bidirectional iterators.

```
template <typename InputIterator>
typename iterator_traits<InputIterator>::difference_type
distance(InputIterator first, InputIterator last);
```

> Returns the number of increments necessary to reach `last` from `first`; `last` must be reachable from `first`.

20.8   Istream Iterators

STL provides *stream iterators*, defined by template classes, to allow algorithms to work directly with input/output streams. The `istream_iterator` class defines input iterator types, and the `ostream_iterator` class defines output iterator types. For example, the code fragment

```
istream_iterator<int> end_of_stream;
partial_sum(istream_iterator<int>(cin),
            end_of_stream,
            ostream_iterator<int>(cout, "\n"));
```

reads a file containing integers from the input stream `cin` and sends the partial sums to `cout`, separated by newline characters.

This section is a reference guide for `istream_iterators`, which are used to read values from the input stream for which they are constructed. Section 20.9 covers `ostream_iterators`, which are used to write values into the output stream for which they are constructed.

20.8.1 Files

```
#include <iterator>
```

20.8.2 Class Declaration

```
template <typename T, typename charT = char,
          typename traits = char_traits<charT>,
          typename Difference = ptrdiff_t>
class istream_iterator :
  public iterator<input_iterator_tag, T,
                  Difference, const T*, const T&>
```

20.8.3 Examples

See Examples 4.1, 12.1, 13.1, 14.1, and 15.1.

20.8.4 Description

An `istream_iterator<T>` reads (using `operator>>`) successive elements of type `T` from the input stream for which it was constructed. Each time `++` is used on a constructed `istream_iterator<T>` object, the iterator reads and stores a value of type `T`. The end-of-stream value is reached when `operator void*()` on the stream returns `false`. In this case, the iterator becomes equal to the *end-of-stream iterator value*. This end-of-stream value can only be constructed using the constructor with no arguments: `istream_iterator<T>()`. Two end-of-stream iterators are always equal. An end-of-stream iterator is not equal to a non-end-of-stream iterator. Two non-end-of-stream iterators are equal when they are constructed from the same stream.

One can use `istream_iterators` only to read values; it is impossible to store anything into a position to which an `istream_iterator` value refers.

The main peculiarity of `istream_iterators` is the fact that `++` operators do not preserve equality; that is, `i == j` does not guarantee that `++i == ++j`. Every time `++` is used, a new value is read from the associated istream.

The practical consequence of this fact is that `istream_iterators` can be used only with single-pass algorithms.

20.8.5   Type Definitions

`char_type`

> Type of character (typically `char` or `wchar_t`) contained in the stream (`charT`).

`traits_type`

> Traits of the character type contained in the stream (`traits`). See Section B.2 for more information on character traits.

`istream_type`

> Type of the iterator's underlying stream (`basic_istream<charT, traits>`).

20.8.6   Constructors

`istream_iterator();`

> Constructs the end-of-stream iterator value. Note that two end-of-stream iterators are always equal.

`istream_iterator(istream_type& s);`

> Constructs an `istream_iterator<T>` object that reads values from the input stream `s`. The first value may be read from the stream at this time, but it is not guaranteed to be read until it is referenced.

```
istream_iterator(const istream_iterator<T, charT,
                                   traits, Difference>& x);
```

> Copy constructor.

`~istream_iterator();`

> Destructor.

20.8.7   Public Member Functions

```
const T& operator*() const;
```

> Dereferencing operator. By returning a reference to const T, it ensures that it cannot be used to write values to the input stream for which the iterator is constructed.

```
const T* operator->() const;
```

> Dereferencing operator. By returning a pointer to const T, it ensures that it cannot be used to write values to the input stream for which the iterator is constructed.

```
istream_iterator<T, charT, traits, Difference>& operator++();
```

> Reads and stores a value of T each time it is called.

```
istream_iterator<T, charT, traits, Difference> operator++(int);
```

> Reads and stores a value of T each time it is called.

20.8.8   Comparison Operations

```
template <typename T, typename charT,
          typename traits, typename Difference>
bool operator==(const istream_iterator<T, charT,
                                        traits, Difference>& x,
                const istream_iterator<T, charT,
                                        traits, Difference>& y);
```

> Equality operator. Two end-of-stream iterators are always equal. An end-of-stream iterator is not equal to a non-end-of-stream iterator. Two non-end-of-stream iterators are equal when they are constructed from the same stream.

20.9   Ostream Iterators

20.9.1   Files

```
#include <iterator>
```

20.9.2 Class Declaration

```
template <typename T, typename charT = char,
          typename traits = char_traits<charT> >
class ostream_iterator :
    public iterator<output_iterator_tag, void, void, void, void>
```

20.9.3 Examples

See Examples 10.2, 13.1, and 14.1.

20.9.4 Description

An `ostream_iterator<T>` object writes (using `operator<<`) successive elements onto the output stream for which it was constructed. If it is constructed with `charT*` as a constructor argument, then this *delimiter* string is written to the stream after each T value is written.

It is not possible to read a value with an output iterator. It can only be used to write values to an output stream for which it is constructed.

20.9.5 Type Definitions

`char_type`

> Type of character (typically `char` or `wchar_t`) contained in the stream (`charT`).

`traits_type`

> Traits of the character type contained in the stream (`traits`). See Section B.2 for more information on character traits.

`ostream_type`

> Type of the iterator's underlying stream (`basic_ostream<charT, traits>`).

20.9.6 Constructors

`ostream_iterator(ostream_type& s);`

> Constructs an iterator that can be used to write to the output stream s.

```
ostream_iterator(ostream_type& s, const charT* delimiter);
```

> Constructs an iterator that can be used to write to the output stream s. The character string `delimiter` is written out after every value (of type T) written to s.

```
ostream_iterator(const ostream_iterator<T, charT, traits>& x);
```

> Copy constructor.

```
~ostream_iterator();
```

> Destructor.

20.9.7   Public Member Functions

```
ostream_iterator<T, charT, traits>& operator*();
```

> Dereferencing operator. An assignment `*o = t` through an output iterator o causes t to be written to the output stream, and the stream pointer is advanced in preparation for the next write.

```
ostream_iterator<T, charT, traits>& operator=(const T& x);
```

> Causes the value x to be written to the output stream, and the stream pointer is advanced in preparation for the next write.

```
ostream_iterator<T, charT, traits>& operator++();
ostream_iterator<T, charT, traits> operator++(int x);
```

> Allow ostream iterators to be used with algorithms that both assign through an output iterator and advance the iterator; they actually do nothing, since assignments through the iterator advance the stream pointer also.

20.10   Reverse Iterators

20.10.1   Files

```
#include <iterator>
```

20.10.2   Class Declaration

```
template <typename Iterator>
class reverse_iterator :
    public iterator<
            typename iterator_traits<Iterator>::iterator_category,
            typename iterator_traits<Iterator>::value_type,
            typename iterator_traits<Iterator>::difference_type,
            typename iterator_traits<Iterator>::pointer,
            typename iterator_traits<Iterator>::reference>
```

In subsequent sections we assume the following type definition for the sake of brevity:

```
typedef reverse_iterator<Iterator> self;
```

The class also provides the following type definition for the adapted iterator type.

```
typedef Iterator iterator_type;
```

20.10.3   Examples

See Examples 2.15, 10.1, and 10.2.

20.10.4   Description

The `reverse_iterator` adaptor takes a random access or bidirectional iterator and produces a new iterator for traversal in the opposite of the normal direction. To iterate through elements in some valid range $[i, j)$ in reverse order, start with a reverse iterator initialized with j and increment it j − i − 1 times with `++`. The elements traversed are those that would be obtained by initializing a normal iterator with j − 1 and decrementing it j − i − 1 times with `--`, namely those in positions j − 1, j − 2, ..., i + 1, i. Note that iterator i − 1 might not be defined (in fact, it isn't if i marks the beginning of some container) and so cannot serve as a past-the-end value for reverse iteration. This problem is solved by defining the dereference operator `*` on reverse iterators so that

$$\&*(\texttt{reverse\_iterator}(i)) == \&*(i - 1)$$

This mapping allows the reverse iterator to use iterators j, j − 1, ..., i + 1 as though they were j − 1, j − 2, ..., i + 1, i, and iterator i is then available to use as the past-the-end value.

The `reverse_iterator` adaptor can be used with both random access and bidirectional iterators. The resulting `reverse_iterator` is in the same iterator category as the original. Thus, if any of the member functions `operator+`, `operator-`, `operator+=`, `operator-=`, and `operator[]` or the global operations `operator<`, `operator>`, `operator<=`, `operator>=`, `operator-` and `operator+` is referenced in a way that requires instantiation (treating the `reverse_iterator` as a random access iterator), the adapted iterator type must also be a random access iterator.

20.10.5 Constructor

```
reverse_iterator();
```

Default constructor; produces a singular value.

```
explicit reverse_iterator(iterator_type x);
```

Creates a reverse iterator with current position specified by `x`, according to relation in Section 20.10.4 (`&*(reverse_iterator(x)) == &*(x - 1)`).

```
template <typename U>
reverse_iterator(const reverse_iterator<U>& u);
```

Creates a reverse iterator with current position specified by `u.base()`. This presumes that a conversion exists from `U` to `Iterator`.

20.10.6 Public Member Functions

```
iterator_type base() const;
```

Returns an iterator to the current position (for which `++` and `--` have the opposite meanings from those of this reverse iterator).

```
reference operator*() const;
```

Dereferencing operator; the result must be the same as that of `{iterator_type tmp = base(); return *--tmp;}`.

```
pointer operator->() const;
```

Dereferencing operator; returns `&(operator*())`.

```
self& operator++();
```

> Changes current position to **base()** - **1** and returns the resulting iterator.

```
self operator++(int);
```

> Changes current position to **base()** - **1** but returns an iterator to the former position.

```
self& operator--();
```

> Changes current position to **base()** + **1** and returns the resulting iterator.

```
self operator--(int);
```

> Changes current position to **base()** + **1** but returns an iterator to the former position.

```
self operator+(difference_type n) const;
```

> Returns a reverse random access iterator to **base()** - **n**.

```
self& operator+=(difference_type n);
```

> Changes current position to **base()** - **n** and returns the resulting iterator.

```
self operator-(difference_type n) const;
```

> Returns a reverse random access iterator to **base()** + **n**.

```
self& operator-=(difference_type n);
```

> Changes current position to **base()** + **n** and returns the resulting iterator.

```
reference operator[](difference_type n) const;
```

> Returns ***(*this + n)**.

20.10.7   Global Operations

```
template <typename Iterator>
typename reverse_iterator<Iterator>::difference_type
operator-(const reverse_iterator<Iterator>& x,
          const reverse_iterator<Iterator>& y);
```

Returns `y.base() - x.base()`.

```
template <typename Iterator>
reverse_iterator<Iterator>
operator+(typename reverse_iterator<Iterator>::difference_type n,
          const reverse_iterator<Iterator>& y);
```

Returns `y + n`.

20.10.8   Equality and Ordering Predicates

```
template <typename Iterator>
bool operator==(const reverse_iterator<Iterator>& x,
                const reverse_iterator<Iterator>& y);
```

Returns `(x.base() == y.base())`.

```
template <typename Iterator>
bool operator<(const reverse_iterator<Iterator>& x,
               const reverse_iterator<Iterator>& y);
```

Returns `(y.base() < x.base())`.

20.11   Back Insert Iterators

20.11.1   Files

```
#include <iterator>
```

20.11.2   Class Declaration

```
template <typename Container>
class back_insert_iterator :
public iterator<output_iterator_tag, void, void, void, void>
```

Container must be a type for which `Container::const_reference` is a type and that has a `push_back` member function that takes a single argument of type `Container::const_reference`.

20.11.3 Examples

See Examples 12.1, 13.1, and 14.1.

20.11.4 Description

Insert iterator adaptors take a container (and in some cases an iterator into the container) and produce output iterators that convert assignments through the iterator into insertions instead. There are three types of insert iterator adaptors. One is `back_insert_iterator<Container>`, whose objects use the `Container` class's `push_back` member function to do the insertions at the end of the container. This class is described in this section, along with a template function `back_inserter`, which is usually more convenient to use than the class. The next section describes the corresponding components for using `push_front` to do the insertions, namely the `front_insert_iterator<Container>` class and `front_inserter` template function; Section 20.13 describes the components for using `insert`, namely the `insert_iterator<Container>` class and `inserter` template function.

20.11.5 Constructors

```
explicit back_insert_iterator(Container& x);
```

> Constructs an insert iterator i for converting assignments `*i = value` into use of `x.push_back(value)` instead.

20.11.6 Public Member Functions

```
back_insert_iterator<Container>&
operator=(typename Container::const_reference& value);
```

> Performs `x.push_back(value)`, where x is the container the constructor associates with the iterator. Returns the iterator.

```
back_insert_iterator<Container>& operator*();
```

> Returns the iterator itself (`*this`), so that an assignment `*i = value` uses the = operator of `back_insert_iterator<Container>` described previously rather than that of `Container::value_type`.

```
back_insert_iterator<Container>& operator++();
back_insert_iterator<Container> operator++(int);
```

> These do nothing except return the iterator itself (`*this`).

20.11.7 Corresponding Template Function

```
template <typename Container>
back_insert_iterator<Container> back_inserter(Container& x);
```

> Returns `back_insert_iterator<Container>(x)`. This function is
> provided just as a convenience.

20.12   Front Insert Iterators

20.12.1   Files

```
#include <iterator>
```

20.12.2   Class Declaration

```
template <typename Container>
class front_insert_iterator :
public iterator<output_iterator_tag, void, void, void, void>
```

`Container` must be a type for which `Container::const_reference` is a type
and that has a `push_front` member function that takes a single argument
of type `Container::const_reference`.

20.12.3   Constructors

```
explicit front_insert_iterator(Container& x);
```

> Constructs an insert iterator `i` for converting assignments `*i = value`
> into use of `x.push_front(value)` instead.

20.12.4   Public Member Functions

```
front_insert_iterator<Container>&
operator=(typename Container::const_reference& value);
```

> Performs `x.push_front(value)`, where `x` is the container the con-
> structor associates with the iterator. Returns the iterator.

```
front_insert_iterator<Container>& operator*();
```

> Returns the iterator itself (`*this`), so that an assignment `*i = value`
> uses the `=` operator of `front_insert_iterator<Container>` described
> previously rather than that of `Container::value_type`.

```
front_insert_iterator<Container>& operator++();
front_insert_iterator<Container> operator++(int);
```

> These do nothing except return the iterator itself (`*this`).

20.12.5   Corresponding Template Function

```
template <typename Container>
front_insert_iterator<Container> front_inserter(Container& x);
```

> Returns `front_insert_iterator<Container>(x)`. This function is provided just as a convenience.

20.13   Insert Iterators

20.13.1   Files

```
#include <iterator>
```

20.13.2   Class Declaration

```
template <typename Container>
class insert_iterator :
public iterator<output_iterator_tag, void, void, void, void>
```

`Container` must be a type for which both `Container::iterator` and `Container::const_reference` are types, and that has an `insert` member function with interface

```
typename Container::iterator
insert(typename Container::iterator,
       typename Container::const_reference&);
```

20.13.3   Examples

See Examples 7.3 and 7.4.

20.13.4   Constructors

```
insert_iterator(Container& x, typename Container::iterator i);
```

> Constructs an insert iterator i for converting assignments `*i = value` into use of `x.insert(i, value)` instead.

20.13.5   Public Member Function

```
insert_iterator<Container>&
operator=(typename Container::const_reference& value);
```

Performs `i = x.insert(i, value); ++i;`, where `x` is the container the constructor associates with the insert iterator and `i` is the current value of the iterator passed to the constructor and updated as shown. Returns the insert iterator.

```
insert_iterator<Container>& operator*();
```

Returns the iterator itself (`*this`) so that an assignment `*i = value` uses the `=` operator of `insert_iterator<Container>` described previously rather than that of `Container::const_reference`.

```
insert_iterator<Container>& operator++();
insert_iterator<Container> operator++(int);
```

Do nothing except return the iterator itself (`*this`).

20.13.6 Corresponding Template Function

```
template <typename Container, typename Iterator>
insert_iterator<Container> inserter(Container& x, Iterator i);
```

Returns `insert_iterator<Container>(x, i)` (see Examples 7.3 and 7.4). This function is provided just as a convenience.

CHAPTER 21

Container Reference Guide

21.1 Requirements

21.1.1 Basic Design and Organization of STL Containers

STL containers are divided into two broad families: *sequence containers* and *sorted associative containers*.

Sequence containers include vectors, lists, and deques, which contain elements of a single type organized in a strictly linear arrangement. Although only the three most basic sequence containers are provided, it is possible to construct other sequence containers efficiently using these basic containers through the use of *container adaptors*, which are STL classes that provide interface mappings. STL provides adaptors for stacks, queues, and priority queues.

Sorted associative containers include sets, multisets, maps, and multimaps. Associative containers allow for the fast retrieval of data based on keys. For example, a map allows a user to retrieve an object of type T based on a key of some other type, while sets allow for the fast retrieval of the keys themselves.

All STL containers have three important characteristics:

1. Every container allocates and manages its own storage.

2. Every container provides a minimal set of operations as member functions to access and maintain its storage:

   - *Constructors and destructors* allow users to construct and destroy instances of the container. Most containers have several kinds of constructors.

- *Element access member functions* allow users to access the container elements. In most instances, the element access member functions do not change the container.

- *Insertion member functions* are used to insert elements into the container.

- *Erase member functions* are used to delete elements from the container.

3. Each container has an *allocator* object associated with it. The allocator object encapsulates information about the memory model currently being used and allows the classes to be portable across various platforms.

The same naming convention is used for the member functions of all containers, resulting in a uniform interface to all the classes. Some differences exist between sequence and associative container interfaces, which we examine after taking a look at the common components.

21.1.2 Common Members of All Containers

The public members of STL containers fall into a two-level hierarchy. The first level defines members that are common to *all* containers, while the second level contains two categories:

- Members common to sequence containers (vectors, lists, deques)

- Members common to associative containers (sets, maps, multisets, and multimaps)

The common members of all STL containers fall into two distinct categories: *type definitions* and *member functions*. We take a look at each in turn.

Common Type Definitions in All Containers.   Following are the common type definitions found in each STL container. In the definitions, the following assumptions are made.

- X is a container class containing objects of type T.

- a and b are values of X.

- u is an identifier.

- r is a value of X&.

X::value_type

Type of values the container holds.

X::reference

Type that can be used for storing into X::value_type objects. This type is usually X::value_type&.

X::const_reference

Type that can be used for storing into constant X::value_type objects. This type is usually const X::value_type&.

X::iterator

Iterator type for traversing the elements in X. It may be any category of iterator except output iterator. All STL containers use either a random access iterator type (for vector or deque) or a bidirectional iterator type (for other containers).

X::const_iterator

Iterator type for traversing the elements in a constant container X. It may be any category of constant iterator except output iterator. All STL containers use either a constant random access iterator type (for vector or deque) or a constant bidirectional iterator type (for other containers).

X::difference_type

Type that can represent the distance between any two X iterator objects (varies with the memory model).

X::size_type

Type that can represent the size of X (varies with the memory model).

Common Member Functions in All Containers. The common member functions required to be in each STL container are outlined here. In the descriptions, the following assumptions are made.

- X is a container class containing objects of type T.

- a and b are values of X.

- u is an identifier.

- r is a value of X&.

All these operations take constant time unless otherwise noted.

```
X();
```

> Default constructor.

```
X(a);
X u(a);
```

> Copy constructor. Takes linear time.

```
(&a)->~X();
```

> Destructor. The destructor is applied to every element of a, and all the memory is returned. Takes linear time.

```
a.begin();
```

> Returns an `iterator` (`const_iterator` for constant a) that can be used to begin traversing all locations in the container.

```
a.end();
```

> Returns an `iterator` (`const_iterator` for constant a) that can be used in a comparison for ending traversal through the container.

```
a == b
```

> Equality operation on containers of the same type. Returns **true** when the sequences of elements in a and b are elementwise equal (using `X::value_type::operator==`). Takes linear time.

```
a != b
```

The opposite of the equality operation. Takes linear time.

```
a.size();
```

Returns the number of elements in the container.[1]

```
a.max_size();
```

`size()` of the largest possible container.

```
a.empty();
```

Returns **true** if the container is empty (if `a.size() == 0`).

```
a < b
```

Compares two containers lexicographically. Takes linear time.

```
a > b
```

Returns **true** if `b < a`. Takes linear time.

```
a <= b
```

Returns **true** if `!(a > b)`. Takes linear time.

```
a >= b
```

Returns **true** if `!(a < b)`. Takes linear time.

```
r = a
```

Assignment operator for containers. Takes linear time.

```
a.swap(b);
```

Swaps two containers of the same type.

---

[1] Although `size` is generally a constant time operation, the C++ Standard actually leaves open the possibility that it is linear. One case where this could occur is with lists where determining the size could involve a list traversal. It is usually safe to assume that `size` executes in constant time. The same caveats apply to `max_size` and `swap`.

21.1.3 Reversible Container Requirements

If the iterator type of a container is in the bidirectional or random access category, then the container is *reversible*. All STL containers are reversible. Reversible containers must provide two additional types and two additional element access methods. The additional members are defined here. In the definitions, the following assumptions are made.

- X is a reversible container class (for example, a vector, list, or deque).

- a is a value of X.

`X::reverse_iterator`

> Iterator type for reverse direction traversal of X.

`X::const_reverse_iterator`

> Constant iterator type for reverse direction traversal of X.

`a.rbegin();`

> Returns a `reverse_iterator` (`const_reverse_iterator` for constant a) that can be used to begin traversing through all locations of the container in the reverse of the normal order.

`a.rend();`

> Returns a `reverse_iterator` (`const_reverse_iterator` for constant a) that can be used in a comparison for ending a reverse direction traversal through all locations in the container.

21.1.4 Sequence Container Requirements

All STL sequence containers define two constructors, three insert member functions, and two erase member functions in addition to the common types and member functions mentioned in the previous section. The additional members follow. In the definitions, the following assumptions are made

- X is a sequence class (for example, a vector, list, or deque).

- a is a value of X.

- i and j satisfy input iterator requirements and $[i, j)$ is a valid range.

- n is a value of X::size_type.

- p is a valid iterator to a.

- q, q1, and q2 are valid dereferenceable iterators to a, and $[q1, q2)$ is a valid range.

- t is a value of X::value_type.

```
X(n, t);
X a(n, t);
```

Constructs a sequence with n copies of t.

```
X(i, j);
X a(i, j);
```

Constructs a sequence equal to the contents of the range $[i, j)$.

```
a.insert(p, t);
```

Inserts a copy of t before p. Returns an iterator pointing to the inserted copy.

```
a.insert(p, n, t);
```

Inserts n copies of t before p.

```
a.insert(p, i, j);
```

Inserts copies of elements in $[i, j)$ before p. i and j must not be iterators into a.

```
a.erase(q);
```

Erases the element pointed to by q. Returns an iterator pointing to the element following q prior to its being erased or a.end() if q is the last element in the sequence.

```
a.erase(q1, q2);
```

Erases the elements in the range $[q1, q2)$. Returns an iterator pointing to the element following q2 prior to the elements being erased, or a.end() if q2 is the last element in the sequence.

```
a.clear();
```

Erases all elements in the container. Equivalent to the expression a.erase(a.begin(), a.end()) except that clear has no return value.

21.1.5   Sorted Associative Container Requirements

STL provides four basic varieties of sorted associative containers: `set`, `multiset`, `map`, and `multimap`. Before taking a detailed look at the type definitions and member functions provided by the associative containers, we need to define a few terms and explain some of the ideas behind the design.

All associative containers are parameterized on a type `Key` and an ordering relation `Compare` that induces a strict weak ordering on elements of type `Key`. In addition, `map` and `multimap` associate elements of an arbitrary type `T` with `Key` elements. An object of type `Compare` is called the *comparison object* of the container.

For sorted associative containers, equivalence of keys means the equivalence relation imposed by the comparison, not the `operator==` on keys. Thus, two keys `k1` and `k2` are considered equivalent according to the comparison object `comp` if and only if `comp(k1, k2) == false && comp(k2, k1) == false`.

The `set` and `map` containers support *unique* keys; they can store at most one element of each equivalence class of keys. The `multiset` and `multimap` containers support *equivalent* keys: they can store multiple elements that have the same key equivalence class.

For `set` and `multiset`, the value type is the same as the key type; that is, the values stored in sets and multisets are basically the keys themselves. For `map` and `multimap`, the value type is `pair<const Key, T>`: the elements stored in maps and multimaps are pairs whose first elements are `const Key` values and whose second elements are `T` values.

Finally, an `iterator` of a sorted associative container is bidirectional. The `insert` operations do not affect the validity of iterators and references to the container, and `erase` operations invalidate only iterators and references to the erased elements.

Following is a list of the type definitions and member functions defined by sorted associative containers in addition to the common container members outlined previously. In all the definitions, the following assumptions are made.

- `X` is a sorted associative container class.

- `a` is a value of `X`.

- `a_uniq` is a value of `X` when `X` supports unique keys, and `a_eq` is a value of `X` when `X` supports equivalent keys.

- i and j satisfy input iterator requirements and refer to elements of value_type, and [i, j) is a valid range.

- p is a valid iterator to a.

- q, q1, and q2 are valid dereferenceable iterators to a, and [q1, q2) is a valid range.

- t is a value of X::value_type.

- k is a value of X::key_type.

X::key_type

Type of keys, Key, with which X is instantiated.

X::key_compare

Comparison object type, Compare, with which X is instantiated. This defaults to less<key_type>.

X::value_compare

Type for comparing objects of X::value_type. It is the same as key_compare for set and multiset, while for map and multimap it is a type that compares pairs of Key and T values by comparing their keys using X::key_compare.

The following operations take constant time unless otherwise noted.

```
X();
X a;
```

Constructs an empty container using Compare() as a comparison object.

```
X(c);
X a(c);
```

Constructs an empty container using c as a comparison object.

```
X(i, j, c);
X a(i, j, c);
```

> Constructs an empty container using `c` as a comparison object and inserts elements from the range $[i, j)$ in it. Takes $N \log N$ time in general, where N is the distance from `i` to `j`; time is linear if $[i, j)$ is sorted with `value_comp()`.

```
X(i, j);
X a(i, j);
```

> Same as `X(i, j, c)` and `X a(i, j, c)`, but uses `Compare()` as a comparison object.

```
a.key_comp();
```

> Returns the comparison object, of type `X::key_compare`, out of which `a` was constructed.

```
a.value_comp();
```

> Returns an object of type `X::value_compare` constructed out of the comparison object.

```
a_uniq.insert(t);
```

> Inserts `t` if and only if there is no element in the container with key equivalent to the key of `t`. Returns a `pair<iterator, bool>` whose `bool` component indicates whether the insertion was made and whose `iterator` component points to the element with key equivalent to the key of `t`. Takes time logarithmic in the size of the container.

```
a_eq.insert(p, t);
```

> Inserts `t` into the container and returns the iterator pointing to the newly inserted element.

```
a.insert(p, t);
```

> Inserts `t` if and only if there is no element with key equivalent to the key of `t` in containers that support `unique` keys (sets and maps). Always inserts `t` in containers that support equivalent keys (multisets and multimaps). Iterator `p` is a hint pointing to where the insert should start to search. Takes time logarithmic in the size of the container in general but amortized constant if `t` is inserted right after `p`. Returns an iterator pointing to an element with key equivalent to `t`.

```
a.insert(i, j);
```

Inserts the elements from the range $[i, j)$ into the container if and only if there is no element with an equivalent key for containers with unique keys. Takes $N \log(\texttt{size}()+N)$ time in general, where N is the distance from i to j. Linear if $[i, j)$ is sorted according to `value_comp()`.

```
a.erase(k);
```

Erases all elements in the container with key equal to k. Returns the number of erased elements. Takes $O(\log(\texttt{size}()) + \texttt{count}(k))$ time.

```
a.erase(q);
```

Erases the element to which q points.

```
a.erase(q1, q2);
```

Erases all elements in the range $[q1, q2)$. Takes $O(\log(\texttt{size}()) + N)$ time, where N is the distance from q1 to q2.

```
a.clear();
```

Erases all elements in the container. Equivalent to the expression `a.erase(a.begin(), a.end())` except that `clear` has no return value.

```
a.find(k);
```

Returns an iterator pointing to an element with key equivalent to k or `a.end()` if such an element is not found. Takes logarithmic time.

```
a.count(k);
```

Returns the number of elements with keys equivalent to k. Takes $O(\log(\texttt{size}()) + \texttt{count}(k))$ time.

```
a.lower_bound(k);
```

Returns an iterator pointing to the first element with key not less than k. Takes logarithmic time.

```
a.upper_bound(k);
```

> Returns an iterator pointing to the first element with key greater than
> `k`. Takes logarithmic time.

```
a.equal_range(k);
```

> Returns a pair of iterators (constant iterators if `a` is constant) where
> the first is equal to `a.lower_bound(k)` and the second is equal to
> `a.upper_bound(k)`. Takes logarithmic time.

21.2   Organization of the Container Class Descriptions

The remaining sections of this chapter describe the specific requirements for
the three sequence containers (`vector`, `list`, `deque`) and sorted associative
containers (`set`, `multiset`, `map`, `multimap`). Each of these container class
descriptions contains the following subsections.

21.2.1   Files

This section shows the header file to be included in programs that use the
class.

21.2.2   Class Declaration

The class name and template parameters are shown.

21.2.3   Examples

Cross references are given to programs in Parts I and II that use the containers in a nontrivial manner. The descriptions of each member function
also include cross references to examples when applicable.

21.2.4   Description

This section describes the basic functionality of the class. It serves as a
short introduction to the particular container being described.

21.2.5   Type Definitions

Explains the type definitions in the public interface of the class.

21.2.6   Constructors, Destructors, and Related Functions

Contains descriptions of constructors and destructors in the class. Some classes also have other related functions that deal with allocation and de-allocation issues, and these are explained wherever required.

21.2.7   Comparison Operations

Contains descriptions of all operators that are used for comparing two containers.

21.2.8   Element Access Member Functions

Explains the functionality of all member functions that are used to access elements in the container.

21.2.9   Insert Member Functions

Explains all member functions that are used to insert elements into the container.

21.2.10   Erase Member Functions

Details all member functions that are used to erase elements from the container.

21.2.11   Additional Notes Section(s)

This section or sections contain details such as implementation dependencies, time complexity discussions for insert and erase member functions, memory model dependencies, and so on. Any important information that is not included in the other sections is included in the notes sections.

21.3   Vector

21.3.1   Files

```
#include <vector>
```

21.3.2 Class Declaration

```
template <typename T, typename Allocator = allocator<T> >
class vector
```

We omit any detailed mention of the **Allocator** parameter. See Chapter 24 and the sidebar "Allocators" in this section for a discussion of allocators.

Allocators.

Each STL container is parameterized on an allocator type that defaults to **allocator<T>**. This type parameter defines a memory allocation policy and is used to allocate memory used by the container. Each constructor for the container, other than the copy constructor, takes an optional argument of type **Allocator&**. The copy constructor copies the allocator of the object being copied.

Additionally, each container defines the type **allocator_type** as an alias for **Allocator** and defines a member function called **get_allocator** that returns a copy of the allocator used by the constructor.

Detailed discussion of allocators, including the constructor argument, is deferred until Chapter 24. For completeness, however, we show **allocator_type**, **get_allocator** and the default constructor arguments in this chapter.

21.3.3 Examples

See Examples 6.1, 6.2, 6.3, 6.4, 6.5, 6.6, 6.7, 6.8, 12.1, 13.1, 14.1, and 17.1.

21.3.4 Description

Vectors are containers that arrange elements of a given type in a strictly linear arrangement and allow fast random access to any element (any element can be accessed in constant time).

Vectors allow constant time insertions and deletions at the end of the sequence. Inserting and/or deleting elements in the middle of a vector requires linear time. Further details of the time complexity of vector insertion can be found in the notes section.

The **vector** class is specialized for vectors of **bool** to optimize space requirements by storing each value as a single bit. From a functional standpoint, this specialization is identical to other vectors with the addition of a method called **flip**, which inverts all the values in the vector.

332

Additionally, the `reference` type of the specialization supports a similar `flip` method that inverts a particular element (for example, `v[0].flip()` will change the first vector element). Currently controversy surrounds some seemingly contradictory requirements on the vector's `reference` type. On the one hand, the general requirements on a vector indicate that the type `vector<bool>::reference` must be `bool&`. On the other hand, to support the `flip` method, it must be some class type. Until this issue is resolved, it is perhaps best to avoid use of `flip`.

21.3.5 Type Definitions

`iterator`
`const_iterator`

> The random access iterator type `iterator` refers to T; `const_iterator` is a constant random access iterator type that refers to `const T`. It is guaranteed that there is a constructor for `const_iterator` out of `iterator`.

`reference`
`const_reference`

> `reference` is the type of locations of elements of the container. This is simply `T&` (or `const T&` for `const_reference`).

`pointer`
`const_pointer`

> `pointer` is the type of pointers to elements of the container (usually `T*` but more generally it is determined by the allocator type); `const_pointer` is a corresponding constant pointer type.

`size_type`

> Unsigned integral type that can represent the size of any vector instance.

`difference_type`

> Signed integral type that can represent the distance between any two `vector::iterator` objects.

`value_type`

> Type of values the vector holds. This is simply T.

```
reverse_iterator
const_reverse_iterator
```

Nonconstant and constant reverse random access iterators.

```
allocator_type
```

Type of the allocator used by the vector. Equivalent to `Allocator`.

21.3.6   Vector Constructors, Destructors, and Related Functions

```
vector(const Allocator& = Allocator());
```

Default constructor, which constructs a vector of size zero (see Examples 6.1, 6.2 and 6.3).

```
explicit vector(size_type n, const T& value = T(),
              const Allocator& = Allocator());
```

Constructs a vector of size `n` and initializes all its elements with `value` (see Examples 6.1, 6.2 and 6.3). If the second argument is not supplied, `value` is obtained with the default constructor, `T()`, for the element value type `T`.

```
vector(const vector<T, Allocator>& x);
```

Vector copy constructor, which constructs a vector and initializes it with copies of the elements of vector `x` (see Example 6.4).

```
template <typename InputIterator>
vector(InputIterator first, InputIterator last,
     const Allocator& = Allocator());
```

Constructs a vector of size `last - first` and initializes it with copies of elements in the range [`first, last`), which must be a valid range of elements of type `T` (see Example 6.4).

```
vector<T, Allocator>& operator=(const vector<T, Allocator>& x);
```

Vector assignment operator. Replaces the contents of the current vector with a copy of the parameter vector `x`.

```
template <typename InputIterator>
void assign(InputIterator first, InputIterator last);
```

Equivalent to {clear(); insert(begin(), first, last);}. Makes the vector contain copies of elements in the range [first, last), which must be a valid range of elements of type T.

```
void assign(size_type n, const T& u);
```

Equivalent to {clear(); insert(begin(), n, u);}. Makes the vector contain n elements with value u.

```
void reserve(size_type n);
```

Directive that informs the vector of a planned change in size so that storage can be managed accordingly (see Example 6.6). It does not change the size of the vector, and it takes time at most linear in the size of the vector. Reallocation happens at this point if and only if the current capacity is less than the argument of reserve (**capacity** is a vector member function that returns the size of the allocated storage in the vector). After a call to **reserve**, the capacity is greater than or equal to the argument of **reserve** if reallocation happens, and equal to the previous capacity otherwise.

Reallocation invalidates all the references, pointers, and iterators referring to the elements in the vector. It is guaranteed that no reallocation takes place during the insertions that happen after **reserve** takes place until the time when the size of the vector reaches the size specified by **reserve**.

```
~vector();
```

Vector destructor.

```
void swap(vector<T, Allocator>& x);
```

Swaps the contents of the current vector with those of the input vector x. The current vector replaces x and vice versa.

21.3.7   Comparison Operations

```
template <typename T, typename Allocator>
bool operator==(const vector<T, Allocator>& x,
                const vector<T, Allocator>& y);
```

Equality operation on vectors. Returns `true` if the sequences of elements in `x` and `y` are elementwise equal (using `T::operator==`). Takes linear time.

```
template <typename T, typename Allocator>
bool operator<(const vector<T, Allocator>& x,
               const vector<T, Allocator>& y);
```

Returns `true` if `x` is lexicographically less than `y`, `false` otherwise. Takes linear time.

21.3.8 Vector Element Access Member Functions

```
iterator begin();
const_iterator begin() const;
```

Returns an `iterator` (`const_iterator` for constant vector) that can be used to begin traversing through the vector.

```
iterator end();
const_iterator end() const;
```

Returns an `iterator` (`const_iterator` for constant vectors) that can be used in a comparison for ending traversal through the vector.

```
reverse_iterator rbegin();
const_reverse_iterator rbegin();
```

Returns a `reverse_iterator` (`const_reverse_iterator` for constant vectors) that can be used to begin traversing the vector in the reverse of the normal order (see Examples 10.1 and 10.2).

```
reverse_iterator rend();
const_reverse_iterator rend();
```

Returns a `reverse_iterator` (`const_reverse_iterator` for constant vectors) that can be used in a comparison for ending reverse direction traversal through the vector (see Examples 10.1 and 10.2).

```
size_type size() const;
```

Returns the number of elements currently stored in the vector.

```
size_type max_size() const;
```

Returns the maximum possible size of the vector.

```
void resize(size_type sz, T c = T());
```

Resizes the vector to have **sz** elements by either inserting copies of **c** on the end or erasing elements from the end.

```
size_type capacity() const;
```

Returns the largest number of elements that the vector can store without reallocation (see Example 6.6). See also the **reserve** member function.

```
bool empty() const;
```

Returns **true** if the vector contains no elements (if **begin()** == **end()**), **false** otherwise.

```
reference operator[](size_type n);
const_reference operator[](size_type n) const;
```

Returns the nth element from the beginning of the vector in constant time.

```
reference at(size_type n);
const_reference at(size_type n) const;
```

Returns the nth element from the beginning of the vector in constant time after checking the bounds of the vector. Throws out_of_range if **n >= size()**.

```
reference front();
const_reference front() const;
```

Returns the first element of the vector (the element to which the iterator **begin()** refers). Undefined if the vector is empty.

```
reference back();
const_reference back() const;
```

Returns the last element of the vector (the element to which the iterator **end()** - 1 refers; see Example 6.7). Undefined if the vector is empty.

```
allocator_type get_allocator() const;
```

Returns a copy of the allocator used when constructing the object.

21.3.9   Vector Insert Member Functions

The time complexities of all insert member functions are described in Section 21.3.11.

```
void push_back(const T& x);
```

>   Adds the element x at the end of the vector (see Example 6.5).

```
iterator insert(iterator position, const T& x);
```

>   Inserts the element x at the position in the vector referred to by position (see Example 6.5). Elements already in the vector are moved as required. The iterator returned refers to the position where the element was inserted.

```
void insert(iterator position, size_type n, const T& x);
```

>   Inserts n copies of the element x starting at the location to which position refers.

```
template <typename InputIterator>
void insert(iterator position, InputIterator first,
            InputIterator last);
```

>   Copies of elements in the range [first, last) are inserted into the vector at the location to which position refers. [first, last) must be a valid range of elements of type T.

21.3.10   Vector Erase Member Functions

```
void pop_back();
```

>   Erases the last element of the vector (see Example 6.7). Undefined if the vector is empty.

```
iterator erase(iterator position);
```

>   Erases the element of the vector to which position refers (see Example 6.8). Undefined if the vector is empty. Returns an iterator pointing to the element following the erased value or end() if the last element is erased.

```
iterator erase(iterator first, iterator last);
```

The iterators `first` and `last` are assumed to point into the vector, and all elements in the range [`first`, `last`) are erased from the vector (see Example 6.8). Returns an iterator pointing to the element following the erased values or `end()` if the last element is erased. Takes linear time.

```
void clear();
```

Erases all elements in the vector. Equivalent to `a.erase(a.begin(), a.end())` except that `clear` has no return value.

21.3.11   Notes on Vector Insert and Erase Member Functions

Inserting a single element into a vector is linear in the distance from the insertion point to the end of the vector. The amortized complexity of inserting a single element at the end of a vector is constant (see Section 1.5.2 for a discussion of amortized complexity).

Insertion of multiple elements into a vector with a single call of the `insert` member function is linear in the sum of the number of elements plus the distance to the end of the vector unless the iterators are input iterators. For input iterators the complexity is proportional to the length of the range times the distance to the end of the vector. Therefore it is much faster to insert many elements into the middle of a vector at once than to do the insertions one at a time.

All insert member functions cause reallocation if the new size is greater than the old capacity. If no reallocation happens, all the iterators and references before the insertion point remain valid.

The function `erase` invalidates all iterators and references after the point of the erase. The destructor of `T` is called for each erased element and the assignment operator of `T` is called the number of times equal to the number of elements in the vector after the erased elements.

21.4   Deque

21.4.1   Files

```
#include <deque>
```

21.4.2   Class Declaration

```
template <typename T, typename Allocator = allocator<T> >
class deque
```

We omit any detailed mention of the **Allocator** parameter. See Chapter 24 and the sidebar "Allocators" in Section 21.3.2 for a discussion of allocators.

21.4.3 Examples

See Example 6.9.

21.4.4 Description

This class provides sequences that can be efficiently expanded in both directions: they allow constant time insertion and deletion of objects at either end. Like vectors, deques allow fast random access to any element (constant time).

21.4.5 Type Definitions

Same as for vectors (see Section 21.3.5).

21.4.6 Deque Constructors, Destructors, and Related Functions

```
deque(const Allocator& = Allocator());
```

> Default constructor. Constructs a deque with size zero.

```
explicit deque(size_type n, const T& value = T(),
               const Allocator& = Allocator());
```

> Constructs a deque of size **n** and initializes all its elements with **value**. The default for **value** is set to T(), where T() is the default constructor of the type with which the deque is instantiated.

```
deque(const deque<T, Allocator>& x);
```

> Deque copy constructor. Constructs a deque and initializes it with copies of the elements of deque **x**.

```
template <typename InputIterator>
deque(InputIterator first, InputIterator last,
      const Allocator& = Allocator());
```

> Constructs a deque of size **last - first** and initializes it with copies of elements in the range [**first, last**), which must be a valid range of elements of type T.

```
deque<T, Allocator>& operator=(const deque<T, Allocator>& x);
```

Deque assignment operator. Replaces the contents of the current deque with a copy of the parameter deque **x**.

```
template <typename InputIterator>
void assign(InputIterator first, InputIterator last);
```

Equivalent to {**clear()**; **insert(begin()**, **first**, **last);**}. Makes the deque contain copies of elements in the range [**first**, **last**), which must be a valid range of elements of type **T**.

```
void assign(size_type n, const T& u);
```

Equivalent to {**clear()**; **insert(begin()**, **n**, **u);**}. Makes the deque contain **n** elements with value **u**.

```
~deque();
```

Deque destructor.

```
void swap(deque<T, Allocator>& x);
```

Swaps the contents of the current deque with those of the input deque **x**. The current deque replaces **x** and vice versa.

21.4.7   Comparison Operations

```
template <typename T, typename Allocator>
bool operator==(const deque<T, Allocator>& x,
                const deque<T, Allocator>& y);
```

Equality operation on deques. Returns **true** if the sequences of elements in **x** and **y** are elementwise equal (using **T::operator==**). Takes linear time.

```
template <typename T, typename Allocator>
bool operator<(const deque<T, Allocator>& x,
               const deque<T, Allocator>& y);
```

Returns **true** if **x** is lexicographically less than **y**, **false** otherwise. Takes linear time.

21.4.8   Deque Element Access Member Functions

```
iterator begin();
const_iterator begin() const;
```

> Returns an **iterator** (**const_iterator** for constant deque) that can be used to begin traversing through all locations in the deque.

```
iterator end();
const_iterator end() const;
```

> Returns an **iterator** (**const_iterator** for constant deque) that can be used in a comparison for ending traversal through the deque.

```
reverse_iterator rbegin();
const_reverse_iterator rbegin() const;
```

> Returns a **reverse_iterator** (**const_reverse_iterator** for constant deques) that can be used to begin traversing all locations in the deque in the reverse of the normal order.

```
reverse_iterator rend();
const_reverse_iterator rend();
```

> Returns a **reverse_iterator** (**const_reverse_iterator** for constant deques) that can be used in a comparison for ending reverse direction traversal through all locations in the deque.

```
size_type size() const;
```

> Returns the number of elements in the deque.

```
size_type max_size() const;
```

> Returns the maximum possible size of the deque.

```
void resize(size_type sz, T c = T());
```

> Resizes the deque to have **sz** elements by either inserting copies of **c** on the end or erasing elements from the end.

```
bool empty() const;
```

> Returns **true** if the deque contains no elements (if **begin()** == **end()**), **false** otherwise.

```
reference operator[](size_type n);
const_reference operator[](size_type n) const;
```

> Allows constant time access to the nth element of the deque. Undefined if the deque is empty.

```
reference at(size_type n);
const_reference at(size_type n) const;
```

> Returns the nth element from the beginning of the deque in constant time after checking the bounds of the deque. Throws out_of_range if n >= size().

```
reference front();
const_reference front() const;
```

> Returns the first element of the deque (the element to which the iterator begin() refers). Undefined if the deque is empty.

```
reference back();
const_reference back() const;
```

> Returns the last element of the deque (the element to which the iterator end() - 1 refers). Undefined if the deque is empty.

```
allocator_type get_allocator() const;
```

> Returns a copy of the allocator used when constructing the object.

21.4.9 Deque Insert Member Functions

```
void push_front(const T& x);
```

> Adds the element x at the beginning of the deque (see Example 6.9).

```
void push_back(const T& x);
```

> Adds the element x at the end of the deque (see Example 6.9).

```
iterator insert(iterator position, const T& x);
```

> Inserts the element x at the location in the deque to which position refers. The iterator returned refers to the position that contains the inserted element.

```
void insert(iterator position, size_type n, const T& x);
```

Inserts **n** copies of the element **x** starting at the location to which **position** refers.

```
template <typename InputIterator>
void insert(iterator position, InputIterator first,
            InputIterator last);
```

Copies of elements in the range [**first**, **last**) are inserted into the deque at the location to which **position** refers. [**first**, **last**) must be a valid range of elements of type **T**.

21.4.10 Deque Erase Member Functions

```
void pop_front();
```

Erases the first element of the deque. Undefined if the deque is empty.

```
void pop_back();
```

Erases the last element of the deque. Undefined if the deque is empty.

```
iterator erase(iterator position);
```

Erases the element of the deque pointed to by **position**. Returns an iterator pointing to the element following the erased value, or **end()** if the last element is erased.

```
iterator erase(iterator first, iterator last);
```

The iterators **first** and **last** are assumed to point into the deque, and all elements in the range [**first**, **last**) are erased from the deque. Returns an iterator pointing to the element following the erased values or **end()** if the last element is erased. Takes linear time.

```
void clear();
```

Erases all elements in the deque. Equivalent to **a.erase(a.begin()**, **a.end())** except that **clear** has no return value.

21.4.11 Complexity of Deque Insertion

Deques are specially optimized for insertion of single elements at either the beginning or the end of the data structure. Such insertions always take constant time and cause a single call to the copy constructor of T, where T is the type of the inserted object.

If an element is inserted into the middle of the deque, then in the worst case the time taken is linear in the minimum of the distance from the insertion point to the beginning of the deque and the distance from the insertion point to the end of the deque.

The insert, push_front, and push_back member functions invalidate all the iterators to the deque. References are also invalidated by insertions into the middle of the deque.

21.4.12 Notes on Deque Erase Member Functions

The erase, pop_front, and pop_back member functions invalidate all the iterators to the deque. References are also invalidated by erasing from the middle of the deque. The number of calls to the destructor (of the erased type T) is the same as the number of elements erased, but the number of calls to the assignment operator of T is equal to the minimum of the number of elements before the erased elements and the number of elements after the erased elements.

21.5 List

21.5.1 Files

```
#include <list>
```

21.5.2 Class Declaration

```
template <typename T, typename Allocator = allocator<T> >
class list
```

We omit any detailed mention of the Allocator parameter. See Chapter 24 and the sidebar "Allocators" in Section 21.3.2 for a discussion of allocators.

21.5.3 Examples

See Examples 6.10, 6.11, 6.12, 6.13, and 14.1.

21.5.4   Description

This class implements the sequence abstraction as a linked list. All lists are doubly linked and may be traversed in either direction.

Lists should be used in preference to other sequence abstractions when there are frequent insertions and deletions in the middle of sequences. As with all STL containers, storage management is handled automatically.

Unlike vectors or deques, lists are not random access data structures. For this reason, some STL generic algorithms such as `sort` and `random_shuffle` cannot operate on lists. The list class provides its own `sort` member function.

Besides `sort`, lists also include special member functions for splicing two lists, reversing lists, making all list elements unique, and merging two lists. The special member functions are discussed in Section 21.5.11.

21.5.5   Type Definitions

`iterator`
`const_iterator`

> `iterator` is a bidirectional iterator referring to `T`. `const_iterator` is a constant bidirectional iterator referring to `const T`. It is guaranteed that there is a constructor for `const_iterator` out of `iterator`.

`reference`
`const_reference`

> `reference` is the type of locations in the container. This is simply `T&` (or `const T&` for `const_reference`).

`pointer`
`const_pointer`

> `pointer` is the type of pointers to elements of the container (usually `T*`, but more generally it is determined by the allocator type); `const_pointer` is a corresponding constant pointer type.

`size_type`

> Unsigned integral type that can represent the size of any list instance.

`difference_type`

> Signed integral type that can represent the distance between any two `list::iterator` objects.

`value_type`

> Type **T** of values the list holds.

```
reverse_iterator
const_reverse_iterator
```

> Nonconstant and constant reverse bidirectional iterator types.

`allocator_type`

> The type of the allocator used by the list. Equivalent to `Allocator`.

21.5.6 List Constructors, Destructors, and Related Functions

```
list(const Allocator& = Allocator());
```

> Default constructor. Constructs an empty list.

```
explicit list(size_type n, const T& value = T(),
              const Allocator& = Allocator());
```

> Constructs a list of size **n** and initializes all its elements with **value**.

```
list(const list<T, Allocator>& x);
```

> List copy constructor. Constructs a list and initializes it with copies
> of the elements of list **x**.

```
template <typename InputIterator>
list(InputIterator first, InputIterator last,
     const Allocator& = Allocator());
```

> Constructs a list of size **last** - **first** and initializes it with copies of
> elements in the range [**first**, **last**), which must be a valid range of
> elements of type **T**.

```
list<T, Allocator>& operator=(const list<T, Allocator>& x);
```

> List assignment operator. Replaces the contents of the current list
> with a copy of list **x**.

```
template <typename InputIterator>
void assign(InputIterator first, InputIterator last);
```

> Equivalent to {clear(); insert(begin(), first, last);}. Makes the list contain copies of elements in the range [first, last), which must be a valid range of elements of type T.

```
void assign(size_type n, const T& u);
```

> Equivalent to {clear(); insert(begin(), n, u);}. Makes the list contain n elements with value u.

```
~list();
```

> List destructor.

```
void swap(list<T, Allocator>& x);
```

> Swaps the contents of the current list with those of the input list x. The current list replaces x, and vice versa.

21.5.7 Comparison Operations

```
template <typename T, typename Allocator>
bool operator==(const list<T, Allocator>& x,
                const list<T, Allocator>& y);
```

> Equality operation on lists. Returns true if the sequences of elements in x and y are elementwise equal (using T::operator==). Takes linear time.

```
template <typename T, typename Allocator>
bool operator<(const list<T, Allocator>& x,
               const list<T, Allocator>& y);
```

> Returns true if x is lexicographically less than y, false otherwise. Takes linear time. See Section 22.34 for the definition of lexicographical comparison.

21.5.8 List Element Access Member Functions

```
iterator begin();
const_iterator begin() const;
```

> Returns an `iterator` (`const_iterator` for constant list) that can be used to begin traversing through the list.

```
iterator end();
const_iterator end() const;
```

> Returns an `iterator` (`const_iterator` for constant list) that can be used in a comparison for ending traversal through the list.

```
reverse_iterator rbegin();
const_reverse_iterator rbegin() const;
```

> Returns a `reverse_iterator` (`const_reverse_iterator` for constant lists) that can be used to begin traversing the list in the reverse of the normal order (see Examples 10.1 and 10.2).

```
reverse_iterator rend();
const_reverse_iterator rend() const;
```

> Returns a `reverse_iterator` (`const_reverse_iterator` for constant lists) that can be used in a comparison for ending reverse direction traversal through the list (see Examples 10.1 and 10.2).

```
size_type size() const;
```

> Returns the number of elements currently stored in the list.

```
size_type max_size() const;
```

> Returns the maximum possible size of the list.

```
void resize(size_type sz, T c = T());
```

> Resizes the list to have `sz` elements by either inserting copies of `c` on the end or erasing elements from the end.

```
bool empty() const;
```

> Returns `true` if the list contains no elements (i.e., if `begin()` == `end()`), `false` otherwise.

```
reference front();
const_reference front() const;
```

> Returns the first element of the list (the element pointed to by the iterator `begin()`). Undefined if the list is empty.

```
reference back();
const_reference back() const;
```

> Returns the last element of the list (the element pointed to by the iterator `end() - 1`). Undefined if the list is empty.

```
allocator_type get_allocator() const;
```

> Returns a copy of the allocator used when constructing the object.

21.5.9 List Insert Member Functions

```
void push_front(const T& x);
```

> Inserts the element `x` at the beginning of the list (see Example 6.10).

```
void push_back(const T& x);
```

> Inserts the element `x` at the end of the list (see Examples 6.10 and 15.1).

```
iterator insert(iterator position, const T& x);
```

> Inserts the element `x` at the position in the list to which `position` points. The iterator returned points to the position that contains the inserted element.

```
void insert(iterator position, size_type n,
        const T& x);
```

> Inserts `n` copies of the element `x` starting at the position to which iterator `position` is pointing.

```
template <typename InputIterator>
void insert(iterator position, InputIterator first,
        InputIterator last);
```

> Copies of elements in the range [`first`, `last`) are inserted into the list at the position to which `position` refers. [`first`, `last`) must be a valid range of elements of type T.

21.5.10   List Erase Member Functions

```
void pop_front();
```

Erases the first element of the list. Undefined if the list is empty.

```
void pop_back();
```

Erases the last element of the list. Undefined if the list is empty.

```
iterator erase(iterator position);
```

Erases the element of the list to which the iterator `position` points (see Example 6.11). Undefined if the list is empty. Returns an iterator pointing to the element following the erased value or `end()` if the last element is erased.

```
iterator erase(iterator first, iterator last);
```

The iterators `first` and `last` are assumed to point into the list, and all elements in the range [`first`, `last`) are erased from the list. Returns an iterator pointing to the element following the erased values or `end()` if the last element is erased.

```
void clear();
```

Erases all elements in the list. Equivalent to `a.erase(a.begin(), a.end())` except that `clear` has no return value.

21.5.11   Special List Operations: Splice, Remove, Remove If, Unique, Merge, Reverse, Sort

```
void splice(iterator position, list<T, Allocator>& x);
```

Inserts the contents of list `x` before `position` and removes all elements from `x` (see Example 6.12). Takes constant time. Essentially, the contents of `x` are transferred into the current list. Invalidates all iterators and references to the list `x`.

```
void splice(iterator position, list<T, Allocator>& x, iterator i);
```

Inserts the element pointed to by iterator i in list x before `position` and removes the element from x (see Example 6.12). Takes constant time. i is assumed to be a valid iterator in the list x. Invalidates iterators and references to the spliced element.

```
void splice(iterator position, list<T, Allocator>& x,
            iterator first, iterator last);
```

Inserts the elements contained in the range [`first`, `last`) in list x before `position` and removes the elements from list x (see Example 6.12). The operation takes time proportional to `last` - `first` unless `&x` == `this`; in that case, it takes constant time. The range [`first`, `last`) is assumed to be a valid range in x, and `position` must not be in [`first`, `last`). Invalidates iterators and references to the spliced elements.

```
void remove(const T& value);
```

Erases all elements in the list that are equal (using `T::operator==`) to `value`. The relative order of other elements is not affected. The entire list is traversed exactly once.

```
template <typename Predicate>
void remove_if(Predicate pred);
```

Erases all elements in the list that satisfy `pred` (all x for which `pred(x)` returns true). The relative order of other elements is not affected. The entire list is traversed exactly once.

```
void unique();
```

Erases all but the first element from every consecutive group of equal elements in the list (see Example 6.13). Exactly `size()` - 1 applications of `T::operator==` are done. This function is most useful when the list is sorted so that all elements that are equal appear in consecutive positions. In that case, each element in the resulting list is unique.

```
template <typename BinaryPredicate>
void unique(BinaryPredicate binary_pred);
```

Erases all but the first element from every consecutive group of elements in the list such that `binary_pred` returns `true` when applied to a pair of the elements. Exactly `size() - 1` applications of `binary_pred` are done.

```
void merge(list<T, Allocator>& x);
```

Merges the argument list `x` into the current list. It is assumed that both lists are sorted according to the `operator<` of type `T`. The merge is stable; for equivalent elements in the two lists, the elements from the current list always precede the elements from the argument list `x`. `x` is empty after the merge. At most `size() + x.size() - 1` comparisons are done.

```
template <typename Compare>
void merge(list<T, Allocator>& x, Compare comp);
```

Merges the argument list `x` into the current list. It is assumed that both lists are sorted according to the comparison object `comp`. The merge is stable; for equivalent elements in the two lists, the elements from the current list always precede the elements from the argument list `x`. `x` is empty after the merge. At most `size() + x.size() - 1` comparisons are done.

```
void reverse();
```

Reverses the order of the elements in the list. Takes linear time.

```
void sort();
```

Sorts the list according to the `operator<` of type `T` (see Example 6.13). The sort is stable; the relative order of equivalent elements is preserved. $O(N \log N)$ comparisons are done, where N is the size of the list.

```
template <typename Compare>
void sort(Compare comp);
```

Sorts the list using the ordering determined by the `comp` function object. The sort is stable; the relative order of equivalent elements is preserved. $O(N \log N)$ comparisons are done, where N is the size of the list.

21.5.12   Notes on List Insert Member Functions

List insert operations do not affect the validity of iterators and references to other elements of the list. Insertion of a single element of type T into a list takes constant time and makes only one call to the copy constructor of T. Insertion of multiple elements into a list is linear in the number of elements inserted, and the number of calls to the copy constructor of T is exactly equal to the number of elements inserted.

21.5.13   Notes on List Erase Member Functions

The function `erase` invalidates only the iterators and references to the erased elements. Erasing a single element of type T is a constant time operation with a single call to the destructor of T. Erasing a range in a list takes time linear in the size of the range, and the number of calls to the destructor of type T is exactly equal to the size of the range.

21.6   Set

21.6.1   Files

```
#include <set>
```

21.6.2   Class Declaration

```
template <typename Key, typename Compare = less<Key>,
          typename Allocator = allocator<Key> >
class set
```

We omit any detailed mention of the `Allocator` parameter. See Chapter 24 and the sidebar "Allocators" in Section 21.3.2 for a discussion of allocators.

21.6.3   Examples

See Examples 7.1 and 11.2.

21.6.4   Description

A `set<Key, Compare, Allocator>` stores unique elements of type `Key` and allows for the retrieval of the elements themselves. All elements in the set are ordered by the ordering relation `Compare`, which must induce a strict weak ordering on the elements. (See Section 22.26.)

As with all STL containers, the set container only allocates storage and provides a minimal set of operations (such as `insert`, `erase`, `find`, `count`, etc.). The `set` class does not itself provide operations for union, intersection, difference, and so on. These operations are handled by generic algorithms in STL. (See Section 22.31.)

21.6.5 Type Definitions

`key_type`

> Type of the keys, `Key`, with which the set is instantiated.

`value_type`

> Same as `key_type`.

`reference`
`const_reference`

> `reference` is a constant reference type of locations in the container. This is simply `Key&` (or `const Key&` for `const_reference`).

`pointer`
`const_pointer`

> `pointer` is the type of pointers to elements of the container (usually `Key*` but more generally it is determined by the allocator type); `const_pointer` is a corresponding constant pointer type.

`key_compare`

> The comparison object type, `Compare`, with which the set is instantiated. This type is used to order the keys in the set.

`value_compare`

> Type of the ordering relation used to order the values stored in the set. It is the same as `key_compare`, since the type of a value stored in a set is the same as the type of the key.

`iterator`
`const_iterator`

> `iterator` is a constant bidirectional iterator referring to `const Key`; `const_iterator` is the same type as `iterator`.

`size_type`

> Unsigned integral type that can represent the size of any set instance.

`difference_type`

> Signed integral type that can represent the distance between any two `set::iterator` objects.

`reverse_iterator`
`const_reverse_iterator`

> These are the same constant reverse bidirectional iterator type.

`allocator_type`

> Type of the allocator used by the set. Equivalent to `Allocator`.

21.6.6   Set Constructors, Destructors, and Related Functions

```
explicit set(const Compare& comp = Compare(),
             const Allocator& = Allocator());
```

> Default constructor(see Example 7.1). Constructs an empty set and stores the comparison object `comp` for ordering the elements.

```
set(const set<Key, Compare, Allocator>& x);
```

> Set copy constructor. Constructs a set and initializes it with copies of the elements of set `x`.

```
template <typename InputIterator>
set(InputIterator first, InputIterator last,
    const Compare& comp = Compare(),
    const Allocator& = Allocator());
```

> Constructs an empty set and inserts copies of elements in the range [`first, last`), which must be a valid range of elements of `value_type` (`Key`). The comparison object `comp` is used to order the elements of the set.

```
set<Key, Compare, Allocator>&
operator=(const set<Key, Compare, Allocator>& x);
```

> Set assignment operator. Replaces the contents of the current set with a copy of set `x`.

```
void swap(set<Key, Compare, Allocator>& x);
```

> Swaps the contents of the current set with those of set `x`.

```
~set();
```

> Set destructor.

21.6.7 Comparison Operations

```
template <typename Key, typename Compare, typename Allocator>
bool operator==(const set<Key, Compare, Allocator>& x,
                const set<Key, Compare, Allocator>& y);
```

Equality operation on sets. Returns **true** if the sequences of elements in x and y are elementwise equal (using T::operator==). Takes linear time.

```
template <typename Key, typename Compare, typename Allocator>
bool operator<(const set<Key, Compare, Allocator>& x,
               const set<Key, Compare, Allocator>& y);
```

Returns **true** if x is lexicographically less than y, **false** otherwise. Takes linear time.

21.6.8 Set Element Access Member Functions

```
key_compare key_comp() const;
```

Returns the comparison object of the set.

```
value_compare value_comp() const;
```

Returns an object of type **value_compare** constructed out of the comparison object. For sets, this is the same as the comparison object of the set.

```
iterator begin() const;
```

Returns a constant iterator that can be used to begin traversing through all locations in the set.

```
iterator end() const;
```

Returns a constant iterator that can be used in a comparison for ending traversal through the set.

```
reverse_iterator rbegin() const;
```

Returns a constant reverse iterator that can be used to begin traversing all locations in the set in the reverse of the normal order.

```
reverse_iterator rend() const;
```

Returns a constant reverse iterator that can be used in a comparison for ending reverse direction traversal through all locations in the set.

```
bool empty() const;
```

Returns **true** if the set is empty, **false** otherwise.

```
size_type size() const;
```

Returns the number of elements in the set.

```
size_type max_size() const;
```

Returns the maximum possible size of the set. The maximum size is simply the total number of elements of type **Key** that can be represented in the memory model used.

```
allocator_type get_allocator() const;
```

Returns a copy of the allocator used when constructing the object.

21.6.9 Set Insert Member Functions

```
iterator insert(iterator position, const value_type& x);
```

Inserts the element **x** into the set if **x** is not already present in the set. The iterator **position** is a hint, indicating where the **insert** function should start to search. The search is necessary since sets are ordered containers. The insertion takes $O(\log N)$ time, where N is the number of elements in the set, but it is amortized constant if **x** is inserted right after **position**.

```
pair<iterator, bool> insert(const value_type& x);
```

Inserts the element **x** into the set if **x** is not already present in the set (see Examples 7.1 and 11.2). The returned value is a **pair** whose **bool** component indicates whether the insertion has taken place and whose **iterator** component points to the just inserted element in the set if the insertion takes place, otherwise to the element **x** already present. The insertion takes $O(\log N)$ time, where N is the number of elements in the set.

```
template <typename InputIterator>
void insert(InputIterator first, InputIterator last);
```

> Copies of elements in the range [first, last) are inserted into the set. [first, last) must be a valid range of elements of type value_type (Key). In general, the time taken for these insertions is $O(d \log(N+d))$, where N is the size of the set and d is the distance from first to last. The time is linear if the range [first, last) is sorted according to the ordering relation value_comp().

21.6.10 Set Erase Member Functions

```
void erase(iterator position);
```

> Erases the set element pointed to by position. The time taken is amortized constant.

```
size_type erase(const key_type& x);
```

> Erases the set element equivalent to x, if present. Returns the number of erased elements, which is 1 if x is present in the set and 0 otherwise. Takes $O(\log N)$ time, where N is the size of the set.

```
void erase(iterator first, iterator last);
```

> The iterators first and last are assumed to point into the set, and all elements in the range [first, last) are erased from the set. The time taken is $O(d + \log N)$, where N is the size of the set and d is the distance from first to last.

```
void clear();
```

> Erases all elements in the set. Equivalent to a.erase(a.begin(), a.end()).

21.6.11 Special Set Operations

```
iterator find(const key_type& x) const;
```

> Searches for the element x in the set. If x is found, the function returns the iterator pointing to it. Otherwise, end() is returned. Takes $O(\log N)$ time, where N is the size of the set.

```
size_type count(const key_type& x) const;
```

Returns the number of elements in the set that are equal to **x**. If **x** is present in the set, this number is 1; otherwise, it is 0. Takes $O(\log N)$ time, where N is the size of of the set.

```
iterator lower_bound(const key_type& x) const;
```

Returns an iterator pointing to the first set element that is not less than **x**. If all elements in the multiset are less than **x**, then **end()** is returned. Since set elements are not repeated, the returned iterator points to **x** itself if **x** is present in the set. Takes $O(\log N)$ time, where N is the size of of the set.

```
iterator upper_bound(const key_type& x) const;
```

The **upper_bound** function returns an iterator to the first set element greater than **x**. If no element in the multiset is greater than **x**, then **end()** is returned. Takes $O(\log N)$ time, where N is the size of of the set.

```
pair<iterator,iterator> equal_range(const key_type& x) const;
```

Returns the pair (**lower_bound(x)**, **upper_bound(x)**). Takes $O(\log N)$ time, where N is the size of of the set.

21.7 Multiset

21.7.1 Files

```
#include <set>
```

21.7.2 Class Declaration

```
template <typename Key, typename Compare = less<Key>,
          typename Allocator = allocator<Key> >
class multiset
```

We omit any detailed mention of the **Allocator** parameter. See Chapter 24 and the sidebar "Allocators" in Section 21.3.2 for a discussion of allocators.

21.7.3 Examples

See Examples 7.2, 7.3, 7.4, and 18.1.

21.7.4   Description

A multiset is an sorted associative container that can store multiple copies of the same key. As with sets, all elements in the multiset are ordered by the ordering relation `Compare`, which induces a strict weak ordering on the elements.

Multisets are necessary because we sometimes need to store elements that are alike in most ways but differ in certain known characteristics. For example, a set of cars sorted by the make of the car would be a multiset: all cars in the set would have the same manufacturer, but they would be different in other aspects, such as engine capacity, price, and so on.

The interface of the multiset class is exactly the same as that of the set class. The only difference is that multisets possibly contain multiple values of the same key value. As a result, some of the member functions also have slightly different semantics.

21.7.5   Type Definitions

Same as for the `set` class. (See Section 21.6.5.)

21.7.6   Multiset Constructors, Destructors, and Related Functions

```
explicit multiset(const Compare& comp = Compare(),
                  const Allocator& = Allocator());
```

>   Default constructor (see Example 7.2). Constructs an empty multiset and stores the comparison object `comp` for ordering the elements.

```
multiset(const multiset<Key, Compare, Allocator>& x);
```

>   Multiset copy constructor. Constructs a multiset and initializes it with copies of the elements of multiset x.

```
template <typename InputIterator>
multiset(InputIterator first, InputIterator last,
         const Compare& comp = Compare(),
         const Allocator& = Allocator());
```

>   Constructs an empty multiset and inserts copies of elements in the range [`first`, `last`), which must be a valid range of elements of type `value_type` (`Key`). The comparison object `comp` is used to order the elements of the multiset.

```
multiset<Key, Compare, Allocator>&
operator=(const multiset<Key, Compare, Allocator>& x);
```

> Multiset assignment operator. Replaces the contents of the current multiset with a copy of multiset **x**.

```
void swap(multiset<Key, Compare, Allocator>& x);
```

> Swaps the contents of the current multiset with those of multiset **x**.

```
~multiset();
```

> Multiset destructor.

21.7.7 Comparison Operations

```
template <typename Key, typename Compare, typename Allocator>
bool operator==(const multiset<Key, Compare, Allocator>& x,
                const multiset<Key, Compare, Allocator>& y);
```

> Equality operation on multisets. Returns **true** if the sequences of elements in **x** and **y** are elementwise equal (using **T::operator==**). Takes linear time.

```
template <typename Key, typename Compare, typename Allocator>
bool operator<(const multiset<Key, Compare, Allocator>& x,
               const multiset<Key, Compare, Allocator>& y);
```

> Returns **true** if **x** is lexicographically less than **y**, **false** otherwise. Takes linear time.

21.7.8 Multiset Element Access Member Functions

```
key_compare key_comp() const;
```

> Returns the comparison object of the multiset.

```
value_compare value_comp() const;
```

> Same function as **key_comp**.

```
iterator begin() const;
```

> Returns a constant iterator that can be used to begin traversing through all locations in the multiset.

```
iterator end() const;
```

Returns a constant iterator that can be used in a comparison for ending traversal through the multiset.

```
reverse_iterator rbegin();
```

Returns a constant reverse iterator that can be used to begin traversing all locations in the multiset in the reverse of the normal order.

```
reverse_iterator rend();
```

Returns a constant reverse iterator that can be used in a comparison for ending reverse direction traversal through all locations in the multiset.

```
bool empty() const;
```

Returns **true** if the multiset is empty, **false** otherwise.

```
size_type size() const;
```

Returns the number of elements in the multiset.

```
size_type max_size() const;
```

Returns the maximum possible size of the multiset.

```
allocator_type get_allocator() const;
```

Returns a copy of the allocator used when constructing the object.

21.7.9   Multiset Insert Member Functions

```
iterator insert(iterator position, const value_type& x);
```

Inserts the element **x** into the multiset. The iterator **position** is a hint indicating where the **insert** function should start to search. Returns an iterator pointing to the newly inserted element. Takes $O(\log N)$ time in general, where N is the number of elements in the multiset, but it is amortized constant if **x** is inserted right after the iterator **position**.

```
iterator insert(const value_type& x);
```

> Inserts the element **x** into the multiset (see Example 7.2) and returns an iterator pointing to the newly inserted element. Takes $O(\log N)$ time, where N is the number of elements in the multiset.

```
template <typename InputIterator>
void insert(InputIterator first, InputIterator last);
```

> [**first**, **last**) must be a valid range of elements of type **Key**. Copies of elements in the range [**first**, **last**) are inserted into the multiset. In general, the time taken for these insertions is $O(d \log(N + d))$, where N is the size of the set and **d** is the distance from **first** to **last**. The time is linear if the range [**first**, **last**) is sorted according to the ordering relation **value_comp()**.

21.7.10   Multiset Erase Member Functions

```
void erase(iterator position);
```

> Erases the multiset element pointed to by **position** (see Example 7.3). The time taken is amortized constant. Note that this function erases only a single element, possibly leaving other elements in the multiset with keys equivalent to ***position**. The time taken is amortized constant.

```
size_type erase(const key_type& x);
```

> Erases all elements equivalent to **x** from the multiset (see Example 7.3). Returns the number of erased elements. In general, this function takes time proportional to $d \log(N + d)$, where N is the size of the set and **d** is the number of elements with key equivalent to **x**.

```
void erase(iterator first, iterator last);
```

> The iterators **first** and **last** are assumed to point into the multiset, and all elements in the range [**first**, **last**) are erased from the multiset (see Example 7.4). Takes $O(d + \log N)$ time, where N is the size of the multiset and **d** is the distance from **first** to **last**.

```
void clear();
```

> Erases all elements in the multiset. Equivalent to the expression **a.erase(a.begin(), a.end())**.

21.7.11   Special Multiset Operations

```
iterator find(const key_type& x) const;
```

Searches for the element x in the multiset (see Example 7.3). If x is found, the function returns an iterator pointing to it. Otherwise, end() is returned. Takes $O(\log N)$ time, where N is the size of the multiset.

```
size_type count(const key_type& x) const;
```

Returns the number of elements in the multiset that are equivalent to x. Takes $O(\log(N) + \texttt{count(x)})$ time, where N is the size of the multiset.

```
iterator lower_bound(const key_type& x) const;
```

Returns an iterator pointing to the first multiset element that is not less than x (see Example 7.4). If all elements in the multiset are less than x, then end() is returned. Takes $O(\log N)$ time, where N is the size of the multiset.

```
iterator upper_bound(const key_type& x) const;
```

Returns an iterator to the first multiset element whose key is greater than x (see Example 7.4). If no element is greater than x, then end() is returned. Takes $O(\log N)$ time, where N is the size of the multiset.

```
pair<iterator,iterator> equal_range(const key_type& x) const;
```

Returns the pair (lower_bound(x), upper_bound(x)). Takes $O(\log N)$ time, where N is the size of of the set.

21.8   Map

21.8.1   Files

```
#include <map>
```

21.8.2   Class Declaration

```
template <typename Key, typename T,
          typename Compare = less<Key>,
          class Allocator = allocator<pair<const Key, T> > >
class map
```

We omit any detailed mention of the **Allocator** parameter. See Chapter 24 and the sidebar "Allocators" in Section 21.3.2 for a discussion of allocators.

21.8.3   Examples

See Examples 2.4, 7.6, 14.1, 15.1, 18.1, and 19.1.

21.8.4   Description

A map is a sorted associative container that supports unique keys of a given type **Key** and provides for fast retrieval of values of another type **T** based on the stored keys. As in all other STL sorted associative containers, the ordering relation **Compare** is used to order the elements of the map.

Elements are stored in maps as pairs in which each **Key** has an associated value of type **T**. Since maps store only unique keys, each map contains at most one **Key**, **T** pair for each **Key** value. It is not possible to associate more than one value with a single **key**.

21.8.5   Type Definitions

key_type

> Type **Key** of the keys in the map.

mapped_type

> Type **T** of the associated values.

value_type

> Type of the values stored in the map, **pair<const Key, T>**. The first member of this pair is declared **const** so that it is not possible to change the key using a nonconstant iterator or reference (it is possible to change the second member, the associated value of type **T**).

`key_compare`

> Comparison object type, `Compare`, with which the map is instantiated. It is used to order keys in the map.

`value_compare`

> Type of comparison object for comparing objects of `map::value_type` (objects of type `pair<const Key, T>`) by comparing their keys using `map::key_compare`.

`iterator`
`const_iterator`

> `iterator` is a bidirectional iterator type that refers to `value_type`; `const_iterator` is a constant bidirectional iterator type that refers to `const value_type`. It is guaranteed that there is a constructor for `const_iterator` out of `iterator`.

`reference`
`const_reference`

> `reference` is the type of locations of values stored in the map. This is simply `pair<const Key&, T>&` (or `const pair<const Key&, T>&` for `const_reference`).

`pointer`
`const_pointer`

> `pointer` is the type of pointers to elements of the container (usually `pair<const Key&, T>*` but more generally it is determined by the allocator type); `const_pointer` is a corresponding constant pointer type.

`size_type`

> Unsigned integral type that can represent the size of any map instance.

`difference_type`

> Signed integral type that can represent the distance between any two `map::iterator` objects.

`reverse_iterator`
`const_reverse_iterator`

> Constant and nonconstant reverse bidirectional iterator types.

```
allocator_type
```

Type of the allocator used by the map. Equivalent to `Allocator`.

21.8.6   Map Constructors, Destructors, and Related Functions

```
explicit map(const Compare& comp = Compare(),
          const Allocator& = Allocator());
```

Default constructor. Constructs an empty map and stores the comparison object `comp` for ordering the elements.

```
map(const map<Key, T, Compare, Allocator>& x);
```

Map copy constructor. Constructs a map and initializes it with copies of the elements of map `x`.

```
template <typename InputIterator>
map(InputIterator first, InputIterator last,
    const Compare& comp = Compare(),
    const Allocator& = Allocator());
```

Constructs an empty map and inserts copies of elements in the range [`first, last`). The comparison object `comp` is used to order the elements of the map.

```
map<Key, T, Compare, Allocator>&
operator=(const map<Key, T, Compare, Allocator>& x);
```

Map assignment operator. Replaces the contents of the current map with a copy of map `x`.

```
void swap(map<Key, T, Compare, Allocator>& x);
```

Swaps the contents of the current map with those of the map `x`. The current map replaces `x`, and vice versa.

```
~map();
```

Map destructor.

21.8.7 Comparison Operations

```
template <typename Key, typename T,
          typename Compare, typename Allocator>
bool operator==(const map<Key, T, Compare, Allocator>& x,
                const map<Key, T, Compare, Allocator>& y);
```

Equality operation on maps. Returns `true` if the sequences of elements in x and y are elementwise equal (using `T::operator==`). Takes linear time.

```
template <typename Key, typename T,
          typename Compare, typename Allocator>
bool operator<(const map<Key, T, Compare, Allocator>& x,
               const map<Key, T, Compare, Allocator>& y);
```

Returns `true` if x is lexicographically less than y, `false` otherwise. Takes linear time.

21.8.8 Map Element Access Member Functions

```
key_compare key_comp() const;
```

Returns the comparison object of the map.

```
value_compare value_comp() const;
```

Returns an object of type `value_compare` constructed out of the comparison object. The returned object compares pairs in the map by comparing their keys using `key_comp()`.

```
iterator begin();
const_iterator begin() const;
```

Returns an `iterator` (`const_iterator` for a constant map) that can be used to begin traversing through all locations in the map.

```
iterator end();
const_iterator end() const;
```

Returns an `iterator` (`const_iterator` for a constant map) that can be used in a comparison for ending traversal through the map.

```
reverse_iterator rbegin();
const_reverse_iterator rbegin() const;
```

Returns a `reverse_iterator` (`const_reverse_iterator` for constant maps) that can be used to begin traversing all locations in the map in the reverse of the normal order.

```
reverse_iterator rend();
const_reverse_iterator rend() const;
```

Returns a `reverse_iterator` (`const_reverse_iterator` for constant maps) that can be used in a comparison for ending reverse direction traversal through all locations in the map.

```
bool empty() const;
```

Returns `true` if the map is empty, `false` otherwise.

```
size_type size() const;
```

Returns the number of elements in the map.

```
size_type max_size() const;
```

Returns the maximum possible size of the map.

```
T& operator[](const key_type& x);
const T& operator[](const key_type& x) const;
```

Returns a reference to the type `T` value associated with the key `x`. In the case of a constant map, a constant reference to it is returned. The map-subscripting operator is different from the subscripting operator of vectors and deques in that if the map contains no element of type `T` associated with key `x`, then the pair (`x`, `T()`) is inserted into the map. Takes $O(\log N)$ time.

```
allocator_type get_allocator() const;
```

Returns a copy of the allocator used when constructing the object.

21.8.9   Map Insert Member Functions

```
iterator insert(iterator position, const value_type& x);
```

> Inserts the value x into the map if no element already present in the map has an equivalent key. The iterator position is a hint indicating where to start to search. This insertion takes $O(\log N)$ time in general, where N is the number of elements in the set, but it takes amortized constant time if x is inserted right after the iterator position.

```
pair<iterator, bool> insert(const value_type& x);
```

> Inserts the value x into the map if no element already present in the map has an equivalent key. The returned value is a pair whose bool component indicates whether the insertion has taken place and whose iterator component points to the just inserted value in the map if the insertion takes place, otherwise to the value x already present. Note that the type of x is pair<const Key, T>, not Key. The function takes $O(\log N)$ time, where N is the number of elements in the set.

```
template <typename InputIterator>
void insert(InputIterator first, InputIterator last);
```

> Copies of elements in the range [first, last) are inserted into the map. [first, last) must be a valid range of elements of value_type (pair<Key, T>). In general, the time taken for these insertions is $O(d \log(N + d))$, where N is the size of the map and d is the distance from first to last. The time is linear if the range [first, last) is sorted according to the ordering relation value_comp().

21.8.10   Map Erase Member Functions

```
void erase(iterator position);
```

> Erases the map element pointed to by the iterator position. The time taken is amortized constant.

```
size_type erase(const key_type& x);
```

> Erases the map element with key equivalent to x, if present. Returns the number of erased elements, which is 1 if there is an element with key equivalent to x, 0 otherwise. Takes $O(\log N)$ time, where N is the size of the map.

```
void erase(iterator first, iterator last);
```

> The iterators **first** and **last** are assumed to point into the map, and all elements in the range [**first**, **last**) are erased from the map. The time taken is $O(d + \log N)$, where N is the size of the map and **d** is the distance from **first** to **last**.

```
void clear();
```

> Erases all elements in the map. Equivalent to **a.erase(a.begin(), a.end())**.

21.8.11 Special Map Operations

```
iterator find(const key_type& x);
const_iterator find(const key_type& x) const;
```

> Searches the map for an element with key equivalent to **x** (see Example 7.6). If such an element is found, the function returns the **iterator** (**const_iterator** for constant maps) pointing to it. Otherwise, **end()** is returned. Takes $O(\log N)$ time, where N is the size of the map.

```
size_type count(const key_type& x) const;
```

> Returns the number of elements in the map with key equivalent to **x**. This number is 1 or 0. Takes $O(\log N)$ time, where N is the size of of the map.

```
iterator lower_bound(const key_type& x);
const_iterator lower_bound(const key_type& x) const;
```

> Returns an **iterator** (**const_iterator** for constant maps) pointing to the first map element whose key is not less than **x**. If the map contains an element with key not less than **x**, then the returned iterator points to this element. If the keys of all elements in the map are less than **x**, **end()** is returned. Takes $O(\log N)$ time, where N is the size of the map.

```
iterator upper_bound(const key_type& x);
const_iterator upper_bound(const key_type& x) const;
```

> Returns an **iterator** (**const_iterator** for constant maps) to the first map element whose key is greater than **x**. If no element has a key greater than **x**, **end()** is returned. Takes $O(\log N)$ time, where N is the size of the map.

```
pair<iterator, iterator> equal_range(const key_type& x);
pair<const_iterator, const_iterator>
equal_range(const key_type& x) const;
```

Returns the pair ($lower\_bound(x)$, $upper\_bound(x)$). Takes $O(\log N)$ time, where N is the size of the map.

21.9 Multimap

21.9.1 Files

```
#include <map>
```

21.9.2 Class Declaration

```
template <typename Key, typename T,
          typename Compare = less<Key>,
          typename Allocator = allocator<pair<const Key, T> > >
class multimap
```

We omit any detailed mention of the **Allocator** parameter. See Chapter 24 and the sidebar "Allocators" in Section 21.3.2 for a discussion of allocators.

21.9.3 Examples

See Example 15.1.

21.9.4 Description

A multimap is an associative container that stores multiple equivalent keys of a given type **Key** and allows efficient retrieval of values of another type **T** based on the stored **Key**. As in all other STL associative containers, the ordering relation **Compare** is used to order the elements of the map. Elements are stored in multimaps as pairs in which each **Key** has an associated value of type **T**.

21.9.5 Type Definitions

Same as for the **map** class. (See Section 21.8.5.)

21.9.6 Multimap Constructors, Destructors, and Related Functions

```
explicit multimap(const Compare& comp = Compare(),
                  const Allocator& = Allocator());
```

> Default constructor. Constructs an empty multimap and stores the comparison object `comp` for ordering the elements.

```
multimap(const multimap<Key, T, Compare, Allocator>& x);
```

> Multimap copy constructor. Constructs a multimap and initializes it with copies of the elements of multimap `x`.

```
template <typename InputIterator>
multimap(InputIterator first, InputIterator last,
         const Compare& comp = Compare(),
         const Allocator& = Allocator());
```

> Constructs an empty multimap and inserts copies of elements in the range [`first`, `last`). The comparison object `comp` is used to order the elements of the multimap.

```
multimap<Key, T, Compare, Allocator>&
operator=(const multimap<Key, T, Compare, Allocator>& x);
```

> Multimap assignment operator. Replaces the contents of the current multimap with a copy of multimap `x`.

```
void swap(multimap<Key, T, Compare, Allocator>& x);
```

> Swaps the contents of the current multimap with those of the multimap `x`. The current multimap replaces `x` and vice versa.

```
~multimap();
```

> Multimap destructor.

21.9.7 Comparison Operations

```
template <typename Key, typename T,
          typename Compare, typename Allocator>
bool operator==(const multimap<Key, T, Compare, Allocator>& x,
                const multimap<Key, T, Compare, Allocator>& y);
```

Equality operation on multimaps. Returns **true** if the sequences of elements in **x** and **y** are elementwise equal (using **T::operator==**). Takes linear time.

```
template <typename Key, typename T,
          typename Compare, typename Allocator>
bool operator<(const multimap<Key, T, Compare, Allocator>& x,
               const multimap<Key, T, Compare, Allocator>& y);
```

Returns **true** if **x** is lexicographically less than **y**, **false** otherwise. Takes linear time.

21.9.8   Multimap Element Access Member Functions

```
key_compare key_comp() const;
```

Returns the comparison object of the multimap.

```
value_compare value_comp() const;
```

Returns an object of type **value_compare** constructed out of the comparison object. The returned object compares pairs in the multimap by comparing their keys using **key_comp()**.

```
iterator begin();
const_iterator begin() const;
```

Returns an **iterator** (**const_iterator** for a constant multimap) that can be used to begin traversing through all locations in the multimap.

```
iterator end();
const_iterator end() const;
```

Returns an **iterator** (**const_iterator** for a constant multimap) that can be used in a comparison for ending traversal through the multimap.

```
reverse_iterator rbegin();
const_reverse_iterator rbegin() const;
```

Returns a **reverse_iterator** (**const_reverse_iterator** for constant multimaps) that can be used to begin traversing all locations in the multimap in the reverse of the normal order.

```
reverse_iterator rend();
const_reverse_iterator rend() const;
```

Returns a **reverse_iterator** (**const_reverse_iterator** for constant multimaps) that can be used in a comparison for ending reverse direction traversal through all locations in the multimap.

```
bool empty() const;
```

Returns **true** if the multimap is empty, **false** otherwise.

```
size_type size() const;
```

Returns the number of elements in the multimap.

```
size_type max_size() const;
```

Returns the maximum possible size of the multimap.

```
allocator_type get_allocator() const;
```

Returns a copy of the allocator used when constructing the object.

21.9.9 Multimap Insert Member Functions

```
iterator insert(iterator position, const value_type& x);
```

Inserts the value **x** into the multimap. Note that the type of **x** is **pair<const Key, T>**. The iterator **position** is a hint indicating where the **insert** function should start to search to do the insert. The insertion takes $O(\log N)$ time in general, where N is the number of elements in the multimap, but it is amortized constant if **x** is inserted right after the iterator **position**.

```
iterator insert(const value_type& x);
```

Inserts the value **x** into the multimap and returns the iterator pointing to the newly inserted value (see Example 15.1). Note that the type of **x** is **pair<const Key, T>**. The insertion takes $O(\log N)$ time, where N is the number of elements in the multimap.

```
template <typename InputIterator>
void insert(InputIterator first, InputIterator last);
```

Copies of elements in the range [`first`, `last`) are inserted into the multimap. [`first`, `last`) must be a valid range of elements of type `value_type`, that is, `pair<Key, T>`. In general, the time taken for these insertions is $O(d \log(N + d))$, where N is the size of the multimap and `d` is the distance from `first` to `last`. The time is linear if the range [`first`, `last`) is sorted according to the ordering relation `value_comp()`.

21.9.10   Multimap Erase Member Functions

`void erase(iterator position);`

> Erases the multimap element pointed to by the iterator `position`. The time taken is amortized constant.

`size_type erase(const key_type& x);`

> Erases all multimap elements with key equivalent to `x`. Returns the number of erased elements. In general, this function takes time proportional to $d \log(N + d)$, where N is the size of the set and `d` is the number of elements with key equivalent to `x`.

`void erase(iterator first, iterator last);`

> The iterators `first` and `last` are assumed to point into the multimap, and all elements in the range [`first`, `last`) are erased from the multimap. Takes $O(d + \log N)$ time, where N is the size of the multiset and `d` is the distance from `first` to `last`.

`void clear();`

> Erases all elements in the multimap. Equivalent to the expression `a.erase(a.begin(), a.end())`.

21.9.11   Special Multimap Operations

`iterator find(const key_type& x);`
`const_iterator find(const key_type& x) const;`

> Searches the multimap for an element with key equivalent to `x`. If such an element is found, `find` returns the `iterator` (`const_iterator` for constant multimaps) pointing to it. Otherwise `end()` is returned. Takes $O(\log N)$ time, where N is the size of the multimap.

```
size_type count(const key_type& x) const;
```

Returns the number of elements in the multimap with key equivalent to x. Takes $O(\log(N) + \texttt{count(x)})$ time, where N is the size of the multimap.

```
iterator lower_bound(const key_type& x);
const_iterator lower_bound(const key_type& x) const;
```

Returns an `iterator` (`const_iterator` for constant multimaps) pointing to the first multimap element whose key is not less than x. If the multimap contains an element with key not less than x, then the returned iterator points to this element. If the keys of all elements in the multimap are less than x, `end()` is returned. Takes $O(\log N)$ time, where N is the size of the multimap.

```
iterator upper_bound(const key_type& x);
const_iterator upper_bound(const key_type& x) const;
```

Returns an `iterator` (`const_iterator` for constant multimaps) to the first multimap element whose key is greater than x. If no element has a key greater than x, `end()` is returned. Takes $O(\log N)$ time, where N is the size of the multimap.

```
pair<iterator, iterator> equal_range(const key_type& x);
pair<const_iterator, const_iterator>
equal_range(const key_type& x) const;
```

Returns the pair (`lower_bound(x)`, `upper_bound(x)`). Takes $O(\log N)$ time, where N is the size of the multimap.

21.10 Stack Container Adaptor

21.10.1 Files

```
#include <stack>
```

21.10.2 Class Declaration

```
template <typename T, typename Container = deque<T> >
class stack
```

21.10.3 Examples

See Example 9.1.

21.10.4 Description

A stack is a data structure that allows the following operations: *inserting* at one end, *deleting* from the same end, *retrieving* the value at the same end, and testing for *emptiness*. Thus, stacks provide a last-in, first-out service. The element deleted or retrieved is always the last one inserted.

STL provides a `stack` container adaptor, which can be used to implement a stack with any container that supports the following operations on sequences: `empty`, `size`, `back`, `push_back`, and `pop_back` (the default is to use a `deque`). In particular, vectors, lists, and deques can be used to implement stacks:

- `stack<char, vector<char> >` Stack of characters with an underlying vector implementation.

- `stack<int, list<int> >` Stack of integers with an underlying list implementation.

- `stack<float>` Stack of floats with an underlying deque implementation.

The difference between `stack` and these sequence abstractions is that `stack` has a much more restricted interface, one that disallows any operations on its objects other than the usual stack operations.

21.10.5 Type Definitions

`value_type`

> Type of the values stored in the stack. This is usually `T`, but more generally it is the `value_type` of `Container`.

`size_type`

> Defined to be the `size_type` of `Container`.

`container_type`

> Type `Container` representing the underlying container.

21.10.6 Constructors

`explicit stack(const Container& cont = Container());`

> Default constructor. Constructs an empty stack and uses the container `cont` for storing the elements.

21.10.7   Public Member Functions

```
bool empty() const;
```

> Returns **true** if the stack is empty, **false** otherwise.

```
size_type size() const;
```

> Returns the number of elements in the stack.

```
void push(const value_type& x);
```

> Inserts the value **x** at the top of the stack.

```
void pop();
```

> Removes the element at the top of the stack. Undefined if the stack is empty.

```
value_type& top();
const value_type& top() const;
```

> Returns the element most recently pushed on the stack. The stack remains unchanged.

21.10.8   Comparison Operations

```
template <typename T, typename Container>
bool operator==(const stack<T, Container>& x,
                const stack<T, Container>& y);
```

> Equality operation on stacks. Returns **true** if the sequences of elements in **x** and **y** are elementwise equal (using **T::operator==**). Takes linear time.

```
template <typename T, typename Container>
bool operator<(const stack<T, Container>& x,
               const stack<T, Container>& y);
```

> Returns **true** if **x** is lexicographically less than **y**, **false** otherwise. Takes linear time.

21.11   Queue Container Adaptor

21.11.1   Files

```
#include <queue>
```

21.11.2   Class Declaration

```
template <typename T, typename Container = deque<T> >
class queue
```

21.11.3   Examples

See Example 9.2.

21.11.4   Description

A queue is a data structure in which elements are inserted at one end and removed from the opposite end. The order of removal is the same as the order of insertion (first-in, first-out).

STL provides a `queue` container adaptor, which can be used to implement a queue with any sequence container that supports the following operations: `empty`, `size`, `front`, `back`, `push_back`, and `pop_front` (the default is to use a `deque`). In particular, lists and deques can be used to implement queues:

- `queue<int, list<int> >`   Queue of integers with an underlying list implementation.

- `queue<float>`   Queue of floats with an underlying deque implementation.

Note that vectors cannot be used with the `queue` adaptor since they do not provide a `pop_front` function. This function is not provided for vectors because it would be inefficient for long vectors.

21.11.5   Type Definitions

`value_type`

Type of the values stored in the queue. This is usually `T`, but more generally it is the `value_type` of `Container`.

`size_type`

Defined to be the `size_type` of `Container`.

`container_type`

Type `Container` representing the underlying container.

21.11.6   Constructors

```
explicit queue(const Container& cont = Container());
```

Default constructor. Constructs an empty queue and uses the container `cont` for storing the elements.

21.11.7   Public Member Functions

```
bool empty() const;
```

Returns `true` if the queue is empty, `false` otherwise.

```
size_type size() const;
```

Returns the number of elements in the queue.

```
void push(const value_type& x);
```

Inserts the element `x` at the end of the queue.

```
void pop();
```

Removes the element at the front of the queue.

```
value_type& front();
const value_type& front() const;
```

Returns the element at the front of the queue. The queue remains unchanged.

```
value_type& back();
const value_type& back() const;
```

Returns the element at the end of the queue. This is the element that was last inserted into the queue. The queue remains unchanged.

21.11.8   Comparison Operations

```
template <typename T, typename Container>
bool operator==(const queue<T, Container>& x,
                const queue<T, Container>& y);
```

Equality operation on queues. Returns `true` if the sequences of elements in `x` and `y` are elementwise equal (using `T::operator==`). Takes linear time.

```
template <typename T, typename Container>
bool operator<(const queue<T, Container>& x,
               const queue<T, Container>& y);
```

Returns **true** if **x** is lexicographically less than **y**, **false** otherwise. Takes linear time.

21.12   Priority Queue Container Adaptor

21.12.1   Files

```
#include <queue>
```

21.12.2   Class Declaration

```
template <typename T, typename Container = vector<T>,
          typename Compare =
              less<typename Container::value_type> >
class priority_queue
```

21.12.3   Examples

See Example 9.3.

21.12.4   Description

A priority queue is a container in which the element immediately available for retrieval is the largest of those in the container for some particular way of ordering the elements.

STL provides a **priority_queue** container adaptor, which can be used to implement a priority queue with any container that supports random access iterators and the following operations: **empty**, **size**, **front**, **push_back**, and **pop_back** (the default is to use a **vector**). In particular, vectors and deques can be used with the **priority_queue** adaptor.

Note that since a **priority_queue** involves an ordering on it elements, a comparison function object **comp** needs to be supplied:

- **priority_queue<int, vector<int>, less<int> >**   Priority queue of integers with a vector implementation using the built-in **<** operation for integers to compare the objects.

- **priority_queue<char, deque<char>, greater<char> >**   Priority queue of characters with a deque implementation using the **>** operation

383

on characters for comparisons. Note that since > is used instead of <, the element available for retrieval at any time is actually the smallest element rather than the largest.

21.12.5   Type Definitions

value_type

Type of the values stored in the priority queue. This is usually T, but more generally it is the value_type of Container.

size_type

Defined to be the size_type of Container.

container_type

Type Container representing the underlying container.

21.12.6   Constructors

```
explicit priority_queue(const Compare& comp = Compare(),
                    const Container& cont = Container());
```

Constructs an empty priority queue and stores the comparison function object comp for ordering the elements. Initializes the underlying container c with a copy of cont and calls make_heap(c.begin(), c.end(), comp).

```
template <typename InputIterator>
priority_queue(InputIterator first, InputIterator last,
            const Compare& comp = Compare(),
            const Container& cont = Container());
```

Constructs a priority queue and inserts copies of elements in the range [first, last). The comparison object comp is used to order the elements of the priority queue. Calls make_heap(c.begin(), c.end(), comp) on the underlying container after inserting the elements.

21.12.7 Public Member Functions

```
bool empty() const;
```

Returns **true** if the priority queue is empty, **false** otherwise.

```
size_type size() const;
```

Returns the number of elements in the priority queue.

```
const value_type& top() const;
```

Returns the element with the highest priority from the priority queue.
The priority queue remains unchanged.

```
void push(const value_type& x);
```

Inserts the element **x** in the priority queue.

```
void pop();
```

Removes the element with the highest priority from the priority queue.

21.12.8 Comparison Operations

Equality and less-than operations are not provided for priority queues.

CHAPTER 22

Generic Algorithm Reference Guide

The STL generic algorithms can be divided into four main categories:

1. Nonmutating sequence algorithms

2. Mutating sequence operations

3. Sorting-related operations

4. Generalized numeric algorithms

All the library algorithms are *generic*, in the sense that they can operate on a variety of containers. The algorithms are not directly parameterized in terms of containers. Instead, they are parameterized by *iterator types*. This allows the algorithms to work with user-defined data structures, as long as these containers have iterator types satisfying the assumptions on the algorithms. The semantic descriptions of the algorithms are thus written in terms of iterator types and iterator objects.

The header file for all of the STL generic algorithms is `<algorithm>`.

22.1 Organization of the Algorithm Descriptions

Within the main categories, we divide the algorithm descriptions into sections, grouping together in each section all algorithms with similar purpose and semantics. Each of these algorithm sections is divided into three parts: Prototypes, Description, and Time Complexity.

22.1.1   Prototypes

This part shows the function prototypes for all algorithms described in the section. In most sections there are several algorithms with the same name, distinguished by their parameter types (function overloading). The most frequent case of overloading is functions that have predicate versions. These take a function object that returns a `bool` value, and they use that predicate in place of an operator, such as `==` or `<`.

In a few cases there are two functions that have the same basic purpose (such as `find` and its predicate version `find_if` in Section 22.4 and `fill` and `fill_n` in Section 22.18) and thus might have been given the same name. The name difference is necessary since they cannot be distinguished by their parameter types. See Chapter 5, especially Section 5.1, for further discussion of algorithm names.

One of the most crucial parts of the specification of STL generic algorithms is the requirements on its iterator template parameters. This information is given implicitly in the prototypes, and usually without additional discussion in the Description section, through the naming convention used for template parameters that are supposed to be iterator types. The names used (`InputIterator`, `OutputIterator`, `ForwardIterator`, `BidirectionalIterator`, and `RandomAccessIterator`) correspond to the classification of iterator types in five categories. See also Chapter 4, especially Section 4.6.

22.1.2   Examples

When applicable, the Examples section includes cross references to programs in Parts I and II that use the algorithms. In cases where an example applies to a specific overloaded variation of the functions, we make the distinction. In most situations, however, the different forms of an algorithm are similar enough that the examples work equally well for all of them.

22.1.3   Description

Under this heading we describe the semantics of each algorithm in the group, always in terms of the parameter names and types used in the Prototypes. Our description includes the effect (if any) of the algorithm on its parameters and the return value (if any).

Almost all STL generic algorithms take at least two iterator parameters that define a *range* of elements in some container (some take two more defining another range or one more defining the beginning of another range). For definition and discussion of the range concept and notation, see the introduction to Chapter 4, and the introduction to Chapter 20.

Some of the predicate versions of algorithms need the predicate function objects passed to them to have certain semantic properties. In particular, all of the sorting-related algorithms assume that the comparison function objects passed to them define *strict weak orderings*. This term is defined in the overview section for that category in Section 22.26; see also Section 5.4.

No examples are given in this chapter, but Chapter 5 has examples of most of the STL generic algorithms. Consult the index for pointers to examples in other chapters.

22.1.4   Time Complexity

In this section bounds on the computing time for each algorithm are given. The terminology and notation (big-Oh notation) used in these descriptions are discussed in Section 1.5. In many cases more precise bounds are given on the number of applications of operators or function objects used by the algorithm.

22.2   Nonmutating Sequence Algorithm Overview

Nonmutating sequence algorithms do not directly modify the containers on which they operate. There are ten subcategories of algorithms in this category:

- for_each applies a given function to each element.

- find does a linear search.

- find_first_of does a linear search for any of a set of values.

- adjacent_find does a linear search for adjacent equal elements.

- count computes the number of occurrences of a given value.

- mismatch scans two sequences to find the first position where they disagree.

- equal scans two sequences checking for elementwise equality.

- search scans a sequence for a match with another.

- **search_n** scans a sequence for a series of identical elements matching a given value.

- **find_end** scans a sequence for the last match with another sequence.

Each of these algorithms, except **for_each**, has two versions: one that uses **==** for comparisons and a predicate version, which uses a predicate function object for comparisons. There are no semantic requirements on the predicate objects, although if they do not define an equality relation, the use of the word equality in stating the results of the algorithms should be reinterpreted in light of this fact. For example, the description of **adjacent_find** in Section 22.6 uses the term *consecutive duplicate* and describes it as "an element equal to the element immediately following it in the range." With the predicate version, consecutive duplicate should be interpreted as "consecutive elements x and y such that **binary_pred(x, y) == true**." This formulation is meaningful even if **binary_pred** does not define an equality relation.

22.3   For Each

22.3.1   Prototype

```
template <typename InputIterator, typename Function>
Function for_each(InputIterator first, InputIterator last,
                  Function f);
```

22.3.2   Examples

See Example 5.7.

22.3.3   Description

The **for_each** algorithm applies the function **f** to each element in the range [**first, last**). The return value of **for_each** is the function argument **f**.

The function **f** is applied to the result of dereferencing every iterator in the range [**first, last**). It is assumed that **f** does not apply any nonconstant function through the dereferenced iterator. **f** is applied exactly **last - first** times. If **f** returns a result, the result is ignored.

22.3.4 Time Complexity

Linear. If N is the size of [first, last), then exactly N applications of f are made.

22.4 Find

22.4.1 Prototypes

```
template <typename InputIterator, typename T>
InputIterator find(InputIterator first,
                   InputIterator last, const T& value);

template <typename InputIterator, typename Predicate>
InputIterator find_if(InputIterator first, InputIterator last,
                      Predicate pred);
```

22.4.2 Examples

See Examples 2.5, 2.6, 2.7, 2.8, 4.1, and 10.2 for find and Examples 5.4, 13.1, and 14.1 for find_if.

22.4.3 Description

The first version of the algorithm traverses the range [first, last) and returns the first iterator i such that *i == value. The second version returns the first iterator i such that pred(*i) == true. In either case, if such an iterator is not found, then the iterator last is returned.

22.4.4 Time Complexity

Linear. The maximum number of applications of != (or pred, for find_if) is the size of the range [first, last). If a match is found, the number of comparisons (or applications of pred) done is one more than the size of the range [first, i).

22.5 Find First

22.5.1 Prototypes

```
template <typename ForwardIterator1, typename ForwardIterator2>
ForwardIterator1 find_first_of(ForwardIterator1 first1,
```

```
                                ForwardIterator1 last1,
                                ForwardIterator2 first2,
                                ForwardIterator2 last2);

        template <typename ForwardIterator1, typename ForwardIterator2,
                typename BinaryPredicate>
        ForwardIterator1 find_first_of(ForwardIterator1 first1,
                                ForwardIterator1 last1,
                                ForwardIterator2 first2,
                                ForwardIterator2 last2,
                                BinaryPredicate pred);
```

22.5.2 Description

This algorithm is similar to find except that rather than searching for a single value, it looks for any of the values in the range [first2, last2). The first version of the algorithm traverses the range [first1, last1) and returns the first iterator i such that, for some iterator j in the range [first2, last2), *i == *j. In the second version, rather than *i == *j the required condition is pred(*i, *j) == true. In either case, if such an iterator is not found, then the iterator last1 is returned.

22.5.3 Time Complexity

Quadratic. If N is the size of the range [first1, last1) and M is the size of the range [first2, last2), then the number of applications of == (or pred, for the predicate version) is at most NM.

22.6 Adjacent Find

22.6.1 Prototypes

```
        template <typename ForwardIterator>
        ForwardIterator adjacent_find(ForwardIterator first,
                                ForwardIterator last);

        template <typename ForwardIterator, typename BinaryPredicate>
        ForwardIterator adjacent_find(ForwardIterator first,
                                ForwardIterator last,
                                BinaryPredicate binary_pred);
```

22.6.2 Examples

See Examples 5.5, 13.1, 14.1, and 15.1.

22.6.3 Description

The `adjacent_find` algorithm returns an iterator `i` referring to the first consecutive duplicate element in the range [`first`, `last`) or `last` if there is no such element. A consecutive duplicate is an element equal to the element immediately following it in the range.

Comparisons are done using `==` in the first version of the algorithm and a function object `binary_pred` in the second version.

22.6.4 Time Complexity

Linear. The number of comparisons done is the size of the range [`first`, `i`).

22.7 Count

22.7.1 Prototypes

```
template <typename InputIterator, typename T>
typename iterator_traits<InputIterator>::difference_type
count(InputIterator first, InputIterator last, const T& value);

template <typename InputIterator, typename Predicate>
typename iterator_traits<InputIterator>::difference_type
count_if(InputIterator first, InputIterator last,
        Predicate pred);
```

22.7.2 Examples

See Example 5.6.

22.7.3 Description

The `count` algorithm returns the number of elements in the range [`first`, `last`) that are equal to `value`.

The `count_if` algorithm returns the number of iterators in the range [`first`, `last`) for which `pred(*i)` `==` `true`.

22.7.4 Time Complexity

Linear. The number of comparisons done is the size of the range [`first`, `last`).

22.8 Mismatch

22.8.1 Prototypes

```
template <typename InputIterator1, typename InputIterator2>
pair<InputIterator1, InputIterator2>
mismatch(InputIterator1 first1, InputIterator1 last1,
         InputIterator2 first2);


template <typename InputIterator1, typename InputIterator2,
          typename BinaryPredicate>
pair<InputIterator1, InputIterator2>
mismatch(InputIterator1 first1, InputIterator1 last1,
         InputIterator2 first2,
         BinaryPredicate binary_pred);
```

22.8.2 Examples

See Example 5.8.

22.8.3 Description

The `mismatch` algorithm compares corresponding pairs of elements from two ranges and returns the first mismatched pair. The algorithm finds the first position at which a value in the range [`first1`, `last1`) disagrees with the value in the range starting at `first2`. It returns a pair of iterators i and j that satisfy the following conditions:

- i points into the range [`first1`, `last1`).

- j points into the range beginning at `first2`.

- i and j are both equidistant from the beginning of their corresponding ranges.

- `!(*i == *j)`, or `binary_pred(i, j) == false`, depending on the version of `mismatch` invoked. In the first version comparisons are made with `==`, and in the second version they are made with function object `binary_pred`.

22.11   Search N

22.11.1   Prototypes

```
template <typename ForwardIterator, typename Size, typename T>
ForwardIterator search_n(ForwardIterator first,
                         ForwardIterator last,
                         Size count, const T& value);


template <typename ForwardIterator, typename Size, typename T,
         typename BinaryPredicate>
ForwardIterator search_n(ForwardIterator first,
                         ForwardIterator last,
                         Size count, const T& value,
                         BinaryPredicate binary_pred);
```

22.11.2   Description

The algorithm search_n traverses the range [first, last - count) looking for a series of count elements matching value. If so, the iterator i that represents the start of the subsequence is returned. For all integers $n <$ count, $*(i + n)$ equals value. Otherwise, last1 is returned.

In the first version of the algorithm, comparisons are made with ==, while in the second they are made with function object binary_pred.

22.11.3   Time Complexity

Time complexity is quadratic. If N is the size of the range [first, last), then the number of applications of == or binary_pred is at most Ncount.

22.12   Find End

22.12.1   Prototypes

```
template <typename ForwardIterator1, typename ForwardIterator2>
ForwardIterator1
find_end(ForwardIterator1 first1, ForwardIterator1 last1,
         ForwardIterator2 first2, ForwardIterator2 last2);


template <typename ForwardIterator1, typename ForwardIterator2,
         typename BinaryPredicate>
ForwardIterator1
find_end(ForwardIterator1 first1, ForwardIterator1 last1,
```

```
                    ForwardIterator2 first2, ForwardIterator2 last2,
                    BinaryPredicate binary_pred);
```

22.12.2 Description

Like search, find_end checks whether the sequence in the second range [first2, last2) is a subsequence of the first range [first1, last1). The difference is that while search returns the first matching subsequence, find_end returns the last such subsequence. If there is no match, last1 is returned.

In the first version of the algorithm, comparisons are made with ==, while in the second they are made with function object binary_pred.

22.12.3 Time Complexity

Time complexity is quadratic. If N is the size of the range [first1, last1) and M is the size of the range [first2, last2), then the number of applications of == or binary_pred is at most $(N - M + 1)M$.

22.13 Mutating Sequence Algorithm Overview

Mutating sequence algorithms typically modify the containers on which they operate. There are twelve subcategories of algorithms in this category.

- copy copies elements to another (possibly overlapping) sequence.

- swap exchanges the elements of one sequence with those of another.

- transform replaces each element with the value returned by applying a given function to the element.

- replace replaces each element equal to a given value with a copy of another given value.

- fill replaces each element with copies of a given value.

- generate replaces each element with the value returned by calling a function.

- remove eliminates elements equal to a given value.

- unique eliminates consecutive equal elements.

- **reverse** reverses the relative order of the elements.

- **rotate** does a circular shift of the elements.

- **random_shuffle** reorders the elements pseudo-randomly.

- **partition** reorders the elements so that elements satisfying a given predicate precede those that don't.

Of these algorithms, **replace**, **remove**, and **unique** have both a version that uses == for comparisons and a version that uses a given predicate object. See Section 22.2 regarding semantic requirements on the predicate object. The **partition** algorithm has a second version that is stable (it preserves the relative order of the elements in each group).

22.14 Copy

22.14.1 Prototypes

```
template<typename InputIterator, typename OutputIterator>
OutputIterator copy(InputIterator first1, InputIterator last1,
                OutputIterator first2);

template <typename BidirectionalIterator1,
          typename BidirectionalIterator2>
BidirectionalIterator2
copy_backward(BidirectionalIterator1 first1,
            BidirectionalIterator1 last1,
            BidirectionalIterator2 last2);
```

22.14.2 Examples

See Examples 5.10, 12.1, 12.1, 13.1, and 14.1.

22.14.3 Description

These algorithms copy elements from one range to another. The **copy** algorithm copies [first1, last1) to [first2, last2), where last2 == first2 + (last1 - first1) and returns last2. The algorithm proceeds forward, copying source elements in the order first1, first1 + 1, ..., last1 - 1, with the consequence that the destination range can overlap with the source range provided that it doesn't contain first2. Thus, for example, **copy** can be used to shift a range one position toward the beginning of the sequence but not toward the end.

The opposite is true of copy_backward, which copies [first1, last1) to [first2, last2), where first2 == last2 - (last1 - first1), and returns first2. It proceeds backward, copying source elements in the order last1 - 1, last1 - 2, ..., first1. The copying thus works properly as long as the source range doesn't contain last2.

22.14.4 Time Complexity

Linear for both copy algorithms. Exactly N assignments are performed, where N is the size of the range [first1, last1).

22.15 Swap

22.15.1 Prototypes

```
template <typename T>
void swap(T& x, T& y);

template <typename ForwardIterator1, typename ForwardIterator2>
ForwardIterator2 swap_ranges(ForwardIterator1 first1,
                             ForwardIterator1 last1,
                             ForwardIterator2 first2);

template <typename ForwardIterator1, typename ForwardIterator2>
void iter_swap(ForwardIterator1 a, ForwardIterator2 b);
```

22.15.2 Examples

See Example 5.18 for swap and Example 5.19 for swap_ranges.

22.15.3 Description

swap exchanges the values stored in locations x and y. swap_ranges exchanges the elements in the range [first1, last2) with those in the range of size N = last1 - first1 beginning at first2. swap_ranges returns the past-the-end iterator, first2 + N.

iter_swap(a, b) is identical to swap(*a, *b) and exists purely for technical reasons, due to the fact that some compilers are unable to properly perform the type deduction required to interpret swap(*a, *b).

22.15.4   Time Complexity

Amortized constant for `swap` and `iter_swap`; linear for `swap_ranges`, which performs N element exchanges.

22.16   Transform

22.16.1   Prototypes

```
template <typename InputIterator, typename OutputIterator,
        typename UnaryOperation>
OutputIterator transform(InputIterator first,
                         InputIterator last,
                         OutputIterator result,
                         UnaryOperation unary_op);

template <typename InputIterator1, typename InputIterator2,
        typename OutputIterator, typename BinaryOperation>
OutputIterator transform(InputIterator1 first1,
                         InputIterator1 last1,
                         InputIterator2 first2,
                         OutputIterator result,
                         BinaryOperation binary_op);
```

22.16.2   Examples

See Example 5.20.

22.16.3   Description

The first version of `transform` generates a sequence of elements by applying a unary function `unary_op` to each element of the range [`first`, `last`). The second version of `transform` accepts a range [`first1`, `last1`) and a range of length N = `last1` - `first1` starting at `first2` and generates a range by applying a binary function `binary_op` to each corresponding pair of elements from the ranges.

For both versions of `transform`, the resulting sequence is placed starting at the position `result`, and the past-the-end iterator, `result` + N, is returned. `result` may be equal to `first` in the case of unary transform or to `first1` or `first2` in the case of binary transform.

`unary_op` and `binary_op` must not have any side effects.

22.16.4 Time Complexity

Linear. The number of applications of **unary_op** is the size of the range [**first**, **last**) and the number of applications of **binary_op** is the size of the range [**first1**, **last1**).

22.17 Replace

22.17.1 Prototypes

```
template <typename ForwardIterator, typename T>
void replace(ForwardIterator first, ForwardIterator last,
             const T& old_value, const T& new_value);

template <typename ForwardIterator, typename Predicate,
          typename T>
void replace_if(ForwardIterator first, ForwardIterator last,
                Predicate pred, const T& new_value);

template <typename InputIterator, typename OutputIterator,
          typename T>
OutputIterator replace_copy(InputIterator first,
                            InputIterator last,
                            OutputIterator result,
                            const T& old_value,
                            const T& new_value);

template <typename InputIterator, typename OutputIterator,
          typename Predicate, typename T>
OutputIterator replace_copy_if(InputIterator first,
                               InputIterator last,
                               OutputIterator result,
                               Predicate pred,
                               const T& new_value);
```

22.17.2 Examples

See Example 5.16.

22.17.3 Description

The **replace** algorithm modifies the range [**first**, **last**) so that all elements equal to **old_value** are replaced by **new_value**, while other elements remain unchanged.

402

replace_if modifies the range [first, last) so that all elements that satisfy the predicate **pred** are replaced by **new_value**, while other elements remain unchanged.

The algorithms **replace_copy** and **replace_copy_if** are similar to **replace** and **replace_if** except that the original sequence is not modified. Rather, the altered sequence is placed in the range of size $N =$ **last - first** beginning at **result**. The past-the-end iterator, **result + N**, is returned.

result must not be in the range [first, last).

22.17.4 Time Complexity

Linear. The number of **==** operations performed, or of applications of the predicate **pred**, is N.

22.18 Fill

22.18.1 Prototypes

```
template <typename ForwardIterator, typename T>
void fill(ForwardIterator first, ForwardIterator last,
        const T& value);

template <typename OutputIterator, typename Size, typename T>
void fill_n(OutputIterator first, Size n, const T& value);
```

22.18.2 Examples

See Example 5.11.

22.18.3 Description

fill places **value** in all positions in the range [first, last). **fill_n** places **value** in all positions in the range [first, first + n).

22.18.4 Time Complexity

Linear. The number of assignments for both versions of the algorithm is the size of the range [first, last).

22.19   Generate

22.19.1   Prototypes

```
template <typename ForwardIterator, typename Generator>
void generate(ForwardIterator first, ForwardIterator last,
              Generator gen);

template <typename OutputIterator, typename Size,
          typename Generator>
void generate_n(OutputIterator first, Size n, Generator gen);
```

22.19.2   Examples

See Example 5.12.

22.19.3   Description

generate fills the range [first, last) with the sequence generated by last
- first successive calls of the function object gen. generate_n fills the
range of size n beginning at first with the sequence generated by n successive calls of gen.

22.19.4   Time Complexity

Linear. The number of assignments and calls of gen for generate is the size
of the range [first, last), while for generate_n the number of assignments
is n.

22.20   Remove

22.20.1   Prototypes

```
template <typename ForwardIterator, typename T>
ForwardIterator remove(ForwardIterator first,
                       ForwardIterator last,
                       const T& value);

template <typename ForwardIterator, typename Predicate>
ForwardIterator remove_if(ForwardIterator first,
                          ForwardIterator last,
                          Predicate pred);

template <typename InputIterator, typename OutputIterator,
```

```
                    typename T>
OutputIterator remove_copy(InputIterator first,
                           InputIterator last,
                           OutputIterator result,
                           const T& value);

        template <typename InputIterator, typename OutputIterator,
                  typename Predicate>
        OutputIterator remove_copy_if(InputIterator first,
                           InputIterator last,
                           OutputIterator result,
                           Predicate pred);
```

22.20.2 Examples

See Example 5.15.

22.20.3 Description

The function **remove** removes those elements from the range [first, last) that are equal to **value** and returns the location i that is the past-the-end iterator for the resulting range of values that are not equal to **value**.

The function **remove_if** removes those elements from the range [first, last) which satisfy the predicate **pred**, and it returns the location i that is the past-the-end iterator for the resulting range of values that do not satisfy **pred**.

It is important to note that neither **remove** nor **remove_if** alters the size of the original container: the algorithms operate by copying (with assignments) into the range [first, i). No calls are made to the **insert** or **erase** member functions of the containers on which the algorithms operate.

remove_copy and **remove_copy_if** are similar to **remove** and **remove_if**, except that the resulting sequences are copied into the range beginning at **result**.

All versions of remove are stable; that is, the relative order of the elements that are not removed is the same as their relative order in the original range.

22.20.4 Time Complexity

Linear. The number of assignments is the number of elements not removed, at most the size of the range [first, last), and the number of applications of == or pred is exactly [first, last).

22.21   Unique

22.21.1   Prototypes

```
template <typename ForwardIterator>
ForwardIterator unique(ForwardIterator first,
                       ForwardIterator last);

template <typename ForwardIterator, typename BinaryPredicate>
ForwardIterator unique(ForwardIterator first,
                       ForwardIterator last,
                       BinaryPredicate binary_pred);

template <typename InputIterator, typename OutputIterator>
OutputIterator unique_copy(InputIterator first,
                           InputIterator last,
                           OutputIterator result);

template <typename InputIterator, typename OutputIterator,
          typename BinaryPredicate>
OutputIterator unique_copy(InputIterator first,
                           InputIterator last,
                           OutputIterator result,
                           BinaryPredicate binary_pred);
```

22.21.2   Examples

See Example 5.21.

22.21.3   Description

The algorithm **unique** eliminates consecutive duplicates from the range
[**first**, **last**). An element is considered to be a consecutive duplicate if it
is equal to an element in the location immediately subsequent in the range.

In the first version of **unique**, equality checks are made with **operator==**,
while in the second they are made using the function object **binary_pred**.

unique_copy is similar to **unique** except that the resulting sequence
is copied into the range starting at **result**, leaving the original sequence
unmodified.

All versions of **unique** return the end of the resulting range.

The **unique** algorithms are typically applied to a sorted range, since in
this case all duplicates are consecutive duplicates.

22.21.4   Time Complexity

Linear. Exactly `last - first - 1` (or 0 if the range is empty) applications of the corresponding predicates are done by both versions of `unique`. `unique_copy` applies the predicates `last - first` times.

22.22   Reverse

22.22.1   Prototypes

```
template <typename BidirectionalIterator>
void reverse(BidirectionalIterator first,
             BidirectionalIterator last);

template <typename BidirectionalIterator,
          typename OutputIterator>
OutputIterator reverse_copy(BidirectionalIterator first,
                            BidirectionalIterator last,
                            OutputIterator result);
```

22.22.2   Examples

See Examples 2.1, 2.2, 2.3, 5.22, and 6.5 for `reverse` and Example 5.2 for `reverse_copy`.

22.22.3   Description

The `reverse` algorithm reverses the relative order of elements in the range [`first, last`).

The `reverse_copy` algorithm places the reverse of the range [`first, last`) into the range beginning `result`, leaving [`first, last`) unmodified. It returns the past-the-end iterator `result + last - first`.

22.22.4   Time Complexity

Linear. For `reverse`, exactly $N/2$ element exchanges are performed, where N is the size of [`first, last`). For `reverse_copy`, exactly N assignments are done.

22.23 Rotate

22.23.1 Prototypes

```
template <typename ForwardIterator>
void rotate(ForwardIterator first, ForwardIterator middle,
            ForwardIterator last);

template <typename ForwardIterator, typename OutputIterator>
OutputIterator rotate_copy(ForwardIterator first,
                           ForwardIterator middle,
                           ForwardIterator last,
                           OutputIterator result);
```

22.23.2 Examples

See Example 5.17.

22.23.3 Description

The `rotate` algorithm shifts elements in a sequence toward the beginning as follows: for $N = $ `last - first`, $M = $ `middle - first`, and each nonnegative integer $i < N$, `rotate` places the element from the position `first + i` into the position `first + (i + M)%N`.

`rotate_copy` is similar to `rotate` except that it places the elements of the resulting sequence into the range [`result, result` $+ N$), leaving [`first, last`) unmodified. It returns `result` $+ N$.

22.23.4 Time Complexity

Linear. `rotate` performs at most N swaps (and therefore $3N$ assignments); `rotate_copy` performs exactly N assignments.

22.24 Random Shuffle

22.24.1 Prototypes

```
template <typename RandomAccessIterator>
void random_shuffle(RandomAccessIterator first,
                    RandomAccessIterator last);

template <typename RandomAccessIterator,
          typename RandomNumberGenerator>
```

```
void random_shuffle(RandomAccessIterator first,
                    RandomAccessIterator last,
                    RandomNumberGenerator& rand);
```

22.24.2 Examples

See Examples 5.14, 8.3, and 8.4.

22.24.3 Description

The random_shuffle algorithm randomly reorders the elements in the range [first, last), using a pseudo-random number-generating function. The permutations produced by random_shuffle are approximately uniformly distributed; the probability of each of the $N!$ permutations of a range of size N is approximately $1/N!$. The second version takes a random number-generating function object rand such that each call to rand(N) returns a pseudo-randomly chosen integer in the interval $[0, N)$.

22.24.4 Time Complexity

Linear. Performs exactly (last - first) - 1 swaps (and therefore three times that many assignments).

22.25 Partition

22.25.1 Prototypes

```
template <typename BidirectionalIterator, typename Predicate>
BidirectionalIterator
partition(BidirectionalIterator first,
          BidirectionalIterator last, Predicate pred);

template <typename BidirectionalIterator, typename Predicate>
BidirectionalIterator
stable_partition(BidirectionalIterator first,
                 BidirectionalIterator last,
                 Predicate pred);
```

22.25.2 Examples

See Example 5.13.

22.25.3 Description

The `partition` algorithm places all elements in the range [`first, last`) that satisfy `pred` before all elements that do not satisfy it.

Both algorithms return an iterator `i` such that for any iterator `j` in the range [`first, i`), `pred(*j) == true`, and for any iterator `k` in the range [`i, last`), `pred(*k) == false`.

With `stable_partition`, the relative positions of the elements in both groups are preserved. `partition` does not guarantee this stability property.

22.25.4 Time Complexity

Linear for `partition`; linear or $O(N \log N)$ for `stable_partition`, depending on whether extra memory is available for a workspace.

`partition` performs approximately $N/2$ element exchanges, where N is the size of [`first, last`), and exactly N applications of `pred`. If extra memory for N elements is available, `stable_partition` performs $2N$ assignments. If not, it does at most $N \log N$ swaps. In either case, it does exactly N applications of `pred`.

22.26 Sorting-Related Algorithms Overview

There are nine subcategories of algorithms related in some way to sorting.

- `sort`, `stable_sort`, and `partial_sort` permute the elements of a sequence into ascending order.

- `nth_element` finds the Nth smallest element of a sequence.

- `binary_search`, `lower_bound`, `upper_bound`, and `equal_range` search a sorted sequence using repeated bisection.

- `merge` merges two sorted sequences into one.

- `includes`, `set_union`, `set_intersection`, `set_difference`, and `set_symmetric_difference` are set operations on sorted structures.

- `push_heap`, `pop_heap`, `make_heap`, and `sort_heap` perform ordering operations on a sequence organized as a heap (providing priority queues, among other uses).

- `min`, `max`, `min_element`, and `max_element` find the minimum or maximum of a pair or sequence of elements.

- `lexicographical_compare` compares two sequences lexicographically.

- `next_permutation` and `prev_permutation` generate permutations of a sequence, based on lexicographical ordering of the set of all permutations.

All nine algorithms have two versions: one that uses < for comparisons and another that uses a function object `comp` of type `Compare`.

`Compare comp` must be a function object that accepts two arguments, returns `true` if the first argument is less than the second, and returns `false` otherwise. `Compare comp` is used throughout for algorithms assuming an ordering relation. It is assumed that `comp` will not apply any nonconstant function through the dereferenced iterator.

For all algorithms that take `Compare`, there is a version that uses < instead. That is, `comp(*i, *j) == true` defaults to `*i < *j == true`.

Any *strict weak ordering* may be used for `comp`. "Strict" means an irreflexive relation, so, for example, we may use < or > on type `int` (or any built-in numeric type) but not <= or >=. "Weak" refers to requirements that are weaker than a total ordering (but stronger than a partial ordering). The exact requirements ([18], p. 33) for a relation R to be a strict weak ordering are as follows:

1. R must be a *partial ordering*:

   - (Transitive) For all x, y, z, if xRy and yRz, then xRz.
   - (Irreflexive) For all x, xRx is false.

2. The relation E defined by "xEy if and only if both xRy and yRx are false" must be transitive. When these requirements are met, E is in fact an *equivalence relation*:

   - (Transitive) For all x, y, z, if xEy and yEz, then xEz.
   - (Symmetric) For all x, y, if xEy, then yEx.
   - (Reflexive) For all x, xEx.

It can be shown that R induces a well-defined comparison relation R/E on the equivalence classes defined by E, such that R/E is a total ordering. Thus R itself is not required to be a total ordering, but R/E is.

Stated directly in terms of `comp`, the definition of the equivalence relation E is

$$xEy \text{ if and only if } !(\texttt{comp(x, y)}) \text{ \&\& } !(\texttt{comp(y, x)}).$$

The equivalence relation E is used not only in stating the requirements on `comp` but also in stating other requirements on the sorting-related algorithms. For example, we define stability of a sorting algorithm as the property that the relative order of equivalent elements is preserved. The equivalence referred to is the relation E.

A sequence is *sorted with respect to a comparison function* `comp` if for any iterator `i` pointing into the sequence and any nonnegative integer N such that `i + N` is a valid iterator pointing to an element of the sequence, `comp(*(i + n), *i) == false`.

22.27 Sort

22.27.1 Prototypes

```
template <typename RandomAccessIterator>
void sort(RandomAccessIterator first,
        RandomAccessIterator last);

template <typename RandomAccessIterator, typename Compare>
void sort(RandomAccessIterator first,
        RandomAccessIterator last, Compare comp);

template <typename RandomAccessIterator>
void stable_sort(RandomAccessIterator first,
            RandomAccessIterator last);

template <typename RandomAccessIterator, typename Compare>
void stable_sort(RandomAccessIterator first,
            RandomAccessIterator last, Compare comp);

template <typename RandomAccessIterator>
void partial_sort(RandomAccessIterator first,
            RandomAccessIterator middle,
            RandomAccessIterator last);

template <typename RandomAccessIterator, typename Compare>
void partial_sort(RandomAccessIterator first,
            RandomAccessIterator middle,
            RandomAccessIterator last, Compare comp);

template <typename InputIterator,
        typename RandomAccessIterator>
RandomAccessIterator
```

```
partial_sort_copy(InputIterator first, InputIterator last,
                  RandomAccessIterator result_first,
                  RandomAccessIterator result_last);

template <typename InputIterator,
          typename RandomAccessIterator,
          typename Compare>
RandomAccessIterator
partial_sort_copy(InputIterator first, InputIterator last,
                  RandomAccessIterator result_first,
                  RandomAccessIterator result_last,
                  Compare comp);
```

22.27.2 Examples

See Examples 5.1, 5.3, 8.3, 8.4, 11.1, 13.1, 14.1, 17.1, and 19.1 for sort and Examples 5.22 and 19.2 for all three sorting algorithms.

22.27.3 Description

For sorting, there are three principal algorithms: sort, stable_sort, and partial_sort. A copying version of partial_sort is also provided.

sort sorts the elements in the range [first, last).

stable_sort sorts the elements in the range [first, last) and ensures that the relative order of the equivalent elements is preserved.

For partial_sort, middle should point into the range [first, last). If $M =$ middle - first, the algorithm places in [first, middle) the M elements that would appear there if the entire range [first, last) were sorted. The order in which it leaves the rest of the elements (those in the range [middle, last)) is undefined.

For partial_sort_copy, let $N =$ last - first and $R =$ result_last $-$ result_first. There are two cases:

1. If $R < N$, partial_sort_copy places in [result_first, result_last) the R elements that would appear in [first, first + R) if the entire range [first, last) were sorted. The range [first, last) is not modified. result_last is returned.

2. Otherwise, it places in [result_first, result_first + N) the elements from [first, last) in sorted order. The ranges [first, last) and [result_first + N, result_last) are left unmodified. result_first + N is returned.

22.27.4 Time Complexity

The `sort` algorithm sorts a sequence of length N using $O(N \log N)$ comparisons and assignments on the average. However, there are a few input sequences that cause it to blow up to quadratic time.

For guaranteed $O(N \log N)$ behavior, one can use `partial_sort` with `middle == last`. In general, if $M = $ `middle - first`, `partial_sort` takes $O(N \log M)$ time.

The time for `partial_sort_copy` is $O(N \log K)$, where $K = \min(N, R)$.

The time for `stable_sort` is $O(N \log N)$ or $O(N(\log N)^2)$, depending on whether extra memory is available for a workspace. If extra memory for at least $N/2$ elements is available, the time is $O(N \log N)$.

22.28 Nth Element

22.28.1 Prototypes

```
template <typename RandomAccessIterator>
void nth_element(RandomAccessIterator first,
                RandomAccessIterator position,
                RandomAccessIterator last);

template <typename RandomAccessIterator, typename Compare>
void nth_element(RandomAccessIterator first,
                RandomAccessIterator position,
                RandomAccessIterator last, Compare comp);
```

22.28.2 Examples

See Example 5.23.

22.28.3 Description

The `nth_element` algorithm places an element of a sequence in the location where it would be if the sequence were sorted.

In the first version of the algorithm, element comparisons are done using <, while in the second version they are done using the function object `comp`.

After a call to `nth_element`, the element placed in `position` is the Nth smallest element of the range, where $N = $ `position - first`. Furthermore, for any iterator i in the range [`first`, `position`) and any iterator j in the range [`position`, `last`), either !(*j < *i) (in the first version) or `!comp(*j, *i)` (in the second version). That is, the algorithm partitions the elements of the sequence according to size: elements to the left of `position` are all less than or equivalent to those to its right. The order in which the elements appear in each partition is undefined.

22.28.4   Time Complexity

Linear on the average, quadratic in the worst case.

22.29   Binary Search

All algorithms in this section are versions of binary search. Although binary search is typically efficient (it performs in logarithmic time) only for random access sequences (such as vectors, deques, or arrays), the algorithms here have been written to work even on nonrandom access sequences (such as lists). For nonrandom access sequences, the total time taken is linear in the size of the container, but the number of comparisons is still only logarithmic.

22.29.1   Prototypes

```
template <typename ForwardIterator, typename T>
bool binary_search(ForwardIterator first,
                   ForwardIterator last, const T& value);

template <typename ForwardIterator, typename T,
          typename Compare>
bool binary_search(ForwardIterator first,
                   ForwardIterator last, const T& value,
                   Compare comp);

template <typename ForwardIterator, typename T>
ForwardIterator
lower_bound(ForwardIterator first, ForwardIterator last,
            const T& value);

template <typename ForwardIterator, typename T,
          typename Compare>
ForwardIterator
lower_bound(ForwardIterator first, ForwardIterator last,
            const T& value, Compare comp);

template <typename ForwardIterator, typename T>
```

```
ForwardIterator
upper_bound(ForwardIterator first, ForwardIterator last,
            const T& value);

template <typename ForwardIterator, typename T,
          typename Compare>
ForwardIterator
upper_bound(ForwardIterator first, ForwardIterator last,
            const T& value, Compare comp);

template <typename ForwardIterator, typename T>
pair<ForwardIterator, ForwardIterator>
equal_range(ForwardIterator first, ForwardIterator last,
            const T& value);

template <typename ForwardIterator, typename T,
          typename Compare>
pair<ForwardIterator, ForwardIterator>
equal_range(ForwardIterator first, ForwardIterator last,
            const T& value, Compare comp);
```

22.29.2   Examples

See Examples 5.24 and 12.1.

22.29.3   Description

For each of these algorithms, the range [first, last) must be sorted according to < or according to comp in the case of those that take a Compare argument.

The binary_search algorithms return true if value is in the range [first, last), false otherwise.

The lower_bound algorithms return an iterator referring to the first position in [first, last) into which value may be inserted while maintaining the sorted ordering.

The upper_bound algorithms return an iterator referring to the last position [first, last) into which value may be inserted while maintaining the sorted ordering.

The equal_range functions return a pair of iterators, those that would be returned by lower_bound and upper_bound.

22.29.4 Time Complexity

Logarithmic for random access sequences, linear otherwise. The number of comparison operations is only logarithmic in either case. For nonrandom access sequences, the number of traversal operations (++) is linear, making the total time linear.

For `lower_bound` and `upper_bound`, the number of comparisons is at most $\log N + 1$, for `binary_search` it is at most $\log N + 2$, and for `equal_range` it is at most $2 \log N + 1$, where N is the size of the range [`first`, `last`).

22.30 Merge

22.30.1 Prototypes

```
template <typename InputIterator1, typename InputIterator2,
        typename OutputIterator>
OutputIterator
merge(InputIterator1 first1, InputIterator1 last1,
    InputIterator2 first2, InputIterator2 last2,
    OutputIterator result);

template <typename InputIterator1, typename InputIterator2,
        typename OutputIterator, typename Compare>
OutputIterator
merge(InputIterator1 first1, InputIterator1 last1,
    InputIterator2 first2, InputIterator2 last2,
    OutputIterator result, Compare comp);

template <typename BidirectionalIterator>
void inplace_merge(BidirectionalIterator first,
                BidirectionalIterator middle,
                BidirectionalIterator last);

template <typename BidirectionalIterator, typename Compare>
void inplace_merge(BidirectionalIterator first,
                BidirectionalIterator middle,
                BidirectionalIterator last,
                Compare comp);
```

22.30.2 Examples

See Examples 2.9, 2.10, and 5.25.

417

22.30.3   Description

The merge algorithm merges two sorted ranges [first1, last1) and [first2, last2) into the range [result, result + N), where $N = N1 + N2$, $N1 =$ last1 - first1, and $N2 =$ last2 - first2. The merge is stable; that is, for equivalent elements in the two ranges, the elements from the first range always precede the elements from the second. merge returns result + N. The result of merge is undefined if the resulting range overlaps with either of the original ranges.

   inplace_merge merges two sorted consecutive ranges [first, middle) and [middle, last) putting the result into the range [first, last). The merge is stable.

22.30.4   Time Complexity

Linear in the case of merge. With in_place_merge, the time complexity depends on whether there is extra memory available for a workspace. If extra memory for $N =$ last - first elements is available, the time taken is $O(N)$; otherwise it is $O(N \log N)$.

   With both algorithms the number of comparisons is at most N.

22.31   Set Operations on Sorted Structures

Five algorithms for set operations are provided: includes, set_union, set_intersection, set_difference, and set_symmetric_difference.

   These operations work on sorted structures, including STL sorted associative containers.

   The algorithms even work with multisets containing multiple equivalent elements. The semantics of the operations have been generalized to multisets in the standard way, by defining union to contain the maximum number of occurrences of an element, intersection to contain the minimum number of occurrences, and so on.

22.31.1   Prototypes

```
template <typename InputIterator1, typename InputIterator2>
bool includes(InputIterator1 first1, InputIterator1 last1,
              InputIterator2 first2, InputIterator2 last2);

template <typename InputIterator1, typename InputIterator2,
          typename Compare>
```

```
bool includes(InputIterator1 first1, InputIterator1 last1,
              InputIterator2 first2, InputIterator2 last2,
              Compare comp);

template <typename InputIterator1, typename InputIterator2,
          typename OutputIterator>
OutputIterator
set_union(InputIterator1 first1, InputIterator1 last1,
          InputIterator2 first2, InputIterator2 last2,
          OutputIterator result);

template <typename InputIterator1, typename InputIterator2,
          typename OutputIterator, typename Compare>
OutputIterator
set_union(InputIterator1 first1, InputIterator1 last1,
          InputIterator2 first2, InputIterator2 last2,
          OutputIterator result, Compare comp);

template <typename InputIterator1, typename InputIterator2,
          typename OutputIterator>
OutputIterator
set_intersection(InputIterator1 first1,
                 InputIterator1 last1,
                 InputIterator2 first2,
                 InputIterator2 last2,
                 OutputIterator result);

template <typename InputIterator1, typename InputIterator2,
          typename OutputIterator, typename Compare>
OutputIterator
set_intersection(InputIterator1 first1, InputIterator1 last1,
                 InputIterator2 first2, InputIterator2 last2,
                 OutputIterator result, Compare comp);

template <typename InputIterator1, typename InputIterator2,
          typename OutputIterator>
OutputIterator
set_difference(InputIterator1 first1, InputIterator1 last1,
               InputIterator2 first2, InputIterator2 last2,
               OutputIterator result);

template <typename InputIterator1, typename InputIterator2,
          typename OutputIterator, typename Compare>
OutputIterator
```

```
set_difference(InputIterator1 first1, InputIterator1 last1,
               InputIterator2 first2, InputIterator2 last2,
               OutputIterator result, Compare comp);

template <typename InputIterator1, typename InputIterator2,
          typename OutputIterator>
OutputIterator
set_symmetric_difference(InputIterator1 first1,
                         InputIterator1 last1,
                         InputIterator2 first2,
                         InputIterator2 last2,
                         OutputIterator result);

template <typename InputIterator1, typename InputIterator2,
          typename OutputIterator, typename Compare>
OutputIterator
set_symmetric_difference(InputIterator1 first1,
                         InputIterator1 last1,
                         InputIterator2 first2,
                         InputIterator2 last2,
                         OutputIterator result, Compare comp);
```

22.31.2 Examples

See Example 5.26.

22.31.3 Description

The includes algorithm returns true if every element in the [first2, last2) is contained in [first1, last1), false otherwise. Each of the remaining algorithms places its result in the range beginning at result and returns the past-the-end iterator.

set_union constructs a sorted union of the elements from the two ranges. set_union is stable; that is, if an element in the first range is equivalent to one in the second range, the one from the first range is copied.

set_intersection constructs a sorted intersection of the elements from the two ranges. set_intersection is guaranteed to be stable.

set_difference constructs a sorted difference of the elements from the two ranges. This difference contains elements that are present in the first set but not in the second.

set_symmetric_difference constructs a sorted symmetric difference of the elements from the two ranges, which means that all elements that are in the first range but not in the second and all that are in the second but not in the first.

The result of each of these algorithms is undefined if the resulting range overlaps with either of the original ranges.

22.31.4 Time Complexity

Linear. In all cases, at most $2(N1 + N2) - 1$ comparisons are performed, where $N1 = $ `last1 - first1` and $N2 = $ `last2 - first2`.

22.32 Heap Operations

A *heap*, in the context of sorting, is a particular organization of a sequence that allows certain selection and sorting operations to be done in logarithmic time. Given a range [`first, last`), where `first` and `last` are random access iterators, we say that the range is a heap if two key properties are satisfied:

- The value to which the iterator `first` points is the largest element in the range.

- The value to which the iterator `first` points may be removed by **pop_heap** or a new element added by **push_heap** in logarithmic time, and in both cases the resulting range is a heap.

These properties allow heaps to be used as priority queues.

In addition to **pop_heap** and **push_heap**, there are two more heap algorithms: **make_heap**, for creating a heap out of an arbitrary range, and **sort_heap**, for putting a heap into sorted order.

22.32.1 Prototypes

```
template <typename RandomAccessIterator>
void push_heap(RandomAccessIterator first,
          RandomAccessIterator last);

template <typename RandomAccessIterator, typename Compare>
void push_heap(RandomAccessIterator first,
          RandomAccessIterator last, Compare comp);

template <typename RandomAccessIterator>
void pop_heap(RandomAccessIterator first,
          RandomAccessIterator last);
```

```
template <typename RandomAccessIterator, typename Compare>
void pop_heap(RandomAccessIterator first,
              RandomAccessIterator last, Compare comp);

template <typename RandomAccessIterator>
void make_heap(RandomAccessIterator first,
               RandomAccessIterator last);

template <typename RandomAccessIterator, typename Compare>
void make_heap(RandomAccessIterator first,
               RandomAccessIterator last, Compare comp);

template <typename RandomAccessIterator>
void sort_heap(RandomAccessIterator first,
               RandomAccessIterator last);

template <typename RandomAccessIterator, typename Compare>
void sort_heap(RandomAccessIterator first,
               RandomAccessIterator last, Compare comp);
```

22.32.2 Examples

See Example 5.27.

22.32.3 Description

If the range [first1, last - 1) is a heap, push_heap permutes the elements in [first, last) into a heap. We say that the element at last - 1 is "pushed into the heap."

If the range [first, last) is a heap, pop_heap swaps the value in the location first with the value in the location last - 1 and permutes the range [first, last - 1) into a heap.

make_heap rearranges the elements in the range [first, last) into a heap.

sort_heap sorts the elements in the heap in the range [first, last).

22.32.4 Time Complexity

Let N be the size of the range [first, last).

push_heap and pop_heap take logarithmic time. push_heap performs at most $\log N$ comparisons, pop_heap at most $2 \log N$ comparisons.

422

make_heap takes linear time and does at most $3N$ comparisons.

sort_heap takes $O(N \log N)$ time and does at most $N \log N$ comparisons.

22.33   Min and Max

22.33.1   Prototypes

```
template <typename T>
const T& min(const T& a, const T& b);

template <typename T, typename Compare>
const T& min(const T& a, const T& b, Compare comp);

template <typename T>
const T& max(const T& a, const T& b);

template <typename T, typename Compare>
const T& max(const T& a, const T& b, Compare comp);

template <typename ForwardIterator>
ForwardIterator
min_element(ForwardIterator first, ForwardIterator last);

template <typename ForwardIterator, typename Compare>
ForwardIterator
min_element(ForwardIterator first, ForwardIterator last,
            Compare comp);

template <typename ForwardIterator>
ForwardIterator
max_element(ForwardIterator first, ForwardIterator last);

template <typename ForwardIterator, typename Compare>
ForwardIterator
max_element(ForwardIterator first, ForwardIterator last,
            Compare comp);
```

22.33.2   Examples

See Example 5.28.

22.33.3 Description

The `min` algorithm returns the smaller of its two arguments, while `max` returns the larger. If the two arguments are equivalent, the first is returned.

`min_element` returns the first iterator referring to a minimal element in the range [`first`, `last`).

`max_element` returns the first iterator referring to a maximal element in the range [`first`, `last`).

22.33.4 Time Complexity

Constant for `min` or `max`, linear for `min_element` or `max_element`.

The number of element comparisons for `min_element` or `max_element` is exactly $\max(N - 1, 0)$, where $N = $ `last - first`.

22.34 Lexicographical Comparison

22.34.1 Prototypes

```
template <typename InputIterator1, typename InputIterator2>
bool lexicographical_compare(InputIterator1 first1,
                             InputIterator1 last1,
                             InputIterator2 first2,
                             InputIterator2 last2);

template <typename InputIterator1, typename InputIterator2,
          typename Compare>
bool lexicographical_compare(InputIterator1 first1,
                             InputIterator1 last1,
                             InputIterator2 first2,
                             InputIterator2 last2,
                             Compare comp);
```

22.34.2 Examples

See Example 5.29.

22.34.3 Description

The lexicographical comparison of two sequences [`first1`, `last1`) and [`first2`, `last2`) is defined as follows: traverse the sequences, comparing corresponding pairs of elements e1 and e2; if e1 < e2, stop and return true; if e2 < e1, stop and return `false`; otherwise, continue to the next corresponding pair of elements. If the first sequence is exhausted but the second is not, then return `true`; otherwise, return `false`.

22.34.4 Time Complexity

Linear. The number of comparisons done is at most i, where `first + ` i is the first position at which a disagreement occurs.

22.35 Permutation Generators

Two permutation generation algorithms are provided: `next_permutation` and `prev_permutation`. Each takes a sequence and produces a distinct permutation of it in such a way that $N!$ successive applications yield all permutations of N elements. A strict weak ordering on the elements, given by < or `comp`, is required. Using such an ordering, let the permutations of a sequence be ordered lexicographically. In this ordering of the permutations, the first (smallest) permutation is the one in which elements are in ascending order and the last (largest) permutation is the one in which elements are in descending order. `next_permutation` permutes a sequence into its successor in this lexicographical ordering of permutations, and `prev_permutation` permutes it into its predecessor.

22.35.1 Prototypes

```
template <typename BidirectionalIterator>
bool next_permutation(BidirectionalIterator first,
                      BidirectionalIterator last);

template <typename BidirectionalIterator, typename Compare>
bool next_permutation(BidirectionalIterator first,
                      BidirectionalIterator last,
                      Compare comp);

template <typename BidirectionalIterator>
bool prev_permutation(BidirectionalIterator first,
                      BidirectionalIterator last);

template <typename BidirectionalIterator, typename Compare>
bool prev_permutation(BidirectionalIterator first,
                      BidirectionalIterator last,
                      Compare comp);
```

22.35.2 Examples

See Examples 5.30 and 12.1.

22.35.3 Description

The `next_permutation` algorithm permutes the sequence in [`first`, `last`) into its successor in the lexicographical ordering of all permutations. If such a permutation exists, the algorithm returns true. Otherwise, it transforms the sequence into the smallest permutation (the one in ascending order) and returns `false`.

   `prev_permutation` permutes the sequence in [`first`, `last`) into its predecessor in the lexicographical ordering of all permutations. If such a permutation exists, it returns true. Otherwise, it transforms the sequence into the largest permutation (the one in descending order) and returns `false`.

22.35.4 Time Complexity

Linear. At most $N/2$ swaps and $N/2$ comparisons are done, where $N =$ `last` - `first`.

22.36   Generalized Numeric Algorithms Overview

The library provides four subcategories of algorithms for numeric processing:

- `accumulate` computes the sum of the elements in a sequence.

- `inner_product` computes the sum of the products of corresponding elements in two sequences.

- `partial_sum` computes the partial sums of the elements of a sequence and stores them in another (or the same) sequence.

- `adjacent_difference` computes the differences of adjacent elements and stores them in another (or the same) sequence.

In each case, a second version is provided that allows using other binary operators instead of the usual operators. For example, one can compute the product of the integers in a sequence by calling `accumulate` with the `multiplies<int>` function object so that it uses * instead of +.

   As the category name *generalized* numeric algorithms suggests, the elements and operators are not necessarily numeric. For example, `accumulate` could be used to merge all the lists in a vector of lists by passing it a function object that encapsulates the list `merge` member function.

22.37 Accumulate

22.37.1 Prototypes

```
template <typename InputIterator, typename T>
T accumulate(InputIterator first, InputIterator last,
            T initial_value);

template <typename InputIterator, typename T,
         typename BinaryOperation>
T accumulate(InputIterator first, InputIterator last,
            T initial_value, BinaryOperation binary_op);
```

22.37.2 Examples

See Examples 2.11, 2.12, 2.13, 2.14, 2.15, and 5.31.

22.37.3 Description

The first version of `accumulate` initializes a variable (call it `accumulator`) with `initial_value`, modifies it with

```
accumulator = accumulator + *i
```

for every iterator i in [`first`, `last`) in order, and returns `accumulator`.

The second version is the same except that `binary_op` is used instead of +, as follows:

```
accumulator = binary_op(accumulator, *i)
```

`binary_op` is assumed not to cause any side effects.

22.37.4 Time Complexity

Linear. The number of applications of + or `binary_op` is the size of the range [`first`, `last`).

22.38 Inner Product

22.38.1 Prototypes

```
template <typename InputIterator1, typename InputIterator2,
          typename T>
T inner_product(InputIterator1 first1, InputIterator1 last1,
                InputIterator2 first2, T initial_value);

template <typename InputIterator1, typename InputIterator2,
          typename T,
          typename BinaryOperation1, typename BinaryOperation2>
T inner_product(InputIterator1 first1, InputIterator1 last1,
                InputIterator2 first2, T initial_value,
                BinaryOperation1 binary_op1,
                BinaryOperation2 binary_op2);
```

22.38.2 Examples

See Example 5.34.

22.38.3 Description

The first form of `inner_product` initializes a variable (call it `accumulator`) with `initial_value`, modifies it with

```
accumulator = accumulator + (*i1) * (*i2)
```

for every iterator `i1` in the range [`first1, last2`) and every iterator `i1` in the range [`first2, first2 + (last1 - first2)`) in order, and returns `accumulator`.

The second version is the same except that `binary_op1` is used instead of `+` and `binary_op2` is used instead of `*`, as follows:

```
accumulator =
  binary_op1(accumulator, binary_op2(*i1, *i2))
```

`binary_op1` and `binary_op2` are assumed to cause no side effects.

22.38.4 Time Complexity

Linear. The number of applications of `+` or `binary_op1` and the number of applications of `*` or `binary_op2` is the size of the range [`first, last`).

22.39 Partial Sum

22.39.1 Prototypes

```
template <typename InputIterator, typename OutputIterator>
OutputIterator
partial_sum(InputIterator first, InputIterator last,
        OutputIterator result);

template <typename InputIterator, typename OutputIterator,
        typename BinaryOperation>
OutputIterator
partial_sum(InputIterator first, InputIterator last,
        OutputIterator result,
        BinaryOperation binary_op);
```

22.39.2 Examples

See Example 5.32.

22.39.3 Description

Let $x_k = $ `*(first + `k`)`, for $k = 0, 1, \ldots, N-1$, where $N = $ `last - first`. Then the kth *partial sum* of the elements in the range [`first`, `last`) is defined as

$$s_k = (\ldots ((x_0 + x_1) + x_2) + \ldots) + x_k.$$

The first form of `partial_sum` places s_k in `result + `k for $k = 0, 1, \ldots, N-1$. The second version does the same thing except that it computes the kth partial "sum" with `binary_op`:

$$s_k = \text{binary\_op}(\ldots \text{binary\_op}(\text{binary\_op}(x_0, x_1), x_2), \ldots, x_k).$$

`binary_op` is expected not to have any side effects.

In both cases, `partial_sum` returns `result + `N.

Note that `result` may be equal to `first`: it is possible for the algorithm to work "in place," meaning that the algorithm can generate the partial sums and replace the original sequence with them.

22.39.4 Time Complexity

Linear. The number of applications of + or `binary_op` is exactly $N - 1$.

22.40   Adjacent Difference

22.40.1   Prototypes

```
template <typename InputIterator, typename OutputIterator>
OutputIterator
adjacent_difference(InputIterator first,
                    InputIterator last,
                    OutputIterator result);


template <typename InputIterator, typename OutputIterator,
          typename BinaryOperation>
OutputIterator
adjacent_difference(InputIterator first,
                    InputIterator last,
                    OutputIterator result,
                    BinaryOperation binary_op);
```

22.40.2   Examples

See Example 5.33.

22.40.3   Description

Let $x_k = $ `*(first + k)`, for $k = 0, 1, \ldots, N - 1$, where $N = $ `last - first`. Then, for $k = 1, \ldots, N - 1$, the kth *adjacent difference* of the elements in the range [`first`, `last`) is defined as

$$d_k = x + k - x_{k-1}.$$

The first version of `adjacent_difference` places d_k in `result + k` for $k = 1, \ldots, N-1$. The second version does the same thing except that it computes the kth adjacent "difference" with `binary_op`:

$$d_k = \text{binary\_op}(x_k, x_{k-1}).$$

In both cases, `adjacent_difference` places `*first` in `*result` and returns `result + ` N.

result may be equal to `first`; that is, the algorithm can work "in place."

22.40.4   Time Complexity

Linear. The number of applications of - or `binary_op` is exactly $N - 1$.

CHAPTER 23

Function Object and Function Adaptor Reference Guide

23.1 Requirements

All the classes and functions discussed in this chapter are found in the header file `<functional>`.

23.1.1 Function Objects

A class-defined function object encapsulates a function in an object for use by other components. This is done by overloading the function call operator, `operator()`, of the corresponding class (see Examples 2.13, 8.2, 8.3, 8.4, 11.1, and 17.1).

Passing a class-defined function object to an algorithm is similar to passing a pointer to a function with one important difference. Class-defined function objects are classes that have `operator()` overloaded, which makes it possible to do the following:

- Pass function objects to algorithms at compile time

- Increase efficiency by inlining the corresponding call

- Locally encapsulate information used by the function object. With a pointer to a function, this would need to be implemented using static or global data (see Example 18.1).

The first two factors make a difference when the functions involved are very simple ones, such as integer additions or comparisons. The last can be significant in a much broader set of situations.

23.1.2   Function Adaptors

Function adaptors are STL classes that allow users to construct a wider variety of function objects. Using function adaptors is often easier than directly constructing a new function object type with a struct or class definition. There are four subcategories of function adaptors:

1. *Binders* are function adaptors that convert binary function objects into unary function objects by binding an argument to some particular value.

2. *Negators* are function objects that reverse the sense of predicate function objects.

3. *Adaptors for pointers to functions* allow pointers to (unary and binary) functions to work with function adaptors the library provides.

4. *Adaptors for pointers to member functions* allow pointers to (unary and binary, including the implicit **this** pointer) member functions to work with function adaptors the library provides.

23.2   Base Classes

A unary function object passed as an argument to an adaptor must define the types `argument_type` and `result_type`, naturally corresponding to the type of the function's argument and its return value. Similarly, binary functions must define `first_argument_type`, `second_argument_type`, and `result_type`. To facilitate making these definitions, two base classes are provided from which function objects can be derived.

```
template <typename Arg, typename Result>
struct unary_function {
  typedef Arg argument_type;
  typedef Result result_type;
};
template <typename Arg1, typename Arg2, typename Result>
struct binary_function {
  typedef Arg1 first_argument_type;
  typedef Arg2 second_argument_type;
  typedef Result result_type;
};
```

See Examples 8.3, 8.4, 11.1, 17.1, and 18.1 and the file `ps.h` used in Examples 13.1 and 14.1 for uses of `binary_function`.

23.3 Arithmetic Operations

STL provides basic function object classes for all the arithmetic operators in the language. The functionality of the operators is described here.

```
template <typename T> struct plus;
```

> Accepts two operands of type T and returns their sum.

```
template <typename T> struct minus;
```

> Accepts two operands of type T and returns the result of subtracting the second operand from the first.

```
template <typename T> struct multiplies;
```

> Accepts two operands of type T and returns their product (see Example 2.14).

```
template <typename T> struct divides;
```

> Accepts two operands of type T and returns the result of dividing the first operand by the second.

```
template <typename T> struct modulus;
```

> Accepts two operands, x and y, of type T and returns the result of the computation x % y.

```
template <typename T> struct negate;
```

> Unary function object that accepts a single operand of type T and returns its negated value.

23.4 Comparison Operations

STL provides basic function object classes for all the comparison operators in the language. The basic functionality of the comparison objects is described here.

```
template <typename T> struct equal_to;
```

> Accepts two parameters, x and y, of type T and returns **true** if x ==
> y, **false** otherwise.

```
template <typename T> struct not_equal_to;
```

> Accepts two parameters, x and y, of type T and returns **true** if x !=
> y, **false** otherwise.

```
template <typename T> struct greater;
```

> Accepts two parameters, x and y, of type T and returns **true** if x >
> y, **false** otherwise (see Example 5.3).

```
template <typename T> struct less;
```

> Accepts two parameters, x and y, of type T and returns **true** if x <
> y, **false** otherwise.

```
template <typename T> struct greater_equal;
```

> Accepts two parameters, x and y, of type T and returns **true** if x >=
> y, **false** otherwise.

```
template <typename T> struct less_equal;
```

> Accepts two parameters, x and y, of type T and returns **true** if x <=
> y, **false** otherwise.

23.5   Logical Operations

STL provides basic function object classes for the following logical operators
in the language: *and, or, not.* The basic functionality of the logical operators
follows.

```
template <typename T> struct logical_and;
```

> Accepts two parameters, x and y, of type T and returns the Boolean
> result of the logical *and* operation: x && y.

```
template <typename T> struct logical_or;
```

Accepts two parameters, `x` and `y`, of type `T` and returns the Boolean result of the logical *or* operation: `x || y`.

```
template <typename T> struct logical_not;
```

Accepts a single parameter, `x`, of type `T` and returns the Boolean result of the logical *not* operation: `!x`.

23.6 Negator Adaptors

Negators are function adaptors that take a predicate and return its complement. STL provides the negators `not1` and `not2`, which take a unary and binary predicate, respectively, and return their complements.

```
template <typename Predicate> class unary_negate;

template <typename Predicate>
unary_negate<Predicate> not1(const Predicate& x);
```

The `not1` function accepts a *unary* predicate `x` as input and returns its complement, `!x` in the form of an instance of **unary_negate** (see Example 13.1). Objects of type **unary_negate** may also be instantiated directly. The constructor takes a unary predicate **pred**.

```
template <typename Predicate> class binary_negate;

template <typename Predicate>
binary_negate<Predicate> not2(const Predicate& x);
```

This function accepts a *binary* predicate `x` as input and returns its complement, `!x` (see Examples 11.1 and 15.1). Again, **binary_negate** may be instantiated directly with a constructor that takes a binary predicate **pred**.

23.7 Binder Adaptors

Binders are function adaptors that convert binary function objects into unary function objects by binding an argument to some particular value. STL provides two binders, `bind1st` and `bind2nd`:

```
template <typename Operation> class binder1st;

template <typename Operation, typename T>
binder1st<Operation>
bind1st(const Operation& op, const T& x);
```

Accepts a function object `op` of two arguments and a value `x` of type T. Returns a function object of one argument constructed out of `op` with the *first* argument bound to `x` (see Examples 13.1 and 15.1). The `binder1st` type has a constructor with similar arguments to `bind1st`—a `const Operation&` and a `const T&`.

```
template <typename Operation> class binder2nd;
```

```
template <typename Operation, typename T>
binder2nd<Operation>
bind2nd(const Operation& op, const T& x);
```

Accepts a function object `op` of two arguments and a value `x` of type T. Returns a function object of one argument constructed out of `op` with the *second* argument bound to `x`. The constructor for `binder2nd` takes a `const Operation&` and a `const T&` as arguments.

23.8   Adaptors for Pointers to Functions

Adaptors for pointers to functions are provided to allow pointers to unary and binary functions to work with the function adaptors provided in the library. They also can help avoid the "code bloat" problem arising from multiple template instances in the same program (see Section 11.3 and Example 11.2).

```
template <typename Arg, typename Result>
class pointer_to_unary_function;
```

```
template <typename Arg, typename Result>
pointer_to_unary_function<Arg, Result>
ptr_fun(Result (*x) (Arg));
```

Accepts a pointer to a unary function that takes an argument of type `Arg` and returns a result of type `Result`. A function object of type `pointer_to_unary_function<Arg, Result>` is constructed out of this argument and then returned. The `pointer_to_unary_function` constructor takes a function pointer of the appropriate type as an argument.

```
template <typename Arg1, typename Arg2, typename Result>
class pointer_to_binary_function;
```

```
template <typename Arg1, typename Arg2, typename Result>
pointer_to_binary_function<Arg1, Arg2, Result>
ptr_fun(Result (*x) (Arg1, Arg2));
```

Accepts a pointer to a binary function that takes arguments of type `Arg1` and `Arg2` and returns a result of type `Result`. A function object of type `pointer_to_binary_function<Arg1, Arg2, Result>` is constructed out of this argument and then returned. The constructor for `pointer_to_binary_function` takes a function pointer of the appropriate type as an argument. See Example 11.2.

23.9   Adaptors for Pointers to Member Functions

Adaptors for pointers to member functions are provided to allow pointers to member functions to work with the function adaptors provided in the library. When a member function is adapted to a regular function object, the `this` pointer becomes an argument of the new function. Thus, a member function of class `X` that takes no arguments is turned into a function that has a single argument of type `X*` (or `X&` if the `mem_fun_ref` adaptor is used). Adaptors are provided for member functions with zero or one arguments.

```
template <typename Result, typename T>
class mem_fun_t;

template <typename Result, typename T>
mem_fun_t<Result, T> mem_fun(Result (T::*x) ());
```

Accepts a pointer to a member function of class `T` that takes no arguments and returns a result of type `Result`. A function object of type `mem_fun_t<Result, T>` is constructed out of this argument and then returned. If the function object is invoked as `f(p)` where p is a `T*`, it returns the result of `(p->*x)()`.

```
template <typename Result, typename T, typename Arg>
class mem_fun1_t;

template <typename Result, typename T, typename Arg>
mem_fun1_t<Result, T, Arg> mem_fun(Result (T::*x) (Arg));
```

Accepts a pointer to a unary member function of class `T` that takes an argument of type `Arg` and returns a result of type `Result`. A function object of type `mem_fun_t<Result, T>` is constructed out of this argument and then returned. If the function object is invoked as `f(p, arg)` where p is a `T*` and `arg` is an `Arg`, it returns the result of `(p->*x)(arg)`.

```
template <typename Result, typename T>
class mem_fun_ref_t;

template <typename Result, typename T>
mem_fun_ref_t<Result, T> mem_fun_ref(Result (T::*x) ());
```

> Accepts a pointer to a member function of class T that takes no arguments and returns a result of type Result. A function object of type mem_fun_ref_t<Result, T> is constructed out of this argument and then returned. If the function object is invoked as f(r) where r is a T&, it returns the result of (r.*x)().

```
template <typename Result, typename T, typename Arg>
class mem_fun1_ref_t;

template <typename Result, typename T, typename Arg>
mem_fun1_ref_t<Result, T, Arg>
mem_fun_ref(Result (T::*x) (Arg));
```

> Accepts a pointer to a unary member function of class T that takes an argument of type Arg and returns a result of type Result. A function object of type mem_fun_ref_t<Result, T> is constructed out of this argument and then returned. If the function object is invoked as f(r, arg) where r is a T& and arg is an Arg, it returns the result of (r.*x)(arg).

```
template <typename Result, typename T>
class const_mem_fun_t;

template <typename Result, typename T>
const_mem_fun_t<Result, T> mem_fun(Result (T::*x) () const);
```

> Accepts a pointer to a const member function of class T that takes no arguments and returns a result of type Result. A function object of type const_mem_fun_t<Result, T> is constructed out of this argument and then returned. If the function object is invoked as f(p) where p is a const T*, it returns the result of (p->*x)().

```
template <typename Result, typename T, typename Arg>
class const_mem_fun1_t;

template <typename Result, typename T, typename Arg>
const_mem_fun1_t<Result, T, Arg>
mem_fun(Result (T::*x) (Arg) const);
```

Accepts a pointer to a const unary member function of class T that takes an argument of type Arg and returns a result of type Result. A function object of type const_mem_fun_t<Result, T> is constructed out of this argument and then returned. If the function object is invoked as f(p, arg) where p is a const T* and arg is an Arg, it returns the result of (p->*x)(arg).

```
template <typename Result, typename T>
class const_mem_fun_ref_t;

template <typename Result, typename T>
const_mem_fun_ref_t<Result, T>
mem_fun_ref(Result (T::*x) () const);
```

Accepts a pointer to a const member function of class T that takes no arguments and returns a result of type Result. A function object of type const_mem_fun_ref_t<Result, T> is constructed out of this argument and then returned. If the function object is invoked as f(r) where r is a const T&, it returns the result of (r.*x)().

```
template <typename Result, typename T, typename Arg>
class const_mem_fun1_ref_t;

template <typename Result, typename T, typename Arg>
const_mem_fun1_ref_t<Result, T, Arg>
mem_fun_ref(Result (T::*x) (Arg) const);
```

Accepts a pointer to a const unary member function of class T that takes an argument of type Arg and returns a result of type Result. A function object of type const_mem_fun_ref_t<Result, T> is constructed out of this argument and then returned. If the function object is invoked as f(r, arg) where r is a const T& and arg is an Arg, it returns the result of (r.*x)(arg).

CHAPTER 24

Allocator Reference Guide

24.1 Introduction

Every STL container class uses an `Allocator` class to encapsulate information about the memory allocation model the program is using. For example, a debugging allocator might do bounds checking or leak detection on allocated memory.

An allocator is a template class parameterized on the type of object it can allocate. The `Allocator` class encapsulates information about pointers, constant pointers, references, constant references, sizes of objects, difference types between pointers, allocation and deallocation functions, and some other functions. The exact set of types and functions defined within the allocator is explained in Section 24.3.

Since allocation model information can be encapsulated in an allocator, STL containers can be made to work with different allocation models simply by providing different allocators. All allocator operations are expected to take amortized constant time.

24.1.1 Passing Allocators to STL Containers

Once an allocator class for a particular allocation model has been written, it must be passed on to the STL container for that container to work properly in the concerned allocation model. This is done by passing the allocator to the STL container as a template parameter.

For example, the `vector` container has the following interface:

```
template <typename T, typename Allocator = allocator<T> >
class vector
```

Here the `Allocator` parameter defaults to `allocator<T>`, which is the default allocator type provided by the library.

24.2 Allocator Requirements

Common Type Definitions in All Allocators. Following are common type definitions that must be found in all allocator classes. It is assumed that X is an allocator class for objects of type T and Y is an allocator class for objects of type U.

`value_type`

> Type of objects the allocator creates. This type is identical to T.

`reference`

> Type that can be used for storing into **value_type** objects. This type is identical to T&.

`const_reference`

> Type that can be used for storing into constant **value_type** objects. This type is identical to **const T&**.

`pointer`

> Type that can be used for the address of **value_type** objects.

`const_pointer`

> Type that can be used for the address of constant **value_type** objects.

`difference_type`

> Type that can represent the difference between any two pointers in the allocation model (usually `ptrdiff_t`).

`size_type`

> Type that can represent the size of the largest object in the allocation model (usually `size_t`).

```
template rebind<U>::other
```

Provides a mechanism for obtaining an allocator type, `Y`, for objects of type `U`, which uses the same memory model as `X`. This is essentially a template typedef such that if `X` is `SomeAllocator<T>`, then `rebind<U>::other` is the same type as `SomeAllocator<U>`. Transitivity holds, so `Y::template rebind<T>::other` is `X`.

Container implementations are permitted to assume that `pointer` is `T*`, `const_pointer` is `const T*`, `size_type` is `size_t` and `difference_type` is `ptrdiff_t`.

Common Member Functions in All Allocators. The common member functions required in each allocator follow. In the descriptions, the following assumptions are made.

- `T` and `U` are any type.

- `X` is an allocator class for objects of type `T`.

- `Y` is an allocator class for objects of type `U`.

- `t` is a value of type `const T&`.

- `a`, `a1`, and `a2` are values of `X&`.

- `b` is a value of type `Y`.

- `p` is a value of type `X::pointer` obtained by calling `a1.allocate`, where `a1 == a`.

- `q` is a value of type `X::const_pointer` obtained by conversion from a value `p`.

- `r` is a value of type `X::reference` obtained by the expression `*p`.

- `s` is a value of type `X::const_reference` obtained by the expression `*q` or by conversion from a value `r`.

- `u` is a value of type `Y::const_pointer` obtained via `Y::allocate`, or else 0.

- `n` is a value of type `X::size_type`.

All these operations take amortized constant time.

`X();`

> Default constructor.

`X a(b);`

> Constructs an allocator for type `T` from an allocator for type `U`. Note that as a special case, types `T` and `U` may be the same, in which case `X a(b)` is the copy constructor. As a postcondition, `Y(a) == b` must be true.

`a.address(r);`
`a.address(s);`

> Returns the address of the object `r` (or `s`, a constant reference) as a `X::pointer` (`X::const_pointer` for `s`).

`a.allocate(n);`

> Returns a `X::pointer` to the initial element of an array of `n` objects of type `T`. The objects are not constructed.

`a.allocate(n, u);`

> Like `a.allocate(n)`, returns a `X::pointer` to the initial element of an array of `n` objects of type `T`. The objects are not constructed. The second argument, `u`, represents a hint that may be used to improve locality of reference. In the case of containers, `this` or a pointer to an ajacent element is often a good choice.

`a.deallocate(p, n);`

> Deallocates memory for `n` objects of type `T` at location `p`. The destructors must be invoked prior to calling `deallocate`. `n` must match the value passed to `allocate`, and `p` may not be null.

`a.max_size();`

> Returns a value of type `X::size_type` representing the largest value that can meaningfully be passed to `X::allocate`.

444

```
a1 == a2
```

> Returns true if and only if storage allocated from each can be deallocated from the other. Container implementations are permitted to assume that this will always be true for instances of the same allocator type.

```
a1 != a2
```

> Same as `!(a1 == a2)`.

```
a.construct(p, t);
```

> Constructs a copy of `t` in the memory address given by `p`. This is the same as `new ((void*)p) T(t)`.

```
a.destroy(p);
```

> Destroys the object in the memory address given by `p`. Same as `((T*)p)->~T()`.

24.3 Default Allocator

24.3.1 Files

```
#include <memory>
```

24.3.2 Class Declaration

```
template <typename T> class allocator
```

24.3.3 Description

A default allocator implementation with the class name `allocator` is provided by the library and is used by the container classes when the allocator type is not explicitly specified. This allocator uses `::operator new(size_t)` and `::operator delete(void *)` for allocation and deallocation, respectively.

24.3.4   Type Definitions

`size_type`

> Type that can represent the size of the largest object in the allocation model, `size_t`.

`difference_type`

> Type that can represent the difference between any two pointers in the allocation model, `ptrdiff_t`.

`pointer`
`const_pointer`

> `pointer` is the type of memory addresses of allocated objects, `T*`. `const_pointer` is the corresponding constant pointer type, `const T*`.

`reference`
`const_reference`

> `reference` is the type of locations of allocated objects, `T&`, and `const_reference` is the corresponding constant reference type, `const T&`.

`value_type`

> Type of object, `T`, that will be created by the allocator.

`template rebind<U>::other`

> Gives a default allocator for the type U. Equivalent to `allocator<U>`.

24.3.5   Constructors, Destructors and Related Functions

`allocator();`

> Default constructor.

`allocator(const allocator&);`

> Copy constructor.

`template <typename U> allocator(const allocator<U>&);`

> Constructs an allocator of objects of `T` from an allocator of objects of type U.

`~allocator();`

> Destructor.

24.3.6   Other Member Functions

```
pointer address(reference x) const;
const_pointer address(const_reference x) const;
```

> Returns a pointer to the referenced object **x**. In particular, it returns
> **&x**.

```
pointer allocate(size_type n,
                 typename allocator<void>::const_pointer hint = 0);
```

> Allocates memory for **n** objects of type **value_type**, but the objects
> are not constructed. Uses the global **new** operator. Note that different
> allocation models require different **allocate** functions (which is why
> the function has been encapsulated in the memory allocator class).
> **allocate** may raise an appropriate exception. The pointer **hint** can
> be used as an aid for locality of reference. In a container member
> function, the self-reference pointer **this** is usually a good choice to
> use for **hint**. It is not specified when or how often **::operator new**
> will be invoked.

```
void deallocate(pointer p, size_type n);
```

> Deallocates all storage pointed to by the pointer **p** using the global
> **delete** operator. All objects in the area pointed to by **p** should be
> destroyed before the call of **deallocate**. It is not specified when or
> how often **::operator delete** is actually invoked.

```
size_type max_size();
```

> Returns the largest positive value N for which **allocate**(N) might
> succeed.

```
void construct(pointer p, const T& val);
```

> Constructs a copy of **val** in the memory indicated by **p** by executing
> **new ((void*)p) T(val)**.

```
void destroy(pointer p);
```

> Destroys the object indicated by **p** by executing **((T*)p)->~T()**.

24.3.7 Comparison Operations

```
template <typename T1, typename T2>
bool operator==(const allocator<T1>&, const allocator<T2>&);
```

Always returns `true`.

```
template <typename T1, typename T2>
bool operator!=(const allocator<T1>&, const allocator<T2>&);
```

Always returns `false`.

24.3.8 Notes on Void

A specialization is defined for `void` since references to `void` and allocation of objects of type `void` are not possible.

```
template <> class allocator<void> {  // specialization
 public:
  typedef void*       pointer;
  typedef const void* const_pointer;
  typedef void        value_type;
  template <typename U> struct rebind {
    typedef allocator<U> other;
  };
};
```

24.4 Custom Allocators

As an example of a custom allocator, we present an allocator that logs all memory allocations and deallocations to `cerr`. This could also be used in conjunction with a debugger by setting breakpoints in the `allocate` and `deallocate` functions.

Our logging allocator will use some other allocator as a base to do the actual memory allocation. The logging allocator is actually an allocator adaptor that adds the logging behavior to any existing allocator class.

We place the code into a header file, `logalloc.h`, which is shown in its entirety. The details of the implementation are discussed in the paragraphs that follow the header file.

```
"logalloc.h" 448 ≡
    #include <memory>
    #include <iostream>
    using namespace std;
```

```
template <typename T, typename Allocator = allocator<T> >
class logging_allocator
{
private:
  Allocator alloc;

public:
  typedef typename Allocator::size_type size_type;
  typedef typename Allocator::difference_type difference_type;
  typedef typename Allocator::pointer pointer;
  typedef typename Allocator::const_pointer const_pointer;
  typedef typename Allocator::reference reference;
  typedef typename Allocator::const_reference const_reference;
  typedef typename Allocator::value_type value_type;
  template <typename U> struct rebind {
    typedef logging_allocator<U,
          typename Allocator::template rebind<U>::other> other;
  };

  logging_allocator() {}
  logging_allocator(const logging_allocator& x)
    : alloc(x.alloc) {}
  template <typename U>
  logging_allocator(const logging_allocator<U,
          typename Allocator::template rebind<U>::other>& x)
    : alloc(x.alloc) {}
  ~logging_allocator() {}

  pointer address(reference x) const {
    return alloc.address(x);
  }
  const_pointer address(const_reference x) const {
    return alloc.address(x);
  }
  size_type max_size() const  { return alloc.max_size(); }
  void construct(pointer p, const value_type& val) {
    alloc.construct(p, val);
  }
  void destroy(pointer p) { alloc.destroy(p); }

  pointer allocate(size_type n, const void* hint = 0) {
    ios::fmtflags flags = cerr.flags();
```

```
      cerr << "allocate(" << n << ", "
            << hex << hint << dec << ") = ";
      pointer result = alloc.allocate(n, hint);
      cerr << hex << result << dec << endl;

      cerr.setf(flags);
      return result;
    }

    void deallocate(pointer p, size_type n) {
      ios::fmtflags flags = cerr.flags();

      cerr << "deallocate(" << hex << p << dec << ", "
            << n << ")" << endl;
      alloc.deallocate(p, n);

      cerr.setf(flags);
    }
};

template <typename T, typename Allocator1,
          typename U, typename Allocator2>
bool operator==(const logging_allocator<T, Allocator1>& x,
                const logging_allocator<U, Allocator2>& y) {
  return x.alloc == y.alloc;
}

template <typename T, typename Allocator1,
          typename U, typename Allocator2>
bool operator!=(const logging_allocator<T, Allocator1>& x,
                const logging_allocator<U, Allocator2>& y) {
  return x.alloc != y.alloc;
}
```

We define our new allocator, **logging_allocator**, as a template class with both the value type and the adapted allocator type as parameters. This allows the logging class to be used conveniently with the default allocator without preventing the use of other custom allocators.

To use the logging allocator to allocate **ints** with the default allocator, we simply say **logging_allocator<int>**. To use another allocator, say **MyAllocator**, we say **logging_allocator<int, MyAllocator<int> >**, passing both the value type and the allocator type as template parameters.

The types required for allocators are simply defined in terms of the adapted **Allocator** template parameter. The **rebind** template is somewhat unusual, since we need to redefine both template parameters in terms of the new value type.

The constructors, destructor, and all member functions except `allocate` and `deallocate` simply defer to the base allocator to do the actual work. The same is done for the comparison operations that compare the base allocator to determine equality.

The `allocate` function prints its arguments and return value on `cerr` while calling the base allocator's `allocate` method to do the actual work. We save and restore `cerr`'s formatting flags, since they are changed to print the pointer in hexadecimal notation.

```
pointer allocate(size_type n, const void* hint = 0) {
  ios::fmtflags flags = cerr.flags();

  cerr << "allocate(" << n << ", "
       << hex << hint << dec << ") = ";
  pointer result = alloc.allocate(n, hint);
  cerr << hex << result << dec << endl;

  cerr.setf(flags);
  return result;
}
```

The `deallocate` function is similar to `allocate`. It prints its arguments, calling the base allocator's `deallocate` method to actually return the memory. Again, the formmatting flags for `cerr` are kept intact by saving them before printing the log message and restoring them afterwards.

```
void deallocate(pointer p, size_type n) {
  ios::fmtflags flags = cerr.flags();

  cerr << "deallocate(" << hex << p << dec << ", "
       << n << ")" << endl;
  alloc.deallocate(p, n);

  cerr.setf(flags);
}
```

The following example demonstrates the use of the logging allocator. We create three vectors, one using the default allocator and two that use a logging allocator. We then insert ten elements into each vector. In the third case we call `v3.reserve(10)` first to reserve space for the elements before doing the insertions. Note that only the declaration of the vector's

type (and the call to **reserve**) is different for each of the cases. The code
that inserts the elements is identical.

Example 24.1: Demonstrating use of a custom allocator

"ex24-01.cpp" 452 ≡

```
#include <iostream>
#include <vector>
using namespace std;

#include "logalloc.h"

int main()
{
  cout << "Demonstrating use of a custom allocator." << endl;

  cout << "-- Default allocator --" << endl;
  vector<int> v1;
  for (int i = 0; i < 10; ++i) {
    cout << "   Inserting " << i << endl;
    v1.push_back(i);
  }
  cout << "-- Done. --" << endl;

  cout << "\n-- Custom allocator --" << endl;
  vector<int, logging_allocator<int> > v2;
  for (int i = 0; i < 10; ++i) {
    cout << "   Inserting " << i << endl;
    v2.push_back(i);
  }
  cout << "-- Done. --" << endl;

  cout << "\n-- Custom allocator with reserve --" << endl;
  vector<int, logging_allocator<int> > v3;
  v3.reserve(10);
  for (int i = 0; i < 10; ++i) {
    cout << "   Inserting " << i << endl;
    v3.push_back(i);
  }
  cout << "-- Done. --" << endl;

  return 0;
}
```

In the following sample output from the program, note that the exact sequence of allocations may vary depending on the specific STL implementation used, as will the specific memory locations.

Output from Example 24.1

```
Demonstrating use of a custom allocator.
-- Default allocator --
    Inserting 0
    Inserting 1
    Inserting 2
    Inserting 3
    Inserting 4
    Inserting 5
    Inserting 6
    Inserting 7
    Inserting 8
    Inserting 9
-- Done. --

-- Custom allocator --
    Inserting 0
allocate(1, 0x0) = 0x46213e8
    Inserting 1
allocate(2, 0x0) = 0x46213e0
deallocate(0x46213e8, 1)
    Inserting 2
allocate(4, 0x0) = 0x4621480
deallocate(0x46213e0, 2)
    Inserting 3
    Inserting 4
allocate(8, 0x0) = 0x4621528
deallocate(0x4621480, 4)
    Inserting 5
    Inserting 6
    Inserting 7
    Inserting 8
allocate(16, 0x0) = 0x46217e8
deallocate(0x4621528, 8)
    Inserting 9
-- Done. --

-- Custom allocator with reserve --
allocate(10, 0x0) = 0x4621a48
    Inserting 0
    Inserting 1
```

```
     Inserting 2
     Inserting 3
     Inserting 4
     Inserting 5
     Inserting 6
     Inserting 7
     Inserting 8
     Inserting 9
  -- Done. --
  deallocate(0x4621a48, 10)
  deallocate(0x46217e8, 16)
```

The first case, of course, does not produce any output regarding memory allocation, since it uses the default allocator. The second and third cases, however, print a message each time memory in the vector is allocated or deallocated. From the second part, we can see that the vector's size grows geometrically as we add more elements. Each time we insert an element that fills the amount of space available, the vector allocates space for twice as many elements as before.

For example, when the fourth element is inserted, after `Inserting 4` is printed, the vector has room for exactly four elements. Therefore, memory is allocated for twice as many elements (`allocate(8, 0x0) = 0x46214c8`), the old values are copied to the new space, and the previous memory is returned (`deallocate(0x4621420, 4)`).

The third case shows how **reserve** causes a single allocation of space for ten elements. We are then able to insert the values without any additional calls to `allocator` or `deallocate`.

The final two calls to **deallocate** are from the destructors of **v2** and **v3**.

CHAPTER 25

Utilities Reference Guide

25.1 Introduction

The file `<utility>` defines a number of template functions and classes that are of general use to C++ programmers but that do not fit into any of the categories discussed in previous chapters. These can be divided into two subcategories, comparison function templates and `pair` class templates.

25.2 Comparison Functions

To simplify the definition of a full set of comparison functions for new types, template functions are provided for `operator!=`, `operator>`, `operator>=`, and `operator<=`. These functions are implemented in terms of `==` and `<`. Thus, for any type it is necessary only to explicitly define equality and less-than comparisons to obtain a full complement of comparison operations.

These functions are in the namespace `std::rel_ops`. To access them, it may be necessary to include **using namespace std::rel_ops** in your program.

```
template <typename T> bool operator!=(const T&x, const T& y);
```

   Returns `!(x == y)`.

```
template <typename T> bool operator>(const T&x, const T& y);
```

   Returns `y < x`.

```
template <typename T> bool operator<=(const T&x, const T& y);
```

Returns !(y < x).

```
template <typename T> bool operator>=(const T&x, const T& y);
```

Returns !(x < y).

25.3   Pairs

25.3.1   Files

```
#include <utility>
```

25.3.2   Class Declaration

```
template <typename T1, typename T2> struct pair
```

25.3.3   Examples

See Examples 13.1 and 14.1.

25.3.4   Description

The `pair` class provides a data structure for storing ordered pairs of arbitrary types. The elements are stored in two member variables, `first` and `second`.

25.3.5   Type Definitions

`first_type`

Type of values in the `first` element of the pair, T1.

`second_type`

Type of values in the `second` element of the pair, T2.

25.3.6   Member Variables

`first`

First element of the pair.

`second`

Second element of the pair.

25.3.7 Constructors

```
pair();
```

> Default constructor, which constructs a pair with each element initialized by its own default constructor.

```
pair(const T1& x, const T2& y);
```

> Constructs a pair with `first` initialized to x and `second` initialized to y.

```
template <typename U, typename V> pair(const pair<U, V> &p);
```

> Constructs a pair initializing `first` and `second` to their corresponding elements in p, performing implicit type conversions as necessary.

```
template <typename T1, typename T2>
pair<T1, T2> make_pair(const T1& x, const T2& y);
```

> This function is defined as a convenience. Since the template parameters are deduced from the function arguments, this function can be syntactically simpler than a constructor invocation in some situations. Compare the expressions `pair<int, double>(5, 3.1415926)` and `make_pair(5, 3.1415926)`.

25.3.8 Comparison Functions

```
template <typename T1, typename T2>
bool operator==(const pair<T1, T2>& x, const pair<T1, T2>& y);
```

> Returns `true` if both elements of the pairs are equal—`x.first == y.first && x.second == y.second`.

```
template <typename T1, typename T2>
bool operator<(const pair<T1, T2>& x, const pair<T1, T2>& y);
```

> Implements a lexicographical comparison of the elements of the pairs. If the `first` element of x is less than that of y, the function returns `true`. Otherwise, if the `first` elements are equal, it returns `x.second < y.second`.

STL Header Files

To use STL components in your programs, you must use the preprocessor `#include` directive to include one or more header files. In all the example programs in this book, we assume that the STL header files are organized and named as in the C++ Standard. C++ library headers in the Standard do not use the `.h` suffix. Headers that are also C library headers are prefixed with a `c` (for example, `stdlib.h` becomes `cstdlib`). The other components are as follows.

1. The `vector`, `list`, and `deque` container classes are in `<vector>`, `<list>`, and `<deque>`, respectively.

2. Both `set` and `multiset` are in `<set>`, and both `map` and `multimap` are in `<map>`.

3. The `stack` adaptor is in `<stack>`, and the `queue` and `priority_queue` adaptors are in `<queue>`.

4. All STL generic algorithms are in `<algorithm>` except generalized numeric algorithms, which are in `<numeric>`.

5. STL iterator classes (other than those defined by container classes) and iterator adaptors are in `<iterator>`.

6. Function object classes and function adaptors are in `<functional>`.

String Reference Guide

Strings in the standard C++ library are implemented as a sequence container of "characters." (See Section 21.1.4 for a detailed definition of sequence container.) This means that like all STL containers, strings support the expressions defined for containers, including iterators (which are analagous to a `char*` in a conventional, null-terminated C string) and can be used with all STL algorithms.

This chapter presents the C++ string classes specifically as they relate to STL. As a result, this is not a comprehensive reference on these classes. For example, the `basic_string` class provides members for appending to a string, finding a character or substring within a string, and replacing a range of characters with another range. Since these operations are not supported by sequence containers in general, they are not discussed here. Our intent is to cover the aspects of strings that are relevant to the use of strings with STL algorithms.

B.1 String Classes

B.1.1 Files

```
#include <string>
```

B.1.2 Class Declaration

```
template <typename charT, typename traits = char_traits<charT>,
        typename Allocator = allocator<charT> >
class basic_string
```

We omit any detailed mention of the `Allocator` parameter. See Chapter 24 and the sidebar "Allocators" in Section 21.3.2 for a discussion of allocators.

B.1.3 Description

Strings are implemented by the `basic_string` template class. For convenience, typedefs are made defining `basic_string<char>` as `string` and `basic_string<wchar_t>` as `wstring`. The `charT` and `traits` template parameters allow for the use of different character types and even for different character semantics such as case-insensitive comparisons or internationally localized collating sequences.

The characters contained in a string are not restricted to the `char` type. In fact, a character can be nearly any type without a constructor for which character traits can be defined. *Character traits* define the properties of the characters, including their ordering in comparisons, how sequences are terminated, and how to copy and move ranges. This provides for a great deal of flexibility in the representation of characters including but not limited to support for multibyte character types used in international character sets. Character traits are discussed in more detail in Section B.2.

The `basic_string` class allocates and deallocates storage as necessary via the allocator. A `basic_string` is a sequence container as defined in Section 21.1.4 and provides random access iterators. As a result, the time complexities of string operations also correspond to the sequence container requirements unless otherwise noted. See Section B.1.10 for details on cases where the iterators may be invalidated.

B.1.4 Type Definitions

`traits_type`

> `traits` template parameter.

`char_type`

> Type of the characters in the string. Same as `charT` and the `char_type` of the `traits` parameter.

`value_type`

> Same as `char_type`.

`size_type`

Unsigned integral type that can represent the size of any `basic_string` instance.

`difference_type`

Signed integral type that can represent the difference between any two `basic_string::iterator` objects.

`reference`
`const_reference`

`reference` is the type of locations of characters in the string, `charT&` (or `const charT&` for `const_reference`).

`pointer`
`const_pointer`

`pointer` is the type of pointers to characters of the string (usually `charT*` but more generally it is determined by the allocator type). `const_pointer` is a corresponding constant pointer type.

`iterator`
`const_iterator`

`iterator` is a random access iterator type referring to `charT`, and `const_iterator` is a constant random access iterator type referring to `const charT`. It is guaranteed that there is a constructor for `const_iterator` out of `iterator`.

`reverse_iterator`
`const_reverse_iterator`

Nonconstant and constant reverse random access iterators.

`allocator_type`

Type of the allocator used by the string. Equivalent to `Allocator`.

B.1.5   Constructors, Destructors, and Related Functions

`basic_string(const Allocator& = Allocator());`

Default constructor for `basic_string`. Creates an empty string with no characters (equivalent to `""`). Takes constant time.

```
basic_string(const basic_string& str, size_type pos = 0,
             size_type n = npos, const Allocator& = Allocator());
```

Constructs a `basic_string` whose contents are a substring of `str`. The substring begins at the position given by `pos` and contains at most `n` characters (fewer if the string is too short). In particular, the new string has size equal to the minimum of `n` or `str.size() - pos`. Note that with the default values for `pos` and `n`, this is the copy constructor. Takes $O(N)$ time where N is the length of the constructed string.

```
basic_string(const charT* s, size_type n,
             const Allocator& = Allocator());
```

Constructs a `basic_string` whose contents are the `n` characters pointed to by `s`. Linear in `n`.

```
basic_string(const charT* s, const Allocator& = Allocator());
```

Constructs a `basic_string` whose value is equal to the array of characters of length `traits::length(s)`. Takes $O(N)$ time where N is the length of the constructed string.

```
basic_string(size_type n, charT c, const Allocator& = Allocator());
```

Constructs a `basic_string` with `n` copies of `c`. Linear in `n`.

```
template <typename InputIterator>
basic_string(InputIterator begin, InputIterator end,
             const Allocator& = Allocator());
```

Constructs `basic_string` from the values in the range [begin, end) unless `InputIterator` is an integral type in which case the result is as if

```
        basic_string(static_cast<size_type>(begin),
                     static_cast<value_type>(end))
```

were applied. In other words, the result has `begin` copies of the character `end`. Takes $O(N)$ time where N is the length of the constructed string.

```
~basic_string();
```

`basic_string` destructor. Returns all allocated storage back to the free store.

```
basic_string& operator=(const basic_string& str);
```

> **basic_string** assignment operator. Replaces the contents of the current sequence with a copy of the parameter string **str**. Linear in the length of **str**.

```
basic_string& operator=(const charT* s);
```

> **basic_string** assignment operator. Produces a result equivalent to ***this = basic_string(s)**.

```
basic_string& operator=(charT c);
```

> **basic_string** assignment operator. Produces a result equivalent to ***this = basic_string(1, c)**.

```
basic_string& assign(const basic_string& str);
```

> Equivalent to **operator=(str)**.

```
basic_string& assign(const basic_string& str,
                     size_type pos, size_type n);
```

> Equivalent to **assign(basic_string(str, pos, n))**. Causes the string to contain a substring of **str** beginning at position **pos** and containing the minimum of **n** and **str.size() - pos** characters.

```
basic_string& assign(const charT* s, size_type n);
```

> Equivalent to **assign(basic_string(s, n))**. Causes the string to contain the **n** characters pointed to by **s**.

```
basic_string& assign(const charT* s);
```

> Equivalent to **operator=(s)**.

```
basic_string& assign(size_type n, charT c);
```

> Equivalent to **{clear(); insert(begin(), n, c);}**. Causes the string to contain **n** characters with the value **c**.

```
template <typename InputIterator>
basic_string& assign(InputIterator first, InputIterator last);
```

> Causes the string to contain copies of characters in the range [`first`, `last`), which must be a valid range of characters of type `charT`. Equivalent to {`clear()`; `insert(begin(), first, last)`;}.

```
void reserve(size_type res_arg = 0);
```

> Directive that informs the string of a planned change in size, so storage can be managed accordingly. It does not change the size of the string, and it takes time at most linear in the size of the string. Reallocation happens at this point if and only if the current capacity is less than the argument of reserve (`capacity` is a string member function that returns the size of the allocated storage in the string). After a call to `reserve`, the capacity is greater than or equal to the argument of `reserve` if reallocation happens.
>
> Reallocation invalidates all the references, pointers, and iterators referring to the characters in the string. It is guaranteed that no reallocation takes place during the insertions that happen after `reserve` takes place until the time when the size of the string reaches the size specified by `reserve`.

```
void swap(basic_string<charT, traits, Allocator>& str);
```

> Swaps the contents of the current string with those of the input string `str`. The current string replaces `str` and vice versa.

B.1.6 Comparison Operations

```
template <typename charT, typename traits, typename Allocator>
bool operator==(const basic_string<charT, traits, Allocator>& lhs,
                const basic_string<charT, traits, Allocator>& rhs);

template <typename charT, typename traits, typename Allocator>
bool operator==(const charT* lhs,
                const basic_string<charT, traits, Allocator>& rhs);

template <typename charT, typename traits, typename Allocator>
bool operator==(const basic_string<charT, traits, Allocator>& lhs,
                const charT* rhs);
```

Equality operation on strings. Returns `true` if the character sequences `lhs` and `rhs` are characterwise equal (using `charT::operator==`). Takes linear time. For the second variant, where `lhs` is a `const charT*`, the result is equivalent to `basic_string(lhs) == rhs`. The third function is similar.

```
template <typename charT, typename traits, typename Allocator>
bool operator!=(const basic_string<charT, traits, Allocator>& lhs,
                const basic_string<charT, traits, Allocator>& rhs);

template <typename charT, typename traits, typename Allocator>
bool operator!=(const charT* lhs,
                const basic_string<charT, traits, Allocator>& rhs);

template <typename charT, typename traits, typename Allocator>
bool operator!=(const basic_string<charT, traits, Allocator>& lhs,
                const charT* rhs);
```

Inequality operation on strings. The `const charT*`s are in effect converted to strings as `basic_string(lhs)` (or `rhs`). Returns `true` if the sequences of characters in `lhs` and `rhs` are not characterwise equal (using `charT::operator!=`). Takes linear time.

```
template <typename charT, typename traits, typename Allocator>
bool operator<(const basic_string<charT, traits, Allocator>& lhs,
               const basic_string<charT, traits, Allocator>& rhs);

template <typename charT, typename traits, typename Allocator>
bool operator<(const charT* lhs,
               const basic_string<charT, traits, Allocator>& rhs);

template <typename charT, typename traits, typename Allocator>
bool operator<(const basic_string<charT, traits, Allocator>& lhs,
               const charT* rhs);
```

Returns `true` if `lhs` is lexicographically less than `rhs`, `false` otherwise. The `const charT*`s are effectively converted to strings as `basic_string(lhs)` (or `rhs`). Takes linear time.

```
template <typename charT, typename traits, typename Allocator>
bool operator>(const basic_string<charT, traits, Allocator>& lhs,
               const basic_string<charT, traits, Allocator>& rhs);

template <typename charT, typename traits, typename Allocator>
bool operator>(const charT* lhs,
```

467

```
                    const basic_string<charT, traits, Allocator>& rhs);

template <typename charT, typename traits, typename Allocator>
bool operator>(const basic_string<charT, traits, Allocator>& lhs,
               const charT* rhs);
```

Returns **true** if **lhs** is lexicographically greater than **rhs**, **false** otherwise. The **const charT***s are effectively converted to strings as **basic_string(lhs)** (or **rhs**). Takes linear time.

```
template <typename charT, typename traits, typename Allocator>
bool operator<=(const basic_string<charT, traits, Allocator>& lhs,
                const basic_string<charT, traits, Allocator>& rhs);

template <typename charT, typename traits, typename Allocator>
bool operator<=(const charT* lhs,
                const basic_string<charT, traits, Allocator>& rhs);

template <typename charT, typename traits, typename Allocator>
bool operator<=(const basic_string<charT, traits, Allocator>& lhs,
                const charT* rhs);
```

Returns **true** if **lhs** is lexicographically less than or equal to **rhs**, **false** otherwise. The **const charT***s are in effect converted to strings as **basic_string(lhs)** (or **rhs**). Takes linear time.

```
template <typename charT, typename traits, typename Allocator>
bool operator>=(const basic_string<charT, traits, Allocator>& lhs,
                const basic_string<charT, traits, Allocator>& rhs);

template <typename charT, typename traits, typename Allocator>
bool operator>=(const charT* lhs,
                const basic_string<charT, traits, Allocator>& rhs);

template <typename charT, typename traits, typename Allocator>
bool operator>=(const basic_string<charT, traits, Allocator>& lhs,
                const charT* rhs);
```

Returns **true** if **lhs** is lexicographically greater than or equal to **rhs**, **false** otherwise. The **const charT***s are in effect converted to strings as **basic_string(lhs)** (or **rhs**). Takes linear time.

B.1.7   Element Access Member Functions

```
iterator begin();
const_iterator begin() const;
```

Returns an `iterator` (`const_iterator` for constant string) that can be used to begin traversing through the string.

```
iterator end();
const_iterator end() const;
```

Returns an `iterator` (`const_iterator` for constant string) that can be used in a comparison for ending traversal through the string.

```
reverse_iterator rbegin();
const_reverse_iterator rbegin() const;
```

Returns a `reverse_iterator` (`const_reverse_iterator` for constant strings) that can be used to begin traversing the string in the reverse of the normal order.

```
reverse_iterator rend();
const_reverse_iterator rend() const;
```

Returns a `reverse_iterator` (`const_reverse_iterator` for constant strings) that can be used in a comparison for ending reverse direction traversal through the string.

```
size_type size() const;
```

Returns the number of characters currently stored in the string.

```
size_type max_size() const;
```

Returns the maximum possible size of the string.

```
size_type capacity() const;
```

Returns the largest number of characters that the string can store without reallocation. See also the **reserve** member function.

```
bool empty() const;
```

Returns **true** if the string is empty (if `begin() == end()`), **false** otherwise.

```
reference operator[](size_type pos);
const_reference operator[](size_type pos) const;
```

Returns the Nth character from the beginning of the string in constant time.

```
reference at(size_type n);
const_reference at(size_type n) const;
```

> Returns the nth character from the beginning of the string in constant time after checking the bounds of the string. Throws out_of_range if n >= size().

```
allocator_type get_allocator() const;
```

> Returns a copy of the allocator used when constructing the object.

B.1.8   Insert Member Functions

```
void push_back(const charT c);
```

> Adds the character c at the end of the string.

```
basic_string& insert(size_type pos1, const basic_string& str);
```

> Inserts the characters in str at the position in the string referred to by pos1.

```
basic_string& insert(size_type pos1, const basic_string& str,
                     size_type pos2, size_type n);
```

> Inserts a substring of str at the position in the string referred to by pos1. The substring begins at position pos2 and contains the minimum of n and str.size() - pos2 characters.

```
basic_string& insert(size_type pos, const charT* s,
                     size_type n);
```

> Inserts the n characters pointed to by s at the position in the string referred to by pos1.

```
basic_string& insert(size_type pos, const charT* s);
```

> Inserts traits::length(s) characters pointed to by s at the position in the string referred to by pos1.

```
basic_string& insert(size_type pos, size_type n, charT c);
```

> Inserts n copies of the character c starting at the location to which pos refers.

```
iterator insert(iterator p, charT c);
```

> Inserts the character c at the position in the string referred to by p. Characters already in the string are moved as required. The iterator returned refers to the position where the character was inserted.

```
void insert(iterator p, size_type n, charT c);
```

> Inserts n copies of the character c starting at the location to which position refers.

```
template <typename InputIterator>
void insert(iterator p, InputIterator first,
        InputIterator last);
```

> Equivalent to insert(p, basic_string(first, last)). Note the special treatment by the string constructor of first and last when InputIterator is an integral type.

B.1.9   Erase Member Functions

```
basic_string& erase(size_type pos = 0, size_type n = npos);
```

> Removes the xlen characters at position pos, where xlen is the minimum of n and size() - pos. With the default arguments, this is equivalent to clear().

```
iterator erase(iterator position);
```

> Erases the character of the string to which position refers. Undefined if the string is empty. Returns an iterator pointing to the character following the erased value or end() if the last character is erased.

```
iterator erase(iterator first, iterator last);
```

> The iterators first and last are assumed to point into the string, and all characters in the range [first, last) are erased from the string. Returns an iterator pointing to the character following the erased values, or end() if the last character is erased.

```
void clear();
```

> Erases all characters in the string. Equivalent to a.erase(a.begin(), a.end()) except that clear has no return value.

B.1.10 Additional Notes

All references, pointers, and iterators to a `basic_string` are invalidated by the following operations.

- Use as an argument to the nonmember functions `swap`, `operator>>` and `getline`.

- Use as an argument to `basic_string::swap`.

- A call to `c_str` or `data`.

- A call to any nonconst member function other than `operator[]`, `at`, `begin`, `rbegin`, `end` and `rend`.

B.2 Character Traits

B.2.1 Files

```
#include <string>
```

B.2.2 Description

Character traits are used to define the properties of a particular character type. A character traits class specifies the ordering of character values and types and functions for manipulating characters.

There are two predefined character traits classes: `char_traits<char>` and `char_traits<wchar_t>`. They are generally used as template parameters to other classes, such as `basic_string` (see Section B.1). There is no reason and it is not generally possible to create an object of type `char_traits`, since the `char_traits` classes contain only typedefs and member functions but no data.

B.2.3 Type Definitions

`char_type`

> Character type whose traits are described.

`int_type`

> Type large enough to represent all legal values of `char_type` along with an end-of-file value.

`pos_type`

> Type that can be used to represent the position of a character within a file. Usually `streampos`.

`off_type`

> Type that can be used to represent the difference between two `pos_type` values. Usually `streamoff`.

`state_type`

> Type that can be used to record state information during encoding and decoding of multi-byte characters. Usually `mbstate_t`.

B.2.4 Character Manipulation Functions

All functions defined for a character traits type are static. Except where otherwise noted, all operations require constant time.

`void assign(char_type& c, const char_type& d);`

> Assigns `d` to `c`.

`bool eq(const char_type& c, const char_type& d);`

> Returns `true` if `c` is equivalent to `d`, `false` otherwise.

`bool lt(const char_type& c, const char_type& d);`

> Returns `true` if `c` is considered less than `d`, `false` otherwise.

`int compare(const char_type* p, const char_type* q, size_t n);`

> Generalization of the C function `strcmp`. Compares the arrays of length `n` given by `p` and `q`. If for all i in $[0, n)$ `eq(p[i], q[i])` is `true`, the function returns 0. Otherwise, if there exists some j in $[0, n)$ such that `lt(p[j], q[j])` and `eq(p[i], q[i])` is `true` for all i in $[0, j)$, it returns a negative integer. If neither condition succeeds, a positive integer is returned. Runs in linear time.

```
size_t length(const char_type* p);
```

> Generalization of the C function `strlen`. Returns the smallest integer i such that `eq(p[i], char_type())` is `true`. Runs in linear time.

```
const char_type* find(const char_type* p,
                      size_t n, const char_type& c);
```

> Generalization of the C function `strchr`. Returns the smallest pointer q in [p, p + n) such that `eq(*q, c)` is `true`. Unlike the generic `find` algorithm (but like `strchr`), this function returns 0, a null pointer, if no character matching `c` is found. Runs in linear time.

```
char_type* move(char_type* s, const char_type* p, size_t n);
```

> Generalization of the C function `memmove`. Moves the characters in the range [p, p + n) to the range [s, s + n), working properly even if the ranges overlap. Returns `s` and runs in linear time.

```
char_type* copy(char_type* s, const char_type* p, size_t n);
```

> Generalization of the C function `memcpy`. Like `move`, it copies the characters in the range [p, p + n) to the range [s, s + n), but for `copy` the two ranges may not overlap. Returns `s` and runs in linear time.

```
char_type* assign(char_type* s, size_t n, const char_type& c);
```

> Generalization of the C function `memset`. Assigns the character `c` to each location in the range [s, s + n). Returns `s` and runs in linear time.

```
int_type not_eof(const int_type& e);
```

> Returns `e` if `eq_int_type(e, eof())` is `false`. Otherwise, returns some value of `int_type` other than `eof()`.

```
char_type to_char_type(const int_type& e);
```

> If `e` corresponds to a legal value for `char_type`, that value is returned. If `e` is `eof()`, the return value is unspecified.

```
int_type to_int_type(const char_type& c);
```

Converts c to int_type.

```
bool eq_int_type(const int_type& e, const int_type& f);
```

If e and f correspond to legal values for char_type (some values c and d exist such that e is to_int_type(c) and f is to_int_type(d)), then the result is the same as eq(c, d). Otherwise, the function returns true if both e and f are eof() but false if only one is eof().

```
int_type eof();
```

Returns a value representing end of file. This value must be distinct from all legal char_type values. Thus, eq_int_type(to_int_type(c), eof()) must be false for all values of c.

STL Include Files Used in Example Programs

C.1 Files Used in Example 17.1

These files are replicated directly from Stroustrup ([20], Section 6.4). The files are available online as described in Appendix D.

`"screen.h"` 477a ≡

```
const int XMAX=40;
const int YMAX=24;
struct point {
   int x,y;
   point() {}
   point(int a, int b) { x=a; y=b; }
};
extern void put_point(int a, int b);
inline void put_point(point p) { put_point(p.x, p.y); }
extern void put_line(int, int, int, int);
inline void put_line(point a, point b)
   { put_line(a.x, a.y, b.x, b.y); }
extern void screen_init();
extern void screen_destroy();
extern void screen_refresh();
extern void screen_clear();
```

`"screen.cpp"` 477b ≡

```
#include "screen.h"
#include <iostream>
using namespace std;
```

```
enum color { black='*', white=' ' };

char screen[XMAX][YMAX];

void screen_init()
{
    for (int y=0; y<YMAX; y++)
        for (int x=0; x<XMAX; x++)
            screen[x][y] = white;
}

void screen_destroy() {}

inline int on_screen(int a, int b)    // clipping
{
    return 0<=a && a<XMAX && 0<=b && b<YMAX;
}

void put_point(int a, int b)
{
    if (on_screen(a, b)) screen[a][b] = black;
}

void put_line(int x0, int y0, int x1, int y1)
/*
    Plot the line (x0, y0) to (x1, y1).
    The line being plotted is b(x-x0) +a(y-y0) = 0.
    Minimize abs(eps) where eps = 2*(b(x-x0) + a(y-y0)).
    See Newman and Sproull:
    ''Principles of Interactive Computer Graphics''
    McGraw-Hill, New York, 1979.  pp. 33-44.
*/
{
    register int dx = 1;
    int a = x1 - x0;
    if (a < 0) dx = -1, a = -a;

    register int dy = 1;
    int b = y1 - y0;
    if (b < 0) dy = -1, b = -b;

    int two_a = 2*a;
    int two_b = 2*b;
```

```
        int xcrit = -b + two_a;
        register int eps = 0;

        for(;;) {
            put_point(x0,y0);
            if (x0==x1 && y0 == y1) break;
            if (eps <= xcrit) x0 += dx, eps += two_b;
            if (eps>=a || a<=b) y0 += dy, eps -= two_a;
        }
    }

    void screen_clear() { screen_init(); }

    void screen_refresh()
    {
        for (int y=YMAX-1; 0<=y; y--) {      // top to bottom
            for (int x=0; x<XMAX; x++)         // left to right
                cout << screen[x][y];
            cout << '\n';
        }
    }
```

"shape.h" 479 ≡

```
    #include "screen.h"

    inline int max(int a, int b) { return a<b ? b : a; }
    inline int min(int a, int b) { return a<b ? a : b; }

    struct shape {
      static shape* list;
      shape* next;
      shape() { next = list; list = this; }

      virtual point north() const = 0;
      virtual point south() const = 0;
      virtual point east() const = 0;
      virtual point west() const = 0;
      virtual point neast() const = 0;
      virtual point seast() const = 0;
      virtual point nwest() const = 0;
      virtual point swest() const = 0;
      virtual void draw() = 0;
      virtual void move(int, int) = 0;
    };
```

479

```
class line : public shape {
/*
    The line from "w" to "e".
    north() is defined as ``above the center,
    as far north as the northernmost point.''
*/
  point w, e;
 public:
  point north() const
    { return point((w.x+e.x)/2, max(e.y,w.y)); }
  point south() const
    { return point((w.x+e.x)/2, min(e.y,w.y)); }
  point east() const
    { return point(max(e.x, w.x), (w.y+e.y)/2); }
  point west() const
    { return point(min(e.x, w.x), (w.y+e.y)/2); }
  point neast() const
    { return point(max(e.x, w.x), max(e.y, w.y)); }
  point seast() const
    { return point(max(e.x, w.x), min(e.y, w.y)); }
  point nwest() const
    { return point(min(e.x, w.x), max(e.y, w.y)); }
  point swest() const
    { return point(min(e.x, w.x), min(e.y, w.y)); }
  void move(int a, int b)
    { w.x += a; w.y += b; e.x += a; e.y += b; }
  void draw() { put_line(w,e); }
  line(point a, point b) { w = a; e = b; }
  line(point a, int len)
    { w = point(a.x + len - 1, a.y); e = a; }
};

class rectangle : public shape {
/*
    nw ---- n ---- ne
    |                |
    w       c        e
    |                |
    sw ---- s ---- se
*/
    point sw, ne;
 public:
  point north() const
    { return point((sw.x+ne.x)/2, ne.y); }
```

```
        point south() const
          { return point((sw.x+ne.x)/2, sw.y); }
        point east() const
          { return point(ne.x, (ne.y+sw.y)/2); }
        point west() const
          { return point(sw.x, (ne.y+sw.y)/2); }
        point neast() const { return ne; }
        point seast() const { return point(ne.x, sw.y); }
        point nwest() const { return point(sw.x, ne.y); }
        point swest() const { return sw; }
        void move(int a, int b)
          { sw.x += a; sw.y += b; ne.x += a; ne.y += b; }
        void draw();
        rectangle(point, point);
    };

    void shape_refresh();        // draw all shapes
    void stack(shape* p, const shape* q); // put p on top of q
"shape.cpp" 481 ≡
    #include "shape.h"

    rectangle::rectangle(point a, point b)
    {
        if (a.x <= b.x) {
            if (a.y <= b.y) {
                sw = a;
                ne = b;
            }
            else {
                sw = point(a.x, b.y);
                ne = point(b.x, a.y);
            }
        }
        else {
            if (a.y <= b.y) {
                sw = point(b.x, a.y);
                ne = point(a.x, b.y);
            }
            else {
                sw = b;
                ne = a;
            }
        }
    }
```

```
void rectangle::draw()
{
   point nw(sw.x, ne.y);
   point se(ne.x, sw.y);
   put_line(nw,ne);
   put_line(ne,se);
   put_line(se,sw);
   put_line(sw,nw);
}

void shape_refresh()
{
   screen_clear();
   for (shape* p = shape::list; p; p=p->next) p->draw();
   screen_refresh();
}

void stack(shape* p, const shape* q)  // put p on top of q
{
   point n = q->north();
   point s = p->south();
   p->move(n.x-s.x, n.y-s.y+1);
}

shape* shape::list = 0;
```

APPENDIX D

STL Resources

D.1 Web Address for SGI STL

At the time of publication, the SGI documentation and implementation of STL were available on the Internet at the following site:

http://www.sgi.com/tech/stl/

The version at the SGI site is the latest release by SGI. Older versions and documentation are also available.

D.2 Web Address for Source Code for Examples in this Book

Files and information related to this book are available at Addison-Wesley's Web site:

http://www.awl.com/cseng/titles/0-201-37923-6/

Among the files available at this site are the following:

- Source files for all example programs in this book

- Dictionary file used as input to the example programs in Part II

- The Theoretical Computer Science Genealogy text file used as input to the example programs in Part II

D.3   STL-Compatible Compilers

The book's examples have all been tested successfully with the following compilers:

>Borland C++, version 5.5 for DOS/Windows
>SGI C++, version 7.3.1.1m
>Comeau C/C++, version 4.2.45.2 for Solaris Unix and version
>>4.2.45.2b for Windows 2000

The examples have also been tested with the Free Software Foundation's compiler,

>GNU C++, version 2.95.2

which is available on many platforms and comes with its own adaptation of SGI STL. All the example programs compile and execute properly with this version. For information on obtaining this free compiler, see

>*http://www.gnu.ai.mit.edu*

With

>Microsoft Visual C++, version 6.0, with Service Pack 5 installed,

all but two of the example programs compile: Examples 16-1 and 24-1.

For more details and updated information on these and other compilers, follow the Source Code link on the Web site mentioned in Section D.2.

D.4   Other Related STL and C++ Documents

ANSI/ISO C++ Standard. Available for purchase online at

>*http://www.ansi.org*

ANSI/ISO C++ Draft Standard. Note that this is not the actual Standard and is significantly out of date in many respects. It is, however, free.

>*http://www.cygnus.com/misc/wp/dec96pub/*

References

[1] Accredited Standards Committee X3 (American National Standards Institute). Working paper for draft proposed international standard for information systems—programming language C++. Technical Report X3J16/95-0185, WG21/N0785, Information Processing Systems, 1995.

[2] Matthew H. Austern. *Generic Programming and the STL: Using and Extending the C++ Standard Template Library.* Addison-Wesley, Reading, MA, 1999.

[3] Preston Briggs. Nuweb, a simple literate programming tool. Version 0.87, 1989.

[4] Margaret A. Ellis and Bjarne Stroustrup. *The Annotated C++ Reference Manual.* Addison-Wesley, Reading, MA, 1990.

[5] ISO/IEC. International standard, programming languages—C++. Technical Report ISO/IEC 14882:1998(E), American National Standards Institute, 1998.

[6] M. Jazayeri. Component programming—a fresh look at software components. In *Proc. 5th European Software Engineering Conference*, Sitges, Spain, September 25–28, 1995.

[7] Nicolai M. Josuttis. *The C++ Standard Library: A Tutorial and Reference.* Addison-Wesley, Reading, MA, 1999.

[8] D. Kapur, D. R. Musser, and A. A. Stepanov. Operators and algebraic structures. In *Proc. of Conference on Functional Programming Languages and Computer Architecture*, Portsmouth, NH, October 1981.

[9] D. Kapur, D. R. Musser, and A. A. Stepanov. Tecton, a language for manipulating generic objects. In *Proc. of Workshop on Program Specification*, Aarhus, Denmark, August 1981. Also published in *Lecture Notes in Computer Science*, Springer-Verlag, New York, Vol. 134, 1982.

[10] Donald E. Knuth. Literate programming. *Computer Journal*, 27:97–111, 1984.

[11] D. McIlroy. Mass-produced software components. Technical report, Petrocelli/Charter, 1976.

[12] D. R. Musser. Introspective sorting and selection algorithms. *Software—Practice and Experience*, 8:983–993, 1997.

[13] D. R. Musser and G. V. Nishanov. A fast generic sequence matching algorithm. *http://www.cs.rpi.edu/˜musser/gp*, 1998.

[14] D. R. Musser and A. A. Stepanov. *The Ada Generic Library: Linear List Processing Packages*. Springer-Verlag, New York, 1989.

[15] D. R. Musser and A. A. Stepanov. Algorithm-oriented generic libraries. *Software Practice and Experience*, 24(7):623–642, July 1994.

[16] D. R. Musser and A. A. Stepanov. Generic programming. In P. Gianni, editor, *ISSAC '88 Symbolic and Algebraic Computation Proceedings*, 1988. Also published in *Lecture Notes in Computer Science*, Springer-Verlag, New York, Vol. 358.

[17] P. J. Plauger, Alexander A. Stepanov, Meng Lee, and David R. Musser. *The C++ Standard Template Library*. Prentice Hall, Upper Saddle River, NJ, 2001.

[18] F. S. Roberts. Measurement theory. In Gian-Carlo Rota, editor, *Encyclopedia of Mathematics and Its Applications*, volume 7. Addison-Wesley, Reading, MA, 1979.

[19] A. A. Stepanov and M. Lee. The standard template library. Technical Report HP-94-34, Hewlett-Packard, April 1994. Revised July 7, 1995.

[20] Bjarne Stroustrup. *The C++ Programming Language, Third Edition*. Addison-Wesley, Reading, MA, 1997.

[21] Bjarne Stroustrup. *The Design and Evolution of C++*. Addison-Wesley, Reading, MA, 1994.

486

[22] Bjarne Stroustrup. Making a `vector` fit for a standard. *The C++ Report*, October 1994.

Index

B

C

F

Q

R

U

V

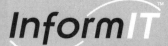
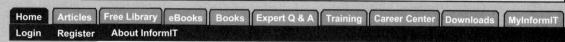